CASSANDRA AND THE POETICS OF PROPHECY IN GREEK AND LATIN LITERATURE

This book explores the miscommunications of the prophet Cassandra – cursed to prophesy the truth but never to be understood until too late – in Greek and Latin poetry. Using insights from the field of translation studies, the book focuses on the dialogic interactions that take place between the articulation and the realisation of Cassandra's prophecies in five canonical ancient texts, stretching from Aeschylus' to Seneca's *Agamemnon*. These interactions are dogged by confusion and misunderstanding, but they also show a range of interested parties engaged in creatively 'translating' meaning for themselves from Cassandra's ostensibly nonsensical voice. Moreover, as the figure of Cassandra is translated from one literary work into another, including into the Sibyl of Virgil's *Aeneid*, her story of tragic communicative disability develops into an optimistic metaphor for literary canon formation. Cassandra invites us to reconsider the status and value of even the most riddling of female prophets in ancient poetry.

EMILY PILLINGER is Lecturer in Classics at King's College London. Her research interests range across Latin (and some Greek) poetry and poetics, focusing on themes that describe the power and fragility of both spoken and written communications: she has written on poetry associated with the utterance of prophecies and curses, with letter-writing, and with inscribed monuments. She also works on the reception of the ancient world, and particularly on the influence of Graeco-Roman myth and history in music composed after the Second World War.

T0370782

CASSANDRA AND THE POETICS OF PROPHECY IN GREEK AND LATIN LITERATURE

EMILY PILLINGER

King's College London

CAMBRIDGE
UNIVERSITY PRESS

Shaftesbury Road, Cambridge CB2 8EA, United Kingdom

One Liberty Plaza, 20th Floor, New York, NY 10006, USA

477 Williamstown Road, Port Melbourne, VIC 3207, Australia

314–321, 3rd Floor, Plot 3, Splendor Forum, Jasola District Centre, New Delhi – 110025, India

103 Penang Road, #05–06/07, Visioncrest Commercial, Singapore 238467

Cambridge University Press is part of Cambridge University Press & Assessment,
a department of the University of Cambridge.

We share the University's mission to contribute to society through the pursuit of
education, learning and research at the highest international levels of excellence.

www.cambridge.org
Information on this title: www.cambridge.org/9781108462990
DOI: 10.1017/ 9781108564007

First published 2019
First paperback edition 2022

A catalogue record for this publication is available from the British Library

Library of Congress Cataloging-in-Publication data
Names: Pillinger, Emily J., 1978– author.
Title: Cassandra and the poetics of prophecy in Greek and Latin literature / Emily Pillinger.
Description: Cambridge: Cambridge University Press, 2019. |
Includes bibliographical references and index.
Identifiers: LCCN 2018048890 | ISBN 9781108473934 (hardback) |
ISBN 9781108462990 (paperback)
Subjects: LCSH: Cassandra (Legendary character) – In literature. |
Prophecy in literature. | Classical literature – History and criticism.
Classification: LCC PA3015.R5C377 2019 | DDC 881/.0109351–dc23
LC record available at https://lccn.loc.gov/2018048890

ISBN   978-1-108-47393-4   Hardback
ISBN   978-1-108-46299-0   Paperback

For Clio and George

Contents

Acknowledgements

This project began as part of a doctoral dissertation in the Department of Classics at Princeton, and I owe a huge debt of thanks to my advisors there, Denis Feeney and Andrew Feldherr. Both leaven their intellectual brilliance with warmth, wit and humour, making it a delight to work with them. Adding to the joy of studying at Princeton were more teachers and friends than can possibly be listed here, but include: Rosa Andújar, Yelena Baraz, Mark Buchan, Andrew Ford, Constanze Guthenke, Bob Kaster, Jake Mackey, Carey Seal, Brent Shaw, Anna Uhlig, Leah Whittington, Michael Wood, Tom Zanker, Froma Zeitlin, and for wonderful conversations that continue across the globe, Michelle Coghlan. I am grateful to David Bellos for organising the Princeton Translation Lunch Series, which addressed in eye-opening ways the obscure enunciations of everything from Derrida to dolphins.

Through the long process of turning the dissertation into a book I have been indebted to Michael Sharp at Cambridge University Press, and to the two anonymous readers for the Press who were exceptionally generous with their time and suggestions. My thanks to Philippa Jevons, too, for her indexing wizardry. The material in this book benefited from road-testing before kind and helpful audiences in the departments of Classics at Exeter, Bristol and Swansea (at a congenial KYKNOS seminar), and at the Classical Association annual conferences in Cardiff and Bristol. Further thoughts were refined during the conference 'The Author-Translator in the European Literary Tradition' held at Swansea, and the 'Text / Performance Workshop on Don Fowler's unpublished *Unrolling the Text*' organised in Oxford by Francesca Martelli.

Since leaving Princeton I have had the support of several universities: the Institute of Greece, Rome, and the Classical Tradition at Bristol; Balliol College, Oxford; and most recently the Department of Classics at King's College London, where I have found the happiest of academic homes.

I am also grateful for various kinds of intellectual and moral support over the past few years from Tim Whitmarsh, William Fitzgerald, Greta Hawes, Deborah Steiner, Alessandro Barchiesi, Helen Van Noorden, Helen Lovatt, Edith Hall, Hugh Bowden, Dan Orrells, Victoria Moul, Danielle Frisby, Ismene Lada-Richards, Lucy Jackson, Paul Cheetham, Kathleen Mysberg, Anik Monoury, Soo-Lin Lui, Vanessa Naish, and finally A. E. Stallings, who provided poetic inspiration at a late stage in the project.

Above all, this book owes its existence to the support of a wonderful family: my remarkable parents Edward and Suzanne, my brilliant brother Toby and my beloved Pavlos. In fact Pavlos Avlamis should rightly be footnoted on every page, since there is no sentence that has not benefited from his wisdom and learning, his patient discussions, frequent hilarity and unwavering encouragement. Above all, to him I owe the dedicatees of this book, our future translated: Clio and George.

Introduction
Translating Cassandra

Τοῦτο μὲν ὀρθῶς ἔλεξας, ὦ Ἄπολλον, ἐπαινέσας τοὺς σαφῶς
λέγοντας, εἰ καὶ μὴ πάνυ ποιεῖς αὐτὸ σὺ ἐν τοῖς χρησμοῖς λοξὸς
ὢν καὶ γριφώδης καὶ ἐς τὸ μεταίχμιον ἀσφαλῶς ἀπορρίπτων
τὰ πολλά, ὡς τοὺς ἀκούοντας ἄλλου δεῖσθαι Πυθίου πρὸς τὴν
ἐξήγησιν αὐτῶν.

You spoke rightly, Apollo, when you praised those who speak clearly,
even if you don't exactly do the same in your prophecies, being
ambiguous and riddling and tossing virtually everything firmly into
no man's land, so that those listening to you need another oracle to
explain them.

(Lucian Iupp. trag. 28)

Quorum omnium [oraculorum quae instinctu diuino adflatuque
funduntur] interpretes, ut grammatici poetarum, proxume ad eorum
quos interpretantur diuinationem uidentur accedere.

The interpreters of all of these [prophecies that are poured out by
divine prompting and inspiration], just like the commentators of
poets, seem to approach very closely to the divine element of those
they are interpreting.

(Cic. Div. 1.34)

The meaning of a poem can only be another poem.

(Bloom (1997) 94)

Translating Cassandra: Who's Translating Whom?

According to the mythic tradition, Cassandra's biography is short and
bleak.[1] The life story of Priam's daughter is shaped by three narratives of
sexual assault or attempted assault, involving one god and two mortal

---

[1] For general treatments of Cassandra see Davreux (1942); Mason (1959); Neblung (1997); Brault
(1990); Mazzoldi (2001 and 2002); Racine (2003). Mazzoldi's work, in which she identifies Cassandra

men: Apollo, Locrian Ajax (the 'lesser' Ajax) and Agamemnon, son of Atreus. Each attack pushes Cassandra into a more vulnerable and isolated position, while imposing a long trail of consequences on the wider communities in which she lives. Apollo grants Cassandra true visions of the future, but after she refuses his sexual advances he undermines her prestige as a prophet by stripping her of the ability to persuade others of her information regarding the future. This is the essence of what may be dubbed Cassandra's 'prophetic paradox'. As Troy falls at the end of the Trojan War – an outcome vainly predicted by Cassandra – Ajax attacks her in the Trojan temple to Athena in which the prophet had taken refuge, prompting the goddess to impose dire punishments upon the returning Greek warriors. Finally, Cassandra is forcibly transported to Mycenae as part of Agamemnon's spoils of war. In the process she becomes a foreigner in Greece, a slave in a ruling household, and ultimately a catalyst for, and collateral damage in, the violence that has engulfed the house of Atreus.

Cassandra's life story tells of repeated marginalisation in every respect: sexual, social, cultural and linguistic. Even in the extant ancient texts that tell her story she is generally found on the periphery of the narrative, rather than at its centre. Her rambling narratives, wandering as they do backwards and forwards through time and space, are the product of a prophet who is always displaced, no matter where she is.[2] Yet even as Cassandra is repeatedly victimised and marginalised, she boldly resists every act of oppression she faces.[3] Her speech, in particular, both heightened and hobbled in its reach, is the weapon with which she asserts her authority, and its delivery and reception form the subject of this book.

---

as containing aspects of both the *mantis* and the *prophētēs*, is particularly valuable. The series of essays in Goudot (1999a) and Monrós Gaspar and Reece (2011) tackle some of the most important features of Cassandra's cultural reception. Cassandra's characterisation as a prophet, rather than simply as a daughter of Priam, is not explicitly marked in Homer, though *Il.* 24.697–702 hints at her prophetic abilities when she becomes the first of the Trojans to see Priam returning to the city with Hector's body. See Richardson (1993) ad loc., and Moreau (1989) 145–6. Cassandra has a 'pitiable voice' in Agamemnon's recollection of her death at *Od.* 11.421, though the dead warrior does not repeat her words. Proclus has Cassandra prophesying in the *Cypria* of the Epic Cycle, and she is clearly a prophet by the time of Pindar (*Pyth.* 11.33).

[2] It is a neat (if serendipitous) fact that Cassandra's biographical move from east to west reflects her literary heritage, in which the oral tales emerging from Asia Minor were fixed under a Greek-speaking authority (see e.g. West (1997) and Nagy (1996)) before ending up in a corpus of texts proliferating from library cultures first in Alexandria and later in Rome.

[3] Brault (1990) makes the point that recent feminist thought and literature has tended to make Cassandra a figure of subjugated womanhood, while the ancient works, particularly those of fifth-century Athens, push back against this characterisation. For Mazzoldi (2001) 18–19, Cassandra's unique knowledge of (her) fate gives her a radical freedom from human oppression.

Cassandra's marginalisation is the very point of her role in mythic narrative. The marginal can speak of straightforward exclusion, but it can also mark a certain exclusive privilege. This privilege resides in the understanding granted to those who live on the limits of one or more societies, those whose skewed perspective and wider world view grants them a unique perceptiveness. Such privileged knowledge is explicit in Greek and Roman didactic modes – poetic, philosophical or historiographical – which revolve around the wisdom of the *metanastēs*, the *hermēneus*, the *exēgētēs*; the *praeceptor*, the *interpres*, the *uates*. 'Mental wandering does not tolerate physical confinement', notes Montiglio, embracing in her observation the experiences of madness and of genius.[4] These thinkers are figures of authority, and often authorship, whose physical and mental peregrinations have left them dwelling on the boundaries of the society to which their privileged insight is valuable.[5] As Hartog puts it, 'The traveler's tale translates what is other, and the rhetoric of otherness is the means by which the translation is effected.'[6] Their existence on the periphery is what shapes their unique knowledge, and this hard-to-grasp knowledge is what keeps them on the boundary; at the moment when their knowledge becomes fully understood and incorporated into the society they address, they lose their exceptional status in relation to that community. This is a vital aspect of the 'prophetic paradox' that characterises Cassandra. Her marginalisation is a result of her exceptional prophetic knowledge, but it is not the knowledge itself, so much as the fact that her message is never fully understood by her peers, that keeps her apart. Her failure to communicate all that she knows keeps her on the limits of society, and her existence there allows her to expand on and even celebrate the very knowledge that she fails to communicate.[7]

One of the recurring features of all the works that tell Cassandra's story is their tendency to link her communicative difficulties to her status as a

---

[4] Montiglio (2005) 39. Mazzoldi (2001) 18 describes Cassandra as 'wandering' in body and mind.
[5] Martin (1992); Volk (2002).
[6] Hartog (1988) 260.
[7] It might be argued that Cassandra's audience disbelieves, rather than misunderstands, the prophet's words, and that the challenge she faces is one of trust, not of language. In fact, in almost all the texts in which she appears, Cassandra's difficulty in convincing her auditors of her prophetic narratives is identified with semantic confusion, rather than good faith, from Aeschylus' seminal portrayal onwards. Even where Cassandra's credibility is explicitly at stake, as in Euripides' *Trojan Women*, the issues remain interlinked, because while her articulation is clearer to both internal and external audiences, it is still situated within a wider context of thwarted comprehension. Her internal audiences, in particular, fail to trust her because of their inability to make sense of her words and behaviour according to their limited understanding of the events to come.

stranger, a native of somewhere foreign, though she is never uncomplicatedly 'other'. In her work on the Greek construction of the 'barbarian', Hall points out that Cassandra is part of a favoured group of barbarians, even in the polarised world of fifth-century Greek tragedy, who escape censure.[8] Being alien is a valuable part of Cassandra's role, not something to be stigmatised. The barbarian ('ba ba') sound of Cassandra's speech is also a surprisingly literal feature of her characterisation: it is ultimately through linguistic difference that her position as an outsider is most clearly articulated. Cassandra's barbarian identity is regularly highlighted in texts narrating her story once she has arrived in Greece, where she is a foreigner and might plausibly be presented as encountering a basic difficulty in communicating in Greek. Yet Cassandra has just as many problems communicating her prophecies when she lives in Troy as she does in Greece, and it transpires that the same tropes of linguistic failure are used to describe her situation there: she is a mystifying stranger even in her own home.[9]

A peculiar characteristic of Greek and Latin literature comes to play a useful part in allowing the theme of linguistic difference to represent Cassandra's difficulties regardless of her geographical location. There is very little representation of foreign speech in Greek literature or its Latin descendants, particularly outside the world of comedy; all protagonists speak Greek or Latin regardless of their purported origins.[10] Cassandra is no exception to this convention: she speaks fluent Greek – and indeed fluent Latin, later on. All the misunderstandings she provokes are expressed in the language of her immediate interlocutors and of her external audience, even when those misunderstandings are identified with the complications of multilingualism. Cassandra sounds familiar whether she is supposed to be at home in Troy or abroad in Greece, and whether she is performed (or read or recited) in Athens, Alexandria or Rome. The result is that the

---

[8] Hall (1991) 211–12. Moreau (1989) also identifies Cassandra's ambiguous and intermediary position as granting her unusual status within Greek myth. Sourvinou-Inwood (1997) 286 notes that Cassandra is never portrayed in 'oriental' costume on Greek vases, and concludes that other aspects of her characterisation trump her barbarian origins. Connelly (1993) makes the important observation that vase paintings of Cassandra's rape by Ajax in Athena's temple change over the course of the fifth century, focusing with increasing intensity on the experience of the prophet as opposed to the insult done to Athena. Connelly reads this partly as a response to the Persian invasion, but even here Cassandra represents not so much the foreign 'other', as the plight of all young women in war.

[9] Goudot (1999b) 11.

[10] Feeney (2015) 17–44. Willi (2002) addresses the situation with regard to Greek comedy; Bettini (2012) 1–31 discusses Roman comedy. An irresistible modern example of this can be found in the 1980s British sitcom 'Allo 'Allo, set in wartime France, where everyone speaks English, be they German, Italian, French or British, but with caricatured accents that indicate their nationalities and allow them to illustrate their varying ability to comprehend each other.

curse Apollo laid on Cassandra, that her prophetic speech should never be properly grasped by her listeners, is granted a significant twist in literary presentations of the situation: external audiences of her story tend to understand her better than the apparently obtuse family members or enemy captors who constitute her internal audiences. Moreover, not only would those external audiences in Greece or Rome have known the mythic trajectory of her story, but they are also likely to have had a good grasp of the issues at stake in Cassandra's linguistic situation. As Mullen points out, 'in the ancient world, as in the modern, monolingualism was a minority trait'.[11]

The marginalised Cassandra's struggles to communicate her prophecies are, then, sympathetically portrayed as analogous to the communicative difficulties suffered by someone who does not speak the language of their interlocutors. The natural consequence to this is the activation of the metaphor of translation in order to illustrate and explore Cassandra's impossible situation. Cassandra's failure to communicate prompts her interlocutors in Aeschylus' *Agamemnon*, the earliest extant text to establish Cassandra's character in real depth, to invite the services of a *hermēneus* – an interpreter, or translator.[12] There is an irony in this, however, for Cassandra's own behaviour as a mouthpiece of Apollo already makes her a *hermēneus* in her own right: she has an exceptional understanding of multiple languages, including at the very least her own and that of the gods, even though her ability to bridge those languages is compromised. The portrayal of Cassandra as a barbarian in Greece therefore both relies upon and complicates the notion of translation. As a translator who still needs to be translated, as an interpreter who still needs further interpretation, Cassandra illustrates not just the communication (or miscommunication) of information from one realm to another, but also the difficulty in identifying at what point such communication (or communicative breakdown) takes place.

The title of this introductory chapter, 'Translating Cassandra', embraces this central ambiguity surrounding Cassandra's relationship with language. Each time that Cassandra prophesies, is she doing the translating, or are others translating her? She may be trying to translate a divine message for a mortal audience, but that same audience is also trying to translate her impenetrable speech. Cassandra's role as translator and translated, and the endless chain of reworked words and delayed comprehension that

---

[11] Mullen (2012) 5. See also Adams (2003) and Adams, Janse and Swain (2002).
[12] *LSJ* s.v. ἑρμηνεία. On this passage (Aesch. *Ag.* 1062–3) see Bettini (2012) 126–7.

she sets in motion, relate to several aspects of her characterisation. It is most obviously a function of the 'prophetic paradox' with which she is cursed, but it is also implicated in the multiple dichotomies she straddles, and the many social realms on whose boundaries she exists. Cassandra challenges the distinctions between communities marked by different capacities for knowledge, most strikingly between mortals and immortals with their differing understanding of the past, present and future. Then Cassandra's status as a woman invites speculation on the distinctive, or not so distinctive, ways in which men and women are perceived as communicating and miscommunicating amongst themselves and with each other. Cassandra's prophecies blur the line between those within the story and those consuming it, too. As Goff notes of Cassandra's role in Euripides' *Trojan Women*, 'If all the spectators see is confusion on the part of the characters, how can they be sure that they are not also caught up in its dynamic? Kassandra's scene thus asks quite aggressively where the stage ends and the spectator begins.'[13]

Above all, Cassandra stages a confrontation between different ethnic, linguistic and literary communities, whilst showing how porous the boundaries are between those various groups. The events of the Trojan War in which she is implicated, and the journey she is forced to make from Troy to Greece, make this an obvious tale of Trojan-Greek clash, but her story turns out to be more universal than that. Not only does Cassandra's tale go on to be told in Alexandria and Rome, but her role expands uncontrollably when many of her characteristics become diffused through the Graeco-Roman prophetic figures found in Latin texts. Through this process she undergoes a kind of metempsychosis from the Greek into the Roman world, without losing her outsider status. *The* Cassandra now becomes *a* Cassandra. This happens most overtly in literary portrayals of the prophet whose words were believed to have shaped the future of the nascent Roman people: the Cumaean Sibyl. In Roman representations of their own riddling prophet, the 'translating' that accompanies the Sibyl's words gains a more specific social edge, occurring as it does within a cultural scene that defines itself as an ongoing act of translation from Greek.

In fact, all the elements of translation with which Cassandra and her related prophets engage in Greek and Latin literature have a metapoetic dimension that is directly dependent on the association between prophetic and literary inspired vision. The portrayal of Cassandra's divinely sanctioned utterance clearly evokes aspects of poetic inspiration and

---

[13] Goff (2009) 54.

interpretation. Meanwhile, with varying degrees of self-consciousness, her words also invite reflection upon issues of generic development; upon the rich cross-fertilisation that occurs when foreign languages and literatures intersect; upon the relationship between history and literary history, between oral and written narrative; and upon the distinctions between life and literature, between lived and literary experience.

Vernant once observed that 'the tragic message, when understood, is precisely that there are zones of opacity and incommunicability in the words that men exchange'.[14] In and of itself, Cassandra's speech does little more than exemplify this truism, but the assimilation of Cassandra's prophesying to a form of translation offers a positive way to represent and read her flawed verbal exchanges. As Cassandra shares and explains her visions, through their delivery and their imperfect reception, the prophet and her interlocutors have to embrace the inevitability of mis-communication. In the process, they show the way to celebrating some of miscommunication's unexpected virtues. Poetry's focus on the search for meaning in Cassandra's speech emphasises not so much the value of her prophetic message, but rather the value of every effort to grasp and reframe that endlessly deferred message. There turns out to be a net gain in Cassandra's odd communicative process, a gain in which 'uncertainty of meaning is incipient poetry'.[15]

In the poetry of Greece and Rome, Cassandra and her prophetic associates play endlessly upon versions of this theme of communicative confusion and proliferation. As such, it is on the dynamics of prophetic communi-cation, rather than the prophecies themselves, that this book focuses. The most interesting moments in forward-looking narratives occur in the space between the articulation of a prophecy and its ultimate realisation. Indeed, the polysemy of the term 'realisation' is vital here. 'Realisation' means not just the point in time when a prophecy has moved from a description of future events to a 'real' occurrence; it also encompasses interlocutors' often extended efforts to comprehend the original prophecy and to make it fit their experience or knowledge to their own satisfaction. As their efforts include speculations, assumptions, reconsiderations and actions, many prophecies turn out to be 'realised' through the very act of interpreting them.[16]

---

[14] Vernant (1990) 43, quoted and discussed further by Goldhill (2006).
[15] Steiner (1998) 246.
[16] A point made by both literary scholars and historians: see e.g. Burkert (1991); Wood (2003); Flower (2008). Detienne (1996) 71 discusses the 'realisation' of prophecy in the Homeric *Hymn to Hermes*.

This book is therefore about exploring a peculiar kind of narrative space that is created by the function of inspired prophecy. It is a space that is dependent on a prophecy's ability to struggle free from the normal constraints of chronology, describing diachronically occurring events of the future in terms of a baffling synchronic present vision, before events resolve back into order through the interpretative efforts and actions of those responding to the prophecy.[17] Cassandra and the Cumaean Sibyl are both paradigmatic figures when it comes to the production of such richly ambiguous prophecies. Each is a prophet who manages to be at once insider and outsider, commentator and actor, purveyor of glosso-lalia and of truth, Greek-speaker and non-Greek-speaker, interpreter and interpreted, virgin and mistress, a traveller through time and space and yet still a mortal constrained by her own life's fated trajectory.

Prophecy as Poetry, Prophets as Poets

According to Pliny the Elder and Plutarch, the Pythia at Delphi invented the hexameter.[18] In the third book of Sibylline Oracles the author predicts, rather indignantly, that Homer will copy both her words and her metre in his tales of Troy.[19] Diodorus Siculus claims that Manto, the inspired prophet and daughter of Tiresias, was an excellent poet whose written verses Homer borrowed.[20] Occasionally, too, oracles might be found in iambic trimeter, the metre of tragic speech.[21] Across the Greek and Roman world, in literary representations and beyond, prophetic utterances were by default packaged in the rhythmic structures of poetic metre.[22] The elevated performativity of verse must have been the prime reason for this, but Plutarch points out that the mnemonic function of metre was also significant for prophecy.[23] Just as events in the past are made memorable

---

[17] Franke (2011) also makes the point that past, present and future all coincide in prophetic discourse, and that this mythic time manages to 'break open the present towards possibilities that it can never encompass but can nevertheless strive after in a movement of ecstatic self-transcendence' (55).
[18] Plin. *HN* 7.56.205; Plut. *De Pyth. or.* 402d; Paus. 10.5.7. Thanks to Alessandro Barchiesi for first pointing out to me this connection. In Plutarch's dialogue it is the Pythia's late adoption of prose, and the questionable quality of her verse, that prompts the extensive questioning of her whole pro-phetic enterprise.
[19] *Or. Sib.* 3.419–25. This is the earliest datable book of Sibylline Oracles, dating to the first or possibly even second century BCE.
[20] Diod. Sic. 4.66.5f.
[21] Potter (1990b) 474.
[22] Not to mention the magical powers attributed to the hexameter in the popular domain, as in curse tablets. See Faraone (2011).
[23] Plut. *De Pyth. or.* 407f.

through faithful repetitions enabled by metrical narrative, so the precise repetition of metrical oracles concerning the future keeps such narratives alive until they can be accurately matched with the events they predict.

At the same time, classical poetry bears the weight of prophetic authority because of its relationship with certain divine figures. The Muses, inspirers of poetry, have their own insight into 'present, future and past events' (Hes. *Theog.* 38). For Plutarch, the Muses are also the 'fellows and guardians of prophecy [*mantikēs*]' (Plut. *De Pyth. or.* 402d). More importantly still, the cultivation of Apollo by both poets and prophets brings their works into a close symbiosis. Apollo inspires and validates the words of the poet as he does the words of the prophet, and grants both mortal figures privileged access to a language that harnesses time through narrative. Indeed, at least by the time of imperial Rome and throughout late antiquity and the Byzantine and medieval worlds, epic poetry itself becomes credited with prophetic potential for every reader through the *sortes Vergilianae* and the *homeromanteion*.[24]

Poets and prophets, then, share in a world of divine inspiration and linguistic power. Their common ground is more marked in the characterisation of the possessed seer, the visionary *mantis*, than in representations of the intellectual sign-reader, the interpreting *prophētēs*. Across the vast range of practices that constitute prophecy in the ancient world, many have at their heart an act of skilled sign-reading: haruspicy, oneiromancy, cleromancy, augury, necromancy, to mention only a few. The task of the sign-reader is largely explicative: what has been divinely fated is already on display as a message embedded in some manifestation of the natural world, and it is the sign-reader's work to interpret these portents, to gloss them in clear and comprehensible language. This may be less a job of translating the message itself, and more one of suggesting rituals or practical steps that will allow interested parties to take action in the face of ominous warnings. Ambiguity is inherent in the signs, but the sign-reader's task is to limit and control this ambiguity, to the best of his or her ability.[25] At times the sign-reader may be asked to interpret a message that has been delivered by a human figure and is already technically in human language, but is still not comprehensible to ordinary men or women. This is the scenario outlined in Plato's *Timaeus*, in which a figure described as a *prophētēs* explains the

---

[24] Ekbom (2013) addresses the *sortes Vergilianae* (as a literary game more than as prophetic material), as does Hardie (2014) 9–10; Karanika (2011) 274 writes of the *homeromanteion* that: 'multiple meanings are integral to the semiotics and poetics of texts that preserve Homeric lines as divination'.

[25] Struck (2004) 166–7.

utterance of an inspired figure called a *mantis*.²⁶ Though not all authors apply the terms *prophētēs* and *mantis* according to Plato's schema, and though some sign-reading does get assimilated to literary practices, it is a variation on the figure of the possessed *mantis* or, in Latin, the visionary *uates*, that plays the most prominent role in constructions of the poet in literary works. There are some cultural differences between the Greek *mantis* and the Roman *uates*, but they are both essentially mouthpieces for a mysterious divine force of truth. Their prophetic utterances are delivered in a mode that is depicted as analogous to the inspired production of poetry, while the features of these prophets' possession influence the representation of poets' inspiration.²⁷

One important dimension to this association between inspired prophets and poets lies in the fact that *manteis* and *uates* are largely, though not completely, deprived of agency in the delivery of their prophecies. While sign-readers explain and assign meaning to a message, to the point where they may be held responsible for an incorrect reading, inspired prophets simply articulate a message. In Plato's *Ion*, Socrates explains the 'magnetic' force of divine meaning as it is passed on through poets and prophets. He points out to Ion that the meaning does not belong to the speaker, but that he simply provides one unwitting link in a chain of communicative acts:

> the god, carrying away the mind of these poets, uses them as his servants [*hupēretais*], as he does soothsayers and divine seers [*tois mantesi tois theiois*], so that we who are listening to them may know that it is not the men – who have lost their minds – who are speaking these so very valuable words, but that it is the god himself who is speaking [*ho theos autos estin ho legōn*], and he is communicating with us through them. (534c–d)

Later Quintus Cicero in *De divinatione* says something similar of Cassandra's modulation into inspired speech in Ennius' *Alexander*: *deus inclusus corpore humano iam, non Cassandra loquitur* – 'contained within a human body the god, not Cassandra, now speaks' (Cic. *Div.* 1.67). We

---

²⁶ Pl. *Ti.* 71e–72b.
²⁷ Nagy (1989) 23–9 and (1990); Newman (1967). Nagy sees a gradual division between the roles of poet and prophet with the emergence of the Greek *polis*, and suggests that later confusion between the roles is simply a 'trace' of a prior age. Nagy also probes the distinctions between *mantis* and *prophētēs*, but overplays the identification of the *mantis* with the Muse and the uninspired *prophētēs* with the poet, basing this comparison partly on the suggestion that priests may have turned the Delphic oracles into verse, *contra* the claim elsewhere that the Pythia invented the hexameter herself. Maurizio (1995) offers a spirited and convincing rebuttal. Struck (2004) 165–70 also points out the distinction between inspired speaker and interpreter across the Greek and Roman realms. Ford (2002) 167–72 brings a wealth of philosophical material to bear on the question. Mazzoldi (2001) 96 places Cassandra somewhere between the two figures of Plato's *Timaeus*. See also [Longinus] *Subl.* 13.2.

should take into account the undercurrent of Socratic irony in the *Ion*, and we must remember too that Cassandra and her sibylline sisters in fact always insist on delivering their prophecies in the first person (see below), but nonetheless such philosophical theories of divine utterance do the important work of detaching the words of inspired figures from the constraints of authorial intention.[28] These prophets impose no solutions, close no interpretative doors and claim no responsibility for the multiplicity of readings that may be imposed on their utterance by the next link(s) in the chain of interpretation. A poet who identifies as a *mantis* or *uates* claims privileged divine knowledge with an invulnerability to criticism if that knowledge turns out to have been misconstrued. As Feeney points out, 'The "truth" of the Muses and their poets is indeed a protean thing.'[29]

Another vital dimension to the connection between poets and prophets lies in the inherent value attributed to their verbal productions, even if they are misunderstood. The most explicit articulation of this appears again in Plato: in the *Ion*, and also in the *Phaedrus*. In one of Socrates' most striking speeches in the *Phaedrus*, he celebrates various kinds of *mania* – 'madness' or 'possession'. In his comparison of prophetic *mania* with poetic *mania*, Socrates explicitly celebrates inspired rather than technically skilled prophets, then draws a similar connection between inspired and uninspired poets:

> As much as inspired prophecy [*mantikē*] is more authoritative and more valued than augury, both in reputation and in fact, so the ancients attest that madness [*manian*] sent by a god is much finer than common sanity … Whoever arrives at the gates of poetry without the madness [*manias*] of the Muses, trusting that he will be a sufficiently good poet with skill, he will be a failure and his poetry, coming as it is from a sane man, will fade into obscurity compared with that of men who are madly inspired [*mainomenōn*]. (244d, 245a)

This attitude is not limited to Socrates, nor even to the fifth- or fourth-century Greeks. No less potent a model in written than in oral performance cultures, Rome continues to celebrate poets gifted with *ingenium* ('filled with a kind of divine inspiration', as Cicero describes it in his *Pro Archia*), even as its literary system appears increasingly devoted to making carefully honed skill, *ars*, the central boast in authorial self-promotion.[30]

---

[28] Murray (1996) 119 mentions the ironic undertow at work here in the *Ion*.

[29] Feeney (1991) 16. His broader discussion shows that this does not mean poets are not, at times, condemned for the unreliability and deceptiveness of their works.

[30] *Quasi diuino quodam spiritu inflari* (Cic. *Arch.* 18). On Roman poetic self-presentation see Lowrie (2009) esp. 1–23. Horace's light mockery of the *uesanus poeta*, the 'crazed poet' (Hor. *Ars P.* 455), only goes to prove the endurance of the stereotype.

A little earlier in the *Phaedrus*, Socrates had illustrated the power of inspired *mania* by referring to the benefits granted to Greece through the efforts of a few legendary prophetic figures:

> For the prophetess at Delphi and the priestesses at Dodona, when mad [*maneisai*], have achieved many great things for Greece both in the private and the public domain, but few or none when they have been in their right minds; and if we are to speak of the Sibyl and all the others [*allous*] who by inspired prophecy have predicted many things to many people and guided them well with regard to the future, it is clear to everyone that we would be dragging our conversation out a long time. (244b)

Here Socrates makes no mention of Cassandra, but he does cite the Pythia at Delphi, the priestesses at Dodona, a sibyl and various unnamed 'others'.[31] It is immediately striking that all the named figures are female. Plato offers no explanation, and gives his readers no indication that he finds it odd or worth remarking upon. Indeed, the 'others' to whom Socrates also attributes inspired prophecy may include male prophets, for he describes them with a masculine collective pronoun (*allous*), but without adducing any specific names. A few famous female figures, it transpires, dominate the mythological world of prophetic inspiration.[32] At the same time, the titles of the inspired role, *mantis* and *uates*, remain open to both male and female appropriation.

The Prophetic Female Voice and Body

Cassandra's life is defined by her sex, then, not only because of the horrors she is forced to undergo as a woman in a patriarchal and war-torn world, but also because of her gendered experience of prophecy. Plato's illustration of prophetic *mania* with a canon of women draws attention to the peculiar association between inspiration and the female body.[33]

---

[31] See the discussion in Dodds (1951) 68ff. For a less female-dominated list see Cic. *Div.* 1.34, citing Bacis and Epimenides as well as the Erythraean Sibyl.

[32] This discussion has been focused strictly on the literary realm. Flower (2008) 84–91, in his subtle and wide-ranging study of the historical seer in ancient Greece, cautions against creating a typology of prophets that relies too heavily on the claims of theoretical and ideologically motivated writers such as Plato. He points out that Plato may have been citing a limited all-female line-up of inspired prophets as part of his agenda to diminish the status of most prophetic practices in society (85). When it comes to delineating the experiences of prophecy in the ancient historical world, Flower softens the edges of the 'inspired' and 'artificial' dichotomy, and with it the tendency to identify women as peculiarly associated with the 'inspired' realm. At the same time, much of his discussion of female seers (211–39) *does* focus on a central figure of inspiration: the Pythia at Delphi.

[33] Bremmer (1996) 98 writes: 'In Archaic Greece, it is only women who prophesy in a state of madness.' See also Crippa (1998) 184–9; Iriarte (1999) 45–6.

Stereotypically female physical and mental characteristics found in Greek and Roman constructions of womanhood contribute to the gendered models of prophetic inspiration, at least as they are portrayed in literary sources. These characteristics include: irrationality, mental fragility or submissiveness; alternative and often uncontrolled sexuality, including a body that is vulnerable or receptive to penetration and a vessel for child-bearing; affiliation with the domestic rather than public sphere; and a marked relationship to speech and language, which includes a propensity for trickery. The representation of inspired prophets toys with these stereotypes even when it rejects them, and in at least some cases the prophetic role transforms into qualities those very characteristics that are normally presented as feminine handicaps. The marginalised status and 'otherness' of women, in both Greek and Roman literary representations, allows fictional female figures to perform outlandish roles that would be both more, and less, challenging when associated with men, particularly with conforming male citizens.[34]

The most notable exception to the female gendering of inspired prophecy comes in the figure of the long-lived Tiresias, but his is the case that proves the rule. Like Phineus in Apollonius' *Argonautica*, Tiresias is characterised by a blindness that offsets his heightened sensitivity in his sixth sense, his prophetic vision.[35] Blindness also appears in the paradigmatic myth of the male inspired poet, Homer, 'who' tells of Tiresias' skills in the tenth and eleventh books of the *Odyssey*. These male versions of prophetic and poetic inspiration involve a model of inversely impaired and enhanced senses that is not found in the female prophet. Moreover, Tiresias' mythic biography contains episodes of transsexuality that put a question mark over any claim that he represents a purely male form of inspired prophecy. As a figure who has lived as both man and woman, who has embodied and evaluated their differences, his biography is, to an extent, an exploration of the gender default for inspired prophecy.[36] In the end, his portrayal as a prophet in

---

[34] On the oppressions and privileges of female 'otherness' see Zeitlin (1996) esp. 87–119 and 341–74; Foley (1998) 49 on Greek male writers 'using fictional women to think with'; Hallett and Skinner (1997). Hall (2002) 22–4 makes some interesting observations on the use of male performers to sing female parts in tragedy on stage.

[35] Apollonius suffers from no lack of male prophets, but other prominent male characters with the gift of prophecy, including Idmon and Mopsus, are clearly marked as sign-readers, not inspired prophets.

[36] Tiresias lived for a spell as a woman, and during his role as adjudicator in a debate between Zeus and Hera, Tiresias identifies with Zeus's interests and rules that women have more pleasure in sex than men (*BNP* 215–16). Detailed analysis can be found in Brisson (1976).

Greek tragedy is scarcely one that plays upon the feminised ecstasy of inspiration. Aélion shows how Tiresias is placed firmly within the male sphere of prophecy, assimilated to the realm of masculine interpretation rather than feminine inspiration, when she notes that Sophocles chooses to represent 'the wisdom of Tiresias over the transports of Cassandra'.[37]

If the paradigmatic male poet-prophet possesses a visual disability that both complements and tempers the man's visionary abilities, the paradigmatic female (poet-)prophet is defined by the expected limitations of her voice. At least in the world of fifth-century Athens, silence is the default adornment of femininity. As Montiglio reflects on Pericles' famous speech in Thucydides, 'Feminine reputation paradoxically rests on silence: it is inversely correlated with the woman's *kleos*, whether it be around her virtue or her defects.'[38] Every female representation must eschew Pericles' exhortation, must defy the idealised absence of her voice, in order to present her perspective on the world. In reality, though, words swirl around women in ways that evoke a public presence even when the women themselves are at their most effaced. Loraux notes, for example, the way in which verbal descriptions anticipate women's deaths on stage: just before they are to be silenced for good, they are celebrated (for good or ill). 'Everything starts by being spoken, by being heard, by being imagined. For seeing is born from words and is closely bound up with them.'[39] Indeed, if 'seeing is born from words', it is through words that women display, even parade, their greatest human and divine powers – including in the realm of prophecy.

No matter how controlled and regulated female speech might be in Greek or Roman life, a range of mythic instantiations suggest that women were perceived as possessing a loaded relationship with language and speech or song.[40] As Fates, Muses, Sirens and Bee-maidens, as sibyls and priestesses such as Plato's Diotima, women are permitted to demonstrate their powerful voices. The interest in these women's utterances lies in their combination of exceptional understanding with the ability to deceive.

---

[37] Aélion (1983) II, 222: 'Il semble que Sophocle … ait préféré la sagesse de Tirésias aux transports de Cassandre.' In a further twist on this paradigm, in Seneca's *Oedipus*, Tiresias presides over a reported Odyssean necromancy, but he also interprets the signs described by his daughter Manto. She is not inspired, but she is strangely physically moved by the process of a (rather Roman) priestly sign-reading: 'I shudder as I watch' (323); 'the disturbed entrails quiver | not with a gentle movement, as they do normally | but they are shaking my whole hands' (353–5).
[38] Montiglio (2000) 83, on Thuc. 2.45.2. For a slightly different view of the 'authority' given women by their everyday work, and in specific realms such as those of captivity and lament, see Karanika (2014).
[39] Loraux (1987) vii.
[40] Hall (1999) esp. 112–18 discusses the close affinity between high-status women and lyric production in fifth-century tragedy.

Bergren explains: 'In these figures we see a degree of knowledge attributed to the female that results in a capacity for double speech, for both truth and the imitation of truth, a paradoxical speech hopelessly ambiguous to anyone whose knowledge is less than the speaker's.'[41] Ancient myth-makers' interest in women's power of speech appears to combine an appreciation of their ordinarily suppressed potential with a fear of how they might put it into subversive practice from their position as political outsiders, sexual submissives and social inferiors. This tension then informs the literary representations of these female figures, which can be used to mirror and explore poets' own risky claims to exceptional knowledge.

Much recent work has focused on the role of the Muses in this process. These figures of inspiration, powerfully immortal but vulnerably female, provide an ideal zone for poets to model their uncontrolled, out-of-body experience of divine possession.[42] Some of these dynamics also feed into the representation of female prophetic voices, but there is an important difference. The female bodies of the Muses are always purely symbolic, which is one of the reasons that poets can toy with them and even pretend to identify with them without posing a profound challenge to their masculinity. When it comes to mortal prophets, however, the women's bodies matter in real terms – and in ways that show how high the stakes are for those who give themselves over to the articulation of inspired words. Cassandra and her descendants demonstrate this starkly. One of the constant refrains in descriptions of Cassandra's prophecies is a reference to Cassandra's physical response to the mental inspiration she receives. The inhuman communicative difficulties she faces place terrible stresses on her body. Cassandra's female body is always central to her story: it was her body that invited Apollo's lust and whose inviolability was punished by the curse of not being believed; the same body is destined to suffer the horrors of Ajax's and Agamemnon's violations.[43] But for Cassandra the inherent paradox of her situation, of knowing but never passing on that knowledge, is also played out on a huge scale within her human frame. The enormous stretches of time and space that her mind is forced to comprehend wreak havoc on an already frail body with frustratingly limited vocal capacities. In the case of the Cumaean Sibyl, another victim of Apollo's promises and

---

[41] Bergren (1983) 70. See also Segal (1993b); McClure (1999); Spentzou (2002); Gera (2003) 203–6; Crippa (1998). Crippa (1990) and (1999) focus on Cassandra's privileged form of glossolalic speech.

[42] Fowler and Spentzou (2002) *passim*. See also Calame (1995) 58ff.; Detienne (1996) 39ff.; and more recently LeVen (2014).

[43] See Sissa (1990) 37–8. On the imagery of childbirth within Cassandra's prophetic domain see Iriarte (1999) 43–4.

another traveller across the Mediterranean, her body is forced to carry her prophetic capacity to term, as it were: her thousand years of life reach out to encompass her visions of the distant future.

Cassandra and the Cumaean Sibyl are both physically bound up in their own prophecies. Cassandra in particular is personally involved, as the cruel brevity of her lifespan is predicated on the very prophecies she delivers. By articulating the future she cannot but guarantee that it happens; as a true prophet, her every speech is a performative speech act and, as such, dangerous.[44] Cassandra's efforts to communicate information about the future are rooted in a human desire to avert those future events, but knowing that her message will be misunderstood regardless, she also recognises the value in not articulating it at all. Her periods of silence, or her streaks of riddling nonsense, can all be read as illustrations of these paradoxes, as well as strategies for combating them. When Cassandra does clearly describe the events to come she is no longer just delivering a narrative, but committing herself to living through, and dying in, that narrative.[45] In turn, the Graeco-Roman Sibyl at Cumae, whose *sortes* or 'lots' are associated with scraps of writing, embeds her skills in a dismembered representation of prophetic utterance. This creates a durability through time and an ambiguity on which her prophecies' authority relies. However, manhandled by their priest-readers and imprisoned in silence and secrecy, immortality in the form of written texts comes at the expense of her bodily form, which dissipates as her prophetic ambiguities are channelled by the enforcers of Roman 'destiny'.

Translation, Prophecy, Literary History

Translation, literally the 'bringing across' of a message from one sphere to another, embraces a wide range of activities. Jakobson describes translation as a term that encompasses three possible semiotic manoeuvres (not in this order): 'interlingual' translation, the interpretation of verbal signs from

---

[44] The speech act theory of Austin (1975) identifies perlocutionary statements as ones that have an effect on their audience. This implies that a prophet's speech is performative if it has the ability to influence listeners in such a way as to change the future: see the discussion in Moberly (2006) 87–8. For a truthful but powerless prophet like Cassandra, however, an ability to change the future and defy the very narrative already predicted would take away her status as a true prophet. Cassandra's performativity lies in the fatal inevitability of her words bringing about a future event, not bringing about an audience response.

[45] Schein (1982) 11–12 glances at this peculiarity of Cassandra's prophecies: 'What is different about Cassandra is that she is … actually seeing and emotionally responding to exceptionally gruesome and vividly described events, including her own murder.'

a foreign language; 'intralingual' translation, the interpretation of signs within a single language through paraphrase; and 'intersemiotic translation' or 'transmutation', in which verbal signs are interpreted by nonverbal signs, i.e. across different media.[46] The term 'translation' covers a spectrum of activities (including quotation, commentary and dramatisation) that all function as a productive form of interpretation, a subjective mediation between different languages that results in a new creation. What makes translation so potent a concept is the tension it builds between its promise that a unique message can be *successfully* conveyed in different languages, different words, different modes, and its acknowledgement that the message can never be *perfectly* conveyed – that is to say, that there are an infinite number of ways in which the message's transformation may take place and none will evoke exactly the same response as the original.

One of the more unusual activities that may be considered to sit within the field of translation is prophecy.[47] Acts of prophecy claim to translate from a source language that is unknowable, under normal circumstances, into a target language that is purportedly comprehensible to mortal audiences. This source language takes one of two notional forms. One is the language of the foreseeing gods, the divine narrative that describes the trajectory of fate.[48] This invites an interlingual translation on the part of the prophet, even though such a narrative of fate is barely conceivable in terms of human language. The other form can be imagined to be the trajectory of fate itself, the actual events that are to happen in the future. This requires a kind of intersemiotic translation that takes action into the realm of description – or rather prescription. Whichever model is evoked, prophecy is dependent on the imperfection that is inherent in the claim to any act of translation, an imperfection that demands to be corrected and updated over time through repeated retranslation. It is a rare prophetic

---

[46] Jakobson (1959) 233. For the application of these ideas in an ancient context see Most (2003).

[47] Light-hearted episodes that underline the association between prophecy and translation include Pseudolus' warning that he will answer Simo 'in Delphic utterance' before he then switches into Greek (Plaut. *Pseud.* 480–9). Apuleius also makes a wittily knowing reference to his own Latin telling of the Greek myth of Cupid and Psyche when Apollo gives an oracle: 'Apollo, though Greek and from Ionia, taking into account the author of the Milesian tale, replied thus with a Latin prophecy' (Apul. *Met.* 4.32).

[48] This divine 'comprehension' of the future may be, but does not have to be, identified with the notion that the gods speak a language different from that of humans. Ross (2005) 309–11 discusses the passage in the Homeric *Hymn to Delian Apollo* (156–64) that describes the divine power of a hymn that is comprehensible to all humans, even those whose own languages are mutually unintelligible. See also Gera (2003) 49–54. Perhaps the clearest representation of this divine narrative of the future is found in Jupiter's privileged knowledge, and selective sharing, of the fates in the first book of the *Aeneid* (see Chapter 4).

utterance that does not require a further act of interpretation to explain the meaning of the prophecy in terms that make sense to the audience. Prophecies – as highly imperfect interlingual or intersemiotic translations from a mystical source language into a human language of sorts – tend to deliver an easily misconstrued message that lends itself to a multiplicity of further interpretations; that is, to further intralingual translations. As the future plays out, this flurry of translation work concludes when specific events come to pass that more or less satisfactorily render in action the repeatedly reworked words of the prophecy. However, the truly ambiguous prophetic message, like a classic text, continues to flaunt the possibility that it has not yet revealed its true meaning. It never completely relinquishes a level of indeterminacy that suggests it may need another attempt at translation at a later point in time.

Even when a prophecy is narrated as part of an apparently fixed mythological narrative in which the fulfilment of the prediction is well known, the language of a prophecy invites an open process of interpretation. Although prophecies imply that the future is predestined and that petitioners have no free will, their ambiguities encourage those petitioners to respond freely, to act in their efforts to uncover a prophecy's truth or to prove it false. Protagonists often construct their prophecy's fulfilment as they actively engage with the words' semantic stretch. As Steiner puts it, 'Men move, as it were, in the interstices, in the lacunae of misunderstanding left by the oracle; or in a space of necessity made coherent, made logical by foresight.'[49] Or, in the context of the Delphic oracle, Maurizio explains it well:

> The client's response, especially when it is a misreading, spurs observation not on the efficacy of Apollo's prophecy, but on how oracles mean, because the search for what will come to be the correct interpretation is tantamount to the search for the future. The dramatic endings of oracular tales suture the gap between word and thing that an oracle initially presents.[50]

When a prophecy is embedded in a literary text, this 'gap between word and thing' invites an open and active engagement on the part of external audiences too. For audiences of a mythic story, this is not simply a moment of dramatic irony in which their superior knowledge of the likely narrative trajectory distances them from the pathetic hopes of the blind protagonists. It can also be a chance for an audience to indulge its own desire to invest in narrative alternatives, or what Wood calls 'the entertainment of

[49] Steiner (1998) 157, with wider discussion at 145–69.
[50] Maurizio (2013) 113.

possibilities'.[51] Ancient authors, entering as readers as well as writers into a literary scene driven by strong narrative and generic traditions, had their own balancing act to walk between the limitations of their chosen literary field and the creative need to design new 'possibilities'. This is often evident in scenes that play with the sequence of mythic narrative in counterpoint with the sequence of literary history, particularly through prophetic episodes. In his reading of Ovid's *Heroides*, texts purportedly produced by mythic women at a crucial turning point in their histories, Barchiesi explores the peculiarity of passages that imagine variations on events that technically lie in the central characters' future, but whose detailed outcome has already been recounted and implicitly fixed in earlier canonical texts. He dubs this the 'future reflexive': a self-conscious technique that 'hints at the prospect of a parallel world, still open to different possibilities and deaf to the claims of the tradition'.[52] Writers, protagonists and readers alike all invest in this parallel world that depends so heavily on the deployment of the future tense and the freedom of interpretation it temporarily invites. To return to Steiner: 'Future tenses ... are a part of the capacity of language for the fictional and illustrate the absolutely central power of the human word to go beyond and against "that which is the case".'[53]

True prophecies are translations of the future that are always successful in setting up a core correspondence in meaning, and always not-quite-perfect, just like any other kind of translation. Though the central message correctly constructs the events to come, ambiguities and misreadings resist those same events. Some insights from modern translation theorists show how this apparently flawed function can have real value – a value based on translation's ability to support the 'entertainment of possibilities'. Venuti acknowledges the danger associated with translation succinctly: 'translation provokes the fear of inauthenticity, distortion, contamination'.[54] But he goes on to argue that these slippages and transformations, which form an inevitable part of the process of translating, do not necessarily diminish the message that is being conveyed. On the contrary: there is a controlled but rich proliferation of meaning at the point of the message's imperfect reformulation. This can be deliberately harnessed through translation that showcases the alienness of its source material, an approach known as 'foreignising' or 'minoritising' translation. When the traces of neither the

---

[51] Wood (2005) 4. Compare Aristotle *Poetics* 1451a36–8.
[52] Barchiesi (1993) 335.
[53] Steiner (1998) 168.
[54] Venuti (1998) 31.

original code nor of the translation process itself are fully effaced, then
there emerge places in a translation where the host language can be openly
seen to map imprecisely, even uncomfortably, onto its source. These jarring
moments strip the host language – especially a hegemonic language – of its
complacent fluency, creating instead a space for new linguistic, social and
cultural constructions.[55]

For the translation process to be perceptible, in all its troubling and
provocative inadequacy, literalism comes into its own. This flies in the
face of ancient theories on successful literary translation. In the writings
of literary critics such as Cicero and Horace, translators are advised to
respect the spirit, rather than the letter, of their source. Word-for-word
efforts (*uerbum e uerbo*) are considered the mark of a clumsy translator
(*indisertus interpres*) who loses the underlying force (*uis*) of the original.[56] But for modern theorists such as Benjamin and Derrida, it is
presumptuous to believe that a text's underlying meaning can ever be
adequately paraphrased; it implies that the translators have identified
both a semantic and a stylistic poverty in their chosen source text. These
theorists embrace literal translation as a means of fully engaging with
the challenge of an individual text and with the process of translation
itself: the awkwardness of literalism exposes the presence of multiple
layers of language in a translation, and in the process it reveals the translator as a true mediator – possibly even a medium. For Benjamin, with
his philosophical and mystical approach to translation in 'The Task of
the Translator', the moment of suspension between languages moves the
translator beyond specific languages: an engagement with 'the element
that does not lend itself to translation' takes him or her into the realm
of 'pure language' ('reine Sprache').[57] Derrida focuses on the new life
bestowed on a text by a translation process that recognises the spectrum
of the source text's meanings and neither aims for a perfectly complete
act of translation nor gives up in despair:

[55] In order to identify and celebrate the potential creativity in rebarbative 'foreignising' translation,
Venuti (1998) develops the Derridean concept of the 'supplement' and the notion of the 'remainder'
articulated in Lecercle (1990) – that is, the use of non-standard linguistic forms to subvert and ener-
gise stale language usage. Chaudhuri (1999) follows Derrida (1979) even more closely in order to
show how a deconstructive approach reveals translation as the generative linguistic function that it
is, and Niranjana (1992) unpicks the value of this approach in redressing the imbalances of cultural
and political power in postcolonial contexts.
[56] See Brock (1979), Kytzler (1989), Traina (1989), following most closely the terms of the debate set up
by Cicero and Horace; also Bettini (2012), McElduff (2013), Feeney (2015) 45–64.
[57] Benjamin (1999) 76. Benjamin (1989) suggests that this 'pure language' is in fact 'translatability',
which is to say, language itself.

Totally translatable, it disappears as a text, as writing, as a body of language. Totally untranslatable, even in what is believed to be one language, it dies immediately. Thus triumphant translation is neither the life or the death of the text, only or already its living *on*, its life after life, its life after death.[58]

This argument does not lack a political dimension, either. Literal translation and unconcealed evidence of translation breakdown – moments where untranslatable qualities in an original text are allowed to disrupt the fluency of its translated version – have also found champions in more recent sociocultural approaches to translation, particularly those emerging from postcolonial studies.[59] 'Foreignising' or 'minoritising' acts of translation that do not over-naturalise the style of a text sustain the character of a source language and culture in its new target language. The result is a more respectful acknowledgement of the source text and the translation process, and an enrichment of the target language and the cultural experience of those operating in it.

This approach to translation may seem to privilege words over meaning, to celebrate alien stylistics and awkward, rebarbative language over straightforward communication. In fact, such 'foreignising' translation work is honest and democratic. It does not conceal the ways in which meaning is contingent on myriad acts of reception, and it insists on a wider and more active participation in the construction of that meaning by its various readers and interpreters. Such translations create an opportunity to revitalise tired, exclusive and limiting forms of language and literature. A similar challenge and reward is offered by the ambiguous prophecies of ancient literature. The failure of easy comprehension, the discomfiting sense of confusion and estrangement triggered by the prophecies' uncertain meaning: these difficulties slow down and enrich (though they certainly do not always improve) the language and the lived experience of all the prophets and petitioners who engage with them.

Cassandra's Foreignising Translations

The function of translation matches Cassandra's prophetic function in each of the several ways outlined by Jakobson. She appears to perform interlingual translation in her delivery of the divinely couched narrative of the future (fate, or in Latin *fatum/fata*, 'that which has been spoken'), offering the kind of translation from one language to another that matches

---

[58] Derrida (1979) 102–3, discussed by Ertel (2011).
[59] E.g. Robinson (1997); Bermann and Wood (2005).

her characterisation as a Trojan foreigner in Greece. When her story goes from being told in Greece to being told in Rome, her language undergoes a real process of interlingual translation as she goes from speaking Greek to speaking Latin – as is also the case with the Cumaean Sibyl. In practice, though, Cassandra mostly provides intralingual translations in the monolingual texts of Greece and Rome, framing and reframing her account of the future in the same language from one text to another, and regularly provoking further acts of commentary, paraphrase and quotation among her audiences. Cassandra is also presented as engaging with intersemiotic translation in the way she transforms future events into words and back again, and this is even more true of the Cumaean Sibyl, whose narratives move fluidly between the written, spoken and lived word; between books, staged utterance and the prophet's physical implication in the history she prophesies.

In other words, Cassandra is not just a translator, she is also an embodiment of the very function of translation: her prophetic speech often appears to be suspended between languages, like Benjamin's translator who operates in the realm of 'pure language' that is beyond any single linguistic code.[60] Cassandra takes and reformulates an incomprehensible message from the future and becomes incomprehensible in the process, (re)producing a message in such a way that it demands a second, or third or fourth translation. Sometimes she descends from a trance-like state of prophecy to initiate the next link in the chain of interpretations herself, reframing her own message in more prosaic language, only to find that this speech too is received with confusion.[61] Her utterance is always both a target and a source text at the same time. The proliferation of translation acts within her single body evokes a kind of never-ending self-translation; like the self-translator, Cassandra suffers a splitting of the self, one part of which is committed to the spirit of the original composition, while the other struggles to reframe it for a new audience that can never grasp the meaning of the original.[62]

---

[60] Dalgarno (2012) 9 notes the importance of Benjamin's emphasis on translator, rather than translation: 'By titling his text "The Task of the Translator" rather than "The Task of Translation" Benjamin kept the emphasis on the subjectivity of the translator, where the tension between experience and theory plays out.'
[61] Mazzoldi (2002) explores Cassandra's fluctuations between ecstatic and rational speech in Aeschylus' *Agamemnon*, arguing that in doing this the prophet actually combines elements of the *mantis* and the *prophētēs*, with the chorus grasping rather more of her meaning as she increases in rationality. See also Goudot (1999b) 9. Bettini (2008) 166 notes Cassandra's 'auto-interpretazione' at work in Aeschylus' *Agamemnon* (see Chapter 1).
[62] Chaudhuri (1999) 47–8. See also Venuti (1998) 5–6 on Kundera and his self-translations.

Like the self-translator, too, Cassandra is not without a measure of authorial claim on her narrative, despite her inability to impose a final form on the message for which she is a conduit. Where the Pythia speaks as Apollo, ventriloquising the voice of the god himself, Cassandra and all sibyls speak on their own account and stand behind the first person in their delivery of prophecies.[63] They may resent the prophetic role imposed on them, but they are not passive in their performance of it. Nor do they normally perform at the whim of others. Where the Pythia responds only to questions, or at least is surrounded by a machinery that turns her inspired words into answers to specific questions, Cassandra and the sibyls speak spontaneously. The Sibylline Books become a source of answers for Roman questioners, but they are distanced in time and medium from the 'original' mythic sibyl whose inspired stream of unprompted Greek prophecy they purportedly document. Virgil's reconstruction of the Cumaean Sibyl's compositional practice makes it clear that her priorities do not usually include indulging her audience.[64]

What is strange about Cassandra's approach to translation, across whatever linguistic boundaries it occurs, is that she appears to defy ancient norms concerning 'good' naturalistic translation practice, at least as it was practised in the literary sphere. Instead she embraces an ostensibly inelegant literalism, one that engages with the principles of foreignising translation. Cassandra's flawed prophecies translate the future without smoothing down the rough edges, the 'foreignness' of her source text. She cannot cater to her audience's desire for a straightforward narrative that lacks any traces of either its incomprehensible source or the mysterious act of translation that she is performing. Her prophecies are a form of translation that grates and baffles, but it also sustains a wealth of provocative meanings that expand the mind, if not the understanding, of her many audiences.

The shortcomings of Cassandra's approach to translating the future are undeniable. Her relentlessly detailed and truthful prophecies are over-exact replicas of the enigmatic visions to which only she has access, of the divine language in which future events are wrapped. Not conceding enough to the language of her auditors, not imposing her own interpretation of the 'meaning' contained within her visions, Cassandra's translations are more than inelegant; they sustain the original's incomprehensibility. In Lycophron's representation of Cassandra's speech, in particular, literalism dogs her words even once they have been taken from her mouth;

---

[63] Lightfoot (2007) 8–16; Parke (1988) 9–10; Graf (1985) 347–8.
[64] See Chapter 4, especially on Helenus' description of the Cumaean Sibyl in *Aeneid* 3.

the messenger who quotes her prophecy replicates every obscure detail of her speech. In the Cumaean Sibyl's case, according to Virgil, her words that tell of the future are transcribed accurately but not selected or placed in order for the benefit of the petitioners. The Sibyl thus sustains in her written prophetic translation the confused diachrony that marked her original prophetic vision.[65]

At the same time, the extreme foreignisation that takes place in Cassandra's translations also allows them to take poetic flight. Suspended as she so often is between languages, Cassandra enables a linguistic experience whereby, through a single language, a single body, a single moment in time, the gears between authorship and reception spin and a moment of wild speculation is allowed, away from the contingent details of the narrative. Cassandra's translations bring her audiences close to the visions she sees, but in making insufficient modifications to their strangeness she forces her audiences to attempt their own translation of her visions. Their divergent readings of Cassandra's tortuously cribbed future productively delay the narrative, extending the life of the prophet and expanding the narrative in which she is placed. Meanwhile Cassandra is creating her own temporary refuge from her performative voice by failing to deliver the direct speech act that would condemn her all the more inescapably to her fate.

Though Cassandra's attempts to translate across multiple dimensions of time, space and language ultimately prove too much for one mortal body, her foreignising prophecies have a real and enduring literary value. The same is true of the Sibyl, who translates knowledge into her own 'sibylline' language, as Crippa says, and in so doing exposes 'the possible forms of communication and experimentation, the limits and possibilities of language'.[66] The process of translating the future allows each Cassandra to reach out to engage with the interpretative capacities of her immediate and her extended family of audiences and readers. Her obscurities expose her role as a translator and open up its workings for appropriation by her interlocutors within the myths and by the external readers and writers who shape those myths. Throughout her verbal experiments, in which meaning itself tends to be replaced by the search for meaning, Cassandra teaches, by example, the authority and the creativity of the foreignising translator.

---

[65] Lucan's Pythia, Phemonoe, who is closely modelled on Virgil's Sibyl, shows how 'all time piles up' for a prophet: *uenit aetas omnis in unam | congeriem* (*BC* 5.177–8).

[66] Crippa (1998) 177: 'La voce oracolare della Sibilla ... evoca le possibili forme di comunicazione e di sperimentazione, i limiti e le possibilità del linguaggio'; and on the Sibyl's translation work: 'traduce la conoscenza in un linguaggio "sibillino"' (180).

Cassandra and the Poetics of Prophecy

This book is about the ways in which Cassandra (mis)communicates the future. The focus is not on the content of her prophecies, but on the dialogic interactions that occur in the time and space between their articulation and their realisation. These interactions are dogged by confusion and misunderstanding. At the same time, they show every link in the chain of narrative production – source of inspiration, author, protagonist and reader – actively engaged in making meaning for themselves out of ostensibly nonsensical words.

Discussion falls into two broad categories. The primary focus is on the various efforts to transmit information regarding the future between the characters inhabiting individual works. In these readings the main aim is to identify how Cassandra and her interlocutors tackle the inaccessibility or instability of Cassandra's prophetic message, and how even the most poignant of communicative failures, the most disastrous and frustrating of misunderstandings, can still contribute something of value to the narrative.

The secondary focus is on how Cassandra, as a character, develops over multiple literary appearances, and how this transformation makes explicit the ways in which one text interacts with another. Cassandra is not just a translator of future events; her own narrative is repeatedly translated from one work to another, in a kind of canonisation process.[67] Cassandra's situation develops into a metaphor for literary influence that challenges some of the other models of literary history presented by ancient poets. Literary models expressed through metaphors of monumentality, genealogy or memory (for example) privilege the power of the poet, a power that is asserted by insisting on narrowing interpretative options. Such models illustrate poets appropriating and celebrating, or condemning, past works by locking their semantic riches into the service of a new vision that boasts its inviolability to future transformations.[68] By contrast, Cassandra's prophetic scenes, embedded in confusion, anticipation, delay and creative discussion, show a more flexible approach to the development of a canon across time and space. Without relinquishing her claim to extraordinary knowledge, Cassandra fails to assert the primacy of any single reading and actively embraces the certainty of better interpretations in the future. She acknowledges the impossibility of ever providing the last word in a tradition

---

[67] Venuti (2008) offers a rich exploration of the relationship between translation and canonicity.
[68] Among the most influential works are the seminal theories propounded in Conte (1986) and, beyond the confines of Classics, Bloom (1997) and (2003).

and instead celebrates her claim to be an influence on the future, albeit in ways she cannot fully control, embracing the collaborative efforts of future audiences and writers. It is no accident that Quintus of Smyrna calls her *polumuthos*: 'much talked of', but also 'full of story' (Quint. Smyrn. 12.557).

Cassandra's telescopic abilities allow her to move through time in extraordinary ways: she looks forwards and backwards within her own lifespan, she digs deep into the mythical past whence her city and family emerged, and she peers into a future that merges into the history of the Greek and Roman poets that tell her story. This mental time travel adds a further dimension to her literary biography. While the character of Cassandra exists only for one short human lifespan, her recurrence in one text after another also makes her an enduring inhabitant of Graeco-Roman literary time. In each appearance, her visions are produced from a different moment in her mythic biography, making a kaleidoscope of her prophetic narratives that grows increasingly complex over time. One largely (but not completely) serendipitous feature of the extant canon means that as Greek literary history moves forwards, from Aeschylus through Euripides to Lycophron, Cassandra's life story plays backwards. Aeschylus describes her on the point of death, Euripides at the moment of the fall of Troy, and Lycophron before the Trojan War has even begun. Each of these three major poets plays on an oddity resulting from Cassandra's genius and its interaction with her age and experience: a younger Cassandra is more prophetically gifted than an older Cassandra, since she sees before her more of the future, just as a 'younger' literary work has more past versions of a mythic narrative to which it may respond. Roman literary history embraces this temporal complexity when Cassandra's voice is taken over by the mortally ageing but textually enduring Cumaean Sibyl and her books, and when Cassandra returns in Seneca's *Agamemnon* at the exact same age she was in Aeschylus' play, only to implicate a contemporary Roman readership in the construction of her mythic visions.[69]

Chapter 1 introduces the Cassandra of Aeschylus' *Agamemnon*, which offers the first extended presentation of her loaded prophetic language. The play, set in Greek Argos, sets the displaced Trojan prophet on a trajectory that takes her from silence, through nonsense, to the strange meaning found in music, and ultimately, as she is about to meet her death, into a state of sympathy, if not understanding, with the chorus. Chapter 2 tackles an early retelling of Cassandra's story at the point of Troy's fall: Euripides'

---

[69] Heirman (1975) already links, albeit briefly, the glossolalic speech of the Greek Cassandras to that of Virgil's Sibyl and Seneca's Cassandra, and Racine (2003) also connects the figures.

Trojan Women. Here the performative power of Cassandra's voice begins to make itself felt. The prophet anticipates the events experienced by her older self in Aeschylus' play, and deliberately uses clear and optimistic – and as such alienatingly inappropriate – language to bring about the disasters that await her in Greece. In Chapter 3, Cassandra's story is retold with the gloss of Hellenistic scholarship in Lycophron's *Alexandra.* This bizarre work, with its intricate layering of narrative voices, purports to represent a literal quotation of Cassandra's words. The failure of interpretation is embedded in the circular text itself, whose words confuse event and narrative, original and commentary. Chapter 4 explores how elements of Cassandra's prophetic gifts are diverted into the more mainstream representation of the Greek-speaking Sibyl of Cumae in Augustan literature. Cassandra's vocally challenged body becomes the Sibyl's disembodied voice, whose precarious relationship with the interpretation of written texts mirrors Roman poets' own exploratory self-positioning within contemporary literary and political hierarchies of reception. Finally, Chapter 5 sees the resuscitation of Cassandra in Seneca's *Agamemnon,* in which the prophet appears on the Senecan 'stage' with a new, cosmic-imperial perspective. Cassandra's painfully transparent speech and agency here make it clear that there is a problematic lack of room for mistaken translation in this Stoically predetermined and tyrannically autocratic world, but there is space for a resistant sharing of each other's visions. Cassandra's narration of the future implicates the immediate and the external audience in her prophetic madness and prophesies its durability. Cassandra's task of translating the future, and our task of translating Cassandra, will go on.

CHAPTER I

Understanding Too Much:
Aeschylus' Agamemnon

Κα. καὶ μὴν ἄγαν γ᾽ ῞Ελλην᾽ ἐπίσταμαι φάτιν.

Cassandra: And yet I know the Greek language only too well.

(Aesch. *Ag.* 1254)[1]

One of the most powerful lines in Aeschylus' *Agamemnon* comes towards the end of the play, when Cassandra wearily responds to a thoroughly confused chorus: καὶ μὴν ἄγαν γ᾽ ῞Ελλην᾽ ἐπίσταμαι φάτιν – 'And yet I know the Greek language only too well' (1254). The force of ἄγαν, set among the delicately idiomatic particles, gives the line a weight of sadness and bitterness; yet it also, despite Cassandra's desperate circumstances, offers a hint of rueful or ironic wit. For Cassandra, a claim to knowing 'too much' Greek encapsulates the paradox of her prophetic role: her communications are always expert and futile at the same time, while she is both an insider and an outsider to the linguistic and social communities in which she is placed.

Cassandra is a foreigner in Greece. Though she was already characterised as a prophet in the Epic Cycle, as well as in Pindar's eleventh Pythian ode, Aeschylus appears to have been the first poet to explore in any detail her role as a prophet after her journey across the Aegean from Troy to Greece. To some extent, his emphasis on Cassandra's dislocation responds to the Athenian self-examination through drama that occurred in the aftermath of the Persian Wars. Aeschylus had fought in these wars and his *Persians* acknowledges the social and political power of the defeated foreign enemy in a Greek cultural form. Through Hall's work on fifth-century tragedy it has become clear that the *Persians* was only part of a wider construction of a foreign 'other', the *barbaros*, whose foreign language and customs were exhibited to sharpen the communal identity of the Athenians.[2] Greek

---

[1] Quotations from the *Agamemnon* are from the edition of West (1991) except where noted. Translations here and throughout the book are my own.

[2] Hall (1991) 1–11; 76–9; 117–21.

dramatists, particularly Aeschylus, turned the Greeks' and Persians' recent history into the material of myth, while they imagined Trojan myths in terms of the contemporary Persian court. Differentials in time as well as space became culturally valuable: 'a rich source of tragic irony was provided by the tension between the "past" and the "elsewhere" '.[3]

Aeschylus' Cassandra explores these tragic ironies within her own story: as a prophet and a traveller in the *Agamemnon* she is implicated in a wealth of odd juxtapositions of time and space.[4] Locating her at an explicitly transitional moment in her mythic biography, Aeschylus identifies the point of interest in her story as occurring when she moves from the narratives of Troy to those of Greece, from the barbarian city of her birth to the Greek city of her death, and from the realm of Homeric epic to that of Athenian tragedy, the genre that Aeschylus played such a part in shaping.[5] For Rehm, Troy itself pervades the Greek language of the *Agamemnon* until 'the fallen city finally appears in the person of Cassandra'.[6] It is against this boundary-breaching background that Cassandra's communicative troubles are set, and it is through the crucial assertion of her linguistic competence – exceptional competence – that they are elaborated.

When Cassandra says that she knows Greek 'too well', she cleverly engages with and complicates the notion of the barbarian 'other', for as a foreign prophet her engagement with Greek is both defective and yet more insightful than that of a native speaker. Her claim to excessive knowledge is, on a personal level, a lament for her searing clarity of prophetic understanding which leaves no room for comfortable doubt: she is burdened with the devastating vision of her own impending death, among other horrors. However, her claim to abnormal expertise in the Greek language describes not only what she understands, but also what she communicates to others. When it is articulated, even in a language that should be comprehensible to her audience, Cassandra's unusual knowledge

---

[3] Hall (1991) 211.

[4] Taplin (2003) 111–12: 'The Cassandra scene in *Agamemnon* is perhaps the most daring stroke in a play which tries language and theatre to their limits. The act is firmly fixed within the tragedy … and yet at the same time it stands outside the tragedy through Cassandra's freedom of vision, which ranges without restraint in time or language.' The radical boldness of Aeschylus' Cassandra is underplayed by McClure (1999), who tames her by assimilating her to the male point of view in the play.

[5] See Knox (1979) 39–55 on Aeschylus' use of the third actor as Cassandra to extend the scope of the play: 'Aeschylus has taken the third actor Sophocles introduced to make the dialogue more flexible, complicated, and realistic, and has used him to make the drama transcend the limits of space and time' (45). See also Vernant (1990) 23–8 on the historical 'moment' of tragedy.

[6] Rehm (2002) 240.

spills over beyond the conventional borders of understanding. She is delivering a Greek speech that baffles her Greek interlocutors.

Aeschylus' emphasis on the fact that Cassandra communicates in a mortal and recognisable language bears on the wider issue of Cassandra's difficulties in making herself understood, and how this relates to the role of language throughout the play. Goldhill's seminal deconstructive readings of the play have already drawn attention to the importance of prophetic speech in Aeschylus' thematisation of language more generally, arguing that 'mantic prophecy, metaphor and the *griphos* function in similar and interrelated ways, drawing attention to the process whereby language and narrative sense are produced, and are at risk'.[7] Goldhill reads prophecy as a system for combating the polyvalence of language, paying particular attention to the role of the sign-reader Calchas. By contrast, Goldhill largely dismisses the prophetic model offered by Cassandra on the grounds that she suffers from a lack of narrative control and passes this on to the ineffectual chorus.[8] Certainly Cassandra displays a fundamentally different model of prophetic utterance from Calchas; in direct contrast to his sign-reading, her mantic prophecies hinge on her *inability* to close off the rampant polysemy of language, and her consequent communication of 'too much' Greek.

This is not, however, a failure on all counts. Because Cassandra's speech is both articulated in and marked as Greek, what the chorus identifies as nonsense cannot simply be dismissed as meaningless. Cassandra's language, even her glossolalia, is richer and more complex than the message it fails to convey, for its polyvalence forces her audience to grapple actively with many layers of potential meaning.[9] Even if her interlocutors are doomed to misunderstand her, the efforts they expend on her difficult language grant it a certain value. This is the same value as that found by Lecercle in

---

[7] Goldhill (1984a) 24.

[8] Goldhill here does not have the advantage of Nagy (1990), who draws out the distinction between the roles of the *mantis* and the *prophētēs* (see the Introduction). This is not to say that the distinction always maps perfectly onto that between inspired and sign-reading prophets, for Calchas is also sometimes called a *mantis*, but Nagy at least highlights the default tasks of the different kinds of prophet. Schein (1982) 11–12 also explores the difference between Cassandra and Calchas: he contrasts Calchas' interpretations of bird signs with Cassandra's experience as a witness of her own death, and hence her 'transcendence' of the most fundamental marker of mortality.

[9] Crippa (1990) 490 offers a clear and helpful definition of ancient glossolalia as a form of nonsense: 'it does not signal an incomprehensible language, but a spontaneous language that is characterised by the fact that it does not produce a meaning that is immediately intelligible to those who are listening' (my translation). She goes on to show how the linguistic features of Cassandra's speech illustrate this. For Bettini (2008), Cassandra's glossolalia creates the space for the 'truth' that she expresses. See also Heirman (1975).

the nonsense poetry of authors such as Edward Lear: as long as the opacity of nonsense poetry is identifiable as specific to a particular language, it invites the audience to engage in a concerted investigation of what it *might* mean, and allows a proliferation of interpretation and reconstruction to take place:

> The lack of meaning turns out to be a kind of excess; the floundering of any global meaning, or global structure, reveals a proliferation of partial meanings and structures, as if the failure of analysis did not put a stop to it but on the contrary prevented it from stopping.[10]

In the case of Cassandra's prophecies in the *Agamemnon*, this offers a vital counterpoint to the notion that prophecy must always strive to produce a 'correct' and monovalent interpretation that ties characters to a predestined future. Instead the multiplicity of interpretations encouraged by her prophecies empower Cassandra and those who interact with her to reflect upon, imaginatively recreate and defer the otherwise unswerving path of fate. Confused and enriched by the barbarian prophet's translation across mortal and immortal languages, Cassandra's language is nonetheless that of her Greek hosts, and as such it demands their (and our) interpretative efforts.

Translating Silence

Cassandra, the prophet defined by her relationship with language, arrives on the Greek tragic stage in complete silence. The introduction of a silent character was a feature of Aeschylus' plays that Aristophanes gleefully mocked as an obvious attempt to mystify the audience, and certainly the speechless figure sitting in Agamemnon's chariot must have been intriguing to the viewers.[11] What Cassandra's silence really does, however, is to demonstrate programmatically how a lack of communication on her part will operate for the rest of the play. Firstly, it obstructs the actions of those wanting to press on with the action of the play, most notably Clytemnestra, who impatiently tries to hurry Cassandra into the house (1035–71). Montiglio notes of Clytemnestra in this scene that 'her *logos*, far

---

[10] Lecercle (1990) 4, developing a discussion of a nonsense 'letter' written by Edward Lear (or, as he signs himself, 'Slushypipp').

[11] Ar. *Ran.* 832–4. Taplin (1977) 316 notes that Cassandra's silence replaces the cries of Agamemnon being murdered, the sound that the audience might have expected after his loaded departure into the house. Knox (1979) 42–3 makes the important point that as the third actor, Cassandra's silence might lead the audience to assume that hers is a non-speaking part, thus making her eventual speech all the more astonishing. See also Aélion (1982) 40.

from breaking Cassandra's silence, is broken by it'.[12] Secondly, it provokes speculation from those trying to interact with Cassandra onstage, particularly the chorus, whose thoughtful overtures towards the silent figure introduce many of the themes that will be developed when Cassandra starts to speak later in the play.[13] These interactions are so sympathetic that there is significant crossover in who represents the frustrated communicator; frequently, other figures 'play' Cassandra. In both cases the point is clear: communication in this play – or rather, the lack of communication – shapes and then challenges implicit hierarchies, granting space for creative resistance that delays the narrative's rush to disastrous completion.[14]

Cassandra's initial refusal to move or speak out can be identified as an obstructive move because it responds to one of the most powerful themes structuring the play's narrative progression. The play first begins with a watchman looking out for the beacon fires whose light represents the end of the Trojan War and the return of the Greek soldiers. The beacons, as Goldhill has already pointed out, are a semantic signal paralleling the use of speech in the play. Goldhill reads their signal as a challenge to speech, an 'opposition between direct, visible communication, and language', but the two forms of communication may also be read as complementary semantic functions.[15] As the beacons light their way across the Aegean they also track the movement of the mythical plotline from the coast of Asia Minor to the mainland of Greece, a plotline that Cassandra is forced to follow as a result of her enslavement by Agamemnon. The theme of barbarian movement from east to west is emphasised by the fact that the beacons are at one

---

[12] Montiglio (2000) 214. The same argument is found in McClure (1999) 94. Montiglio's approach to Cassandra is generally convincing, although less compelling is her suggestion (and Thalmann's) that Cassandra's silence is part of a general trope in which prophets reveal their knowledge by remaining silent only when silence is in accordance with the will of the gods. This underplays both her obstructive silence here and her lengthy ravings later in the play. For other discussions of silence in Aeschylus see Taplin (1972) and Thalmann (1985). Winnington-Ingram (1948) 134 also notes Cassandra's moral victory over Clytemnestra: 'Thus the slave proves herself superior to the conqueror, the barbarian to the Greek, the woman to the man.' For Heath (2005) 254, 'Both women are presented as beasts as language fails them.'

[13] Taplin (1977) is one of the few to give the chorus' role in this scene sufficient weight.

[14] This demonstration of creative resistance challenges Rosenmeyer (1982) on Aeschylean communication. He argues that 'the speakers of *Agamemnon* or *Persians* do not listen to one another, but wait patiently until it is their turn to speak; and when they speak their speech continues, or varies, or interprets what has been said by others, but a listener would look in vain for any signs of true responsiveness' (189). On the delays and suspensions of dramatic time in this scene more generally: Knox (1979) 45; Taplin (1977) 292; Mitchell-Boyask (2006) 280.

[15] Goldhill (1984a) 36, describing Clytmenestra's speech at *Ag.* 281–316. Verrall (1904) is vexed by the problem of the beacons which, as he realises, break any hope of realistic chronology by appearing only just before Agamemnon's arrival. But his convoluted explanations serve only to make the beacons' symbolic role all the more transparent. See also Debnar (2010) 134 with n. 37.

point referred to by the term ἄγγαρος – 'courier' (282), which Tracy identifies as a Persian word.[16] Though the beacon fire represents the fall of Troy and the return of the triumphant Greek warriors with captive Trojans, it would doubtless evoke in an Athenian audience an emotional recollection of the Persians' more recent journey to Greece and their destruction of Athens.

Fire and its light is also a metaphorical theme that shapes Cassandra's own prophecies in the *Agamemnon* once she starts to speak and to act. She refers to the burning fire of prophetic inspiration itself (1256). Fire too marks the way in which Cassandra's actions are constrained by her Greek conquerors, by her literary destiny and prophetic understanding of it, and by the plot of the play that stages this particular version. When Clytemnestra invites Cassandra to enter the house and to move towards the fire at its heart (1055–9), she is drawing the captive prophet towards the final beacon of her journey. To reach it Cassandra must leave the stage, and thus acquiesce in the final step towards her end, to her literal and her dramatic death.[17] So Cassandra's refusal to move or engage in conversation with Clytemnestra is an obstructive tactic that holds off the end of the play for a while: the prophet extends the length of her journey, her existence and the creative life of the plot. The beacons measure the story's progression from its origins in the past; Cassandra's initial stillness and silence, her resistance to both the movement and the meaning of the beacon fire, holds off the conclusion to which the story is tending by forcing Clytemnestra and the chorus to spend time attempting to crack her silence with their own speech.

While delay is good for Cassandra, her inscrutable silence makes a failure of every speech addressed to her and turns each one into the kind of disastrous attempt at communication that Cassandra herself is doomed to utter. In the absence of a response to their statements or questions, her interlocutors cannot be sure that any communication has taken place, and as such they are disempowered as speakers and made to question the clarity of their own pronouncements. In this arena of heightened confusion and self-doubt the chorus becomes vital, and its traditional role as slightly detached narrator and mediator is pushed to the fore.[18] When Cassandra

---

[16] Tracy (1986).

[17] Taplin (1972) 67 n. 31 supports Wilamowitz's idea that the *skēnē* building was still novel at the time of Aeschylus' composition of the *Oresteia*. If true, this would make Cassandra's silent rejection of its exit even more noticeable on stage. Taplin (2003) 22 also notes that Clytemnestra is in total control of the threshold throughout the *Agamemnon*, except in the case of Cassandra.

[18] Hall (1991) 115 argues that this essentially marginal role of the chorus is the reason why Greek tragedy increasingly came to depend on choruses that were foreign or female (or both). It is interesting

gives no reaction to Clytemnestra's first invitation to enter the house, the chorus follows up Clytemnestra's welcome with one of its apparently simplistic and yet notoriously difficult to interpret suggestions:

> σοί τοι λέγουσα παύεται σαφῆ λόγον·
> ἐντὸς δ' ἁλοῦσα μορσίμων ἀγρευμάτων
> πείθοι' ἄν, εἰ πείθοι'· ἀπειθοίης δ' ἴσως.

> She has just finished making a clear speech to you;
> captured within the hunting nets of fate
> you should obey, if you could be persuaded to; but perhaps you
>   cannot be persuaded.   (Aesch. *Ag.* 1047–9)

The chorus wants to emphasise the fact that Clytemnestra's argument was clear, but also evidently anticipates communicative confusion and signals this by dwelling on the ambiguities inherent in the verb *peithō* in line 1049.[19] The verb's double meaning in the middle and passive voices of 'obey' and 'be persuaded' shows how difficult it is to identify where communications with Cassandra break down. If the question is whether the prophet will 'obey' Clytemnestra's commands, then the chorus is characterising Cassandra as resistant, stubbornly disobedient in the face of a perfectly comprehensible invitation. If they are wondering if she can 'be persuaded', the emphasis shifts away from Cassandra to the speech addressed to her: in its ineffectiveness it offers a paradoxical inversion of Cassandra's failure to communicate her prophecies to others and a more fundamental sharing of communicative breakdown. Morgan finds in this line a reference to Cassandra's original deceit of Apollo too: her refusal to be 'persuaded' by him to be his lover, and her consequent failures in the rest of her life to 'persuade' others.[20]

The interpretation of the delicate ambiguities in this speech is helped by being careful not to detach line 1049 from the one that precedes it, for taken together they show that the chorus has a grasp on the relationship

---

to note that the *Agamemnon* uses a chorus that is both male and native, but one that shows growing sympathy with the Trojan visitor.
[19] Morgan (1994) 124 sets up the two possible translations as follows: 'Obey, if you are going to obey. Perhaps you may disobey'; 'Be persuaded, if you can be persuaded. Perhaps you cannot be.' The complexities of this line contrast with the abrupt order Clytemnestra gives Agamemnon earlier in the play – πιθοῦ, 'Obey me!' (943) – which is discussed by Buxton (1982) 106–7 as the culmination of a scene dramatising deceitful as opposed to rational *peithō*. On this whole passage see Goldhill (1984a) 82–3, who draws attention to an alternative reading of line 1047, in which παύεται σαφῆ λόγον is taken together and translated as 'she [Clytemnestra] has stopped speaking clearly'. Certainly this reading can be integrated into a broader appreciation of the blurring of comprehensibility throughout the episode.
[20] Morgan (1994) 127.

between prophecy and fate and the significance of the two for Cassandra. In line 1048 the chorus points out that Cassandra is already acting within strong constraints, with a premonitory allusion to the nets that will ultimately bring about Agamemnon's downfall.[21] The chorus sees, albeit unconsciously, that Cassandra cannot fight what is already fated (that is, the 'fatal' snares of Clytemnestra's nets – μορσίμων ἀγρευμάτων, 1048), but she can delay their arrival by allowing linguistic ambiguities to flourish and confound at length.[22] These verbal entanglements defy the proclaimed 'clear speech' (σαφῆ λόγον, 1047) of Clytemnestra. In its subtle appreciation of Cassandra's situation, the chorus demonstrates a sympathy that brings it ever closer to the prophet. In fact, their proximity to each other was foreshadowed earlier in the play. The chorus' vague anxieties and unconscious prophecies are often ironically prescient; indistinct apprehension of the future is precisely what is articulated in the choral stasimon sandwiched between Agamemnon's portentous walk into the house and the Cassandra scene: 'an unwanted, unhired song sings its prophecies [*mantipolei*]' (978).[23] The chorus has also long acknowledged that silence is its own chosen tactic in the face of perceived oncoming danger: 'for a long time I have resorted to silence as protection against harm' (548). The chorus has thus aligned its behaviour with that of Cassandra well before Cassandra arrives onstage, and implicitly identifies Clytemnestra as the shared enemy. In bringing up the possibility of Cassandra's 'disobedience', deliberate or no, the chorus welcomes the linguistic challenge Cassandra poses to Clytemnestra whilst also celebrating its own streak of resistance.

Clytemnestra embraces Cassandra's challenge, picking up smartly on the importance of 'persuading' the prophet:

> ἀλλ' εἴπερ ἐστὶ μὴ χελιδόνος δίκην
> ἀγνῶτα φωνὴν βάρβαρον κεκτημένη,
> εἴσω φρενῶν λέγουσα πείθω νιν λόγωι.

> But unless she is, like a swallow,
> possessed of an unintelligible foreign voice,

---

21 There is also the net thrown over Troy referenced at 357–60, mentioned by Sommerstein (2008), and the net that is the murderous Clytemnestra herself at 1115–16. Loraux (1987) points out, following Bergren (1983), that the net used to kill Agamemnon is 'a bold materialization of every metaphor concerning *mētis*' (10), which in turn has a strong connection to the deadly actions of women.

22 Rehm (2002) 80: 'Figurative and literal nets conjoin, as Cassandra draws together the house of Atreus, its offstage interior, and her distant home whose destruction has bound her to the now doomed Agamemnon.'

23 The chorus here owns its own prophetic abilities, referring in the previous line to its 'prophetic heart' (*kardias teraskopou*). Apollo Loxias is described with the same word by the Pythia in Aesch. *Eum.* 62: 'a healer-seer ... and a prophet' (*iatromantis ... kai teraskopos*).

by speaking within her mind I am persuading her with my
argument.   (Aesch. *Ag.* 1050–2)

The imagery of birds that has permeated the play thus far carries with it
powerful suggestions of loss and destruction at the heart of the home.[24]
Now it is mobilised to represent instead that which is unfamiliar, distant and 'other': the swallow, like the term *barbaros* in its original sense,
represents that which makes a noise but no sense to outsiders; it has an
'unfamiliar' or 'unintelligible voice' (ἀγνῶτα φωνὴν, 1051).[25] The swallow is
also, like the beacons, a semantic symbol: it is the harbinger of spring, and
as such it also plays on the theme of prophecy.[26] In Clytemnestra's application of the simile to Cassandra these themes of foreign speech, semantics
and prophecy are all at work, while Clytemnesta is also exposing the communicative inversions caused by Cassandra's silence. In characterising
any foreign speech as that of a swallow, the implied direction of communication is from the chattering outsider, the *barbaros*, to the native
Greek speaker. A strict application of the simile would suggest that it is
Cassandra's job to speak and Clytemnestra's to respond, but Clytemnestra
demonstrates that her interest is not in what Cassandra can say, but what
she can understand. For Clytemnestra, her power over Cassandra can be
asserted only by getting inside her mind (εἴσω φρενῶν, 1052). With this
achieved, communication and persuasion can be achieved with the simple
application of *logos*, the purest distillation of verbal reason. As signalled by
her use of the present simple conditional, Clytemnestra acknowledges that
the prophet's continuing association with nonsense-chattering animals sets
her, Clytemnestra, up for communicative failure. As long as Cassandra
sustains an association with the foreign, and the animal, she challenges the
authority of those trying to persuade her to surrender to the violence of the
house of Atreus, the new Greek story and the future.

Offering both a parallel and an extension to Cassandra's silence is
the prophet's immobility. Clytemnestra and the chorus already recognise that straightforward communication has been made impossible by
Cassandra's defiant refusal to let Clytemnestra get inside her head, to grant
her access to her silent mind-body. It turns Clytemnestra's hope for one

---

[24] In particular the evocation of the vultures bereaved of their chicks in line 49, or the portent of the
eagles (Agamemnon and Menelaus) eating the pregnant hare (Iphigenia) at line 113. See Heath
(2005) 254 on Cassandra as a bird and a slave in this passage.

[25] Heath (2005) 200–1.

[26] Thanks to Deborah Steiner and Andrew Feldherr for drawing my attention to this connection,
which is especially potent when taken with the imagery of the springtime that Clytemnestra evokes
on drenching herself in Agamemnon's blood (1388–92).

simple *logos* into a requirement for many *logoi*. Faced with the silent figure of Cassandra, Clytemnestra and the chorus are forced into superfluous speech, which comes not only as an ironic inversion of Cassandra's usual futile speech but also as a delay to any movement towards the next episode of the story. Clytemnestra identifies time and words wasted outside the house as an obstruction of her own plans. Cassandra's stillness is therefore as much of a provocation as her silence: it sends the message that the prophet is resisting Clytemnestra's desire to pass straight into the central part of the house, where the sacrificial celebrations are due to take place and where her crimes will, ultimately, be perpetrated. For Clytemnestra, the myth comes from overseas but must be domesticated in every sense. Impatiently she says:

οὔτοι θυραίαι τῆιδ' ἐμοὶ σχολὴ πάρα
τρίβειν. τὰ μὲν γὰρ ἑστίας μεσομφάλου
ἕστηκεν ἤδη μῆλα πρὸς σφαγὰς πάρος ... [27]

I do not have the leisure to waste time here outdoors.
Already by the hearth, the very navel of the house,
the sacrificial sheep are standing ready for slaughter ...
(Aesch. *Ag.* 1055–7)

In Clytemnestra's eagerness to move indoors she describes the hearth at the very centre of the house in terms of a 'navel' (μεσομφάλου, 1056). Verrall spotted the link to the shrine of Apollo at Delphi, traditionally dubbed the navel (*omphalos*) of Greece, reading Clytemnestra's turn of phrase as a teasing reference to Cassandra as a kind of Pythia in her priestly garb.[28] Morgan argues that this link also shows Cassandra being inexorably drawn to join Apollo at the centre of the house, but a more literal-minded viewer of the scene will see that it is really Clytemnestra who is being drawn in – and enthusiastically at that.[29] Hers is a rush towards the realisation of the tragedy. It is Clytemnestra who seeks direct communication, who is ultimately destined to shape the outcome of the play, and who reaches for the narrative control and fulfilment guaranteed by Apollonian prophecy. By contrast, Cassandra at this point chooses to inhabit, to her own advantage, a position on the periphery. When she opens the final play of the trilogy, the Pythia herself will appear onstage. This verbose Greek prophet, rooted firmly at Delphi, will represent the beginning of the end, the untangling of the twisted threads of

---

[27] Following Page (1972) in replacing θυραίαν τήνδ' with θυραίαι τῆιδ'.
[28] Verrall (1904) 128. Fraenkel (1950) is unnecessarily dismissive of the connection.
[29] Morgan (1994) 130.

the house of Atreus. By contrast, here in the first play of the trilogy a Trojan prophet, displaced and silent, resists any such move to closure, provoking as many linguistic contortions as she can through her stubborn refusal to move in word or deed towards the conclusion of her story.

Clytemnestra ends her speech with an apparently baffling couplet:

> εἰ δ᾽ ἀξυνήμων οὖσα μὴ δέχηι λόγον,
> σὺ δ᾽ ἀντὶ φωνῆς φράζε καρβάνωι χερί.

> But if you are uncomprehending and you don't grasp my argument,
> instead of through speech, communicate with your foreign hand.
> (Aesch. *Ag.* 1060–1)

There is a straightforward illogicality to this. Cassandra cannot know to signal with her hand if she cannot understand the order. Fraenkel suggests that under normal circumstances a foreigner would already be signalling by now to show that they cannot understand the words addressed to them, so he finds in this statement a more generalised response to Cassandra's frustrating combination of stillness and silence.[30] But these lines implicate Clytemnestra in a more significant way. In the simile of the swallow, Clytemnestra marked Cassandra as a possible speaker of a foreign language, but she now goes on to identify Cassandra's body signals in terms of her foreignness: it is a 'foreign hand' with which she is supposed to communicate. The word for 'foreign' that Clytemnestra comes up with here – *karbanos* – is highly unusual. It may be of Phoenician origin, and is certainly rare enough in Greek to be striking in its appearance; it may even have needed translating for some in the native Greek audience.[31] Clytemnestra therefore understands Cassandra's foreign identity in terms that extend beyond spoken differences into physical differences. Clytemnestra assumes that Cassandra can understand her quite well enough to signal, and that this signal, should she deign to give it, would represent her foreign mentality just as clearly as her use of spoken language. The barriers between Clytemnestra and Cassandra are not linguistic, strictly speaking; language is only a metaphor for a more fundamental difference, an entirely divergent perception and interpretation of events.

What is exciting about the way in which this metaphor is used in the *Agamemnon* is that it grants misunderstanding a value and a potential that goes beyond blank incomprehension. The different spoken and gestured

---

[30] Fraenkel (1950) 484–5.
[31] Hornblower (2015) 216 on Lycoph. *Alex.* 606 adduces Tzetzes' claim that the word was of Phoenician origin. Hall (1991) 118 describes the word's estranging function in Aeschylus' *Suppliants*.

modes of communication described and invited by Clytemnestra and the chorus represent efforts to breach their misunderstanding of Cassandra, and this struggle to bridge interpretative differences forms as fundamental a part of the metaphor as the basic communicative disjunction that it marks in the first place. While Cassandra's rejection of Clytemnestra's overtures appears to discourage communication, it actually encourages Clytemnestra to continue probing the alien in front of her. Cassandra's passivity makes Clytemnestra explore the silent figure through the resources available to her in her own Greek language, and yet in doing so she ends up turning to foreign terms such as *karbanos*. Even before Cassandra utters a word, the language of the play is being augmented by her presence. Clytemnestra's Greek is effectively enhanced by her effort to engage with Cassandra's foreign identification. The majority language is reaching out to what it identifies as foreign, exposing itself to alternatives, recognising difference and communicative failure, and encompassing it in a way that both estranges and enriches the more powerful language. Clytemnestra is offering an example of the way in which 'foreignising translation' into Greek would work, even though as yet she has none of Cassandra's actual words to interpret.[32] The fact that this can still be identified as a translation, even as a successful translation, is shown through a subtle twist in which Clytemnestra and Cassandra are revealed to be communicating quite well here. When Clytemnestra invites Cassandra to respond with a sign if she *does not* understand, the implication of Cassandra's stillness is that she in fact *does* understand. Already there are glimmers of understanding transmitted and acknowledged, even in these most apparently unpropitious of exchanges.

This point is pushed home by a quick and perceptive response from the chorus:

> ἑρμηνέως ἔοικεν ἡ ξένη τοροῦ
> δεῖσθαι· τρόπος δὲ θηρὸς ὡς νεαιρέτου.

> The foreigner seems to be in need of a clear interpreter;
> her manner is like that of a newly captured wild animal.
> (Aesch. *Ag.* 1062–3)

Morgan suggests that the irony in these lines lies in the fact that the chorus is too foolish to perceive that Cassandra's silence is due to defiance, not to

---

[32] Venuti (1998) 8–30. Venuti outlines the value inherent in the penetration of unsettlingly foreign-sounding terms into a mainstream language, with all the attendant cultural and hegemonic upheavals.

any difficulty in understanding Greek: 'they think on too literal a level'.[33]
Certainly their comparison of Cassandra to a wild animal might seem to
attribute her silence to an inability to speak, rather than to deviousness,
but the chorus deserves more credit for its contextually loaded use of the
term 'interpreter', *hermēneus*. Hall observes that there is a strong irony
in their use of a word 'which can mean an interpreter either of foreign
languages or of obscure oracles'.[34] Knox had already made the point too,
with his pithy remark: 'She needs no interpreter, she *is* the interpreter.'[35]
The fact that Cassandra is already a *hermēneus* of sorts makes the chorus'
suggestion seem redundant, but the chorus is actually revealing a smart
intuition concerning the ways in which Cassandra's prophetic abilities
function and are received. Goldhill defines the *hermēneus* as 'the figure
whose locus is the gap between utterance and receiver of utterance, the
"interpreter"'.[36] In other words, Goldhill's *hermēneus* is a translator, a sign-
reading *prophētēs*, a figure who explains the message of one language in
the terms of another. Cassandra, as an inspired *mantis*, is both more and
less than a *hermēneus* in this sense. She certainly negotiates between the
knowledge of Apollo and the ignorance of her audience, but she does so as
the mouthpiece of the original 'utterance' itself and in a way that does not
adequately bridge the gap between 'utterance and receiver of utterance'.
That is to say, Cassandra is the first to articulate fate's narrative in human
language as well as the first to try (and fail) to frame that incomprehensible narrative so that it makes sense to her audience.[37] As such Cassandra
can be identified as both the producer *and* the interpreter of the message
she bears when she prophesies. The fact that this leads to little more than
confusion on the part of her audience makes her no less of an interpreter.[38]
However, it does make her both overstretched and insufficient in that
interpretative role.

---

[33] Morgan (1994) 124–5.
[34] Hall (1991) 117.
[35] Knox (1979) 44.
[36] Goldhill (1984a) 36.
[37] Mazzoldi (2002) argues that Cassandra does actually represent both the *mantis* and the *prophētēs*
in her prophecies, though she argues that Cassandra shows the workings of the different prophetic
figures in her different kinds of speech, not at the same time.
[38] A description of a *hermēneus* that fits Cassandra rather more closely can be found in Plato *Ion*
(534e) and its description of inspired poets, though here there is no sense that such poets' words
are inaccessible to their audiences: 'Poets are nothing but interpreters [*hermēnēs*] of the gods, each
inspired to speak by whichever god inspires him.' The term *hermēneus* used here is translated as
'mouthpiece' by Murray (1996) 121, emphasising the poet-mediator's minimal control over his or
her divine message.

To modify Knox's comment: Cassandra needs an interpreter, *even though* she is an interpreter. The adjective 'clear' (τορου) is significant in this context too: it may be frequently used to modify *hermēneus* (as it does at 616, where 'clear interpreters' encourage a dangerously generous reading of Clytemnestra's deceitful speech), but in its original meaning of 'sharp' or 'high-pitched' it also describes another conventional characteristic of barbarian voices.[39] In these lines, then, the chorus has deliberately invited the services of a *hermēneus* who represents a reductive stereotype of Cassandra as an incomprehensibly shrieking foreign prophet. In doing so it has identified the fact that the hermeneutic processes within Cassandra's voice are set to fail, but it has also suggested that a solution to this problem may be found in inviting more people to play the role of *hermēneus*, to explore and share different aspects of Cassandra's complex prophetic function and to continue the chain of translating the future that she begins.

The last words of Clytemnestra in this scene make this point clearer. In the face of Cassandra's silence, Clytemnestra resorts to addressing the chorus with an angry speech:

> ἦ μαίνεταί γε καὶ κακῶν κλύει φρενῶν,
> ἥτις λιποῦσα μὲν πόλιν νεαίρετον
> ἥκει, χαλινὸν δ᾽ οὐκ ἐπίσταται φέρειν
> πρὶν αἱματηρὸν ἐξαφρίζεσθαι μένος.
> οὐ μὴν πλέω ῥίψασ᾽ ἀτιμασθήσομαι.

> Indeed she is raving mad and hears only her evil wits,
> she who has come here, leaving her newly captured city,
> and yet does not understand how to bear the bridle
> before she has foamed away her force in blood.
> But I shall not waste any more effort to be dishonoured.
> (Aesch. *Ag.* 1064–8)

The chorus' use of the term *hermēneus* alluded to aspects of Cassandra's prophetic abilities that echoed the process of translation from one language to another, whilst they also hinted that her problems came from being forced to perform too many different aspects of that process simultaneously. Clytemnestra makes a similar point when she describes Cassandra as 'raving mad' (μαίνεταί γε, 1064), and describes the consequences. Clytemnestra is also rationalising Cassandra's uncommunicative stance, but she acknowledges that the problem is not straightforwardly one of operating across different human languages. The 'raving' that Clytemnestra

---

[39] Goldhill (1984a) 83; Hall (1991) 119 n. 59. On Cassandra's pitch in performance see Johnson (2000) 75 n. 35.

identifies might well be the frenzy associated with prophetic behaviour. When Clytemnestra derisively describes Cassandra as listening to her own wits – the very same impregnable mind Clytemnestra had hoped to break into with her *logos* – she points to the internal divisions that characterise Cassandra's role as *hermēneus*, both prophet and interpreter. While Cassandra will later prove to know the Greek narrative 'too well' (ἄγαν ... ἐπίσταμαι, 1254), here she apparently knows too little (οὐκ ἐπίσταται, 1066) how to follow its fateful path. This is exactly the tension between 'too much' knowledge and 'too little' communication that is fundamental to Cassandra's dilatory role at this point in the play. Clytemnestra finds in Cassandra's defiance a waste of energy, a misspent use of her force (μένος, 1067), which does nothing in line with necessity. In this Cassandra has embroiled Clytemnestra, who leaves the stage infuriated by the waste of time or energy or words (the Greek is suggestively silent on this) that she is being asked to expend. The 'extra' work that Clytemnestra has already done to engage with Cassandra, however, is evidence of exactly the creativity – in time, energy *and* words – that Cassandra provokes.

Clytemnestra and the chorus have failed to create any meaningful conversation with Cassandra. What they have started to do, however, is to interact strangely among themselves. Clytemnestra has given up on addressing Cassandra in her final speech and turned instead to the chorus. In doing so she picks up on the chorus' vocabulary: she echoes the chorus' description of Cassandra as 'newly captured' (νεαιρέτου, 1063), this time applying the description to the prophet's city (νεαίρετον, 1065). When Clytemnestra leaves the stage, the chorus makes a last-ditch attempt to persuade Cassandra to leave the chariot. This time it transforms Clytemnestra's speech for Cassandra, rephrasing the request:

> ἴθ᾽ ὦ τάλαινα· τόνδ᾽ ἐρημώσασ᾽ ὄχον,
> ε<ἴ>κουσ᾽ ἀνάγκηι τῆιδε, καίνισον ζυγόν.

> Go, you poor woman; vacate this chariot:
> giving in to fate, try on a new yoke.   (Aesch. *Ag.* 1070–1)

The chorus has tried Cassandra again and again in Greek; now its members finally start to become the interpreters, the *hermēneis* whose services they earlier invited. Here they encourage Cassandra to give in to fate by their act of transforming, or 'translating', both Clytemnestra's previous words and their own. Clytemnestra's bridle (χαλινόν, 1066, itself a repetition of the restraint applied to Iphigenia at line 238) has become a yoke (ζυγόν, 1071). Their words contain acoustic resonances through vowels and sibilance (their own ἑρμηνέως, 1062 has become ἐρημώσασ᾽ ... ε<ἴ>κουσ᾽, 1070–1)

and consonants (Clytemnestra's χαλινόν, 1066, has become καίνισον, 1071).
With the imperative that literally means 'make new' (καίνισον, 1071), the
chorus even encourages Cassandra to resume her job of translation, to try
again. She can 'renew' her situation, following the chorus as it reworks
its own first thoughts and Clytemnestra's orders. As the chorus' function
in tragedy is to bridge the gaps between the protagonists of a drama and
the audience, it is appropriate that the chorus, above all other characters,
should come to adopt and champion the role of the *hermēneus*, but it is
under Cassandra's influence that it has done so. Cassandra has inspired
an interest in the possibilities of different language use, in the function of
translation, and has encouraged speculative and interpretative communities to begin operating around her silent body, even before she has spoken
a single word.

Introducing Apollo: Dialogue/Trialogue

Cassandra is not, in fact, a silent actor, and she must engage with the
words and action of the play at some point. As she suddenly makes her first
movements and sounds, all attention is on her and the way in which she will
now tackle the questions surrounding her use of language, questions that
she has already provoked without moving a muscle or opening her mouth.

Until this point in the play Cassandra's silence has been a delaying tactic
and a challenge to Clytemnestra, but it has also protected the prophet from
herself. Cassandra's prophetic ability is so bound up with her inability to
communicate fully that it becomes hard to categorise the one as a quality
and the other as a curse; it might be argued that Cassandra's biggest curse is
her truthfulness, rather than her failure to be understood. By guaranteeing
her prophecies, Apollo makes Cassandra's speech ineluctably performative: what she says *must* happen.[40] As such, there is a tremendous danger
in Cassandra's speech, in the communication of her clear-sighted vision.
Once Cassandra breaks her silence and engages with her interlocutors, the
obfuscation of her truthful message gains in value. Nonsensical speech
continues the delaying function previously achieved by her silence, and
encourages the same proliferation of interpretative efforts among its
listeners. Nonsense also blurs the performativity of Cassandra's utterances.
As her interlocutors engage in creating some sense from the muddled,

---

[40] See Austin (1975), and the Introduction to this book. This is not quite the same as (though also
not incompatible with) Goldhill's more fatalistic summary of her prophetic situation: 'An absolute
knowledge of the future means an absolutely determined world' Goldhill (1986) 27.

dissonant or confusing sounds they hear, they provide alternatives that defy the heavily predestined narrative that Cassandra would otherwise be clearly prophesying and hence assuring.

The work of traditional philologists as well as contemporary critical theorists can be brought to bear on Cassandra's nonsense and its unusual value. Fraenkel's note on Cassandra's first articulation in the play is perceptive, if regrettably orientalist in tone:

> Now, after the departure of Clytemnestra, the mute and motionless figure on the wagon suddenly stirs, and breaks, not indeed into speech or song, but into something between a song and those wild notes of lamentation which were familiar to the Athenians from the ritual performances of the barbarian mourning women from the East. What we hear are not, of course, crude and formless cries but sounds ennobled by rhythms of Hellenic music: still, they are distinct from articulate language.[41]

Fraenkel cuts straight to the heart of the issue in his effort to identify the odd status of Cassandra's voice which, sliding between noise and language, is an enigma to the Greek speakers who have been speculating on her grasp of their language ever since she arrived on stage. Fraenkel is keen to place it exactly on the right point between speech, song and lament; between barbarian ritual and its Athenian assimilation; between eastern mourning and western music. It is, as he shows through his own western bias, both Greek and not-Greek.

Lecercle describes the delicate balance between noise and language found in nonsense poetry with a commentary that could well be applied to Cassandra's first words: 'language is no longer a mere instrument, it seems to have acquired a life of its own. Language speaks, it follows its own rhythm, its own partial coherence, it proliferates in apparent, and sometimes violent, chaos'.[42] Lecercle argues that nonsense – that is, language that seems to have escaped the control of both speaker and listener – functions as a challenge to conventional language and its users' sense of mastery over it. Such language reaches above and beyond meaning. This unsettling use of language is of interest to scholars of translation, for the potential independence of sound and meaning is crucial to the enterprise of translating sense from one language to another. For Venuti, for example, the moments where a translated text loses fluency, even perhaps a degree

---

[41] Fraenkel (1950) 539.
[42] Lecercle (1990) 5. Prins (2005) gives an excellent reading of Virginia Woolf's interpretation of Cassandra's nonsense words here, and identifies Woolf as coming to similar conclusions about the creative function involved in making sense of them. See also Pillinger (2017).

of sense, are salutary reminders of the very function of translation working behind that text. Such jagged edges in the text actually reduce the 'violence' inherent in wresting a text away from the linguistic and cultural contingencies that shape its meaning in the source language and replacing them wholesale with the new (and inevitably quite different) contingencies of the target language.[43] They avoid the 'domestication' of the text, which resistance in turn serves to undermine cultural hierarchies that are otherwise reinforced by the casual imperialism of hegemonic languages such as English or, in the case of Athenian tragedy, Greek. It is significant, therefore, that Fraenkel hears Cassandra's voice in terms of a blurring of boundaries between the world of Hellenic control and the barbarian east. She is using language that goes beyond meaning to draw attention to her foreignness, to the power and authenticity of her source knowledge and yet to the likelihood of its incomprehensibility in a new setting, and she is asking her interlocutors to engage with all of this.

The whole process is presided over by Apollo, who is invoked in Cassandra's first stuttering and practically untranslatable words:

> ὀτοτοτοτοῖ πόποι δᾶ·
> ὤπολλον ὤπολλον.
>
> Otototototoi popoi da;
> Ahpollo Ahpollo.   (Aesch. *Ag.* 1072–3)

Sense only emerges from Cassandra's truly swallow-like chattering sounds when the name Apollo rises out of the elision of her inarticulate laments. Her second attempt at speech, a re-articulation that Bettini interestingly dubs 'self-interpretation', sees her develop this sound by sliding into a neat pun on 'Apollo': ἀπώλεσας γὰρ οὐ μόλις τὸ δεύτερον – 'for you have completely destroyed me a second time' (1082).[44] In her play on the name Apollo and the verb *apollumi*, Cassandra now forces more meaning into one single word than it normally bears: Apollo's name has turned nonsense into multi-sense. The chorus is also quick to jump to the correct assumption that Cassandra is calling upon Apollo in his association with the linguistic trickery of oracles, for it now grants him his cult title Loxias, 'the riddling one' (1074).

---

[43] Venuti (1995) 17–19.
[44] Bettini (2008) 165–6 explores Cassandra's 'auto-interpretazione'. He discusses the possibility that meaning may begin to appear with the Doric δᾶ, for γῆ, but he accepts that her words are certainly shifting between sound and sense here. Heirman (1975) unpicks many of these slippages in Cassandra's first words.

Recognising Cassandra's relationship with Apollo does not make the chorus' communications with her any less subject to confusion; Loxias lives up to his name. Cassandra's tendency to refer all her early cries and questions to Apollo creates a scenario in which the chorus is forced into a triangular conversational position, commenting ineffectively on Cassandra's speech, rather than creating a dialogue. One of the ways in which this is manifest is in the wandering prophet's need to orientate herself in time and space, and in the chorus' initial failure to appreciate this. Through her pun on Apollo/*apollumi*, Cassandra alludes to her past history with Apollo: in claiming that he has destroyed her 'a second time', Cassandra is already building a sense of patterning and repetition into her narrative of past, present and future. Cassandra's first direct question to Apollo, ποῖ ποτ' ἤγαγές με; – 'Where-*ever* have you brought me?' (1087) – contains within it an effort to identify not just the space, but also the temporal circumstances in which Cassandra finds herself.[45] The chorus offers an answer that only explains the location – the house of Atreus. Cassandra, however, responds to images that refer not to the place, but to its history. The house, as she describes it, carries a consciousness (*sunistora*, 1090) of the horrific murders and infanticides that define its past and, indeed, future.

These references to the history of the house encourage the chorus to lay out more firmly its attitude towards Cassandra's prophecies. Having already described her as 'hunting down' (*mateuei*, 1094) the events of the past like a bloodhound, the chorus appropriates that metaphor for itself in order to spell out its feelings about different kinds of prophets:

> καὶ μὴν κλέος σου μαντικὸν πεπυσμένοι
> ἦμεν· προφήτας δ' οὔτινας μαστεύομεν.[46]
>
> Indeed we had already learned of your fame as a seer,
> but we are not hunting for any prophetic interpreters.
>   (Aesch. *Ag.* 1098–9)

The chorus' reference to both the fame of a seer (κλέος μαντικόν, 1098) and to prophets (προφήτας, 1099) acknowledges the semantic distinction between the *mantis*, the inspired seer who has direct contact with the

---

[45] Ποτέ, usually meaning 'ever, at this time' in a question, largely serves just to intensify, so it is hard to gauge its semantic weight here. But it certainly anticipates the historical aspect of the place that Cassandra proceeds to investigate. Mitchell-Boyask (2006) reads the verb of leading here as the first in a series of lexical clues intended to portray Cassandra as the bride of Apollo, rather than of Agamemnon.

[46] Or μστεύομεν, as in Page (1972), picking up the earlier verb even more directly.

gods, and the *prophētēs*, who is the interpreter of such visions, the go-between.[47] In these important two lines the chorus makes it clear that it has little interest in the work of a *prophētēs*. If by this the chorus is just glossing *mantis*, then it appears to be rejecting all prophecy. If, however, the chorus is observing the difference between the two prophetic tasks, then these lines may be read as demonstrating the chorus' interest in a particular sort of prophecy. The chorus rejects mortal interpreters, prophets such as those it describes at line 409, who respond to Helen's abduction with predictions of doom that scarcely represent great insight under the circumstances. The *Oresteia*, with its tales of one generation locked into retribution for the sins of past generations, is easy enough to experience with a sense of foreboding; the chorus already had this feeling just before the arrival of Cassandra (975–8). Moreover the chorus' past experience with a *prophētēs* was with Calchas, whose horrifying order to Agamemnon to slaughter his daughter Iphigenia lies behind much of the chorus' sympathy for Cassandra, the latest sacrifice to the house of Atreus.[48] Cassandra is not a Calchas-type, nor does the chorus view her as such. Her mantic abilities are different from the talents of Calchas, for she does not advocate the horrors to be committed by mortals, but simply (if obscurely) describes them. Cassandra has more authority, and less moral responsibility, despite her performative voice. The chorus does not reject this mantic work; it is willing to engage with her way of reading, or precipitating, the progression of time from the past to the future.

However, as the chorus and Cassandra continue to exchange words, it becomes increasingly clear that Cassandra's communicative confusions begin at the very point where she describes events that lie in the future. The chorus sets up a division between what it can understand and what it cannot, referring first to Cassandra's anxieties for the future and then, with more confidence, to her account of the killing of Thyestes' children in the past:[49]

---

[47] Nagy (1990): see the discussion of the *hermēneus* above. Raeburn and Thomas (2011) 187–8 sum up an interesting, if slightly strained, perspective on the distinction, based on the argument that the two kinds of interpreter operate in a different temporal sphere: the *mantis* predicts the future while the *prophētēs* interprets present signs. According to this reading, the chorus is trying to shut down any revelations about the past, without ruling out the utility of Cassandra's prophetic gifts.

[48] On the pervading theme of Iphigenia's sacrifice in the *Oresteia* see Zeitlin (1965) 466; on Cassandra as a new sacrifice in the mould of Iphigenia see Wohl (1998) 107, and Mitchell-Boyask (2006) 280ff., who also notes the chorus' terror of Calchas.

[49] On children either as sufferers from or bearers of a family curse, particularly with reference to the *Oresteia*, see Jones (1962) 82–111; Ganz (1982); Sewell-Rutter (2007) 15–48. Hall (2010) 217 and (2002) discusses Cassandra's vision of the children of Thyestes. On concepts of family pollution in Greece more generally see Parker (1983).

τούτων ἄϊδρίς εἰμι τῶν μαντευμάτων,
ἐκεῖνα δ' ἔγνων· πᾶσα γὰρ πόλις βοᾷ.

I am ignorant of these prophetic visions,
but those I understood: for the whole city shouts them out loud.
(Aesch. *Ag.* 1105–6)

Cassandra herself goes on to shrink away from describing the horrors to come, implying that the further into the future she looks, the harder it is for her to explain its truths for the benefit of her auditors. She asks, πῶς φράσω τέλος; – 'how do I tell the end?' (1109). The word *telos* is particularly appropriate in this context, for it describes not only the goal, the action that provides the 'end' of the story, but also the 'crux' of the matter. It is the nugget of core information whose transmission represents the most effective communicative act – in Cassandra's case, the most performative statement.[50] Fortunately the articulation of this 'end' eludes Cassandra for now, and the chorus ratifies the delay with a reference to its own deferred comprehension: οὔπω ξυνῆκα – 'I haven't grasped it, yet' (1112).

A similar awareness of the danger inherent in Cassandra's speech about the future is apparent when the chorus responds to Cassandra's increasingly determined prophecies. After Cassandra's inarticulate cries once again resolve into a speech in which she interrogates and describes her prophetic visions – ἒ ἒ παπαῖ παπαῖ, τί τόδε φαίνεται; 'Ah ah papai papai, what is this apparition?' (1114) – the chorus accuses her of invoking a Fury:

ποίαν Ἐρινὺν τήνδε δώμασιν κέληι
ἐπορθιάζειν;

What kind of Fury are you summoning to this house
to raise up a shout?   (Aesch. *Ag.* 1119–20)

As the traditional force of vengeance, Furies represent the endless cycle of tragic violence besetting families such as the house of Atreus. Their activities are ritually brought to a halt in the *Eumenides*, but appear in the *Agamemnon* to stretch indefinitely into the future, based on the crimes of the past.[51] The chorus' reference to a Fury here might therefore be interpreted as a sign that

---

[50] *LSJ* s.v. τέλος. The connection between *telos* as speech and action is reinforced as the noun picks up the verb Cassandra had applied to Clytemnestra as the real performer of the future narrative: ἰὼ τάλαινα, τόδε γὰρ τελεῖς; – 'Oh wretched woman, will you really do this?' (1107). Ford (2002) 9, 21 finds that in ancient literary criticism, particularly Aristotle, the term *telos* describes the aim and function of poetry according to its form, independent of occasion or other contextual goals. See also Goldhill (1984b).

[51] Questions remain over the extent to which the trilogy is brought to a satisfactory ritual, political or artistic conclusion by the *Eumenides*. For excellent summaries of the debate to date see Mitchell-Boyask (2009) 108–24 and Goldhill (2004) 24–41.

the chorus is treating Cassandra's explication of her vision as that of a *prophētēs*, whose reading of horrific portents past or present predicts suitably horrific future events. According to the chorus, however, Cassandra is not reading, or even observing a Fury, but 'calling' or 'summoning' her into the house: her mantic speech brings about the inevitable fulfilment of the very visions it describes. The association between speech and agency is cemented through the chorus' imaginative picture of the Fury, arriving at the house and lifting up her powerful voice to take over Cassandra's narration of ineluctable fate.

The chorus is modest about its abilities to untangle Cassandra's divinely inspired prophecies, but gnomically underlines its own investment in vague foreboding, rather than precisely grasped foresight:

οὐ κομπάσαιμ' ἂν θεσφάτων γνώμων ἄκρος
εἶναι, κακῶι δέ τωι προσεικάζω τάδε.
ἀπὸ δὲ θεσφάτων τίς ἀγαθὰ φάτις
βροτοῖς τέλλεται; κακῶν γὰρ διαὶ
πολυεπεῖς τέχναι
θεσπιωιδῶν φόβον φέρουσιν μαθεῖν.

I would not boast that I am the ultimate interpreter of divine oracles,
but I imagine these represent bad news.
Well, from divine oracles what good speech
does emerge for mortals? For with their bad news
the verbose skills
of the singers of prophecy cause one to learn fear.

(Aesch. *Ag.* 11330–5)

In this passage the chorus acknowledges that its communications with Cassandra are based more on expectations and fears about the power of prophetic speech than on any particular transmission of information. Prophecies are terrifying because of their sheer verbosity, their heightened poetic form (πολυεπεῖς τέχναι, 1134, may perhaps also allude to the composition of hexameter verse), and because they so often bring bad news. The chorus therefore takes refuge in a generalisation that recognises the horrifying realities that probably lie behind (or rather, ahead of) Cassandra's prophetic speech, but also sidesteps responsibility for identifying, or becoming complicit in 'realising', the details of that future horror.[52] The chorus willingly inhabits its own dubious communicative limbo, in which anxious fear of the unknown is better than the gory resolution that must accompany any clarification in the prophetic message.

[52] Knox (1979) 50.

Singsong, Birdsong

Nonsense is language that does not operate according to normal rules of signification; as sound freed from controllable sense it is a linguistic mode that bears some affinity with music. In the *Agamemnon* Cassandra's misunderstood speech is certainly associated more closely with the language of music (*melos*) than of reason (*logos*). This connection with music helps to establish the register of Cassandra's utterance, so mystifying in its sounds that are both truthful and incomprehensible. It also reinforces the suggestion that Cassandra's miscommunications provide a potentially valuable kind of delay: their acoustic complexities are creative and provocative, demanding an emotional response from even the least understanding of her audience members.

Cassandra's voice is embedded in both action and intermission, recitative and aria, and plays upon the tensions between these modes. Her exchanges with the chorus mark these distinctions strongly. During the first conversation between Cassandra and the chorus, the movement between speech and song is already oddly fluid.[53] Epirrhematic exchanges such as this, involving the chorus and one actor, generally involve the chorus singing in lyric metre and the actor speaking, but in this case the exchange has begun with Cassandra singing lyric passages in wild dochmiacs, while the chorus responds in spoken trimeters. The role reversal is not clear-cut, however, for just after asking Cassandra about the Fury she seems to be inviting down upon the house, the chorus starts to pick up the lyric metres (1121; 1132), whilst Cassandra begins to finish each of her stanzas with a couplet in iambic trimeters (1136ff.).[54] Their dialogue is therefore couched within spoken and sung forms that are never quite consonant, but appear to be learned from each other and mutually explored. The exchanges show both Cassandra and the chorus experimenting at different times with the rearrangement of their language in order to bring sound, rather than sense, to the fore.[55]

As Cassandra's voice grows clearer to the audience, the chorus avoids engaging too closely with her meaning by drawing attention to the musical dimension of her articulation:

---

[53] Fraenkel (1950) 487–8, and 539f.
[54] On this shift see Lebeck (1971) 52; Taplin (2003) 138–9 n. 1; Schein (1982) 13–14; Rehm (2002) 80.
[55] On the relationship between word and music in fifth-century drama more generally see Ford (2002) 152ff.

φρενομανής τις εἶ θεοφόρητος, ἀμφὶ δ᾽ αὐτᾶς θροεῖς
νόμον ἄνομον οἷά τις ξουθὰ
ἀκόρετος βοᾶς, φεῦ, φιλοίκτοις φρεσὶν
Ἴτυν Ἴτυν στένους᾽ ἀμφιθαλῆ κακοῖς
ἀηδὼν μόρον.⁵⁶

You are raving, carried away by the god,
and about yourself you voice
unmusical music like a chirruping bird
ceaseless in its cry, oh, with your melancholy mind
like a nightingale groaning 'Itys, Itys' in lament for her son's fate,
a heritage doubly flourishing in evil.   (Aesch. *Ag.* 1140–5)

Having noted that Cassandra is divinely inspired, the chorus suggests that in her lament for her own future she is singing 'unmusical music' (νόμον ἄνομον, 1142). This oxymoronic play on the term *nomos* leans on the tendency of Cassandra's utterance simultaneously to construct and to undermine cultural norms as well as musical forms. Her voice is not completely anarchic, for there are recognisable rules to her utterance, but it is unregulated in its application. This vocal lawlessness is potentially either moral or aesthetic, and the simile that follows, in which the chorus describes Cassandra's voice as like the repetitive cry of the nightingale, evokes a myth that is illustrative of both terrible physical violence and terrible musical beauty. Nonetheless it is sound, above all, that is foregrounded throughout the description of birdlike cries (ξουθὰ | ἀκόρετος βοᾶς ... στένους᾽ ...). Fraenkel appositely cites ad loc. Alcman's poetic boast, 'I know the songs [*nomōs*] of all birds,' further underlining this early association of the term *nomos* with music, and specifically the music of birdsong.⁵⁷ As Hall points out, the very scansion of Aeschylus' phrase νόμον ἄνομον, as five short syllables, produces a twittering-like effect that continues through this dochmiac exchange between Cassandra and the chorus.⁵⁸

The myth of the nightingale tells that when Procne discovered, from her sister Philomela's woven tapestry, that her husband Tereus had raped Philomela and cut out her tongue, Procne killed her son Itys and fed him to her husband in vengeance. Before Tereus could take further revenge, all the characters were turned into birds. Procne became a nightingale, Philomela a swallow and Tereus a hoopoe. The story carries weight for Cassandra in many respects. It is a tale of sexual aggression, emotional and

⁵⁶ Fraenkel's text here.
⁵⁷ Ϝοῖδα δ᾽ ὀρνίχων νόμως | παντῶν (*PMG* fr. 40).
⁵⁸ Hall (2002) 8.

physical torture, a silenced female voice, sacrificed children and the figuration of women as at least part-animal. The chorus hears this myth behind Cassandra's voice: Cassandra, Procne and Philomela share a song that emerges out of isolated mental torture, here described as Cassandra's 'melancholy mind' (φιλοίκτοις φρεσὶν, 1143). The song consists of a chirruping sound ("Ἴτυν "Ἴτυν, 1144) which also expresses grief for a character's fate (μόρον, 1145). Above all, the myth is about the production of song by tragic protagonists when they realise that human action – even human voice – has been exhausted.

The myth of the nightingale was not obscure. Sophocles' lost play *Tereus* was devoted to the tale and included all the grim family details behind the metamorphoses.[59] A version can also be found in the *Odyssey*, which casts Aeschylus' simile into relief:

> ὡς δ' ὅτε Πανδαρέου κούρη, χλωρηῒς ἀηδών,
> καλὸν ἀείδησιν ἔαρος νέον ἱσταμένοιο,
> δενδρέων ἐν πετάλοισι καθεζομένη πυκινοῖσιν,
> ἥ τε θαμὰ τρωπῶσα χέει πολυδευκέα φωνήν,
> παῖδ' ὀλοφυρομένη Ἴτυλον φίλον, ὅν ποτε χαλκῷ
> κτεῖνε δι' ἀφραδίας, κοῦρον Ζήθοιο ἄνακτος·

> As when the daughter of Pandareos, the greeny-brown nightingale,
> sings beautifully as spring just arrives,
> sitting in the thick foliage of the trees,
> she who often modulating pours out her many-toned voice,
> mourning her beloved son Itylus, whom once with a bronze weapon
> she killed out of madness, the son of the lord Zethos.

> (Hom. *Od.* 19.518–23)

In this simile there is little allusion to the details of the story, though the nightingale's acts are explained as due to some 'madness' (ἀφραδίας, 19.523). This is echoed in the *Agamemnon*, where the chorus expresses its concern that Cassandra is 'raving' (φρενομανής, Aesch. *Ag.* 1140) before turning to the myth. Where the texts diverge is in their description of the nightingale and her song. For Homer, both body and voice are marked by their variety, their colour, their aesthetic beauty: 'the greeny-brown nightingale sings beautifully … she who often modulating pours out her many-toned voice'. In Aeschylus, the nightingale's lamenting call ("Ἴτυν

---

[59] For details see Burkert (1983) 179–85. On later responses to the nightingale and music (especially in Aristophanes' *Birds*) see Barker (2004), and for the tradition and link to Cassandra see Segal (1993b) 66–73 and Hall (2002) 8, both of whom note that Cassandra shifts the focus away from the nightingale's voice to her own physical body.

Ἴτυν, 1144) is repetitively monotonous.[60] Yet Cassandra returns to the positive artistic judgement expressed in the *Odyssey* when she responds to the chorus' simile in order to reject its analogy:

> ἰὼ ἰὼ λιγείας μόρος ἀηδόνος·
> περέβαλον γάρ οἱ πτεροφόρον δέμας
> θεοὶ γλυκύν τ' αἰῶνα κλαυμάτων ἄτερ·
> ἐμοὶ δὲ μίμνει σχισμὸς ἀμφήκει δορί.

> Io io, the fate of the clear-sounding nightingale;
> for the gods granted her a feathery form
> and a sweet life without cries of grief;
> for me there awaits butchery by a two-edged weapon.
>
> (Aesch. *Ag.* 1146–9)

Like Homer, Cassandra praises the nightingale's voice when she calls her 'clear-sounding' (λιγείας, 1146), and then she goes further, describing the nightingale as living a life that is 'sweet ... without cries of grief' (γλυκύν ... κλαυμάτων ἄτερ, 1148). This stands in marked contrast with the prophet's own imminent grisly fate.[61] Cassandra hears a beauty in the nightingale's song that she cannot identify with her own terrible music (νόμον ἄνομον, 1142).

Behind this conflict of aesthetic opinions lies the myth's thematisation of communication without language, as well as language without communication. The silent accusation woven by Philomela into her tapestry replaces a spoken indictment, while Procne's lament for her child, her repetition of his name, is absorbed into the meaningless chatter of birds. In the *Agamemnon* the chorus tries to read Cassandra as a nightingale figure, but Cassandra recognises that she is better assimilated to Philomela, the figure whose communications, despite her hideous silencing, remain true and bring about a horrendous conclusion. Cassandra's 'madness' bears no relation to her killing a child, but is based on her victimisation by Apollo: his assault, and his curse on her communication abilities.[62] Philomela is metamorphosed into a swallow and it was, of course, to a swallow that Clytemnestra first likened Cassandra. For these reasons, Cassandra quite rightly implies that she fits the model of the raped Philomela better than that of the murdering Procne.

---

[60] Segal (1993b) 68 draws out the way in which the chorus' articulation of Ἴτυν Ἴτυν momentarily borrows Cassandra's voice, demonstrating both the chorus' compassion and its incomprehension.

[61] See Hall (2002) 22 on the characterisation of sound as *ligus/liguros*.

[62] Though McClure (1999) 95 does associate Cassandra's lament for the children of Thyestes with Procne's lament for Itys.

But the chorus is not being completely illogical either. The repetition of 'Itys, Itys' might certainly be heard as analogous to the onomatopoeic *bar bar* of the *barbaros*, or indeed the *otototototoi* of Cassandra's first cry. Each stuttering sound projects to a mainstream audience an emotional tenor or general sense, rather than a specific reference. 'Itys, Itys' is a birdsong that has no meaning to anyone without knowledge of the myth of Procne and Philomela, while *bar bar* has no referent in Greek and Cassandra's *otototototoi* laments a fate that remains obscure to her interlocutors.[63] So it is fair of the chorus to link Cassandra's voice with a repetitive sound that carries specific meaning only to a few insiders, but it is misguided to identify Cassandra's lived experience with that of Procne. This confusion becomes all the more credible when the myth's later tradition is taken into account, in which the metamorphoses are inverted: Procne becomes the swallow and Philomela the nightingale.[64] The potential muddle in the metamorphosis appears to have been embedded early on in the trickiness of Cassandra's voice. One further poignancy in this entwining of birds, stories and songs may be found in the irony that Cassandra only sounds like (and knows she sounds like) a swallow to her immediate listeners; as far as *she* is concerned, and as far as Aeschylus' external audience can tell so far, her song is indeed as rich and varied as that of the nightingale.

Moving away from its profound but unappreciated simile, the chorus continues to investigate the form of Cassandra's song:

> πόθεν ἐπισσύτους θεοφόρους τ' ἔχεις
> ματαίους δύας,
> τὰ δ' ἐπίφοβα δυσφάτωι κλαγγᾶι
> μελοτυπεῖς ὁμοῦ τ' ὀρθίοις ἐν νόμοις;
> πόθεν ὅρους ἔχεις θεσπεσίας ὁδοῦ
> κακορρήμονας;

> From where do you get the sudden, god-inspired
> and pointless pangs?
> And why with inarticulate cry do you strike up these fearful things
> in musical form, and in high-pitched strains?
> From where do you get the limits to your path of prophetic song –
> limits that are ill-omened?   (Aesch. *Ag.* 1150–5)

---

[63] The song echoes on in John Lyly, Matthew Arnold and T. S. Eliot's Philomel from *The Waste Land*: 'And still she cried, and still the world pursues, | "Jug Jug" to dirty ears.'

[64] This variation is slyly referred to by Ovid in his version, when he writes cryptically: *quarum petit altera siluas,* | *altera tecta subit* – 'of whom one heads for the woods, | the other goes under the roof' (Ovid *Met.* 6.668–9), and is confirmed by Seneca (Sen. *Ag.* 670–7). See Chapter 5.

The chorus wants to know what it is that impels Cassandra still to attempt to convey her prophecies, and not just in speech, but in something more than speech: 'you strike up a melody' (μελοτυπεῖς, 1153). Acknowledging that the pain of prophecy is vain (ματαίους δύας, 1151), that no successful communication is taking place, the chorus skates over the inaccessible meaning contained within Cassandra's prophecies in favour of investigating the prophecies' status and value as pure medium, as sound.

The chorus proves observant in its role as music critic, identifying and discussing the shape, pitch and timbre of Cassandra's articulation. Picking up on its earlier description of Cassandra's voice as providing 'unmusical music' (νόμον ἄνομον, 1142), the chorus goes on to describe her as singing in 'high-pitched strains' (ὀρθίοις νόμοις, 1153) with a cry that is 'unutterable' or 'inarticulate' (δυσφάτωι κλαγγᾶι, 1152), again evoking her high barbarian sound and her tendency to express noise rather than recognisable words.[65] Rather more obscurely, then, the chorus tackles her prophecy's 'path' and its boundary stones or 'limits', which they identify as 'ill-omened' (ὅρους ... θεσπεσίας ὁδοῦ | κακορρήμονας, 1154–5).[66] Normally Cassandra's prophecies are defined by their ability to transcend space and time, not by their confinement within limits, but here the chorus notes that Cassandra's voice is in fact restrained and directed down a path of sorts. This direction shapes her narrative such that her ominous utterance becomes musical, if not comprehensible. The path down which her narrative is forced is described with a word that means 'divinely sweet-sounding' as much as it means 'prophetic' (θεσπεσίας, 1154). Fraenkel once again draws out the importance of the music in Cassandra's voice here, when he points out that the 'path of the song' was a familiar enough notion that may have been evoked by the similarity between the Greek words *oimos* ('road') and *oimē* ('song').[67] The chorus reinforces this association here with a new echo between the words *hodos* ('path') and *horos* ('limit') – in the latter case, a word whose wider sphere of meaning may by now include that of a note that limits an interval in a musical scale.[68] It seems that for the chorus the path of Cassandra's song is bounded and constrained not so much to make narrative sense as to make musical sense.

---

[65] On this *nomos* as one of lament see Fleming (1977).

[66] Sommerstein (2008) 139 translates with nice literalism: 'Whence do you get the direction of your path of prophecy, which speaks of evil?' (and explains in n. 248).

[67] Fraenkel (1950) 530: 'They talk of the "path", because the "path of the song" is a generally familiar idea, whether or no the Greeks of the classical period felt the connexion between οἴμη (specialised in the *Odyssey* so as to mean "song, lay") and οἶμος.'

[68] *LSJ* s.v. ὅρος. The word is used in the musical sense at the very least by the late classical period.

Cassandra picks up this theme of the path and its margins as she expands her narrative to include her own lived experience, delving into the past to identify Paris' marriage as the origin of the disasters at Troy and to make the connection with her childhood, and then flashing forward to anticipate her life after death (1156–61). As she tells these past and future events, she situates herself precisely. She describes herself on the banks of the river Scamander when she was young, and she claims that she will sit on the banks of the underworld's river Acheron and by the river Cocytus when she is dead.[69] Even there, she says, she will still sing her prophecies:

> νῦν δ' ἀμφὶ Κωκυτόν τε κ'Αχερουσίους
> ὄχθους ἔοικα θεσπιωιδήσειν τάχα.

> Now it seems as though I will soon be singing my prophecies
> by Cocytus and the banks of Acheron.   (Aesch. *Ag.* 1160–1)

With this insistence on her prophesying at these specific riverside locations, Cassandra adopts the metaphor of the 'path of prophetic song' (θεσπεσίας ὁδοῦ, 1154) which the chorus has just described. Cassandra replaces the image of an abstract road with an evocation of the specific rivers that accompany her at the beginning and end of her life, and visualises herself inhabiting the liminal space of those rivers' banks. If the chorus felt that 'ill-omened limits' defined the direction and sound of her prophecies, Cassandra knows that it is the 'banks' of worldly and other-worldly rivers that shape her very existence and her understanding of where she sits in relation to events past and future. Figurative paths and mytho-historical rivers alike carve narrative routes through the landscapes of Troy, Greece and the underworld; Cassandra's enigmatic song, composed on the verges of these paths and rivers, must broadly follow their snaking routes, but resists being swept along wholesale by the current.

In the midst of this rhetorical exploration of imagined space and sound, the chorus is shocked by the real implication of Cassandra's words when she describes her life by the rivers in the underworld. Recoiling from the unexpected clarity of meaning, they ask, τί τόδε τορὸν ἄγαν ἔπος ἐφημίσω; – 'What is this statement you have uttered all too clearly?' (1162). The danger of successful communication is once again in evidence. Cassandra is 'too clear' (τορὸν ἄγαν) in a way that evokes the chorus' earlier request for a 'clear interpreter' when she was silent (ἑρμηνέως ... τοροῦ, 1062), and which anticipates Cassandra's own grief at knowing Greek 'too well'

---

[69] Cf. Pindar *Pythian* 11.19–22, where Clytemnestra dispatches Cassandra 'to the shadowy banks of Acheron' (21).

(ἄγαν … ἐπίσταμαι, 1254). The chorus now resists Cassandra's meaning, taking refuge in misunderstanding. On the one hand, it argues that she seems to be so clear that a child might understand her; on the other, its continued questioning suggests that it has failed to understand, or cannot bear to admit that it understands.[70] The chorus responds not to any global meaning behind her voice, but to its disconnected sounds. It is θραύματ' (1166): 'shattering for me to hear' (Fraenkel) or 'it shatters me to hear' (Sommerstein); literally, though, it is 'shattered things for me to hear'.

This fragmentation is the form of Cassandra's prophecy that most fascinates and confuses the chorus, and it once again underlines her mantic role. Though the chorus fails to follow her narrative transitions from the past to the future, it sees the formal patterning in her speech: ἑπόμενα προτέροισι τάδ' ἐφημίσω – 'You have uttered a speech that follows on from what came before' (1173).[71] The chorus understands that she is singing of death in the future, though it cannot see how this will happen: τέρμα δ' ἀμηχανῶ – 'still, I'm at a loss as to the end' (1177). Goldhill reads this as the ultimate expression of the chorus' inability to control the narrative, but this is once again to invest more in the content of Cassandra's prophecies than in their music.[72] In fact the chorus is demonstrating an exceptional engagement with the form of Cassandra's language. When they say 'I'm at a loss as to the end' the chorus is echoing Cassandra's earlier lament, πῶς φράσω τέλος; – 'how do I tell the conclusion?' (1109), to which it had then responded, οὔπω ξυνῆκα – 'I haven't grasped it, yet' (1112). Both Cassandra and the chorus are consciously operating in a temporary safe space that has been constructed by their deferred communication or comprehension of a narrative whose ultimate unfolding must lead to a dreadful finale (*terma, telos*). The chorus' focus on understanding the form of Cassandra's prophecies, rather than their content, aids in the suspension of that finale. Indeed, this tactic proves not only effective, but surprisingly enduring. Despite Clytemnestra's later assertion that Cassandra's death made a 'swan song' of her final lament (1444–5), Cassandra, with the help of the chorus, has constructed a scenario in which she can be imagined as never ceasing to sing her prophecies, even after death. Her songs will

---

[70] McClure (1999) 96 and Thalmann (1985) 229 note the chorus' impulse to suppress Cassandra's message.

[71] Knox (1979) 50 describes Cassandra's prophecy of 'the future, set in its pattern of the past which gives it meaning'. Ahl (1984) 180 also notes that the chorus' trouble is not in grasping Cassandra's accounts of the past, but in detecting 'the relationship of past horror to the present moment'.

[72] Goldhill (1984a) 85 argues that Cassandra's knowledge, which takes away free will, and the chorus' incompetence and fear, leads to equal ineffectiveness.

continue to hover indefinitely on the borders of comprehensibility even as she wanders through the underworld. Cassandra and the chorus have created a tragic exchange that is presented as capable of resisting and outlasting any normal narrative drive. It proves to be a delicate commentary on their lyric dialogue, and the valuable part that this music – more sound, less sense – plays within the tragedy.

Choruses and Clarity

Lyric pause within the tragedy itself cannot continue forever, and it is Cassandra who breaks the spell of the musical interlude. At line 1178 she marks a shift in tone by abandoning lyric completely and beginning a new chapter in iambic trimeter. This moment has always been seen as pivotal for Cassandra, though scholars have explained it according to a wide variety of readings of her sexual and mantic roles.[73] Behind most of these readings is an appreciation of the increasingly evident implication of Cassandra's body with her prophetic ability. As time passes Cassandra's prophetic words inch closer in time and in clarity to her inexorable fate. Her linguistic otherness is less apparent, metaphor approaches reality, and to match this the riddling Apollo Loxias, dedicated to the word, is briefly contrasted with the potentially healing Apollo Paian, focused on the body (1199). Cassandra's strategy, then, as the productive fragmentation in her mind-body starts to resolve, is to mark out new zones of fragmentation, to define different communities beyond her own person to continue the work of proliferating articulation, interpretation and translation. She does so by establishing firmer bonds of trust with her immediate interlocutors, as they have to comprehend and then adopt communicative processes that until now have been taking place within the prophet's body. She also

---

[73] Fraenkel (1950) 539–40 suggests that this is the moment when Cassandra moves from chaotic visions to 'real' prophecy: 'What follows is not vision but prophecy ... It is likely that this different mental attitude is emphasized by the change in the metrical form.' On this as the real moment of shift from confusion to enlightenment in the play see Taplin (2003) 77 and McClure (1999) 96, who identifies this as a movement from involuntary to voluntary speech. Mazzoldi (2002) 148 and 154 reads it as a demonstration of one of the most rational of the four stages she sees Cassandra going through. Lebeck (1971) suggests that only now does Cassandra become aware of the chorus. Morgan (1994) sees this as the point where Cassandra moves from maiden to married woman, while Mitchell-Boyask (2006) sees her more as poised between prophet and bride: 'an inverted system of associations that poignantly capture her predicament: a bride who is not a bride, a prophet who is not a prophet, both roles under the control of Apollo' (278). For Wohl (1998) 114–15 this passage is a marker of Cassandra's 'sexual liminality', leading to the exposure of her violent and deceitful sexual relationship with Apollo and fully implicating her in the betrayals that constitute the narrative of the house of Atreus.

reveals how groups can manifest both unified and fragmented perspectives when they come to relay a narrative, relying in particular on the way in which choral voices draw out the valuable polysemy of tragedy. As Vernant describes it, 'The dialogue exchanged and lived through by the heroes of the drama undergoes shifts in meaning as it is interpreted and commented upon by the chorus and taken in and understood by the spectators, and this constitutes one of the essential elements of the tragic effect.'[74]

Cassandra's first words in this new episode are a mass of imagery:

κα‌ὶ μὴν ὁ χρησμὸς οὐκέτ' ἐκ καλυμμάτων
ἔσται δεδορκὼς νεογάμου νύμφης δίκην,
λαμπρὸς δ' ἔοικεν ἡλίου πρὸς ἀντολῆς
πνέων ἐπᾴξειν, ὥστε κύματος δίκην
κλύζειν πρὸς αὐγὰς τοῦδε πήματος πολὺ
μεῖζον· φρενώσω δ' οὐκέτ' ἐξ αἰνιγμάτων·[75]

Well then, the oracular response no longer will peer out
from behind the veil like a newly married bride,
but brightly it seems to be about to rush down,
breathing from the rising of the sun, so that like a wave
it dashes against the shore a far greater pain than this.
I shall teach no longer through riddles.   (Aesch. *Ag.* 1178–83)

It is immediately evident that the dynamics are shifting at this point in the play. The protean similes of social and cosmic transformation that begin Cassandra's speech – the bride, the sunrise, the wave – resist simple decoding, and thus work against Cassandra's claim that she will no longer speak in riddles. The images do, however, create a tonal shift based on the externalisation of Cassandra's communicative agonies. The oracular response (χρησμὸς, 1178) moves out from behind the (her) veil, and is instantly equated with natural forces far beyond any human control. The prophecy is now blowing from the rising of the sun in the east towards the west, aligning with the direction taken by the narrative (beacons, ships, characters) from the end of the Trojan War.[76] From now on, the story Cassandra is telling becomes easier to understand, but harder to escape. This new clarity means that Cassandra begins to bring her fated destiny upon herself more explicitly, while a plethora of different figures and

---

[74] Vernant (1990) 42. Goldhill (1998) similarly reads the chorus as 'a key dramatic device for setting commentary, reflection, and an authoritative voice in play as part of tragic conflict' (255).
[75] Following Sommerstein (2008) in the adoption of ἀντολῆς (1180) and αὐγὰς (1182).
[76] See Lavery (2004a) 12–13; Raeburn and Thomas (2011) 194.

perspectives join her more regulated speech to create a new kind of interpretative fragmentation.

The first figure to appear is the freshly evoked spectre of Apollo. The
bright oracular response (χρησμός) is 'breathing' or 'blowing' (πνέων) its
prophecy. This evokes the elemental force of the wind, to fit the other
similes from the natural world, but it also prefigures the explanation
Cassandra will soon give the chorus of her prophetic abilities, when she
will recall Apollo's initial attack as 'a wrestler breathing his favour' (1206).
By externalising her prophetic message and associating its blast with the
moment when her body was most explicitly the focus of Apollo's desire,
Cassandra is harking back to the moment just before she lost the clear
physical distinctions between herself, Apollo and the voicing of prophecy.
She reaches for the time before Apollo's curse, before she was forced to
embrace in her overworked mind-body all the various jumbled processes
that make up her prophetic utterance.

After this rather oblique evocation of Apollo, Cassandra starts to
acknowledge her interlocutors more openly:

> καὶ μαρτυρεῖτε συνδρόμως ἴχνος κακῶν
> ῥινηλατούσηι τῶν πάλαι πεπραγμένων.
> τὴν γὰρ στέγην τήνδ' οὔποτ' ἐκλείπει χορὸς
> ξύμφθογγος οὐκ εὔφωνος· οὐ γὰρ εὖ λέγει.
> καὶ μὴν πεπωκώς γ', ὡς θρασύνεσθαι πλέον,
> βρότειον αἷμα κῶμος ἐν δόμοις μένει,
> δύσπεμπτος ἔξω, συγγόνων Ἐρινύων·
> ὑμνοῦσι δ' ὕμνον δώμασιν προσήμεναι
> πρώταρχον ἄτην, ἐν μέρει δ' ἀπέπτυσαν
> εὐνὰς ἀδελφοῦ τῶι πατοῦντι δυσμενεῖς.
> ἥμαρτον, ἢ κυρῶ τι τοξότης τις ὥς;
> ἢ ψευδόμαντίς εἰμι θυροκόπος φλέδων;
> ἐκμαρτύρησον προυμόσας τό μ' εἰδέναι
> †λόγωι† παλαιὰς τῶνδ' ἁμαρτίας δόμων.

> And you bear witness as I sniff out the trail, following close,
> of terrible deeds done long ago.
> For from this house there never leaves a chorus,
> singing in one voice but not harmoniously: for it does not speak
>   of good things.
> Indeed having drunk of human blood, so that it has become
>   even more bold,
> the band of revellers is settling firm in the house,
> impossible to send away, Furies related to the house itself.
> Haunting the place they sing the song

of the blundering sin that began it all, and one by one they spit out
   their hatred
for a brother's marriage bed, full of hostility towards the man who
   trampled on it.
Am I wrong, or have I hit the mark, like some kind of archer?
Or am I a prophet of lies, a door-to-door peddler of nonsense?
Bear witness, swearing a solemn oath, that I know
through my speech the ancient wrongs of this house.

(Aesch. Ag. 1184–97)

As Cassandra gets into her stride, she ceases to attempt rapid-fire dialogue with the chorus, or with another actor. Instead she outlines a new role for the chorus, repeatedly asking it to 'bear witness': μαρτυρεῖτε (1184), ἐκμαρτύρησον (1196). She is inviting another narrative perspective, one that will guarantee rather than interrogate her own tale. This offers both a parallel and a challenge to Apollo, who is the metaphysical guarantor of Cassandra's words. The more substantial body of voices in the orchestra is to remain faithful to its job as a chorus by watching and noting events, and then to use this neutral status to back up Cassandra's spoken activity.[77] Cassandra also uses imagery of hunting (1194), picking up on the imagery that the chorus had earlier used to describe her prophetic impulses and its own engagement with them (1093–4 and 1099, see discussion above). Here Cassandra is attempting to mobilise and align the chorus' perspective with her own, underlining their shared investment in tracking not the path, but the very trail of events (ἴχνος κακῶν, 1184). The adverb συνδρόμως (1184), 'following close' or 'running alongside', is ambiguously placed such that it appears to apply equally well to Cassandra, chasing down the trail, as to the chorus, following Cassandra's lead as best it can.

Another group is also introduced to Cassandra's formulation of her newly shared prophetic authority: the Furies. These figures stand between the vague abstraction of Apollo and the physical presence of the chorus as a further guarantee and externalisation of Cassandra's visionary narrative. Earlier the chorus accused Cassandra of invoking a shrieking Fury by recklessly delivering her performative prophecies (1119–20). Cassandra's more extensive description here of a band of Furies implies (as the rest of the trilogy will confirm) that they are not her own creation, but are in fact embedded with the house and with the events that have taken place in it over the years.[78] Nonetheless there are unsettling links between these

---

[77] On the role of the 'collective' chorus as negotiators of authority, including political authority, see Gould (1998) and Goldhill (1998).
[78] Padel (1992) 181 notes the development of the Erinyes through the *Oresteia*. They are visible initially only to outsiders but are gradually revealed to insiders: they are viewed by Cassandra, then Orestes,

Furies and the prophet. Cassandra claims to hear the actual voices of
the Furies that the chorus had fearfully imagined, and describes them as
singing (ὑμνοῦσι δ' ὕμνον, 1191). The language Cassandra uses to depict
their song aligns them with the terms in which her own lyric song has
been described. The Furies are, as she puts it, 'singing in one voice but not
harmoniously' or even 'singing in unison but not in tune' (ξύμφθογγος
οὐκ εὔφωνος, 1187).[79] The paradox of Cassandra's 'unmusical music' (νόμον
ἄνομον, 1142) is found in the voices of these Furies, though here it is applied
not to the effect of an individual voice but to that of a motley choir that
produces an ugly symphony. The group is, however, more successful in
its processing of meaning. Cassandra's prophetic voice gestured towards
Greek but avoided sense. The Furies' voices sail more dangerously close to
cogency. Being 'in unison' (ξύμφθογγος) they avoid the fragmentation of
Cassandra's message, singing not only unanimously with each other but in
synch with the events they trigger. The result is that their dissonant message
is not incoherent; on the contrary, its horror is evident (οὐκ εὔφωνος). If
Cassandra believes that her voice is channelling that of the Furies, then she
is embracing a move away from the kind of delaying linguistic chaos she
provoked earlier in the play, and towards a performative triggering of the
events being described.

Cassandra follows up her description of this tuneless but powerful chorus
by returning to the real chorus. She looks again to the distinction between
her successful communications with the chorus regarding the past, and
their shared failure to translate that success into meaningful communication about the future. Cassandra aggressively anticipates the accusation
that she is 'a prophet of lies' (ψευδόμαντις, 1195) before demanding that
the chorus at least admit to her accuracy about the house's history, if not
its future. Cassandra needs the chorus to acknowledge that despite coming
from overseas, she has as much knowledge about Argos' past as the native
chorus. Her upbringing in Troy means that she must have had access to
supernatural channels of communication in order to learn the information that the chorus is aware of simply from living in Argos. Once again
Cassandra's foreign status is what proves her extraordinary transtemporal
knowledge.

---

then the Pythia and finally the Athenian spectators. 'It is madness to see them. It may be madness
not to.' This anticipates the implication of the audience in Cassandra's visions – her *furor* – in
Seneca's *Agamemnon* (see Chapter 5).

[79] Prins (1991), who explores the performativity of the Furies' song in the *Oresteia*, translates the phrase
as 'dissonant'.

Cassandra's interlocutors can indeed verify the prophet's truthfulness as a storyteller of Argos' history:

καὶ πῶς ἂν ὅρκου πῆγμα γενναίως παγὲν
παιώνιον γένοιτο; θαυμάζω δέ σου,
πόντου πέραν τραφεῖσαν ἀλλόθρουν πόλιν
κυρεῖν λέγουσαν ὥσπερ εἰ παρεστάτεις.

And yet how could the binding security of an oath honestly secured
be helpful? Then again I am indeed amazed at you,
how, brought up beyond the sea and speaking about a foreign-speaking city,
you are as accurate as if you had been present here.

(Aesch. *Ag.* 1198–1201)

The chorus is astounded at Cassandra's ability to narrate correctly events occurring at a distance from her in space as much as time. In addition, the Greek city she is describing is foreign-speaking to her (ἀλλόθρουν, 1200), so the chorus marks Cassandra's distance from Argos and its past with a reference to the same linguistic barrier that has represented her communicative troubles from the start. Yet while the chorus grants the truth of Cassandra's narrative, it denies its own ability to guarantee her narrative, arguing that a sworn oath would not be 'helpful' or 'healing' (παιώνιον, 1199). Once again the presence of Apollo lurks behind her language, here in his role as healer: Apollo Paian. The chorus rejects the role of guarantor in terms that suggest it should really be performed by the god who created Cassandra's linguistic complications in the first place. Apollo has the power to synthesise not just the fragmented narratives of past and future but also the sundered functions of narrative and reality.

Cassandra and the chorus appear to be communicating so successfully now that, after Cassandra explains the story of Apollo's attack and his curse, the chorus protests that it actually believes her prophecies: ἡμῖν γε μὲν δὴ πιστὰ θεσπίζειν δοκεῖς – 'to us at least you seem to prophesy things we should believe' (1213). But Cassandra shows that Apollo will continue to wreak sadistic havoc on her communications and her destiny. She agrees that Apollo is responsible for everything: μάντις μ' Ἀπόλλων τῶιδ' ἐπέστησεν τέλει – 'the prophet Apollo set me to this goal' (1202). He will, however, offer only a perverted version of the resolution the chorus hoped for. After a passage of wild prophecy Cassandra goes on to observe: ἀλλ' οὔτι Παιὼν τῶιδ' ἐπιστατεῖ λόγωι – 'there is no healing Paian presiding over this narrative' (1248). These two lines (1202 and 1248) delivered by Cassandra mirror each other syntactically and lexically, while pointing to Apollo's cruelty at the beginning and the end of Cassandra's life, before and after she has the gift of prophecy. After describing the moment of horrific physical proximity, when Apollo sexually attacked Cassandra ('a wrestler breathing his favour', 1206) and Cassandra resorted to verbal trickery ('I cheated Loxias', 1208), Apollo becomes notable for his absence, for his failure to 'heal' Cassandra's speech. Apollo set Cassandra on a track to a 'goal', a *telos*, that signifies both her prophetic function and her inevitable demise, and he insists that both are seen through to the bitter end. Apollo stands back from her words so that only Cassandra's bodily 'end' can offer the guarantee, the ultimate proof, of her prophecies. Narrative and reality will resolve, but through Apollo's deliberate failure to intervene in the unfolding horrors, rather than through his healing powers.

Instead of dwelling on the moment of awful synthesis of words and action, voice and body, that she will encounter at the *telos* of her life above ground, Cassandra moves to consider the ongoing acts of verbal resistance that will occur when her interlocutors correctly match word to event after it is all apparently over:

> καὶ τῶνδ' ὁμοῖον εἴ τι μὴ πείθω· τί γάρ;
> τὸ μέλλον ἥξει, καὶ σύ μ' ἐν τάχει παρὼν
> ἄγαν γ' ἀληθόμαντιν οἰκτίρας ἐρεῖς.

> And yet it is all the same if I fail to convince in any of these
>   things: what of it?
> The future will come, and very soon, right here,
> you will pity me and describe me as all too accurate a prophet.
>   (Aesch. *Ag.* 1239–41)

The operations of persuasion and delay are now replaced by Cassandra's exhausted surrender to the inevitable (τὸ μέλλον ἥξει, 1240) and a poignant, but astute, observation about her own function when those future events take place. For at that moment the chorus, or the 'you' represented by the chorus and potentially encompassing a much broader audience, will reflect on Cassandra's story in such a way that it takes over her role as narrator: 'you will describe me as all too accurate a prophet' (ἄγαν γ' ἀληθόμαντιν ... ἐρεῖς, 1241). When the chorus picks up the threads of Cassandra's prophecies, it will identify her as a figure invested in too much sense, not in too much nonsense. The surplus meaning that was created through her misunderstandings will be transformed into a surplus of truth. Or, viewed from another angle, it will be proven simply to be two sides of the same coin. There is always too much truth in Cassandra's misunderstood narrative and in all its reformulations, both before and after her *telos*.

This paradox of 'too much sense' is picked up in Cassandra's delivery of the astonishing line discussed at the beginning of this chapter, and the chorus' response to it. Both are an expression of the continued miscommunications that spill out beyond Cassandra's body:

> Κα. καὶ μὴν ἄγαν γ᾽ Ἕλλην᾽ ἐπίσταμαι φάτιν.
> Χο. καὶ γὰρ τὰ πυθόκραντα, δυσμαθῆ δ᾽ ὅμως.

> Kass. And yet I know the Greek language only too well.
> Chor. And indeed the Pythian Promises, though they are
>   still hard to understand.   (Aesch. *Ag.* 1254–5)

Both Cassandra and the chorus understand, and can speak, Greek. But having a common language does not mean having a common understanding, and having a common understanding (even as the Furies in Cassandra's vision sang in unison) does not mean that the communication itself is desirable. When the issue of Cassandra's competence in Greek was first broached in the tragedy, there was confusion over whether it was more important that she spoke or understood the language (1050–4). Here, towards the end of Cassandra's time onstage, the issue resurfaces. The most natural reading of Cassandra's line assumes that she is plaintively pointing out that her competent Greek *speech* is being misunderstood. Yet in the light of all the other passages discussed, and the chorus' response to Cassandra here, at least one other reading is possible, one that emphasises Cassandra's claim to a kind of *understanding* and relinquishes the role of speech to others.

The Greek language (Ἕλλην᾽ ... φάτιν, 1254) Cassandra knows is the whole Greek story to which she is bound. It is the narrative that she has articulated (with limited success), as well as the narrative that she has comprehended (with more success), as a foreign and prophetic outsider. Meanwhile the chorus, which has been brought to recognise her unusual knowledge and to identify it positively with her foreign origins, responds with a curious swerve. It compares Cassandra's prophetic function with that of the indigenous Greek Pythia – in the process invoking another shady domain of Apollo. The chorus' comment is generally taken to mean 'And so do the Pythian Promises know (= get articulated in) Greek', with πυθόκραντα (1255) in the nominative case. But for the oracular prophecies themselves to 'know' or 'speak' Greek is strained. The chorus has capped Cassandra's ambiguity with an equally ambiguous line that could also mean, 'And indeed you know the Pythian Promises too, though they are still hard to understand', with πυθόκραντα in the accusative case to parallel Cassandra's knowledge of the Greek language (Ἕλλην᾽ ... φάτιν). This ambiguity means that the chorus' reference to the riddling language of the Delphic oracle can be understood as an analogy for either the ambiguities of Cassandra's prophecies or her exceptional understanding of language even in its most convoluted and mystic forms.[80]

With both these readings sitting in the balance, Cassandra is granted a double point of identification. The flexibility of the comparison allows her speech to be identified with the impenetrability and divine power of the Pythia, whose riddling Greek is baffling to its petitioners, while it also allows her to be identified with those human protagonists who are engaged so constantly and against the odds in trying to disentangle the complexities of the Greek language. Cassandra is once again playing multiple hermeneutic roles: prophet and interpreting petitioner, inspired *mantis* and sign-reading *prophētēs*, a *hermēneus* who is both foreign and multi-, even super-lingual, too much a true prophet (ἄγαν γ' ἀληθόμαντιν, 1241) and too knowledgeable of Greek (καὶ μὴν ἄγαν γ' Ἕλλην' ἐπίσταμαι φάτιν, 1254). Cassandra subtly plays on her relationship to the native prophetic sanctuary at Delphi. In her excessive knowledge and her vivid consciousness of this burden (καὶ μὴν ἄγαν ...), she punningly defies one of the proverbial instructions given to visitors to the Pythia: μηδὲν ἄγαν – 'nothing in excess', whilst she embraces another, γνῶθι σεαυτόν – 'know yourself'. Above all, the chorus' sympathetic probing not only exposes the paradoxes of her extravagant knowledge and multiple interpretative roles, but also identifies where her communicative excesses become the responsibility of other characters. It is the chorus that repeatedly hints at Apollo's malign interference (or lack of interference), that first hints at Cassandra's implication with the Furies, that offers the brilliantly slippery analogy with the Delphic oracle and ultimately takes on the task of spreading Cassandra's fame, if only retrospectively, as 'too accurate a prophet'.

Performing Prophecy

It remains only to turn to Cassandra's final moments in the play, where she demonstrates what it really means to be 'too accurate a prophet'. This is the point at which her performative speech is no longer escapable, and the prophet moves to enact what previously she has only described. As

[80] Fraenkel (1950) identifies the semantics of the term πυθόκραντα by considering the verb κραίνειν and suggests that it means 'to pronounce and establish in binding and valid form with the guarantee of fulfilment in the future' (193). It thus stands as a resolution for humans, but for gods it represents a decree of fate, an assurance of a future event – again reflecting the double bind of mortal and divine responses to these events.

her prophetic narrative and her life begin to converge, Cassandra continues to mark the difference between knowledge and experience, a story narrated and a story lived. The question left concerns the level of closure that is imposed by the prophet's fated death, her *telos*. Does it represent the finality of full understanding, or is there still room for the 'excess' created by Cassandra's confusing prophetic speech and song? Throughout this episode Cassandra's assertion of her increasing independence from Apollo, her embrace of his failure to 'heal' her speech even as she bows to the fate he has imposed on her, can be read as an attempt to answer this question.

As Cassandra feels the onset of Apollo for the last time, she addresses him not as Loxias, or Paian, but as Lukeios (1257) – 'the Lycian', or 'the Wolf-god'. The epithet identifies him with Cassandra's past in Asia Minor, not her present in Greece, and has him appearing in his most savage form. With his final onslaught upon Cassandra comes a return to the (in)articulations of prophetic inspiration: παπαῖ· οἷον τὸ πῦρ ἐπέρχεται δέ μοι – 'Ah! What fire comes suddenly upon me' (1256). Like the beacons tracking the progress of Troy's fall and its narrative across the Aegean, the fire of true prophecy alights upon Cassandra's person as her own fall and her narrative of it conjoin. This time Cassandra responds with an unusually bodily response, frenziedly stripping off the accoutrements of Apollo:

τί δῆτ' ἐμαυτῆς καταγέλωτ' ἔχω τάδε
καὶ σκῆπτρα καὶ μαντεῖα περὶ δέρηι στέφη;
σὲ μὲν πρὸ μοίρας τῆς ἐμῆς διαφθερῶ·
ἴτ' ἐς φθόρον πεσόντ', ἐγώ θ' ἅμ' ἕψομαι.
ἄλλην τιν' ἄτης ἀντ' ἐμοῦ πλουτίζετε.
ἰδοὺ δ', Ἀπόλλων αὐτὸς οὐκδύων ἐμὲ
χρηστηρίαν ἐσθῆτ'. ἐποπτεύσας δέ με
κἀν τοῖσδε κόσμοις καταγελωμένην μέγα
φίλων ὑπ' ἐχθρῶν οὐ διχορρόπως, μάτην
⟨τὰ πιστὰ θεσπίζουσαν, οὐδέν ἤρκεσεν,⟩
καλουμένη δέ, φοιτὰς ὡς ἀγύρτρια,
πτωχὸς τάλαινα λιμοθνὴς ἠνεσχόμην·
καὶ νῦν ὁ μάντις μάντιν ἐκπράξας ἐμὲ
ἀπήγαγ' εἰς τοιάσδε θανασίμους τύχας,
βωμοῦ πατρώιου δ' ἀντ' ἐπίξηνον μένει
θερμὸν κοπέντος φοινίωι προσφάγματι.[81]

Why then do I hold on to these ridiculous items,
both the sceptre and the garland of prophecy around my neck?
You, at least, I shall destroy before I meet my fate:

---

[81] Keeping καλουμένη in line 1273.

Go to perdition, dashed to the ground, and I shall follow right after:
make some other rich with ruin in my place.
Look, Apollo himself is the one who is stripping me
of my prophetic dress. Having looked on
while I was horribly mocked, even wearing this outfit,
by friends more like enemies, relentlessly, in vain
<prophesying the truth, he did not defend me in any way,>
and though called, like those religious scroungers who go around
     demanding alms,
a 'wretched, starving beggar', I put up with it:
and now the prophet who has destroyed me, his prophetess,
has led me off to these death-dealing fates,
and instead of the altar of my homeland, the chopping block waits for me,
warm with the previous bloody sacrifice of the man hacked to death.

(Aesch. Ag. 1264–78)

In this passage Cassandra's vulnerability in the face of Apollo's whims is clear: however one translates the verb ἐκπράξας (1275) – 'made', 'unmade', 'ruined', 'killed', 'exacted as his due' – it embraces Apollo's total control over Cassandra, the prophet he both creates and destroys. Yet the phrase as a whole (ὁ μάντις μάντιν ἐκπράξας ἐμέ), with the juxtaposition of Apollo (μάντις) and Cassandra (μάντιν) playing the same prophetic role, implies rather more equality in their power dynamic at this point in the play. As much as Apollo has shaped her fate, Cassandra is moving to enact it by her own volition. This power struggle is also expressed through Cassandra's description of the material symbols of her relationship with Apollo. Containing an eroticised edge, Cassandra's rejection of the symbols of Apollo reflects Apollo's initial attack – as she throws them off, she describes Apollo as stripping her of them – but it also replays her initial rejection of the god.[82] During this simultaneous narrative and performance of her disrobing, Cassandra creates an odd form of 'double motivation' in which actions are conceived of as motivated by a merging of divine influence and mortal decision.[83] The double motivation is unusual here because Cassandra the *actor* is openly cognisant of Apollo's role as *auctor*, 'author', in determining her actions (as well as her speech and her ultimate fate). Moreover, through her deliberate dramatisation of Apollo's interference, particularly her angry deictic 'look' (ἰδού, 1269), Cassandra insists on asserting her own power as an *auctor*, her own ability to shape

[82] Taplin (2003) 43 marks the paradox: 'Cassandra casts her prophet's trappings to the ground (1265); but this defiant rejection of Apollo, who has brought her to misery and death, far from spoiling her prophetic power, seems to unburden and sharpen it.'
[83] Lesky (1961).

the articulation of events. Her overdetermined speech and performance combine such that the prophet appropriates Apollo's mantic authority, while rejecting the god and his symbols.

Laughter, like her silence earlier in the *Agamemnon*, also marks Cassandra's paradoxical power play with Apollo. She describes her Apollonian accoutrements as 'ridiculous' (καταγέλωτ', 1264). Laughter usually marks a power dynamic in which the person laughing diminishes the person or thing being laughed at, but a shared appreciation of the ridiculous also creates a communicative bond. Cassandra's refusal to define firmly the mockery's direction or origin diffuses this potential bond among different communities. For Cassandra to describe Apollo's symbols as ridiculous is a defiant gesture against Apollo himself, but the symbols are a part of her own role and inviting mockery of them is also a form of self-mockery. To reinforce this, the terminology of mockery shifts from the symbols to Cassandra herself (1264, 1271), when the prophet describes herself as laughed at 'by friends more like enemies'. Here her vagueness applies to the community ridiculing the prophet, rather than the object of their ridicule: the boundary between her friends and enemies has slipped, with their new collaboration asserted 'relentlessly' or 'unanimously' (οὐ διχορρόπως, 1272). Like the chorus of Furies, they are in a state of perfect agreement with each other, even while what they communicate is painful to hear. The laughter of these friend-enemies has Apollo's implied approval and participation too, for he was the first to leer at Cassandra, not just 'looking on' but also 'looking her over' (ἐποπτεύσας δέ με, 1270) from the beginning of their association. Apollo is nothing if not a fickle friend and enemy to Cassandra. The result of this confusion of mocking and mocked creates a circular process in which Cassandra embroils Apollo as both subject and object. More significantly, she positions herself as a disempowered, mocked body, but her words assert the power of the comedian, directing the humour bitterly wherever she chooses, and eliciting it from whomever she picks.

With this astonishing outburst Cassandra has defined her social exclusion as starkly as she did with her first taciturn moments onstage. Towards the end of the passage, in order to describe the kind of mockery she faces, she adopts terms that refer to social exclusion based on real experiences of poverty and displacement (1273–4). Her bodily privations are implied in the insults she quotes that address her as a starving beggar (πτωχὸς τάλαινα λιμοθνής, 1274), and she describes herself as the very perversion of an honoured priestess: she is an ἀγύρτρια (1273), a despised religious figure who goes around wheedling alms. Tiresias in Sophocles' *Oedipus Tyrannus* is accused of being just such a deceitful figure.[84] Finally, Cassandra is destined for death far from her father's altar (βωμοῦ πατρώιου, 1277) although, of course, such a paternal altar was no refuge for Agamemnon's daughter Iphigenia, whose sacrificial blood has 'warmed up' the altar for Cassandra as much as Agamemnon's is about to do.

The cumulative effect of these multiple images, conjured up by Cassandra to accompany her shedding of Apollo's regalia, is to highlight a particular kind of simultaneity, a growing synchrony of word and action whose articulation is made possible by Cassandra's position on the margins of society and of normal communication. This synchrony is the inescapable convergence of prophecy and its realisation, and it is one that Cassandra refuses to experience passively. In physically rejecting her ties to Apollo and in adopting descriptive and proactive speech that makes her both subject and object of the enfolding narrative, she works to master the paradoxes of her position: she is an agent and a victim; her friends and enemies work together; Apollo's protectiveness as a prophet is no protection to his own favoured and cursed prophet; the symbols of prophecy are both powerful and ridiculous. The silence that earlier forced Cassandra's interlocutors to supply their own voices and motions in the act of interpreting her description of future events, has now been overtaken by a flood of speech that asserts Cassandra's own control as the gap between narrative and event closes. This control becomes most marked in Cassandra's attitude to her actual death. First she hands over to Orestes not just the task of taking vengeance for her death, but also her very role as a 'fugitive, wanderer and exile' (1282).[85] Then she moves in the opposite direction, approaching the house to accept her oncoming death:

ἰοῦσα πράξω· τλήσομαι τὸ κατθανεῖν·
...
Ἅιδου πύλας δὲ τάσδ' ἐγὼ προσεννέπω·

Going forth, I will suffer what is to come: I will dare to die
...
and I greet these gates as the gates of Hades.   (Aesch. *Ag.* 1289, 1291)

---

[84] Oedipus calls Tiresias δόλιος ἀγύρτης (Soph. *OT* 388). This unjustified outburst suggests that the term is used more as part of a conventional (false) accusation levelled at prophets, rather than as a description of real behaviour: hence a preference for καλουμένη at 1273, rather than any of the emendations.

[85] Orestes will also take over Cassandra's visions of the Furies: where she was the first to see them in the *Agamemnon*, he will be plagued by them in the *Libation Bearers*, before the entire audience sees them in the *Eumenides*.

Though the verb πράξω (1289) – 'I will suffer' – is often read as textually corrupt, it does a lot of work left as it is. With it Cassandra echoes her description of Troy 'suffering as it suffered' (1287) two lines earlier, drawing her own fate and that of the fallen city into an even closer symbiosis. She also uses it to emphasise her agency: 'I will achieve (what is to come)'. Then she adds speech to her deliberate activity, addressing the gates of the house in terms that anticipate her journey to the underworld.

The chorus is discombobulated by Cassandra's sudden assumption of control:

ὦ πολλὰ μὲν τάλαινα, πολλὰ δ᾽ αὖ σοφή
γύναι, μακρὰν ἔτεινας. εἰ δ᾽ ἐτητύμως
μόρον τὸν αὑτῆς οἶσθα, πῶς θεηλάτου
βοὸς δίκην πρὸς βωμὸν εὐτόλμως πατεῖς;

O you who are so wretched a woman, but then again also so wise,
you have stretched your speech out at some length. But if truly
you know your own fate, how can you walk bravely towards the altar,
like a sacrificial cow driven forward by a god's demand?

(Aesch. *Ag.* 1295–8)

The chorus beautifully represents the combination of determination and residual delay in Cassandra's speech. Though clearly still confused by what Cassandra will face inside the house, the chorus comprehends the importance of her speech, and particularly its length (μακρὰν ἔτεινας, 1296). The speech here, like her silence before, creates delay, standing between the prophet and her death, her knowledge (οἶσθα, 1297) and her action (πατεῖς, 1298), with the element of divine compulsion hanging over the whole process (θεηλάτου, 1297). What the chorus sees is the increasing tension as the final seconds tick away between Cassandra's prophecies and the enactment of the events she prophesied: ὁ δ᾽ ὕστατός γε τοῦ χρόνου πρεσβεύεται – 'But the last bit of time, at least, is the most precious' (1300).

As such, Cassandra's last compulsive prayer is perhaps the most valuable hermeneutic key to her speech throughout the play, though its textual problems make it a minefield for interpretation:

ἅπαξ ἔτ᾽ εἰπεῖν ῥῆσιν ἢ θρῆνον θέλω
ἐμὸν τὸν αὑτῆς· ἡλίου δ᾽ ἐπεύχομαι
πρὸς ὕστατον φῶς, δεσπότου τιμαόροις
ἐχθροὺς φόνευσιν τὴν ἐμὴν τίνειν ὁμοῦ,
δούλης θανούσης, εὐμαροῦς χειρώματος.
ἰὼ βρότεια πράγματ᾽· εὐτυχοῦντα μὲν

σκιᾶι τις ἂν πρέψειεν, εἰ δὲ δυστυχῆι,
βολαῖς ὑγρώσσων σπόγγος ὤλεσεν γραφήν.
καὶ ταῦτ' ἐκείνων μᾶλλον οἰκτίρω πολύ.[86]

Just once more I would like to make a speech, or a lament maybe,
for myself, and, facing the last light of the sun,
I pray that to the avengers of my master
my enemies will pay for my death too,
for me dying a slave, an easy conquest.
Oh, mortal affairs are strange: when they are prospering
they may be described as a shadow, but if there is misfortune
a damp sponge deletes the scribble at a stroke.
And these situations I pity far more than those.   (Aesch. *Ag.* 1322–30)

Cassandra's final images are constructed as she faces the setting sun; this
represents her last and furthest move westwards. The beacons from the
beginning of the play that marked the myth's progression from the east
have been swallowed up in the light of the sun, and as the sun's fire dies
for the night Cassandra prays for the next stage of the tragedy to run its
course. She then delivers a gnomic final four lines. In the light provided
by the beacons and the sun are the shadows of mortals' stories, stories that
also look like ephemeral 'scribbles'.

With this final image Aeschylus' Cassandra perfectly poises the balance
between the finality of death and the enduring power of narrative. Earlier
in the play the great lines of mythic narrative lay encapsulated in the image
of the beacons, literal and symbolic by turn, marking and sometimes even
defying mortal time, travel and communication. Cassandra now shows
that the big picture of human and divine existence lies in an even bigger
stream of light: in the endless rising and setting of the sun. The stories of
individual mortals lie poignantly outlined as shadows in the day's sun,
shadows that in adversity are marked as nothing more than a transient
representation, a *graphē*, subject to obliteration. This representative *graphē*
is another image, like Philomela's embroidery, standing for hampered or
modified speech that nonetheless manages to outline a human narrative: it
evokes Cassandra's fragile utterance in visual – maybe even written – form.
Vulnerable though it is, such a scribble fights against the obliteration of
any death that is too clearly identified or passively met.

Cassandra's depiction of human stories as a scribble, an obscure mark
that – however sketchily – transmits a narrative to others, builds on the

---

[86] Following Page (1972) and Sommerstein (2008) for σκιᾶι τις ἂν πρέψειεν (1328).

fact that multiple perspectives and refractions have surrounded the con-
sumption of all her narratives in the play. In her every silence, song and
speech, each mode of communication as abstract and vague as this *graphē*,
Cassandra marks out the space for a flourishing of interpretations and
new constructions of her meanings. The sponge may threaten to obliterate
Cassandra's story and that of the people around her, but while her lived
experience may be blotted out, the representative scribble will live on in
her interlocutors' flawed recollections, reconstructions and (re)interpret-
ations for as long as the sun continues to rise and set.

The paradox of the terrible truthfulness and rich confusion in
Cassandra's speech is ultimately the paradox of a horrifying (and hor-
rifyingly short) life story that is artful and enduring in the telling.
Cassandra's life and prophecy climax in a *telos* that is *the* end of her life,
but only *an* end of her story. Knox argues that the chorus, Cassandra's
main interlocutors, gain from their interactions with Cassandra: 'They
do learn, in the end, and from Cassandra, to face reality, bitter though
it may be, to see things as they actually are and must and will be.'[87] This
may be true to some extent, but in interactions with Cassandra such
monovalence and straightforward comprehension is always marked as
ugly and dangerous. It is the Furies' inescapable singing 'as one' that
is so unpleasant (ξύμφθογγος οὐκ εὔφωνος, 1187), as is the mockery
of friends acting like enemies 'unanimously' (φίλων ὑπ᾽ ἐχθρῶν οὐ
διχορρόπως, 1272). Cassandra's own unmusical music (νόμον ἄνομον,
1142) is certainly no easy listening either, with its dissonant confusions
and its underlying performative ineluctability. However, the imperfect
translation that her baffling voice demands, the endless exchanges that
it provokes, mean that her song illustrates the value that can be found
in sound even without sense: it celebrates and perpetuates the abstract
scribbles in the sun before the obliteration of the sponge, the beauty of
the drama in which the audience can suspend its knowledge of the story's
tragic trajectory to the very end (μακρὰν ἔτεινας, 1296) – and possibly
even beyond that end. What the chorus really learns, or at least exempli-
fies, is how to engage with what is beyond precise comprehension, how
not to reject what is more than any one language can express and how to
see things not necessarily 'as they actually are and must and will be', but
as they *might* be.

---

[87] Knox (1979) 52. Taplin (1977) also argues that Cassandra's speech allows the chorus to move from
aporia to relative clarity of understanding.

CHAPTER 2

Rewriting Her-story: Euripides' Trojan Women

Χο. ὡς ἡδέως κακοῖσιν οἰκείοις γελᾶις.

Chorus: How cheerfully do you laugh at your own evils.
(Eur. *Tro.* 406–7)[1]

More than forty years after the *Oresteia* was first produced, in 415 BCE Cassandra and her prophetic ravings could be found back on the Athenian stage in Euripides' *Trojan Women*. However, the city around Cassandra and her tragic audience had changed radically in the intervening years. In Athens the enduring scars of the Persian Wars had been replaced by the present trauma of the Peloponnesian War, now dragging on well into its second decade. Now that she was pitted against other *poleis* in Greece, Athens' self-definition through cultural exploration of the barbarian 'other' needed to be updated with more introspective analyses of Athenian exceptionalism, power and vulnerability in a Hellenic context.[2] Sparta and her allies were the immediate enemy, and the loyalty (or submissiveness) of Athens' own Greek allies was in question.

Most recently, just a few months before the *Trojan Women* was staged, Athens' relationship with the island of Melos had given a harsh example of this. Athens had tried to expand the Delian League by incorporating the oligarchic Melos, which was founded as a Spartan colony but to date had been largely neutral in the war. The failure of initial negotiations led to Athens invading the island, besieging the city and, after its fall, making the decision to execute all the male citizens of the island and sell the women and children into slavery. Thucydides' imaginative reconstruction of the 'Melian Dialogue' (Thuc. *Hist.* 5.84–116) vividly illustrates the brutal reality of Athenian hegemony. Whether or not Euripides had had time to

---

[1] Quotations from the *Trojan Women* are from Diggle (1981a) except where noted.
[2] Lape (2010). See recent work on Aristophanes' comedies, such as Willi (2002) on Greek dialectal differentiation and its 'Othering' (or 'de-Othering') effect. See also Whitehorne (2005). On Troy's flexible job in constructing Athenian identity across the fifth century see Zeitlin (2009).

take this violent episode of a Greek city's destruction into account when he wrote the *Trojan Women*, there is little doubt that the contemporary audience of the play would have had the event in mind when they watched the play's first staging.[3] It is, as Poole describes it, a play dominated by 'images of an evacuation, a dispersal, a demolition, an obliteration – literally, of a city and its people, but also at a wider level, of a whole set of ideas, ideals and values'.[4] Andromache's cry in the middle of the most heart-rending passage of the play, when she has learned that Astyanax is to be killed, must have left the audience feeling at least some degree of discomfort:

ὦ βάρβαρ' ἐξευρόντες Ἕλληνες κακά,
τί τόνδε παῖδα κτείνετ' οὐδὲν αἴτιον;

Oh Greeks, inventors of barbarian evils,
Why are you murdering this innocent boy?   (Eur. *Tro.* 764–5)

For the character of Cassandra onstage things have changed too. Loraux describes Euripides' Cassandra as 'an interpretation – a reading, we would say today – of Aeschylus' Cassandra'.[5] In fact a wealth of events, themes and characterisations from the *Agamemnon* lie in the background to the *Trojan Women*, but they have been transformed in ways that cast new light on the myth and on the earlier play. For starters, in the *Trojan Women* the dramatic setting has shifted from Cassandra's arrival in Argos to her experiences during the final capture and fall of Troy.[6] This moves against the current found in the *Agamemnon*, in which the narrative drive pushes from east to west, from Troy to Greece. The cultural, temporal and linguistic dislocations suffered by Cassandra in the *Trojan Women* are played out on the other side of the Aegean instead, where the Greeks are the foreigners and the defeated Trojan women are still, for a final few hours, clinging to the coast of their homeland.[7]

To this spatial shift between the *Agamemnon* and the *Trojan Women* is added a temporal shift. Relative to the *Oresteia*, the text emerges later in historical time, but it is set earlier in mythic time. Euripides' play comes four

[3] Croally (1994) 234; Goff (2009) 27–35.
[4] Poole (1976) 260.
[5] Loraux (2002) 75.
[6] Croally (1994) reads Troy as the real subject of the play.
[7] On the liminal space of the Trojan coastline see Gregory (1997) 156. A fragment from the first line of the first play in Euripides' trilogy, the *Alexander*, emphasises the move to Troy: [Τροία μὲν ἥδε] καὶ τὸ κλεινὸν Ἴλιον, supplemented by Scodel (1980) 22. Scodel argues that the prologue to the *Alexander* was spoken by the herdsman who saved Paris, but there are reasons to maintain that it could have been delivered by Cassandra herself – not least because of the faint echo of Cassandra's voice in Thyestes' prologue to Seneca's *Agamemnon* (see Chapter 5), which may possibly in its turn echo a Cassandra speaking the prologue to Ennius' *Alexander*.

decades after Aeschylus', yet his Cassandra is younger and less tested. The intertextuality between the two works becomes marked and self-conscious when the later work foreshadows events that occur in the former. Barchiesi has identified a version of this phenomenon in Latin literature, calling it the 'future reflexive', following Goldhill's lead on Hellenistic examples (indeed a more marked case of this will emerge in Lycophron's *Alexandra*, discussed in Chapter 3).[8] The telling of a well-established myth from a point in the story that knowingly anticipates the events of an older telling allows the later text and its characters to supplement, explain and some-times subvert the action of the earlier text, with various degrees of ironic anticipation or foreboding.[9] Of course, for Cassandra this has particular significance, as her prophetic gift mirrors the knowledge of a well-read external audience. Moreover, the younger she is, the longer the stretch of the future she is condemned to foresee in the presence of her infuriatingly blinkered internal audience.

Despite this fresh setting for Cassandra and her prophecies, it rarely goes unremarked upon by commentators that the *Trojan Women* is a play in which very little actually happens. The two previous plays in the trilogy, as far as their plots can be reconstructed, appear to have been more action-packed.[10] The *Alexander* had staged the story of Paris' triumphant return to the Trojan palace, after Hecuba's dream that she gave birth to a firebrand had led to him being abandoned as a baby.[11] Cassandra's warnings about Paris' role in bringing down the city of Troy are, predictably, ignored. The *Palamedes* had addressed some part of the story concerning the downfall of its eponymous hero, who had invented writing and tricked Odysseus into joining the expedition to Troy. In turn Odysseus framed Palamedes as a traitor to the Greeks and he was put to death, but final vengeance was had by Palamedes' father: he placed false beacons on Euboea to lure returning Greeks to their deaths on the rocky coastline. So the *Trojan Women* comes as a coda to two plays that dramatise events leading up to the fall of Troy (*Alexander*) and the disasters of the Greek *nostoi* (*Palamedes*). The third play of the trilogy embraces the fulfilment of both events, as Troy has fallen just before the *Trojan Women* begins, and the prologue shows Poseidon and Athena forging a new alliance in order to set in motion the punishment of the Greeks for their sacrilegious behaviour when sacking Troy. Yet, despite

---

[8] Barchiesi (1993), Goldhill (1991) 284–333.
[9] Goff (2009) puts it slightly differently: 'the people in the play are improvising in unprecedented situations – they no longer have the characters that they used to have' (58).
[10] Scodel (1980), Kovacs (1999) 4–7.
[11] Pindar has Cassandra retell this dream of Hecuba in his eighth *Paean*: Pind. *Pae.* 8a (P. Oxy. 52i(A)).

all the drama surrounding the *Trojan Women*, the action within the play turns out to be minimal. Indeed, Dunn argues that the long-term post-war strategies being plotted by Poseidon and Athena in the prologue provide more of a conclusion than an introduction to the play, leaving the play itself with nowhere to go and the audience with a sense of being stranded in limbo.[12] The play's identification as 'paratragic' is not unreasonable.[13]

So the *Trojan Women* offers a dramatic 'pause' in which there is little action, partly because the disempowered protagonists have little by way of agency.[14] If Cassandra's silence and speech in the *Agamemnon* offered a moment of pause for productive misunderstanding and for delay of the inevitable, the whole cast of the *Trojan Women* is involved in a similar operation. Words are there to process events, not to trigger them. For Gregory the play is about *logos* itself, 'as alternative to action'.[15] Goldhill agrees: 'in the *Trojan Women*, Cassandra's prophecies, Andromache's mourning, and Hecuba's rationalism in different ways emphasise the insufficiency of words to deal with the violence and suffering of war, as much as the power of language to explain, define and control the narratives of war'.[16] The play is about how the women reformulate the horrors facing them, both for their own battered selves and for their Greek audiences inside and outside the play's fiction – Greek audiences who may have grown too comfortable in their identification with the victors. Torrance puts it well: 'the novelty of *Trojan Women* lies not in the events themselves, but in the drama's perspective that sufferings can function as a muse, and in the sense that history repeats itself in a destructive and cyclical fashion'.[17]

Euripides certainly allows his characters to probe their grief in a rich variety of ways. In this sense he democratises Cassandra's strange way with language, allowing a range of disempowered women to explore their own trauma in whatever way is most meaningful to them and regardless of how it sounds to others. Frequently in the play one character responds inadequately, or antagonistically, to the words pouring out of another character's

---

[12] Dunn (1993) 24: 'The absence of the usual beginning and ending suggests deliberate avoidance of structural unity; and since the play begins with an ending and ends without one, it also frustrates the audience's desire for a goal.' See also pp. 101–14.

[13] The *Trojan Women* has been accused of abandoning dramatic coherence altogether in favour of a new kind of extended 'paratragic' lament or lyric drama. See discussion in Sienkewicz (1978) and Dunn (1993). Hunter and Fantuzzi (2004) 432ff. address the continuity of late classical tragedy and early Hellenistic literary culture, particularly the development of the conception of tragedy as 'literature'.

[14] Gregory (1997) 157.

[15] Gregory (1997) 160.

[16] Goldhill (2006) 149.

[17] Torrance (2013) 219.

mouth, but the impulse to speak their grief is shared among the women. This egalitarianism is partly a reflection of the crushed social order of Troy. While Hecuba is onstage throughout the play and provides the drama's central pivot, as the natural leader to whom most of the women still defer, in reality the women are now equals in slavery.[18] The play has flattened old distinctions and hierarchies. For the figure of Cassandra, this represents an important change in terms of her literary history as much as her lived experience: she was faced with a sympathetic but essentially alien chorus in the *Agamemnon*, but in the *Trojan Women* she is surrounded by people of the same sex, nationality and status. Cassandra gains support in another way too. Her uniquely fatalistic self-consciousness in the *Agamemnon* is now adopted more openly by other characters in the play, whose disastrous experiences have taught them to understand how little control they have over the past or the future.

In the *Trojan Women* the main response to events is through lament.[19] Lament, as Gregory explains, has a twofold function: it appeases the dead, while offering a measure of consolation to the living.[20] But it is also a particularly female counterpoint to the voice of male authority, a socially approved and communal form of witnessing, processing and reframing of unbearable and uncontrollable events.[21] Suter argues compellingly for the significance of the women's collective voice in this mode, even though they exist on the margins of the action: 'lament is the authoritative voice of women'.[22] Before Hecuba's first song in the play, she deliberates carefully over what, and why, to lament:

αἰαῖ αἰαῖ·
τί γὰρ οὐ πάρα μοι μελέαι στενάχειν,
ἧι πατρὶς ἔρρει καὶ τέκνα καὶ πόσις;
…
τί με χρὴ σιγᾶν; τί δὲ μὴ σιγᾶν;

Aiai, aiai!
What is there that is not for me to lament, wretched as I am,
I whose fatherland, whose children, whose husband have all perished?

---

[18] Sienkewicz (1978) makes a good argument for the significance of the chorus in this play.
[19] See especially Dué (2006) and Suter (2003).
[20] Gregory (1997) 161–2, following Alexiou (1974) 165.
[21] Ethnographers and cultural anthropologists have offered rich sources of comparanda. Seremetakis (1991) emphasises the cooperative aspect of female lament, which may help to explain the flattening of hierarchies in the *Trojan Women*: 'Antiphonic reciprocity between women in the mourning ritual entails the intensive interpenetration of collective and individual poetic creation' (3).
[22] Suter (2003) 21.

...
About what must I keep silent? About what must I *not* keep silent?
(Eur. *Tro.* 105–10)

Hecuba may not be able to control the events that trigger the need for lament, but she can shape the lament itself, focusing its force in whatever way she decides is most effective. She has agency over her narrative, if not over her life.

There is also a strong strain of rhetorical practice underpinning the language in the play. The most obvious case of this is the *agōn* between Hecuba and Helen, in which the two characters debate the responsibility Helen bears for the fall of Troy. Here the women engage in a form of speech that is not socially sanctioned for women in the way that lament is, but it is a common enough feature of tragedy.[23] Here too the women turn events into words as an act of appropriation, in the form of a selective commentary designed to persuasively promote their own interests.

The Trojan women of the *Trojan Women* all use speech in ways that could be seen as inspired by Cassandra's own experience of disempowerment in the *Agamemnon*. They use speech not so much to communicate straightforwardly as to delay the inevitable, to assert a measure of verbal authority in the face of their helplessness, to express grief at events past and future. It is still Cassandra whose speech is most strange in the play, however. Her act of 'translation' in the *Trojan Women* is to turn every reasonable response to events upside down. The result is that her language is not nonsensical, at least not in its constituent parts, but her emotional state is. Her language is cogent, but bafflingly inappropriate to the point of incomprehensibility; she projects a kind of emotional illiteracy. She completely eschews lament. Her rhetorical fireworks, which are not inconsiderable, are fired at the most perverse of objects: she argues, for example, that the Greeks are really the victims in the fall of Troy. Her prophecies figure her rape by Agamemnon as a marriage, and her enslavement as a cause for celebration. Above all, she refuses to acknowledge that the events surrounding Troy's destruction represent a disastrous rupture with the past or even a definitive end to the city and its inhabitants. In contrast with the other female characters in the play, Cassandra insists that her voice gives her the agency to influence present and future events, not just the narration of past events.

---

[23] Gregory (1997); Goldhill (2006).

For most of the characters within the *Trojan Women*, the mythical events behind the play are unchangeable and words exist simply to direct attention, to arouse emotion, to repeat and reframe those events in a way that is therapeutic for those onstage and in the audience alike. Cassandra's prophetic language, her ability to project herself into the future with a confidence that defies rationality, belief and even, to an extent, the events that the mythic tradition lays down as canonical, offers a different model of language use. Her presence marks a continuity between the *Agamemnon* and the *Trojan Women*, but her perverse and paradoxical speech rejects the notion of submission to a present drama of victimhood, or a predetermined future of suffering.[24] Cassandra translates lament and defensive rhetoric into celebration and confident agency. Her tone-deaf voice of optimism, incomprehensible as it is under the circumstances, becomes the reason why she is capable of escaping to achieve her goals.

Continuity and Rupture: Dramatic Time

The *Trojan Women* may not have a complex plot, but it has a highly complicated relationship with historical and literary time. This builds a level of self-reflexivity into the play, to which the characters respond on different levels.[25] For example, in the choral ode (lines 511–67) directly following Cassandra's scene, the chorus reconstructs not only the events surrounding the arrival of the Trojan horse and the fall of Troy, but the Trojan singing and dancing that accompanied the drawing of the horse into the city. The chorus invokes the Muse to inspire a funeral ode for the city, a 'new' (*kainos*) kind of hymn (513–14). As Torrance has shown, the reference to novelty through the word *kainos* immediately signals a level of metapoetic awareness.[26] The chorus then moves on to describe the distinctly un-funereal music and singing and dancing that took place around the Trojan horse, and ends up describing its own joyful celebration at the moment of the Greek attack:

ἐγὼ δὲ τὰν ὀρεστέραν
τότ' ἀμφὶ μέλαθρα παρθένον

---

[24] Papadopoulou (2000) identifies Cassandra's empowerment in the *Trojan Women* as resulting from her unique understanding of past, present and future time, and argues that it is therefore not an empowerment that is accessible or appreciable by the other women in the play.
[25] Goldhill (1986) 244–64 discusses this aspect of Euripides' work more generally.
[26] Torrance (2013) 220–9 explores the metapoetic reference to his own novelty that is embedded in Euripides' use of the word *kainos* here and elsewhere. She also notes that the word is used more often in this play than in any other play by Euripides.

Διὸς κόραν ἐμελπόμαν
χοροῖσι·

I, at that point, was celebrating
the wild virgin daughter of Zeus
with song and dance around her temple.   (Eur. *Tro.* 552–5)

Torrance has identified this ode as a reworking of Demodocus' song and
Odysseus' response to it in *Odyssey* 8.[27] It is not just a matter of textual
reworking, however, but also of repetition as it is lived and experienced by
the characters within a myth. It is a version of what Henrichs has dubbed
'choral projection', in which the actual dancing in the orchestra is projected
into the different time and space of the drama, embedding it more fully
in the dramatic action.[28] This is a specific case, in which the chorus' self-
projection allows it not to perform but to re-perform a previous chorus in
which it took part, this time overlaying the joy of the original performance
with the irony and bitterness of hindsight.[29]

This kind of reworking of well-known events and texts manifests
throughout the play. From the very beginning of the *Trojan Women*,
Euripides makes it clear that he is rewriting Homeric myth aggressively
and pointedly.[30] This is signalled in the prologue by the newly defined
alliances of the divine protagonists. Poseidon, a supporter of the Greeks in
the *Iliad*, immediately makes himself known as a friend to the city of Troy
in the *Trojan Women*.[31] This is not presented as a change from his previous
position. On the contrary, Poseidon emphatically states that he was *never*
inimical to Troy:

... οὔποτ' ἐκ φρενῶν
εὔνοι' ἀπέστη τῶν ἐμῶν Φρυγῶν πόλει·

... never from my heart
has goodwill towards the city of the Phrygians ever slipped.
                                        (Eur. *Tro.* 6–7)

Poseidon corrects his portrayal in Homer in a bold move that cannot be
described as opportunism, since he now aligns himself with the losing

[27] Torrance (2013) 220–1.
[28] Henrichs (1995) 74–5.
[29] Torrance (2013) 220–2; Segal (1993a) 18.
[30] Goldhill (1986) 138ff., esp. 165–7; Torrance (2013) 183–265.
[31] Torrance (2013) 231–3 on Poseidon's double-edged relationship to Troy in the *Trojan Women*. Poseidon's single gesture of friendship towards the Trojans in the *Iliad* is at 20.293ff., where he rescues Aeneas from Achilles. He also indicates an investment of sorts in the future of Troy, when he notes the importance of Aeneas' future as a Trojan leader (*Il.* 20.307–8).

side, but one that flatly denies the alliances found in Euripides' great epic ancestor. By contrast, Athena acknowledges that she traditionally supported the Greeks, but announces her newfound enmity by explaining the vital intervening narrative event: Locrian Ajax's desecration of her temple when he attacked Cassandra during the sack of Troy. Through a combination of literary subterfuge and flashback, then, Athena's and Poseidon's allegiances are realigned, and, at least in the case of Athena's flashback, Cassandra is implicated in their new common purpose.[32] She is and will continue to be a catalyst in this play, while in the *Agamemnon* she was an unfortunate bystander.

The early imagery of the play also sets it in a wider literary context, but one in which Aeschylus' *Agamemnon* plays an increasingly significant part. According to Poseidon, the city itself is resounding with cries of grief as the enslavement of the women takes place:

> πολλοῖς δὲ κωκυτοῖσιν αἰχμαλωτίδων
> βοᾷ Σκάμανδρος δεσπότας κληρουμένων.

> The river Scamander shouts out with the many howls
> of the women taken as prisoners and being distributed to masters.
> (Eur. *Tro.* 28–9)

In the *Agamemnon*, the trajectories of Cassandra's life and prophecies were marked out by the imagery of rivers past and future, the rivers of Cassandra's childhood and the rivers she will encounter in the under-world.[33] These rivers – Scamander, Cocytus, Acheron (Aesch. *Ag.* 1157–61) – represented for Cassandra the endlessly flowing passage of time and narrative, along whose banks the prophet travels and sings as a visionary. Here in the *Trojan Women* the river Scamander is not nurturing the young prophet and her voice, but is echoing back the communal voice of the lamenting Trojan women. The howls themselves are described but as yet unheard, like Cassandra's initial silence in the *Agamemnon*; the women's vocal response to the disaster unfolding around them must be imagined by the audience, prompted by Poseidon's reference to the river's sounds. The Scamander has now become a literary constant, embracing a wider range of female voices and flowing through texts as well as time and space, reflecting through its echoes of the many victims' voices the endless mythic narratives as well as the repeated experiences of suffering that connect one play circularly to another.

---

[32] Croally (1994) 70–2 notes the 'fluidity' exposed in the gods' attachments at this point in the play.
[33] See the section 'Singsong, Birdsong' in Chapter 1.

An even more potent symbol marking the continuity between the *Trojan Women* and the *Agamemnon* is that of the beacons. As Scodel has noted, the symbolism of fire pervades Euripides' trilogy and unites the constituent plays in its repeated reminder of the coming destruction of the city of Troy.[34] As the trilogy develops, the imagery becomes less symbolic and more real: from Hecuba's pregnant dream of giving birth to Paris as a firebrand in the *Alexander*, through the promise (if not the actual staging) of the false beacons set on Euboea to deceive the returning Greeks in the *Palamedes*, and ending up with the relentless reference to flames, torches and the blazing city of Troy in the *Trojan Women*. In fact, as Torrance notes, within the *Trojan Women* the city actually burns twice.[35] From Poseidon's description in the prologue onwards, the city is repeatedly described as smouldering after its sack (e.g. καπνοῦται, Eur. *Tro.* 8), and yet at the end of the play the chorus panics over Greek soldiers entering the city with firebrands to burn it to the ground:

> ἔα ἔα·
> τίνας Ἰλιάσιν τούσδ' ἐν κορυφαῖς
> λεύσσω φλογέας δαλοῖσι χέρας
> διερέσσοντας; μέλλει Τροίαι
> καινόν τι κακὸν προσέσεσθαι.

> Ah! Ah!
> Who are these I see on the peaks above Ilion,
> men brandishing hands flaming
> with torches? Some dreadful new event
> is about to be added to Troy. (Eur. *Tro.* 1256–9)

For Torrance, the 'second' burning of Troy creates a sense of closure at the end of the play, but it also introduces a note of artifice. She is certainly right that characters within the drama become increasingly alert to the retellings their story will go through, but it is strange that while the levels of metapoetic awareness seem to multiply as the drama progresses, the layers of symbolism actually peel away. The detached artifice of description is there in the chorus' reference to a 'dreadful new event' (καινόν τι κακὸν, 1259) which echoes the term *kainos* that referenced the literary innovation of a 'new' hymn earlier in the play (513). But this phrase is now also a shocked response to the threat of present events, to the literal fire their city

---

[34] Scodel (1980) 76–9 offers an instructive reading of the symbolism of torches as it recurs throughout Euripides' Trojan trilogy. She argues convincingly that it is a trope used specifically to draw connections between the first play (*Alexander*) and the last (*Trojan Women*).
[35] Torrance (2013) 231–2.

is about to face, not to a symbolic representation of distant troubles as told or experienced by others.

By the end of the trilogy, the imagery of fire as symbol and metaphor is about to become, or rather, revert to, the reality of pyrotechnic destruction, as torches are brought to burn the city. This reifying theme does not simply draw *Alexander*, *Palamedes* and *Trojan Women* into a stronger unity as a trilogy, it reaches out to link the end of Euripides' Trojan story with the beginning of Aeschylus' *Oresteia*. Here, at the very end of the *Trojan Women*, the chorus spots the threatening gleam of light above Troy just as the watchman at the very beginning of the *Agamemnon* had caught sight of the long-expected beacons, beacons that would bring both relief and fear to the speaker. The circularity between the beginning of Aeschylus' play and the end of Euripides' is emphasised by the fact that the chorus still reads the light as a sign, an indication that something, or rather 'something new', is about to happen. Yet these Euripidean flames are not (or not only) a message, but an action. The herald Talthybius, the real message-bearer in the play, orders his soldiers to turn the 'lazy flame' in their hands over to the actual burning of Troy, making it even more explicit that what was once ominously symbolic is now a reality:

> ... μηκέτ᾽ ἀργοῦσαν φλόγα
> ἐν χερσὶ σώιζειν ἀλλὰ πῦρ ἐνιέναι,
> ὡς ἂν κατασκάψαντες Ἰλίου πόλιν
> στελλώμεθ᾽ οἴκαδ᾽ ἄσμενοι Τροίας ἄπο.
> ὑμεῖς δ᾽, ἵν᾽ αὐτὸς λόγος ἔχηι μορφᾶς δύο,
> χωρεῖτε, Τρώων παῖδες, ὀρθίαν ὅταν
> σάλπιγγος ἠχὼ δῶσιν ἀρχηγοὶ στρατοῦ,
> πρὸς ναῦς Ἀχαιῶν, ὡς ἀποστέλλησθε γῆς.

> ... no longer save the flame, lazy
> in your hand, but hurl the fire in,
> so that having flattened the city of Ilium
> we may be satisfied and set out homewards from Troy.
> You, on the other hand, so that the same order may have two aspects,
> go on, you children of Troy, whenever the leaders of the army
> give the high echoing signal on the trumpet,
> go towards the ships of the Achaeans, so that you may set out from
>   the land.   (Eur. *Tro.* 1261–8)

Talthybius is clear: his single order is the trigger for both the burning of Troy and the launching of the Greek ships homewards with the Trojan women on board. Just as the beacons in the *Agamemnon* offered a parallel journey of the story from east to west alongside Agamemnon's return, here too fires from Troy accompany and signal the beginning of a journey westwards. Of course the beacons were intended as a message that would anticipate the returning Greeks by some considerable time, and the *Agamemnon* obscures this fact with the strange chronological contraction whereby the beacons are spotted in Argos only moments before Agamemnon actually arrives. Euripides engages with this confusing simultaneity of the journey and its announcement in the *Agamemnon* by emphasising the more logical simultaneity of light and action at the end of the *Trojan Women*. He marks the moment in the past when a single conflagration was simultaneously both event and message: the fire here *is* the light of burning Troy, but it is also the signal for the Greek men and Trojan women to prepare to set off on their boats, and beyond that it is implicitly the first in the line of beacon fires lit to announce the fall of Troy and the start of the *nostoi* to the awaiting audience in Greece. In this blaze there is not yet any rupture between deed and its glossing through words or symbols. Instead, original horrors are being set up for the rich inconsistencies, anachronisms and misunderstandings that abound when they are recalled and replayed in the *Agamemnon*.

The relationship between the *Trojan Women* and the *Agamemnon* pulls in two directions, then. The *Trojan Women* predates the *Agamemnon* in its dramatic setting, such that the reality of the fire at Troy precedes the journey of the beacons across the Aegean and their adoption in the Greek-set *Agamemnon* as a largely symbolic image. The plays' real chronological relationship to each other, however, has a forward drive, for Aeschylus' wordy symbolism of fire, already somewhat concretised over the course of the *Oresteia* trilogy, becomes increasingly threatening through Euripides' Trojan trilogy and is fully realised in the destructive fires of the *Trojan Women*.[36] This example of the 'future reflexive' has a prophetic element to it, and it is not surprising that it is in the scenes that include Cassandra that these circular temporal dynamics are made most explicit.

With the heavy significance hanging over the imagery of fire in particular and its relationship to temporality in the play, a significance that draws the play into conversation with its predecessors within the trilogy and within the dramatic canon more broadly, Cassandra's control over it becomes all the more important. This is made clear in the lines leading

---

[36] The transformation of imagery from 'metaphorical expression to a concrete embodiment' is already beginning to take place over the course of Aeschylus' trilogy, according to Zeitlin (1965) 488. She notes (489) how the beacons, in particular, are transformed into the lanterns Clytemnestra has lit in the *Libation Bearers*, then into the triumphal procession of the Erinyes in the *Eumenides*.

up to her arrival on stage. The light of fire is a signal of defeat for the Trojan women, but it is also one that the women are conceived of possibly using to their own benefit. They are imagined as being capable of appropriating the job of burning Troy, to the point where the very events of the *Agamemnon* and the other stories of the *nostoi* could be overturned. When Talthybius arrives to take Cassandra away to begin her journey to Greece with Agamemnon, he notices a flame in the living quarters of the Trojan women:

> ἔα· τί πεύκης ἔνδον αἴθεται σέλας;
> πιμπρᾶσιν, ἢ τί δρῶσι, Τρωιάδες μυχούς,
> ὡς ἐξάγεσθαι τῆσδε μέλλουσαι χθονὸς
> πρὸς Ἄργος, αὐτῶν τ᾽ ἐκπυροῦσι σώματα
> θανεῖν θέλουσαι; κάρτα τοι τοὐλεύθερον
> ἐν τοῖς τοιούτοις δυσλόφως φέρει κακά.
> ἄνοιγ᾽ ἄνοιγε, μὴ τὸ ταῖσδε πρόσφορον
> ἐχθρὸν δ᾽ Ἀχαιοῖς εἰς ἔμ᾽ αἰτίαν βάλῃ.

> Ah! What light of a pine torch is gleaming inside?
> Are the Trojan women burning their rooms, or what are they doing,
> since they are about to be led away from this land
> to Argos, and are they setting their own bodies on fire,
> hoping to die? Certainly in such cases
> the free-spirited bear the burden of evils very badly.
> Open, open up, in case something that is good for them
> but bad for the Achaeans ends up being blamed on me.

> (Eur. *Tro.* 298–305)

At this moment just before Cassandra enters the action, Talthybius identifies a danger in the symbol of the city's destruction and the Trojan women's victimhood. What should be a representation of their downfall becomes the potential enactment of their escape from further victimisation by the Greeks. There is a grim paradox behind Talthybius' characterisation of the women's self-immolation as 'something that is good for them but bad for the Achaeans' (304–5). But a still greater ironist than Talthybius will prove him wrong. As Cassandra will explain once she arrives onstage brandishing her own 'wedding' torches, it is her very *escape* from death that will bring about what is really bad for the Greeks. She will reveal this to her interlocutors with impunity through a range of verbal tricks, not least by redirecting, in the face of all logic, the meaning of the flames that elsewhere enact or stand for the destruction of Troy.

Paradoxical Rhetoric

The first chapter in this book showed how Aeschylus' *Agamemnon* portrays Cassandra's prophetic speech as nonsensical, verging on gibberish, to her immediate interlocutors. In the third chapter, on Lycophron's *Alexandra*, Cassandra will be seen to rely even more heavily on linguistic contortions designed to baffle in equal measure the internal and external audiences of the text. In the *Trojan Women*, by contrast, Cassandra demonstrates unusual clarity in her speech. Her words do not cause confusion and consternation in and of themselves. It is her bizarre argumentation, her inappropriate choice of tone and mode, and her apparently illogical construction of events and symbols from the past, present and future that all combine to create an impression of untrustworthiness. Cassandra uses rhetorical strategies that are paradoxical and perverse to the point of incomprehensibility.[37]

The Cassandra of the *Trojan Women* proves to be capable of manipulating symbols with a boldness that outstrips all the other characters, starting with her treatment of the central symbolism of fire. Cassandra makes her first appearance on stage emerging from the same *skēnē* door by which she left to meet her end at Clytemnestra's fiery hearth in the *Agamemnon*.[38] Here in the *Trojan Women* she turns out to be the active bearer of the torches. She is blazing the beacon trail, rather than following it passively:

ἄνεχε, πάρεχε, φῶς φέρε· σέβω φλέγω –
ἰδού, ἰδού –
λαμπάσι τόδ' ἱερόν. ὦ Ὑμέναι' ἄναξ …

Lift up, hand over, bring on the flame: I honour, I am ablaze –
look, look –
setting ablaze this holy locale with torches. O lord Hymenaeus …

(Eur. *Tro.* 308–10)

Cassandra immediately demands an attentive audience to her brandishing of the torches. She plays on the transitive and intransitive meanings of the verb 'to blaze' (φλέγω, 308): her words offer the possibility that she is identifying with the burning flame itself, perhaps in response to

---

[37] Rutherford (2012) 259.
[38] Craik (1990) 3 notes that in the *Trojan Women* the only characters to use the *skēnē* door are Cassandra and Helen, who both enter that way, establishing a curious parallelism between the two characters. In fact there are strong connections between these two women in the play: Helen, like Cassandra, is a catalyst for action, a tricksy wordsmith and an object of sexual desire.

Talthybius' fears of the women's suicide, before the rest of her sentence makes clear that she is directing the flame, and doing so to a very different end.[39] Cassandra dramatically reverses the imagery of marriage and sacrifice that characterised her and Iphigenia in the *Agamemnon*. No longer one of Aeschylus' sacrificial virgins, his brides *manquées*, the flaming torches now signify Cassandra's progression from victim to Euripidean bride, as she runs onstage with a prayer to Hymen, the god of weddings, to celebrate her forthcoming 'marriage' to Agamemnon.[40] From her very first appearance it is clear that, deluded or not, Cassandra presents herself as in confident control of her imagery, her actions and their consequences.

Cassandra also hurries to draw a contrast between her attitude and that of the other women in the play, particularly that of her grieving mother. She does so by refusing, in the face of all reason, to acknowledge any disjunction between events in the past, present or future. Her prophetic gift allows her to experience events synchronically; in this play she adds an emotionally warped response to this knowledge.[41] Cassandra dismisses Hecuba for lamenting her dead husband and beloved fatherland 'with tears and groans' (316), and invites the initiation of a dance to celebrate her marriage. Unlike the choral song and dance that will follow her scene, in which the chorus will re-perform its celebrations over the Trojan horse with a new grief born of hindsight, Cassandra insists that there must be no recognition of Troy's changed circumstances. She asks her followers to dance in a way that shows no difference from the dances of the past: ὡς ἐπὶ πατρὸς ἐμοῦ μακαριωτάταις | τύχαις – 'as in the time of my father's most blessed | fortunes' (327–8). Cassandra's eager anticipation of her 'pseudo-marriage' to come is expressed in terms that insist on an unbroken connection between the past and the present, as well as between the present and the future.[42] Cassandra celebrates ancient Trojan tradition even in

---

[39] Papadopoulou (2000) 519; Loraux (2002) 79.

[40] On the marriage theme in Cassandra's song see Rehm (1994) 128ff. Rabinowitz (1993) 15–17 remarks on the traditional anthropological link between the exchange of women in marriage and the circulation of language, reacting to Lévi-Strauss' *Elementary Structures*. Rabinowitz suspects that Greek women cannot be considered as both 'signs' and 'generators of signs', as Lévi-Strauss suggests, because their public speech was so drastically restricted. However, as Agamemnon's self-proclaimed bride in the *Trojan Women*, Cassandra clearly performs both roles.

[41] *Pace* Aélion (1983) 11, 232, who reads Cassandra's disturbed ravings as purely psychological, rather than prophetic.

[42] The term 'pseudo-marriage' is coined by Croally (1994) 96, who points out that Cassandra's song is explicitly not a lament. Suter (2003) argues that it is still a lament because death and marriage are so closely connected in Greek society and in this particular song, but she underplays the jubilant tone in the speech, which is rightly emphasised by Papadopoulou (2000) 518.

the way she holds up her torch: ἇι νόμος ἔχει – 'as custom has it' (324). In the *Agamemnon*, Cassandra's connection to Greek collective practices and language was tenuous and dangerous; the unstable language of custom or *nomos* lying behind her 'unmusical music' (νόμον ἄνομον, Aesch. *Ag.* 1142) reflected her social and cultural liminality in Greece. In the *Trojan Women*, Cassandra invokes *nomos* to assert her ability to uphold firmly the old socio-cultural norms of Troy, even as Troy has fallen and the practitioners of its customs are to be scattered among new and different Greek communities. Poseidon could rewrite the divine alliances of the *Iliad* by insisting on the continuity of his affection for Troy; Cassandra rewrites the fiery symbolism of Troy's destruction by refusing to see the city's defeat as demanding any change in emotional response or ritual behaviour.[43]

Hecuba, one of several characters in the play to attempt an interpretation of Cassandra's perversity, resists her daughter's appropriation of the literal and symbolic torches. Her remonstration reinforces what is strange about Cassandra's behaviour:

… οὐ γὰρ ὀρθὰ πυρφορεῖς
μαινὰς θοάζουσ', οὐδὲ σαῖς τύχαις, τέκνον,
σεσωφρόνηκας ἀλλ' ἔτ' ἐν ταὐτῶι μένεις.
ἐσφέρετε πεύκας δάκρυά τ' ἀνταλλάσσετε
τοῖς τῆσδε μέλεσι, Τρωιάδες, γαμηλίοις.

… not correctly are you playing the part of torch-bearer
raving and frenzied like this, nor, child, have you faced your fate
with self-control, but instead you are still behaving the same way as before.
Bring in the torches, Trojan women, and replace
her wedding songs with your tears. (Eur. *Tro.* 348–52)

For Hecuba, the consistency of Cassandra's behaviour and her songs is worrying (ἔτ' ἐν ταὐτῶι μένεις, 350). Cassandra's madness lies not in the frenzy of incomprehensible prophecy, but in the inappropriately unmodified glee with which she faces a present, and indeed a future, whose horrors appear to be visible to everyone but her. By contrast, Cassandra's interlocutors are united in the tears (δάκρυα, 351) that the prophet had dismissed but which are a far more appropriate response to circumstances marked by such disastrous change.

During this initial exchange Cassandra has used sung lyrics to express her emotional disorder and inverted symbolism. After Hecuba's reproach, Cassandra shifts into spoken trimeters, and with this change in tone comes

---

[43] Another curious overlap between Cassandra and Poseidon is found in Poseidon's offer of a prophecy in the play (87–91). See Dunn (1993) 29.

a new display of verbal trickery to bewilder her audience. Despite the more straightforward delivery, her use of conditional clauses and tricksy metaphors in her references to the future serves to undermine otherwise straightforward statements, and hints at her inclination to diverge from the ordained mythic narrative. Cassandra's speech in the future tense in the *Trojan Women* ranges from hopes and promises through to outright fabrications.

Cassandra begins by describing events to come purely in terms of her agency behind the unfolding narrative. Without giving any indication of divine inspiration, she uses Apollo as her guarantor for what is, in fact, a commitment to her own future activities:

> ... εἰ γὰρ ἔστι Λοξίας,
> Ἑλένης γαμεῖ με δυσχερέστερον γάμον
> ὁ τῶν Ἀχαιῶν κλεινὸς Ἀγαμέμνων ἄναξ.
> κτενῶ γὰρ αὐτὸν κἀντιπορθήσω δόμους
> ποινὰς ἀδελφῶν καὶ πατρὸς λαβοῦσ᾽ ἐμοῦ.

> ... for if Loxias exists,
> in a marriage that will get more out of hand than that of Helen
> will that famous Agamemnon, leader of the Achaeans, marry me.
> For I will kill him and I will destroy his house as he did mine,
> avenging my brothers and my father.   (Eur. *Tro.* 356–60)

The conditional phrasing of 'if Loxias exists' sets the troubling tone of this passage. It may be a formulaic phrase in normal usage, used to indicate an incontrovertible truth ('as sure as Loxias exists'), but it is a curiously dismissive – even uncertain – appeal to Apollo's authority when it is spoken, as here, by a prophet normally presented as helplessly dependent upon the god's influence. The brief appeal to Apollo is casually subordinated to the fact of Cassandra's marriage, which, she argues, is what actually triggers events. The god is further diminished by his brief confusion with a mortal, when Cassandra delays mentioning Agamemnon's name for a full line until 358, leaving it momentarily unclear whether she is claiming that Apollo or the leader of the Achaeans will marry her.

Having established her own agency as the strongest influence over events to come in the future, Cassandra proceeds to rock these foundations. Cassandra makes what those who remember the traditional story know to be an incorrect prophecy: she will, she says, kill Agamemnon. This unambiguous and deliberate statement (κτενῶ γὰρ αὐτὸν, 359) cannot be explained away on the grounds that her appearance as Agamemnon's concubine will provoke Clytemnestra to murder, even if Euripides does play up the role of sexual jealousy in Clytemnestra's actions.[44] Cassandra is promising a physical act of murder that she will not actually commit. Furthermore, in going on to argue that Agamemnon's death will serve as vengeance for the loss of her brothers and her father Priam, Cassandra appropriates not only the crime committed by Clytemnestra in the *Agamemnon*, but also Clytemnestra's main motive for the crime in that play: vengeance for the sacrifice of a family member (in Clytemnestra's case, her daughter Iphigenia). In this prophecy Cassandra is aggressively, at times implausibly, highjacking the conventional lines of her future story.

After these startling lines Cassandra swerves away from their implication. Instead she moves into a *praeteritio* in which she accurately predicts her own death and the story that follows it exactly as it is told in Aeschylus' *Oresteia*, but couches the narrative in terms of what she will *not* tell:

> ἀλλ' αὔτ' ἐάσω· πέλεκυν οὐχ ὑμνήσομεν,
> ὃς ἐς τράχηλον τὸν ἐμὸν εἶσι χἀτέρων,
> μητροκτόνους τ' ἀγῶνας, οὓς οὑμοὶ γάμοι
> θήσουσιν, οἴκων τ' Ἀτρέως ἀνάστασιν.

> But I will drop this topic: I will not sing of the axe
> which will sink into my neck and that of the others,
> nor the mother-killing struggles which my marriage
> will set in motion, nor the upheaval of the house of Atreus.
> (Eur. *Tro.* 361–4)

Cassandra is well suited to the rhetorical effect of *praeteritio*, in which a speaker disclaims any interest in communicating precise details while making sure that the audience hears the very details she wants them to hear. It mirrors her paradoxical relationship to prophecy. Her prophetic skills can be proven by her comprehensive listing of events to come, but her speech is overlaid by the acknowledgement of its futility: she might as well not bother to articulate the details. In claiming that she will not speak (ἀλλ' αὔτ' ἐάσω, 361), Cassandra alludes to the fact that what she says cannot reach its full potential as speech as long as its meaning is not grasped. At the same time, her use of this rhetorical technique also permits her to assert a measure of control over her communicative situation, not only by describing the future clearly and accurately, but also by insisting

---

[44] Lee (1976) underplays the oddity of Cassandra's claim: 'Cassandra means, of course, only that she would be the *cause* of Agamemnon's doom. She is so involved with her own role in the affair that she uses the first person as if she were the very perpetrator of the disaster' (134–5). Cassandra is in fact consistent in highlighting her direct agency, making the same point just a few lines later (404–5). On Cassandra's role as Agamemnon's influential concubine see Foley (2001) 94–5.

that it is her own choice not to engage in the development of those futile prophecies. In addition to this, by refusing to expand on her prophecies she also pushes a little harder against the performative aspect of her speech. She muffles the detailed authority of her prophetic voice, whilst acknowledging the fact that all her revelations have already been articulated and guaranteed – both in the brief summary offered by her *praeteritio* here, and in earlier versions of the narrative.

Cassandra offers another form of curtailed speech in the *Trojan Women*, through her pointed use of ellipsis. These truncated passages of prophecy do not serve exactly the same purpose as her use of *praeteritio*, in which Cassandra simultaneously parades her prophetic skill and its lack of recognition. Instead these episodes demonstrate how suppressed speech can still have a powerful effect, even if it is not an effect based on the delivery of any straightforwardly useful communication. In this case, Cassandra uses abridgement and elision to impose insults on her enemies, and to award tributes to her loved ones.

Cassandra self-censors when it comes to telling the details of the future that awaits Hecuba. Here she is withholding speech from her mother as an act of kindness, to avoid telling the story of her metamorphosis into a dog before her death: τἄλλα δ' οὐκ ὀνειδιῶ – 'I will not reproach [her] with the other details' (430).[45] Cassandra explores this moderation of her narrating voice from a more hostile perspective when, in her final speech, she begins to hint at the horrors facing Odysseus during his *nostos*. Here her laconicism becomes a weapon designed to cause as much anxiety as possible. Her vindictive brevity has an ironic twist in its application to Odysseus, who is characterised as abounding in verbal gymnastics: earlier in the play Hecuba had despised him for his 'double tongue' (286). Cassandra briefly expresses pity for Odysseus' ignorance, but she projects more sardonic gloating than sympathy: δύστηνος, οὐκ οἶδ' οἷά νιν μένει παθεῖν – 'Poor thing, he does not know of all the sufferings that are waiting for him' (429). In place of this ignorance, Cassandra proceeds to offer an absurd reduction of the *Odyssey*, racing through the most dramatic episodes of Odysseus' journey, and summing up in a prosaic tone: ὡς δὲ συντέμω – 'to cut my story short ...' (441). Συντέμω may also carry some programmatic weight here. Aristophanes later picks up the term when he presents Euripides as parodying Aeschylus' poetry in the *Frogs*; this Aristophanic

---

[45] See e.g. Eur. *Hec.* 1257–74.

Euripides echoes Cassandra's didactic δείξω – 'I will show' (see below on Eur. *Tro.* 365) as well as her abbreviating συντέμω:

> Ευ. πάνυ γε μέλη θαυμαστά· δείξει δὴ τάχα.
> εἰς ἓν γὰρ αὐτοῦ πάντα τὰ μέλη ξυντεμῶ.

> Truly fantastic songs; well this will show it right away.
> For I will cut all his songs down to one.   (Ar. *Ran.* 1261–2)

Like Euripides' mockery of Aeschylus' language in the *Frogs*, Cassandra's ludicrous reduction of the entire *Odyssey* to an epitome of scarcely more than ten lines diminishes the grandeur of the story even as it pitches the narrative as a reality whose length is to be dreaded, at least by the hero who must live through it. Cassandra's terseness towards Hecuba was a mercy, but towards the absent Odysseus it is a scornful snub.

Cassandra's 'unspoken' speech plays on the fact that as an explicitly later addition to a growing literary family of Cassandras, her external audience, having full knowledge of Apollo's curse, may in fact believe her prophecies far too easily. Euripides' Cassandra extricates herself from this dilemma not just by effacing the details of her prophecies, but by replacing her forward-looking speech with narratives designed to baffle in new ways.[46] After her *praeteritio* concerning her own future, she turns to prophecy's opposite: to the narrative of the past – that is, the history of her city and the Greeks' first arrival in Troy (Eur. *Tro.* 365–405). In the *Agamemnon*, Cassandra's discussion of history was generally well understood by her interlocutors, so this might be expected to be a more straightforward episode of communication in the *Trojan Women* too.[47] The prophet is moving from speech as a mystic performance of the future to speech as a commentary on history and its telling. However, Euripides gives a rhetorical spin to Cassandra's historical discussion that adds new communicative complication. Croally rightly describes this speech as 'historical revisionism'.[48] Here Cassandra

---

[46] This gives good reason to retain the sometimes deleted lines in which Cassandra reasserts her decision not to tell of the disasters piling up in Greece: μηδὲ μοῦσά μοι | γένοιτ' ἀοιδὸς ἥτις ὑμνήσει κακά – 'may my Muse not become a singer who sets terrible things in song' (384–5). See also Croally (1994) 245 n. 220.

[47] See the second section of Chapter 1, 'Introducing Apollo: Dialogue/Trialogue' above.

[48] Croally (1994) 123, with discussion at 122–34 and further at 227–31. Croally points out that Euripides' Cassandra 'exploits her main mythical characteristic to question the truth of myth' (231), arguing that her misleading assertions in the *Trojan Women* serve to show that Aeschylus, Cassandra and Euripides cannot all be telling 'the truth'. Perhaps, though, she is showing that they are *all* telling a truth, but one that depends on a specific perspective in each case. Goldhill (1986) suggests that Euripides is still playing on the difficulty audiences were supposed to have in believing Cassandra's voice: 'To many in the city of Athens, great imperialist power, this voice of truth must indeed have seemed eminently unbelievable' (166). Again, though, the language of the chorus that follows

demonstrates a new perversity of argument, first marking the shift with a careful explanation of her mental state:

πόλιν δὲ δείξω τήνδε μακαριωτέραν
ἢ τοὺς Ἀχαιούς, ἔνθεος μέν, ἀλλ' ὅμως
τοσόνδε γ' ἔξω στήσομαι βακχευμάτων·

I will show that this city is luckier
than the Achaeans; I am inspired, but nonetheless
at least to this extent I will stand outside my Bacchic ravings ...

(Eur. *Tro*. 365–7)

Cassandra points out that, whilst remaining inspired (ἔνθεος, 366), she is capable of detaching herself from her inspired body and commenting rationally on the effect of her words.[49] This appeal to rationalism might be expected of Cassandra at the beginning of a non-lyric passage, but she marks the shift only now, after she has already been speaking in trimeters for some time. It is the rhetorical approach she takes to history that demands this new appeal to reason.

Along with this, Cassandra projects the confidence that she will be understood. Knowing that this narrative is historical, not prophetic, and that she is therefore less vulnerable to misunderstanding, she adopts an assured, didactic tone. In fact, until her final couplet envisaging her 'marriage' to Agamemnon, the only prophecy that Cassandra makes is her very insistence that she will manage to convince her audience of her message, with her opening verb δείξω – 'I will show' (365). A marked borrowing from contemporary rhetorical form, Goldhill notes that Cassandra's use of the word 'connotes both "demonstration" as a form of proof and a stylish public performance on a set theme, so-called epideictic rhetoric'.[50] In other words, Cassandra is, for once, using the future tense in a way that is fully transparent to her audience – at least, to members of the fifth-century theatre audience au fait with sophistic rhetorical trends – even as she is adopting a mode of speech-making that is notoriously slippery and unreliable when it comes to representing the truth.[51]

What follows is certainly a bravura rereading of the past, in the course of which Cassandra overturns the dichotomy between barbarian and

suggests that it is comprehension, as much as belief, that is really the problem when it comes to grasping Cassandra's reasoning.
[49] On the Bacchic strain to Cassandra's inspiration in the *Trojan Women* see Papadopoulou (2000) esp. 516–17 and Croally (1994) 133–4.
[50] Goldhill (2006) 134.
[51] Goldhill (2006) 135.

native Greek in her bizarre argument that the Trojan War represents a Trojan success story.[52] She argues that the Greeks acted contrary to their personal interests, abandoning their families in order to die abroad without even gaining the glory of defending their homeland, while the Trojans continued to enjoy time with their families and earned fame and honour through their fighting. Perhaps the most remarkable aspect of this argument is not so much the fact that its formulation challenges the views of Cassandra's Greek and Trojan audience within the play, or her Greek audience in the Athenian theatre, but the fact that it establishes a basis for later Roman triumphalist reconfigurations of the Trojan myth. Cassandra's argument is nonsensical in the context of real Trojan suffering, and yet it will indeed one day find an audience that values her reading of the victims as winners.

The many and varied features of Cassandra's speech in the *Trojan Women* – new appropriation of symbols, deceit, suppression, compression, didacticism and historical revisionism – are united by the strain of weird optimism that runs through them all. Nor is this optimism proved or disproved during the course of the play, as so many of Cassandra's claims embrace time and events beyond the scope of the play and the trilogy as a whole.[53] Other characters in the play also reframe events, often in distorted ways, but their narratives are always keyed in understandable ways to the trauma surrounding them. When they are mistakenly optimistic in their expectations – such as Hecuba's assumption that Astyanax will survive to defend Troy's interests (701–5) – these hopes are dashed before the play ends. The real paradox in the rhetoric of Euripides' Cassandra is that, in this play of unremitting disaster and grief, she neither laments nor seems to believe herself subject to the events that deserve lament.

Making Nonsense of Sense

If Cassandra's speech in the *Trojan Women* is essentially incongruous rather than strictly nonsensical, it is all the more the job of her interlocutors to demonstrate how and where their communication with her breaks down. These characters in the play reveal the impenetrability of Cassandra's prophecies; they show that there is no translating her positive words in a

---

[52] Compare Helen's later negotiation with the Greeks and her suggestion that she saved them from being ruled by 'barbarians' (932–4), and Hecuba's accusations of Helen's own barbarian traits (995) among the barbarian Trojans (1021), discussed below.
[53] Dunn (1996) 67 and 106.

way that makes sense either to the grieving Trojans or to the triumphant Greeks. Beyond this, they wrap her prophecies in the layers of confusion that were lacking in her speech, which had relied on clear, albeit unsuitable, strategies of rhetorical persuasion. In the process they muffle her ominous promises, neutralise potential opposition to her direct threats and hence ultimately bind her prophecies even more tightly to their inevitable fulfilment. In the *Trojan Women*, it is the people around Cassandra who guarantee her paradoxical relationship to truth and misunderstanding. They are also the people who draw out her ability to transcend not only time but also the boundaries between one text and another, most particularly the boundary between the *Trojan Women* and the *Agamemnon*.

The chorus, always Cassandra's most important interlocutor, laces her speech with the ambiguity it otherwise lacks in the *Trojan Women*. For example, faced with her perverse argument concerning the winners and losers of the Trojan War and her joyful embrace of her forthcoming 'marriage', they note:

> ὡς ἡδέως κακοῖσιν οἰκείοις γελᾷς
> μέλπεις θ' ἃ μέλπουσ' οὐ σαφῆ δείξεις ἴσως.

> How cheerfully do you laugh at your own evils
> and sing things that perhaps, through your singing,
> you will show to be unclear.

> (Eur. *Tro.* 406–7)

The chorus cannot understand Cassandra's inappropriate joy in the face of the horrors surrounding her. Nor does it trust her proclaimed clarity of expression. In δείξεις (407), the chorus picks up δείξω (365), with which Cassandra had clearly identified the goal of her historical rereading, but the chorus asserts that what the prophet is really showing is not clear at all: it is οὐ σαφῆ (407), a common description of prophetic riddles.[54] The chorus thus reminds everyone of Apollo's curse, which is otherwise little in evidence within Cassandra's actual speech. Moreover, in another reference to Cassandra's complicated relationship with words, the chorus describes what she says in terms of song, repeating the verb 'to sing' twice: μέλπεις ... μέλπουσ' (407). Since at this point in the play Cassandra has long abandoned lyric for spoken iambic trimeter, this emphasis is bizarre; it is as if the chorus has barely heard the prophet's reasoned argumentation, and perceives her voice purely in terms of sound. The chorus effectively manoeuvres Cassandra back into her baffling prophetic role at

---

[54] Lee (1976) 142. Note also the chorus' description of Clytemnestra's first speech to Cassandra in the *Agamemnon* in the same, but opposite, terms: σαφῆ λόγον (Aesch. *Ag.* 1047).

the conclusion of a rhesis she has delivered with few mystic or prophetic pretensions, forcing her into the incomprehensibility insisted on by her traditional characterisation.

Other characters perform similarly obfuscatory roles around Cassandra in the *Trojan Women*. The herald Talthybius, already an intermediary by virtue of the part he plays as the main messenger in the drama, is a particularly important interlocutor. As a protagonist, messenger and mediator combined, he reflects aspects of Cassandra's own role: both are translators between cultures, tellers of tales from the past or future. Despite belonging to the inimical Greek forces (though he is not unsympathetic to the plight of the Trojan women and children), he manages to support the two fundamental features of Cassandra's prophetic speech: he not only emphasises her incomprehensibility, but also ultimately assures her truthfulness.

Talthybius reacts angrily to Cassandra's threat regarding the destruction her 'marriage' will cause:

εἰ μή σ' Ἀπόλλων ἐξεβάκχευσεν φρένας,
οὔ τἂν ἀμισθὶ τοὺς ἐμοὺς στρατηλάτας
τοιαῖσδε φήμαις ἐξέπεμπες ἂν χθονός.
...
καὶ σοῦ μέν (οὐ γὰρ ἀρτίας ἔχεις φρένας)
Ἀργεῖ' ὀνείδη καὶ Φρυγῶν ἐπαινέσεις
ἀνέμοις φέρεσθαι παραδίδωμ'·

If Apollo had not driven your mind into Bacchic frenzies,
you would not be getting away with sending off our military leaders
from this country with such words.
...
And as for you (since your mind is disturbed)
your insults towards the Argives and your praises of the Phrygians
I give over to the winds to carry away.   (Eur. *Tro.* 408–10, 417–19)

Talthybius, like the chorus, seems more aware of Apollo's influence on Cassandra's speech than the prophet herself. For Talthybius, the result is not so much confusion as untrustworthiness. The effect of Cassandra's words is blunted by her association with Apollo. Apollo does not cloud her words by wrapping them in portentous riddles, nor does he grant them authority; instead his presence behind her speech explains her inappropriate reaction to events as evidence of divinely imposed insanity and makes it pardonable, even negligible. Because of this, Cassandra is permitted to escape punishment. The very evidence of Apollo's inspiration persuades Talthybius to allow Cassandra to live and to make the alliance that she claims will be so disastrous for Agamemnon. Apollo is as crucial as he has ever been, even if Cassandra seems oblivious to this fact. In a new version of the prophetic paradox that the god originally imposed on his prophet, Apollo here guarantees the truth of Cassandra's prophecies by signalling her impotence to Talthybius.

Talthybius is not completely unaware of this contradiction, however, nor of his own unusual position relative to Cassandra's prophetic paradox. The herald's dismissal of Cassandra's words to the winds is a formula that speaks of anxiety, of a sense of ill omen and an effort to absolve himself of responsibility for dealing with her meaning.[55] Like Cassandra's rhetorical appeal to Apollo's existence (εἰ γὰρ ἔστι Λοξίας, 356, discussed above), it is a turn of phrase that is insignificant enough in casual use, but heavily ironic in the context of this play. Just as in the case of the beacon fires, the winds in the narratives of the Trojan War are never neutral – though nor are they partisan. Winds carry Helen from Mycenae to Troy. The winds that obstruct Agamemnon's ships at the very beginning of the war require the sacrifice of Iphigenia, which provides one of the motivations for Clytemnestra's murder of Agamemnon and Cassandra on their return to Greece. The winds that carry the Greek forces back to Greece enable the wealth of *nostos* narratives. Some of these winds will blow Cassandra to Greece, where she will play out the final act of her life. The winds do not diffuse dangerous prophecies; they fill sails. Talthybius' mistrust of Cassandra, and his choice of words in response to this mistrust, embroils him all the more deeply in Cassandra's plots.

There is a coda to Talthybius' reaction to Cassandra, as the prophet pushes even further the significance of his turn of phrase. After Talthybius' dismissal of her words, Cassandra delivers her final speech of the play, beginning with her carefully curtailed references to the travails awaiting Hecuba and Odysseus. As she comes to the end of Odysseus' story, the prophet slips into trochaic tetrameter catalectic, the only passage in that metre in the whole play, and with this her verbal stride lengthens. Cassandra now rushes to embrace her future as Agamemnon's bride, joining action to her speech. She casts off Apollo's symbols, replaying – or rather, anticipating – the undressing scene in the *Agamemnon* and reworking its thematisation of Cassandra as both *actor* and *auctor*, as simultaneously the composer/singer

---

[55] In *Iphigenia Among the Taurians*, Iphigenia has a nightmare the night before Orestes arrives and, while she misinterprets it, she tells it to the air in an effort to stop it from coming true: ἃ καινὰ δ' ἥκει νὺξ φέρουσα φάσματα | λέξω πρὸς αἰθέρ', εἴ τι δὴ τόδ' ἔστ' ἄκος – 'the strange dreams that this night has come bringing with it | I will tell to the ether, if there is any good in doing this' (Eur. *IT* 42–3).

and the real-life enactor of her prophetic narrative (Aesch. *Ag.* 1264–78, discussed in the last section of Chapter 1):

ὦ στέφη τοῦ φιλτάτου μοι θεῶν, ἀγάλματ᾿ εὔια,
χαίρετ᾿· ἐκλέλοιφ᾿ ἑορτὰς αἷς πάροιθ᾿ ἠγαλλόμην.
ἴτ᾿ ἀπ᾿ ἐμοῦ χρωτὸς σπαραγμοῖς, ὡς ἔτ᾿ οὖσ᾿ ἁγνὴ χρόα
δῶ θοαῖς αὔραις φέρεσθαι σοὶ τάδ᾿, ὦ μαντεῖ᾿ ἄναξ.

O garlands of the god dearest to me, honorific symbols
    of my divine inspiration,
goodbye. I have left behind the festivals in which previously
    I took such pride.
Ripped to shreds, leave my skin, so that while my body is still pure
I may give them to the swift winds to carry to you, O lord of
    prophecy.

(Eur. *Tro.* 451–4)

The ambiguous power dynamics that Cassandra exposed when she stripped herself of Apollo's symbols in the *Agamemnon* appear to have here been turned into a proud act of faithfulness towards Apollo, who will now not be dishonoured by Agamemnon's violation of Cassandra's body. This might mean that Ajax cannot have raped Cassandra earlier, as Lee argues, though Athena's furious volte-face in the preface would seem hard to justify without such a strong trigger, and repeated horrors are implied by Andromache's later description of Agamemnon as Cassandra's 'second Ajax' (618).[56] In fact, the very repetition of Cassandra's undressing from the scene in the *Agamemnon* is a sign that the prophet, like Euripides' entire text, is engaged in a process that repeats events in an endless loop which make it difficult to argue for a 'before' and 'after', a 'first' violation or a 'second' violation. However, the point here is that at this moment, when Cassandra *consents* to her union with Agamemnon, she acknowledges a betrayal of her relationship with Apollo. Not even necessarily (or solely) in sexual terms, but because her relationship with Apollo thus far has been predicated upon her failure to communicate his prophecies. In becoming such a willing agent in Euripides' play, she makes a claim to influencing the course of action, not to obstructing it through endless narrative complications, so she unwinds the tortured linguistic power that Apollo has purportedly held over her.

In this act of releasing Apollo's symbols, Cassandra echoes Talthybius' dismissal of her words. Where the messenger said ἀνέμοις φέρεσθαι παραδίδωμ᾿ – 'I give over [your insults/praises] to the winds to carry away'

---

[56] Lee (1976) ad loc. See also Scodel (1980) 67 n. 11. Hornblower (2015) 199–200 discusses the evidence for Cassandra's rape across multiple texts and media.

(419), the prophet announces δῶ θοαῖς αὔραις φέρεσθαι – 'I may give [these symbols] to the swift winds to carry' (454). Talthybius had superstitiously entrusted the prophet's crazily inappropriate words to the winds, creating the very danger he dreaded for Agamemnon on two accounts: as a throwaway expression, he showed that he had wrongly interpreted Apollo's clear influence over Cassandra's speech and was washing his hands of any responsibility to investigate it further; and as an invocation of the power of a natural element, he anticipated, albeit unintentionally, the reality of the winds that would soon be carrying Cassandra over to Greece. In her echo, Cassandra embraces exactly the same danger that Talthybius had tried to avert, with a similar pairing of verbal slipperiness with the reality of the physical world. She casts away on the winds the symbols of Apollo that marked her incomprehensibility to others and deferred the inevitable, and in so doing she shows herself ready to embark on a new journey, literal and metaphorical, towards the punishment of Agamemnon and the fulfilment of her destiny.

As her speech draws to an end, Cassandra develops this language of the wind further, in order to make another loaded allusion to the *Agamemnon*. In her final lines in the play, Cassandra reiterates her eagerness for the winds that will take her across the sea to Greece, and in the process she adopts one more symbol from Aeschylus:

> οὐκέτ' ἂν φθάνοις ἂν αὔραν ἱστίοις καραδοκῶν,
> ὡς μίαν τριῶν Ἐρινὺν τῆσδέ μ' ἐξάξων χθονός.

> No longer are you too early in looking for a breeze for the sails,
> to take one of the three Erinyes, myself, from this land.
> (Eur. *Tro.* 456–7)

Aeschylus' Cassandra and the chorus of the *Agamemnon* had both played with the imagery of the Furies, figures that implicate each new generation in the narrative of the previous one. In these lines, some of her final words in the *Trojan Women*, Cassandra invites the winds to carry her as a Fury, 'one of the three Erinyes', into the next stage of the myth. Cassandra actualises the moment in the *Agamemnon* when the chorus revealed its concern that Cassandra's prophecies were not simply telling the future but actually invoking it:

> ποίαν Ἐρινὺν τήνδε δώμασιν κέλῃ
> ἐπορθιάζειν;

> What kind of Fury are you summoning to this house
> to raise up a shout?
> (Aesch. *Ag.* 1119–20)

Euripides' Cassandra embraces the role, not of a Fury-summoner, but of an actual Fury in her own right: she is fated to bring havoc to Argos, and will do so with enthusiasm.[57] She has managed to align her own motivation and agency with the inevitability of events as they have been constructed by her own voice in the earlier text. This is why, though she is a victim in so many ways, in the *Trojan Women* Cassandra is arguably neither deluded nor sophistic when she twice proclaims herself νικηφόρος – 'victorious' (353, 460). Talthybius' casual casting of Cassandra's words to the winds has not only left her free to pursue the fate she knows lies ahead of her, but the richness of the idiom he used so inadvisably has also allowed the prophet to position herself as the crucial point of contact between the play in which she is currently speaking and the Aeschylean play that lies behind it in literary time and ahead of it in mythic time.

One further character acts as a foil to Cassandra and her troubling clarity, and that is Hecuba. When both characters are onstage in the *Trojan Women*, the exchanges between mother and daughter emphasise their pity and sympathy for each other, but also their mutual misunderstanding and their bafflement at the other's emotional state. However, Hecuba relates more closely to her daughter when Cassandra is not present. After the prophet has left the stage, Hecuba adopts her determination to make sense of the events taking place during the play by seeing them within the wider context of the past and future narratives of Troy. Seneca highlights this connection between the two women in the opening lines of his *Trojan Women*, when Hecuba points out that the visions she saw during her pregnancy with Paris anticipated all those of Cassandra:

> … *quidquid aduersi accidit,*
> *quaecumque Phoebas ore lymphato furens*
> *credi deo uetante praedixit mala,*
> *prior Hecuba uidi grauida nec tacui metus*
> *et uana uates ante Cassandram fui.*

> … Whatever disaster happened,
> and whatever evils the prophet of Phoebus predicted,
> crazed and with frantic speech while the god forbade
>   her to be believed,
> I, Hecuba, saw beforehand when I was pregnant, nor was
>   I silent about my fears,
> and I was the helpless prophet before Cassandra.   (Sen. *Tro.* 33–7)

[57] See Kovacs (1999) 60 on the connection with Eur. *Or.* 408, citing also Diggle (1981b) 62.

Euripides also hints at their parallelism at an early stage in his play. Before Cassandra has even arrived onstage, Hecuba instructs her to cast off Apollo's symbols (Eur. *Tro.* 256–8), anticipating the prophet's later act of undressing in the *Trojan Women*, and setting up that scene's reflection of the similar undressing scene in the *Agamemnon*.

In another layering of roles, Hecuba picks up and tweaks elements of Cassandra's vocal production in the *Agamemnon* as well as in the *Trojan Women*. The chorus' examination of Cassandra's song in the *Agamemnon* had involved an attempt to identify the birdsong most closely aligned with the sound of Cassandra's voice. This allowed them to explore in dialogue with the prophet the songs of the nightingale and the swallow, and the related myth of Procne and Philomela with its horrors of rape, infanticide and lament. When Hecuba announces her own lament in the *Trojan Women* she also evokes birdsong, replicating aspects of that exchange between Aeschylus' Cassandra and the chorus:

> τύφεται Ἴλιον, αἰάζωμεν.
> μάτηρ δ' ὡσεὶ τις πτανοῖς,
> κλαγγὰν ἐξάρξω 'γὼ μολπάν,
> οὐ τὰν αὐτὰν οἵαν ποτὲ δὴ
> σκήπτρωι Πριάμου διερειδομένου
> ποδὸς ἀρχεχόρου πλαγαῖς Φρυγίους
> εὐκόμποις ἐξῆρχον θεούς.[58]

> Troy is smouldering, let us wail 'aiai'!
> Like a mother to her winged ones,
> I shall strike up a song of cries,
> not the same as the one which once,
> when Priam leant on his sceptre,
> by the firm beat of the chorus leader's foot
> I struck up for the Phrygian gods.   (Eur. *Tro.* 145–52)

Hecuba produces 'a song of cries' (κλαγγὰν ... μολπάν, 147), where Cassandra had been described as producing an 'inarticulate cry' (δυσφάτωι κλαγγᾶι, Aesch. *Ag.* 1152); both lose their words, but not their voices, in their horror at events. Hecuba does not explicitly mark her allusion to the *Agamemnon* – how can she when the events of that play have yet to take place? – but she evokes such an act of allusion when she frames her song as the transformation of an earlier one (οὐ τὰν αὐτὰν, Eur. *Tro.* 148). She explains the song she is about to deliver in terms of a new beginning whose initiation offers her a lead role (ἐξάρξω, 147), and she encourages

---

[58] Text of Kovacs (1999).

all the Trojan women to sing it with her (αἰάζωμεν, 145), in the process constructing out of an old tale the bare bones of the play in which she stands: the *Trojan Women*.

While Hecuba may not have Cassandra's prophetic knowledge – which equates to a knowledge of the *Agamemnon* and its contents – she demonstrates a metapoetic awareness similar to that of her daughter, and a pride in their lives as they will be celebrated in songs yet to be sung. Towards the end of the play Hecuba suggests:

> ... εἰ δὲ μὴ θεός
> ἔστρεψε τἄνω περιβαλὼν κάτω χθονός,
> ἀφανεῖς ἂν ὄντες οὐκ ἂν ὑμνηθεῖμεν ἂν
> μούσαις ἀοιδὰς δόντες ὑστέρων βροτῶν.

> ... and yet if the god had not
> perverted it all, burying things that were above underneath the ground,
> we would have been invisible and would not have been set in song
> providing themes to the Muses of later mortals.   (Eur. *Tro.* 1242–5)

Here Hecuba echoes Helen in *Iliad* 6.356–8, but her claim for the literary productivity of even the most disempowered is closer to the theme as it is more obliquely demonstrated by Cassandra in the *Agamemnon*.[59] Hecuba and Cassandra are both wrestling with the contingent ways in which the future they are forced to live through has been, is being and will be described. Hecuba may not have Cassandra's insight into the events of the future and the texts that encode them, but she does have at least a suspicion that her story will be – maybe has already been – told over and over again.

Between the chorus of Trojan women, the herald Talthybius and the enslaved matriarch Hecuba, Cassandra is surrounded by characters who expose and exacerbate the communicative barriers between them – barriers that have been built not by the prophet's language so much as by her attitude, as she appears to be impervious to the changed circumstances in which the Trojans and Greeks are living. Cassandra's interlocutors also reveal the hidden quality in the prophet's insensitivity to the passage of time. Because Cassandra seems to experience the narrative of her life synchronically rather than diachronically, she has an ability to draw connections

---

[59] On the connection with the *Iliad* see Segal (1993a) 32. Papadopoulou (2000) 527 appositely cites Eur. *HF* 1021–2, in which Procne's crime is described as a sacrifice to, or material for, the Muses. For Loraux (2002) 69–70, the futurity of Hecuba's statement is problematic in the context of tragic performance, though it makes sense in an epic context.

between historical and future events and between different literary works that embrace that wider span of time. Her interlocutors may enhance the difficulties surrounding her voice by parading their bewilderment in the face of her inexplicable optimism, but they also validate, in the way they express their sympathy or hostility, the truth of her prophetic visions and the related power she possesses to transcend the boundaries between one text and another – particularly between the *Trojan Women* and Aeschylus' *Agamemnon*.

Troy in Greece

The *Trojan Women* has been criticised for demonstrating little by way of narrative drive within the drama, and for providing even less by way of conclusion to either the play or the trilogy as a whole.[60] Much of this sense of suspension hinges on the status of Troy itself at the end of the play. The smouldering city is facing a second onslaught of fire, posing a question to the audience: does this represent the city's final destruction, or is it doomed to burn over and over again, forever a literary trope signalling the shift of power from barbarian past to Greek future? Zeitlin's summary of Troy's role in Greek tragedy is particularly pertinent here:

> what counts most for the city of Troy on stage is not, as in Homer's *Iliad*, the battlefield and combats, not the domestic life within its walls, but rather its final destiny – its utter ruin – and the shock waves that emanate from its conflagration, which spread far beyond its boundaries in both space and time.[61]

This indeterminacy is also found in the disparate fates of the enslaved Trojan women as the action draws to a close. A group that was initially defined by a shared experience of loss has now become one in which each woman is to be scattered in a different direction across the Mediterranean with her new master. If these women are not destined to die in the city of Troy, whose future lies in Greek literary recreations of its fall, then they are to live out the rest of their lives as rootless barbarians in Greece. The only figures who embrace their future in the west with any measure of agency are Cassandra, who welcomes her new barbarian role, and Helen, who is effectively returning home and will reassimilate as a Greek.

---

[60] Torrance (2013) 233–4; Dunn (1993) 24.
[61] Zeitlin (2009) 711.

Hecuba's final words of grief are fixed not on the loss of her family, but the destruction of the city that defined her and her family.[62] She notes that it is being obliterated in name and story, as well as in physical terms:

ὦ μεγάλα δή ποτ' ἀμπνέουσ' ἐν βαρβάροις
Τροία, τὸ κλεινὸν ὄνομ' ἀφαιρήσηι τάχα.

O Troy, who once upon a time breathed your greatness
    among the barbarians,
you will soon be stripped of your famous name.   (Eur. *Tro.* 1277–8)

Hecuba describes Troy's glorious history 'among the barbarians', ἐν βαρβάροις (1277): the city's greatness was defined by its repute among non-Greek speakers, including its own inhabitants. In this claim Hecuba is tacitly bowing to the fact that the myth of Troy is even now being reconfigured, not just by Greece's victory, but also by Greece's appropriation of the myth itself, for it is the Greek standpoint and the Greek language of the play itself that designate Troy and its neighbouring peoples as barbarian. This alienation of the Trojans from themselves had begun during the *agōn* between Helen and Hecuba (914–1032), in which Helen's claim that she saved the Greeks from being conquered by 'barbarians' (933) is capped by Hecuba's accusation that Helen desired petty power over the 'barbarians' among whom she was living (1021).[63] Now Hecuba's apparent victory in that *agōn* has proved shallow and short-lived, as the audience knows that Helen is to bounce back from Menelaus' condemnation and Hecuba is to suffer the full consequences of her own identification with barbarian Troy, in her future as a barking dog. Nor is the city only a space in which barbarians exist, according to Hecuba. The effortless superiority once 'breathed' by Troy (ἀμπνέουσ', 1277) adds a strangely live dimension to the city, hinting at the traditional force of divine influence – Apollo and his oracles both 'breathed' their mysterious power in the *Agamemnon* (Aesch. *Ag.* 1181, 1206) – and at the thematic winds that have pervaded the *Trojan Women* and complicated any claims to linguistic clarity or agency. Troy is dying as a physical, lived and living space; even its name is under threat of oblivion.

Although Hecuba still believes herself destined for Ithaka, she concludes her speech by encouraging the Trojan women to throw themselves into

---

[62] In its disappearance, the city mirrors the absence of the Trojan War itself in the trilogy. This is discussed by Dunn (1996) 114 with reference to Scodel (1980) and her identification of 'the empty space the poet has placed with such emphasis in the centre of his work' (72).

[63] Hecuba also complicates this dichotomy by accusing Helen of a taste for luxury, a conventionally barbarian trait. See Hall (1991) 201–23.

the flames of Troy. In this effort to combine eternally with the city of Troy
she makes a last-ditch attempt to take herself and her people out of the
narrative westwards. Echoing the way Cassandra in the *Agamemnon* finally
agreed to move towards the hearth of Agamemnon's house, Hecuba tries to
escape into fire, joining Troy in the physical conflagration that from now
on will be replayed in symbolic terms by the returning Greeks in other
Greek narratives. Instead, however, Hecuba and the chorus are restrained
and can only continue to lament the loss of Troy's name to the very end of
the play. The chorus offers a final echo of Hecuba's words:

> ὄνομα δὲ γᾶς ἀφανὲς εἶσιν· ἄλλαι δ᾽
> ἄλλο φροῦδον, οὐδ᾽ ἔτ᾽ ἔστιν
> ἀ τάλαινα Τροία.

> The name of the land will become invisible: in one place
> and then in another something is gone, and no more is
> wretched Troy.   (Eur. *Tro.* 1322–4)

Now, perhaps more than ever, the audience is reminded that this play is
written and performed in Greek, as the chorus reiterates the point that the
city is becoming nothing more than a memory in song, a song that is currently being sung by barbarian Trojan women but in the language to which
they will have to accustom themselves as their own world dies.

Though Cassandra has left the action by this point in the play, her significance only grows during these last discussions of Troy's future. Hecuba
is doomed to die in Thrace long before Odysseus returns to Ithaka, and
the chorus is destined to become even more 'nameless' than Troy itself,
losing its unity and definition as the chorus of 'Trojan women' in its dias-
pora.[64] By contrast, Cassandra has already thrown herself into the next
stage of her life in Greece, but without losing her attachment to the idea,
if not the actual city, of Troy. As Rehm had said of the prophet's role in the
Agamemnon, 'the fallen city … appears in the person of Cassandra'.[65] She
carries the city with her, as Troy's representative and embodiment. Unlike
the other Trojan women, who rightly describe themselves as subject to
the demands of Greek song, Cassandra embraces her role as the barbarian
whose language resists Hellenic control. She will continue to make no
sense in Greek, just as she has always made no sense to the Trojans.

In the *Trojan Women*, Cassandra suggests that her agency is as far-
reaching as her knowledge. She aligns herself and her song with the

---

[64] Eur. *Hec.* 1257–74.
[65] Rehm (2002) 240.

forward movement of events, embracing her ultimate fate from the very beginning of the play. She actively moves towards her forthcoming alliance with Agamemnon in the same way that she ultimately walked into his house and to her own death in Aeschylus' *Agamemnon* – only this time she moves forwards without all the preceding delaying tactics. She even enlists Hecuba, her immediate audience, to help her hasten into the future:

καὶ πέμπε, κἂν μὴ τἀμά σοι πρόθυμά γ᾽ ἦι
ὤθει βιαίως ...

See me off, and if my own self does not seem enthusiastic enough to you,
force me along ...   (Eur. *Tro.* 355–6)

The reason for Cassandra's enthusiasm is that her overarching vision, her understanding of events past and events future, narratives already written and narratives still to be written, makes her appreciate the big mythic picture in which Troy will be neither destroyed nor forever nameless. Croally notes that 'Troy still exists' for Cassandra, because she understands time in a different way from the other characters.[66] In fact, Cassandra is quite right: Troy *does* still exist, not only in the endless Greek reformulations of its story, but also in Cassandra's determination to bring Troy's vengeance to Argos (and ultimately to Rome), and in her resistance to any monolithic Greek reading of Troy's story. The range of perspectives that had been contained within the laments expressed by all the Trojan women in Euripides' play is threatened with suppression as the city falls and the women are enslaved, but Cassandra's confident approach proves that in following the beacon fire of Troy's fall, in being part of the transference of Troy's narrative from Asia Minor to Greece and in bridging the narratives of Euripides and Aeschylus, she can continue to offer a divergent barbarian perspective that will baffle, and trouble, and speak truth to the powerful Greek audiences she encounters. Lament stays with the physical fall of Troy: by contrast, Cassandra takes the city's smouldering language of defiance and brings it westwards, into the as yet incomprehensible and uncomprehending future.

---

[66] Croally (1994) 216.

CHAPTER 3

A Scholarly Prophet: Lycophron's Alexandra

... νεκροῖς στρωφωμένη
τὰ λοίπ' ἀκούσω ταῦθ', ἃ νῦν μέλλω θροεῖν.

... wandering among the dead
I will hear these things, all the rest, which I am now about to voice.
(Lycoph. *Alex.* 1373)[1]

In the *Agamemnon* and the *Trojan Women*, the various interpretations of Cassandra's prophetic voice give rise to a wealth of new perspectives on her prophetic speech, and on the act of voicing and re-voicing her narratives. Lycophron's *Alexandra*, an extraordinary Hellenistic narration of Cassandra's prophecies, offers another angle on her task of translating the future, and on the task of translating her. The *Alexandra* consists of one immensely long monologue: 1,474 lines of relentless iambic trimeter, most of it delivered by a figure approximating the role of the tragic messenger. Priam has locked away a young Cassandra, here given her Spartan name Alexandra, and the king now requires her jailor, the messenger, to listen to her prophetic ravings and to repeat them back to him verbatim. Where Euripides' *Trojan Women* anticipated the events of Aeschylus' *Agamemnon*, Lycophron's *Alexandra* anticipates the events of both plays. The posterior text predates and predicts two anterior texts, offering a further layer of Barchiesi's 'future reflexive'.[2]

---

[1] Quotations from the *Alexandra* are from the edition of Hornblower (2015) except where noted.

[2] Barchiesi (1993). Sens (2010) calls the *Alexandra* 'a "prophecy" of Lycophron's own literary heritage' (305), while Lowe (2004) describes it as 'Greek narrative's longest and most ambitious essay in prior narration' (307). The relevance of Barchiesi's article is also identified by Kolde (2009). Note too the Auden-inspired title of West's article on Lycophron: 'Hindsight as Foresight Makes No Sense' (2000). McNelis and Sens (2016) 63–6 show how the poetics of Aeschylus and Euripides are mixed into Lycophron's *Alexandra* from its very beginning. However, the interactions between the same three texts discussed here make up only a fraction of the *Alexandra*'s rich intertextuality. See e.g. Hornblower (2015) 7–36. West (1984) gives some excellent examples of the influence of Herodotus and Aeschylus' *Prometheus Bound* and *Unbound*, and also considers potential parallels with Near Eastern prophetic texts such as the *Oracle of the Potter*. Further examples are described in Part I of the rich volume of studies on Lycophron edited by Cusset and Prioux (2009) 19–115. Sens (2010) points

Cassandra's interlocutors were crucial to the illustration of her communicative challenges in the *Agamemnon*, and even more so in the *Trojan Women*. By contrast, the form of Lycophron's *Alexandra* removes all the prophet's potential interlocutors, embedding the interpretative multiplicity of Cassandra's speech in a riddling voice-within-a-voice. This phenomenon is alluded to towards the end of the work, when Cassandra offers a disorientating prophecy of her afterlife:

> ... νεκροῖς στρωφωμένη
> τὰ λοίπ' ἀκούσω ταῦθ', ἃ νῦν μέλλω θροεῖν.

> ... wandering among the dead
> I will hear these things, all the rest, which I am now about to voice.

> (1372–3)

Lycophron's Cassandra is her own audience, the beginning and endpoint of her own prophecies. The text thoroughly blurs the lines between the roles of 'author' (or 'speaker') and 'interpreter', and as such the presentation of Cassandra's prophetic paradox, her uncommunicative verbosity, becomes even more self-reflexive than it is in the earlier texts.

Lycophron's Hellenistic rewriting of Cassandra's prophecies makes for a poem that is explicitly textual and scholarly. With a tortuous use of quotation and riddling allusiveness, Lycophron reveals a version of Cassandra's narrative that appears to be spinning beyond the prophet's control even as she packs it full of the abstruse details of a commentary, offering yet another version of Cassandra's unique combination of linguistic vulnerability and empowerment. Above all, the demand for translation and explanation always found in Cassandra's voice becomes, in this work, a meditation on the relationship between the slippery transience of utterance and the ambiguous fixity of writing, and on the significance of this in the self-conscious construction of a canon creatively (in the form of a new poetic voice) and scholastically (in the form of an external commentary on it).

These issues are complicated by the fact that modern readers have unusually limited resources when it comes to establishing the *Alexandra*'s historical context. Smatterings of references to a certain Lycophron do not settle the ongoing debate over when the text was written, and by whom. West (1984), Hurst and Kolde (2008) and Hornblower (2015)

out that resonances with Lycophron in recent papyrological finds (the Cologne Alcaeus, fragments of Sophocles' *Locrian Ajax*) show how many of Lycophron's allusions have also been lost to us.

most clearly set up the major problems, which centre on the fact that
the Lycophron about whom classical scholars know anything, the tragedian from Chalcis and contemporary of Ptolemy Philadelphus, seems
unlikely to have written passages in the text that describe prophecies in
which Rome will come to great power across the Mediterranean.[3] This
must be due to one of three possibilities: (i) Lycophron of Calchis, the
Alexandrian tragedian and librarian, proved exceptionally prescient, correctly identifying the long-term significance of Rome's dramatic recent
successes in the Pyrrhic Wars and alliance with Ptolemy Philadelphus;
(ii) Lycophron of Calchis wrote a text that was subsequently interpolated
after Rome proved its staying power; (iii) the Lycophron who wrote the
Alexandra was not Lycophron of Calchis, but a poet living at a later
date, probably the second century BCE. The second solution, developed
in the nineteenth century, was later endorsed by West, and it is plausible
based on the episodic nature of the text.[4] Some (including Momigliano)
have taken the first view and Hurst and Kolde remind us that it is
still defensible, but it is the third scenario that has had the strongest
support in recent scholarship.[5] Fraser's argument for a second-century
pseudo-Lycophron offers a particularly attractive version of the third
solution: he suggests that an unknown writer was deliberately playing
with the sort of writing Lycophron the tragedian might have produced
a century earlier.[6]

Part of the joy of the *Alexandra* is that this enduring uncertainty over
the work's authorship liberates its readers to embrace a measure of indeterminacy regarding the poem's meaning and purpose, an approach that would
normally require an appeal to Barthesian theory.[7] The *Alexandra* exists in

---

[3] Lycoph. *Alex.* 1226–80; 1446–50.

[4] E.g. Horsfall (2005) offers the ingenious, but extreme, suggestion that lines 1226–80 were written in
response to Virgil's *Aeneid*. The approach is rebutted on good literary critical grounds by McNelis
and Sens (2016) 200.

[5] See Ziegler (1927); Josifović (1968); Fraser (1979) esp. 341–3; Momigliano (1942); Hurst and Kolde
(2008) esp. xiii–xxv; OCD s.v. 'Lycophron'; Hornblower (2014) 101 and more extensively (2015) 36–9.

[6] A more specific historical version of this argument is propounded by Kosmetatou (2000), who
argues for an author who is the grandson of Lycophron of Calchis, living and working for the
Attalids at Pergamon in the early second century BCE and celebrating the Roman-Pergamene alliance
that led to Flamininus' victory over Philip V at Cynoscephalai. Hornblower (2015) 47–9 makes the
case for an author of this period originating from South Italy.

[7] West (1984) suggests that scholars cannot discuss the *Alexandra* without taking a position on its date
and authorship, but this does not hinder many of the contributors to Cusset and Prioux (2009).
Indeed, Hurst and Kolde (2008) xxv rightly note that fixating on the date of the text has, in the past,
impoverished scholarship on the text as a whole.

an authorial vacuum without immediate predecessors or successors, and lacks any obvious generic affiliation, confounding attempts to situate it within the canon of ancient poetry. This *aporia* forces readers to interpret the work on the basis of little more than the text itself. In fact, the few inarguable aspects of the poem's provenance – those that indicate an Alexandrian literary affiliation or heritage of sorts – also suggest that the notion of diffused authority might have been intentionally thematised in the *Alexandr(i)a*. Cusset points to some of the resonances in Lycophron's use of the name 'Alexandra' that reinforce this scattered impression.[8] While Cassandra's biography was almost a synecdoche for 'the myth of Troy' in previous versions of her story, this version uses the Spartan version of Cassandra's name in a bold but unsettling geographical shift.[9] Meanwhile, the tale is set in a Troy of the past but looks towards a dominant Rome in the future. Such a conflation of global and temporal settings is regularly alluded to in the text. The very opening word, the future tense λέξω – 'I will tell', foregrounds semantic play on the themes of speech, futurity and intertextuality, while its aural hint at the Greek name 'Alexandra' reminds the reader of Cassandra's own displacement.[10] Poetic and narrative authority will be scattered among the different voices that are subsumed within the messenger's speech, and those voices will range across time and space.[11] At the same time, this diversity is rooted in the influence of a specifically 'Alexandrian' multicultural literary scene, whether practised in Alexandria itself or as part of the Hellenistic movement elsewhere.[12]

A particular phenomenon of Alexandrian literary culture is, of course, the growth in literary scholarship.[13] The construction of the Mouseion in the early years of the Ptolemaic kingdom and the vibrant bookish culture that grew up around it during the century that followed was predicated upon several important historical factors, but they included a version of cultural imperialism that involved recognising a measure of distance in

---

[8] Cusset (2006) 45–6. See also Fusillo, Hurst and Paduano (1991) 31.
[9] The Spartan connection is confirmed by Hesychius and Pausanias; see Hornblower (2015) 91.
[10] One might compare Cassandra's loaded δείξω – 'I will show' in Euripides' *Trojan Women* (365), discussed in the first section of Chapter 2.
[11] Cusset (2006). On poetic authority see Mazzoldi (2001) 260.
[12] West (2000) 164.
[13] Though Sluiter (2000) connects literary commentary with an older religious exegetical tradition: 'Greek commentary literature originates with the *exēgētai* of sacred texts. There must have been a long oral tradition of interpreting divine signs, meteorological phenomena, and possibly even oracles before the focus became purely textual …' (185).

time and space between the present moment and earlier moments of what was perceived as high culture, and then worked to close those distances and appropriate that culture.[14] Cameron is right to complicate excessively over-schematising tendencies of scholars who want to define the later poetry as purely 'private', 'for a court audience', 'learned' and 'elitist' in explicit contrast with earlier 'public' works, and he also rightly emphasises that not all poetic production occurred only in or around Alexandria.[15] Yet it is generally accepted that the role of the theatre did come to decline after the fourth century BCE, and that the Alexandrians found new ways to channel the dramatic arts through different genres and modes.

The development and use of the scholarly commentary was one of the most potent Alexandrian methods of resolving the tension between the high status granted to the 'classic', which depends on a respect for the integrity of a fixed text, and the constant demand for recontextualisation of that 'classical' text. Commentary retranslates a literary language (its grammar, its social and cultural references, its performance context) for contemporary readers, but without overwriting the original, offering a palimpsestic reading experience that bridges different periods of time without explicitly privileging one over another.[16] Its ultimate goal is to expose the gaps between contemporary and past ways of consuming literature and to suspend the reader in that space of awareness, conscious of and participating in the acts of translation that are taking place. Moreover, as Most and Sluiter have noted, while a commentary translates literary works for and into a new era, the very existence of a commentary also marks the fact that those works are perceived as worthy of such an act of interpretation.[17] Each commentary therefore points to the process of canonisation that it

---

[14] Hutchinson (1988) points out connections between the classical and Hellenistic literary eras but also marks the distinction as vital to the creative works of the Hellenistic poets: 'we see the imposing basis provided by poetry before the fourth century (particularly the classical) ... For the poets of the Hellenistic period who concern us most, these presuppositions form a vital point of reference: they need them to give full force to the strangeness and boldness of their own divergent approach' (8). See also Bing (1988) 75, and Hunter (2006) 3–4, 141–6 on establishing how far this may have influenced Roman poets' sense of literary history and chronology.

[15] Cameron (1995) 24ff. makes the case for the term 'Hellenistic' in place of 'Alexandrian', *pace* Zanker (1987), to point to the fact that many of the poets of the first half of the third century did not live in, or even visit, Alexandria. Hutchinson (1988) too recognises that figures such as Aratus were neither native nor visitors to Alexandria, but simply owed much to the literary traditions associated with that city. In the case of the text under discussion, the affiliation is all the more tenuous.

[16] The melting pot of languages in Alexandria, and the interaction between high and vernacular Greek at the time, may have further enhanced this function: see Stephens (2003).

[17] Most (1999); Sluiter (1998) and (2000). In his introduction, Most (1999) also notes that while a commentary reinforces the authority of the canonised text, it also points to the deficiencies in the original.

enables, implicating in the process its authors, its readers and the original text it complements.

The *Alexandra* does just this with the myth of Cassandra. The composer of the *Alexandra* may or may not have been Lycophron of Chalcis, the tragedian who worked, like Callimachus and Apollonius, in the Alexandrian library. If he was, then in writing tragedies he was already actively engaged in trying to keep alive a dramatic tradition that was losing popularity as a staged form. It is also likely that in his role as librarian he would have been involved in writing, or at least engaging with, commentaries on classical tragedies. But whether the author is the tragedian or not, whether he (or she) lived in Alexandria or not, the *Alexandra* clearly reads *as if* its author were buried deep in a scholarly tradition that was engaged in synchronising works and myths through a great library tradition.[18] The work reflects a literary culture that is engaged in bridging the gaps between a classic and its new audience, mingling the authority of a source text with that of a commentator. It does so by using a form and a style that points to the medium, rather than the message; the riddles and extraneous details rather than the mythological narrative; the text-based explication, rather than the *son et lumière* performance.

The work also opens itself up to the same dangers suffered by commentaries: they are vulnerable to being dipped in and out of, and are not held together by a narrative drive. Indeed, this is the very feature of the text that leads several scholars to believe that any performance context for the *Alexandra* could only have been in the form of excerpts.[19] This empowerment of the reader to draw meaning out of the text for himself or herself based on its episodic – at times even lemmatic – style, works against the form of the messenger speech to which the *Alexandra* initially gestures. A messenger would be expected to deliver a coherent narrative summary of events that have occurred 'offstage', producing a gripping account that bears some common features with epic narrative.[20] But the

---

[18] Gutzwiller (2007) 125 describes the *Alexandra* as 'a *tour de force*, which attempts to rewrite the masterpieces of Hellenic culture in the dark, allegorical style of Sibylline prophecy'.

[19] West (2000) 155 firmly asserts that the text must have been designed to be read rather than performed, but Cameron (1995) 81 claims that some parts might have been performable in the form of excerpts. In trying to establish the performance context and genre of the *Alexandra*, Gutzwiller (2007) 124 points to a probable link between the poem and the popular custom in the Hellenistic era of extracting lyric passages from later tragedies (particularly from female roles), and performing them alone as 'monodrama'. Whitmarsh (2004) 130–2 is characteristically balanced on the issue of text and performance more generally in Hellenistic Alexandria.

[20] Rutherford (2012) 202. McNelis and Sens (2016) 53–5 go into more detail on the role of the messenger speech in Lycophron.

Alexandra's debts to the commentary tradition demand more effort of the reader, and ultimately grant him or her more interpretative power. In fact, as Most points out, the function of commentary ultimately empowers everyone involved in creating a canon: the author who had lost relevance; the reader who is given material that the commentator believes the author had intended him or her to have; and the institutions (libraries, etc.) that bring the author, commentator and reader together.

This is also very much what Venuti claims for the function of translation. While he believes that translation can work to disrupt traditional scholarly canons, he recognises that it can also trace and even shape the development and meaning of such canons as they endure through time:

> The study of translations is truly a form of historical scholarship because it forces the scholar to confront the issue of historical difference in the changing reception of a foreign text. Translation, with its double allegiance to the foreign text and the domestic culture, is a reminder that no act of interpretation can be definitive for every cultural constituency, that interpretation is always local and contingent, even when housed in social institutions with the apparent rigidity of the academy.[21]

The Cassandras of Aeschylus and Euripides had combined multiple different linguistic functions in the momentary utterance of a single frail body onstage. Lycophron's *Alexandra*, a newly textual evocation of the tragic figure, embraces in a single book roll those many functions found in the dramas, along with a more explicit engagement with the issues explored by Most and Venuti in their analyses of commentary and translation. Timeless mythic tale combines with timely explication and, conversely, ephemeral performance is embedded within a text that facilitates endlessly repeatable private reading.

The Instant Messenger

Discussion must begin at the beginning of the text.[22] This is where the work programmatically describes Cassandra's voice, and demonstrates the way in which the form of the *Alexandra* will go on to package and expose the prophet's idiosyncratic language. The only lines of the work that are not a 'quotation' of Cassandra's words are the first thirty and the final fourteen,

---

[21] Venuti (1998) 46.
[22] For excellent discussions of this opening passage see Cusset (2006) and McNelis and Sens (2016) 47–66.

and the introduction in particular offers a densely packed framing of the
text. This rich section begins as follows:

Λέξω τὰ πάντα νητρεκῶς, ἅ μ' ἱστορεῖς,
ἀρχῆς ἀπ' ἄκρας. ἢν δὲ μηκυνθῇ λόγος,
σύγγνωθι, δέσποτ'· οὐ γὰρ ἥσυχος κόρη
ἔλυσε χρησμῶν ὡς πρὶν αἰόλον στόμα·
ἀλλ' ἄσπετον χέασα παμμιγῆ βοὴν
δαφνηφάγων φοίβαζεν ἐκ λαιμῶν ὄπα,
Σφιγγὸς κελαινῆς γῆρυν ἐκμιμουμένη.

I will tell everything exactly, all that you inquire about,
from the very beginning. And if the speech is dragged out at length,
forgive me, master: for not calmly did the girl
unleash her shifty oracular speech, as before,
but pouring out an unspeakable mixed-up shout
she let her Apollonian voice run riot from her bay-eating throat,
copying the cry of the shadowy Sphinx.   (Lycoph. *Alex.* 1–7)

The voice that opens the work is that of the messenger, Cassandra's jailor,
who has been asked to relay Cassandra's words back to her father. The
normal function of a messenger, at least in tragedy, is to report a narrative of
events that could not be effectively portrayed on stage. Here, however, the
messenger reports not action but speech: events occur at a double remove
and dramatic action is twice denied.[23] Even more oddly, the messenger's
audience is as effaced as his informant. There is no reference to anyone
other than Priam as receiving the information, and even Priam's presence
is only alluded to; he has no voice. What for a moment presents itself as a
dialogue promptly devolves into a relentless monologue, marking its precarious formal position, poised between tragedy and epic.[24]

These dynamics are important markers of Cassandra's communicative
activity and its influence over the form of Lycophron's *Alexandra*. Cassandra's
prophecies are presented with extra layers of potential misapprehension, as
they are translated from her already divinely inspired self to the messenger,
to Priam and thence, implicitly, to the reading audience (with or without a
further commentary or two to hand). These layers reinforce the shift from
the immediacy of her appearances in the classical tragedies to the mediated
written version Lycophron is presenting to his audience. At the same time,

---

[23] West (2000) 159. This information is destined to be 'turned over' again in Priam's mind, as noted by Hornblower (2015) 122 on κἀναπεμπάζων (9).
[24] As McNelis and Sens (2016) note, the poem 'plays on the intersection between tragedy and epic, and on the distinction between the dialogic form of the one and the narrative form of the other' (3). See also Fusillo (1984); Cusset (2006) 44; Sens (2010) 300.

the prophecies of Lycophron's Cassandra manage to overwhelm those multiple layers of audiences. The messenger claims to tell her words 'exactly' as he heard them, and 'exactly' is how Priam wants to hear them.[25] For the central 1,430 lines of the text, readers purportedly hear Cassandra's direct speech, all delivered in the first person. This is quotation explicitly stripped of any interpretative function. Stranger still, the idiosyncrasy of Cassandra's language is not limited to the central episode where the messenger 'quotes' her: the messenger's own speech at the beginning and the end of the work is just as full of *hapax legomena* and other unusual verbal tricks. Rather than the messenger glossing Cassandra's prophecies, she interpolates the messenger's speech. As in the case of the *Agamemnon* and the *Trojan Women*, Cassandra's presence shapes a work that first points to, then blurs, the boundaries between inspired speaker, interpreter and audience.

The text begins λέξω ('I will tell') – a packed and pregnant opening.[26] Though the messenger claims to relate Cassandra's words precisely, Cassandra is quoted throughout, so technically this work has gone beyond Cassandra's defiant silence in Aeschylus to the point where she is not granted a voice at all. Yet, as Cusset points out by looking to echoes elsewhere in the thirty-line 'prologue', the word is closely tied to Cassandra's status as a speaking agent, as a falsely etymologised 'A-lex(andra)' – who in turn is implicated in the work of Apollo Loxias.[27] Cassandra/Alexandra may not actually speak, but the messenger relates her words 'exactly', νητρεκῶς, a variant of ἀτρεκῶς attested only here in ancient Greek literature. The alpha privative is therefore pointedly absent twice in the first four words of the work, while the implied α- hints at complications ahead: there will be losses and gains as this 'peculiarly memorious' messenger translates Cassandra through implausibly accurate quotation.[28]

The complications are not limited to the role of the speaker in this work; the target audience of the work is also invoked. At the end of the line the messenger points out that he is speaking in response to a request by Priam (μ' ἱστορεῖς, 1). The enquiries of Cassandra's father resonate with historiographical echoes, as he is described as looking for information from 'the

---

[25] The messenger's subsequent instruction to Priam to listen to as much as the messenger has held διὰ μνήμης, 'in his memory' (8), may imply that he is not relating absolutely everything, but is perforce excerpting. See McNelis and Sens (2016) 58.

[26] McNelis and Sens (2016) 4–5 discuss how this word foregrounds the role of the poet-narrator and the long literary tradition that informs the work.

[27] Cusset (2004) 52. See also Cusset (2006) 45. For more on the etymology, particularly the scholia on Alex-andra as an appropriate name for 'she who wards off men', see West (1984) 136 n. 44 and Hornblower (2014) 118.

[28] Lowe (2004) 308.

very beginning' (ἀρχῆς ἀπ' ἄκρας, 2) even though Priam's investigations into Cassandra's speech might be supposed to concern the future, not the past. In fact, what Priam effectively hears is, at least from the perspective of the external readership, a history not just of the Trojan War, but of the Persian Wars too. The *Alexandra* 'prophesies' Herodotus' *Histories*; not only its subject matter, but also its fascination with the relationship between east and west, and between myth and history. Nor is this the only programmatic theme embedded in the prominent placement of the verb *historeō*. Cameron points out that there is a lesser-known technical meaning of the verb's cognate noun *historia* that dates back to the Alexandrian era: it refers to 'a matter of fact or subject matter in a classical text, as opposed to a detail of language or a rhetorical trope'.[29] Just as *historia* in the common sense means everything from 'inquiry' through to 'the written results of that enquiry', so *historia* in this technical sense means both 'any subject matter requiring explanation' and 'the explanation itself'. As a result, Priam's desire for enlightenment becomes the justification for a punning reference to the text's complex relationship with commentary: it flaunts its status not only as an endlessly deferred search for explanation and a back-to-front history, but also as a work of exegesis and, indeed, 'the explanation itself'.

This conflation of literary functions relates to the *Alexandra*'s totalising impulse, its drive to encompass everything, from beginning to end, within its narrative. Towards the end of Aeschylus' *Agamemnon*, the chorus notes that Cassandra's speech has been extended (μακρὰν ἔτεινας, Aesch. *Ag.* 1293). At the beginning of the *Alexandra* the messenger apologises for the length of his speech (ἢν δὲ μηκυνθῇ λόγος, | σύγγνωθι, δέσποτ', Lycoph. *Alex.* 2–3).[30] Cassandra's tendency to expand beyond the conventional or appropriate bounds of speech has been taken over by the messenger, whose monologue turns out to be as long as an entire classical play or, with equal significance, as long as a single Alexandrian book roll.[31] This overspill reflects the fact that Lycophron's narrative tells of a Cassandra who inhabits an earlier stage in her biography than that described in previous canonical versions of her story, and she proceeds to look further forward in time than in those earlier narratives.[32] The messenger promises to step out on his narrative from the same point as the prophet, telling the story from

---

[29] Cameron (2004) 90, citing Quint. 1.4.4 and Dion. Thrax 1.1.
[30] Hornblower (2015) 121 also probes the Herodotean notes in μηκυνθῇ.
[31] Van Sickle (1980) 8.
[32] Though note the early setting of Euripides' *Alexander*.

the very beginning (ἀρχῆς ἀπ' ἄκρας, 2) as did Cassandra: ἀπ' ἀρχῆς ἦρχ' Ἀλεξάνδρα – 'Alexandra began from the beginning' (30).[33] The layering of narrators works against this parallelism, though, for the messenger has a thirty-line head start on Cassandra, even while Cassandra technically gave the speech first. Once again the issue of primacy is problematised in the text; it is impossible to establish what is the original, and what is the response.

Not only is Cassandra's speech (via the messenger) abnormally long, but her jailor also claims that it is the most complicated yet. That is to say, her oracles have become increasingly convoluted over time: 'not calmly did the girl | unleash her shifty oracular speech, as before' (οὐ γὰρ ἥσυχος κόρη | ἔλυσε χρησμῶν ὡς πρὶν αἰόλον στόμα, 3–4). Though this might plausibly be the first time in her young life that Cassandra has been possessed by such a frenzied form of inspiration, the reader may still be surprised to hear a claim that Cassandra used to be calm in the past (ὡς πρίν, 4). Placed at the beginning of this new text, the messenger's reference to a time 'before' gestures to the existence of previous versions of Cassandra's voice. The messenger is marking his Cassandra out by defining her against 'earlier' Cassandras, describing the convolution of her speech in terms of an escalation over time, despite the fact that no extant canonical dramatic texts have characterised her as 'calm'.

This building of a faux literary tradition is reinforced by an oblique evocation of a different prophetic voice. Cassandra's prophetic 'shifty speech' (αἰόλον στόμα, 4) echoes a passage in Aeschylus' *Prometheus Bound* in which Io – in her own half-crazed words – tells of how her father sent messengers to ask the oracles at Delphi and Dodona to solve the problem of Io's dreams (Aesch. *P.V.* 658–62). She describes the answers that return as αἰολοστόμους – 'shifting-in-speech' (Aesch. *P.V.* 661).[34] The story of Io, evoked here through the messenger's characterisation of Cassandra's voice, harnesses to Cassandra another myth involving a woman whose relationship with her father is destroyed by the cruel attentions of a lecherous god, and has at its centre both prophecy and a woman's hobbled ability to communicate. Io's punishment comes from a distant oracle and destines her to be sent away from her home. In Cassandra's case, the oracles come from her own mouth and cause her to be imprisoned by her father, although she

[33] Fusillo, Hurst and Paduano (1991) 31. McNelis and Sens (2016) 49–50 discuss other ways in which the narratives of the messenger and Cassandra are paralleled.
[34] Sens (2010) 300–1, and now McNelis and Sens (2016) 54–5, also map Prometheus' introductory words at *P.V.* 609–11 onto Cassandra's first words in Lycophron's text.

too will ultimately travel far from her father's home. Above all, though, the appearance of Io's ghost behind Cassandra foregrounds the uncertain autonomy always surrounding oracular voices. Unlike Io, Cassandra has ownership of her own oracular 'shifty speech', and she knows her future, whereas Io has to request further information from Prometheus. However, Io was at least the narrator of her own story in *Prometheus Bound*. In the *Alexandra*, the messenger has taken over Cassandra's 'shifty speech'. Indeed, he has doubly appropriated it, for in characterising it with the allusivity of the words αἰόλον στόμα, he has forcibly mapped Cassandra's literary biography onto Io's through the women's shared vulnerability to ambiguous prophetic language. As the messenger constructs it, the literary heritage of the *Alexandra* is no more straightforward, and no more straightforwardly Cassandra's, than the language in which it is framed.

The messenger goes on to explain that Cassandra's speech is ἄσπετον – 'unspeakable' (5). Once again the alpha privative reappears, here not to describe the accuracy of the messenger's report (cf. νητρεκῶς, 1) but to assert the essential impossibility of the report in the first place. To reinforce this oddity, the messenger proceeds to describe his speech, or rather Cassandra's, as παμμιγῆ – 'all mixed up' (5). This is a *recherché* term found until this point only in extant ancient texts exercised by expressing the voice of the linguistic and cultural 'other': Aeschylus' and Timotheus' *Persians*.[35] The speech is indeed mixed up, for reasons that relate both to the generic Cassandra and to this specific Cassandra. As always, Apollo's curse has muddled Cassandra's speech, but the muddle is multiplied in the *Alexandra* by the fact that the messenger's speech and Cassandra's have been mingled and confused. The messenger now replicates not just Cassandra's speech but also the effect of her speech: its defining incomprehensibility. This effect is necessitated and caused by the absence of any representation of the messenger's audience. In Aeschylus' and Euripides' dramas, internal interlocutors proved vital to expose the moments where Cassandra's speech was misunderstood, since her words were often clear enough to the external audience. For misunderstandings to be marked in the *Alexandra*, they must be embedded in Cassandra's speech; only then can they be recognised by the audience outside the text. For this reason the messenger cannot translate the original 'meaning' of Cassandra's speech, or even project its discombobulating effect on him by paraphrasing her inaccurately. It is crucial that he be *literally* accurate in his reporting in

[35] Aesch. *Pers.* 269; *PMG* 791; Timoth. *Pers.* fr. 15, 175. See now McNelis and Sens (2016) 66.

order to convey both her truth and her linguistic confusion, the vital multiplicity of her voice.

In these exceptionally packed first lines, then, the messenger performs an exercise that takes Cassandra's voice out of the dramatic mode and places it firmly within the world of Alexandrian scholarly activity, even as he claims not to be changing a thing. Sluiter points out that:

> If we remember the essentially oral nature of teaching, the paraphrastic mode adopted by some commentators takes on an interesting dimension: it means that the teacher appropriates the voice of 'his' author wholesale. This is signalled in the commentators themselves by their comparison of exegetes to actors who adopt the persona of the author and perform his or her text.[36]

In taking on Cassandra, word for word, the messenger is not explaining, but demonstrating, the complexity of her voice.

Second Sight

There is no diminution in the allusive metapoetry when the messenger first begins to ventriloquise Cassandra. The 'belatedness' of this text relative to Aeschylus' *Agamemnon* and Euripides' *Trojan Women* sees it pick up on themes found in those works, particularly themes that have already served to illustrate the endless iterability of mythic narratives. Troy once again becomes the exemplar of a city that falls, a city whose fall is repeated in the cultural imagination over and over again. Cassandra's own words emphasise the relationship between each event and its replaying through narrative, and she develops a powerful metaphor based on the interplay between land and sea to explore this iterability and to reflect her own unique understanding of the ebb and flow of time.

The first word the messenger quotes is αἰαῖ – 'Aiai!' (31) – an evocation of the first inarticulate noises produced by Cassandra in Aeschylus' *Agamemnon* as well as a generic non-linguistic expression of grief found (for example) in Hecuba's first lament in the *Trojan Women* (Eur. *Tro.* 105).[37] In the *Agamemnon*, Cassandra's first stuttering sounds devolve

---

[36] Sluiter (2000) 191.

[37] Ovid offers an interesting take on these connections in his *Metamorphoses*, which depends in its own way on the tension between the singular and the generic in terms of both its content and its literary self-definition. At *Met.* 10.214–6 Apollo inscribes his grief for Hyacinthus by marking 'AI AI' on the flower that will bear his name, the hyacinth. The passage is reworked in *Met.* 13, when the same flower appears from the blood of Ajax: *Aias: littera communis mediis puero uiroque | inscripta est foliis, haec nominis, illa querellae* – 'writing that applies to both boy [Hyacinthus] and man [Ajax] | is inscribed on the petals, in one case referring to a name, in the other to a lament' (*Met.* 13.398). The names of a specific hero and a specific grief are connected and made endlessly repeatable in

into a pun on Apollo's name, whereupon Cassandra invokes the god and reproaches him for having destroyed her 'a second time' (τὸ δεύτερον, Aesch. *Ag.* 1082). Aeschylus' Cassandra then asks Apollo to tell her where she is, signalling her disorientation in space and time. In the *Alexandra* the messenger has already delivered the pun on a name with λέξω, and in the first words that Lycophron gives Cassandra in the *Alexandra* there is no mention of Apollo.[38] Instead this new Cassandra refers immediately to the city in which she is situated. First she outlines Troy's past sufferings at the hands of Heracles: τάλαινα θηλαμὼν, κεκαυμένη – 'wretched nurse, burned down' (Lycoph. *Alex.* 31). Then she summarises the city's destiny, which is to have this disaster repeated: λεύσσω σε, τλῆμον, δεύτερον πυρουμένην – 'I see you, miserable city, burned up a second time' (52). As in Euripides' *Trojan Women*, both Troy and Cassandra appear to be defined by the inherently repetitious nature of their downfalls, and the iteration of events and of their narratives becomes a crucial part of the *Alexandra*'s construction.

As in the *Agamemnon* and the *Trojan Women*, too, the fall of Troy is marked by conflagration, fire that is a literal facet of the city's destruction as well as a symbol of that destruction, to be lit and lamented, and to be rehearsed and recalled across multiple texts. Cassandra's adoption of fiery imagery in the *Alexandra* allows her to do more than simply contribute to the repetitions of Troy's fall in the earlier plays. The span of Cassandra's prophetic vision in the *Alexandra* embraces the very multiplicity of Troy's fall by encompassing several mytho-historical instances of the city's destruction, and in her speech the overlaps between actual and literary repetition become thematised in their own right. Moreover, the reflexivity of her prophecies, Cassandra's personal investment in Troy's survival, also triggers the human response to each iteration of the tragic event. Now Cassandra picks up the lamenting role that she had rejected in the *Trojan Women*, and magnifies it yet further:

> στένω, στένω σε δισσὰ καὶ τριπλᾶ δορὸς
> αὖθις πρὸς ἀλκὴν καὶ διαρπαγὰς δόμων
> καὶ πῦρ ἐναυγάζουσαν αἰστωτήριον.

---

the natural world. Note also the phrasing of Lycophron's Cassandra in her lament for Troilus: αἰαῖ, στενάζω καὶ σὸν εὔγλαγον θάλος – 'Aiai, I sigh for your blooming youth, drenched in milk' (Lycoph. *Alex.* 307).

[38] In fact Cassandra is described as speaking from a βακχεῖον στόμα – 'Bacchic mouth' (28). For more on the Bacchic aspects of Cassandra's representation see Mazzoldi (2001).

> I lament, I lament for you twice and three times,
> beholding as you do the spear's violence and the plundering of houses
> and destructive fire again.   (Lycoph. *Alex.* 69–71)

Through her prophetic visions Cassandra lives through each time that Troy is destroyed. Her visions are linked to the city of Troy itself through the participial ἐναυγάζουσαν (71), normally meaning 'illuminating' but here also 'beholding', in the sense that it sees its own destruction as clearly as Cassandra does (cf. λεύσσω σε, 52).[39] The repeated collapse of Troy is circularly connected to Cassandra's repeated act of lament, which both predicts and responds to the image of the firing of the city. Her grief is repeated not each time the events happen in real time, but rather each time she narrates her prophetic vision of the events. As the versions of Cassandra's narrative multiply across several texts and (in the case of the *Alexandra*) across several layers of narrative authority, Cassandra pointedly and programmatically laments for a second time, then a third (δισσὰ καὶ τριπλᾶ, 69). As well as repeatedly describing the same events, each time this lamenting Cassandra narrates an event, she sandwiches it between two narrative perspectives, creating a logically impossible synchronisation of visionary anticipation and retrospective regret.

Moreover, the performativity of Cassandra's prophetic voice, as always, ties her narrative to the fulfilment of the events she repeatedly describes. In an extension to the *Alexandra*'s exploration of the relationship between original and commentary, the text is fascinated by the complex, sometimes causal, relationship between event and narrative. It highlights this connection by returning to the images of fire already found in the *Agamemnon* and *Trojan Women*. The *Trojan Women* made the largely symbolic home fires, city fires and beacon fires of the *Agamemnon* more concrete, more real. In the *Alexandra*, Cassandra synthesises the literal and the metaphorical, deed and word, in her references to fire. The image also becomes personal, as it is linked all the more strongly to the perceived catalyst for most of the events in the text: to Paris, the firebrand. Finally, the image is expanded by the addition of fire's opposite: water. By focusing on the role played by floods or seas, Cassandra's prophetic voice situates the blazing fires of human activity and the burning beacons of human communication within the bigger forces and spaces of the natural world. These waters that divide countries and cities afford an opportunity for pause, or for journeys, in the course of which the forward-looking plans and backward-looking

---

[39] Compare Cassandra's play on the transitive and intransitive meanings of φλέγω at Eur. *Tro.* 308–9, which also uses the imagery of firelight to create confusion between the subject's vulnerability to the events taking place and its dispassionate observation – even incitation – of those events.

narratives concerning land-based events are given the time and space to be formulated.

An early example of this theme at work appears immediately after Cassandra's prophetic lament for the fiery fall of Troy. She proceeds with a flashback to the city's foundation, which sets in relief the apocalyptic events surrounding the city's destruction. According to its foundation myth, Dardanus swam to the Troad through a flood sent by Zeus. The flood's transformative power battered the whole earth with its noise: the rain is described as καχλάζων (80) – 'plashing' – a word that comes to be used to describe overflowing eloquence.[40] Next, Cassandra's narrative springs forward through time again as she sees Paris, the 'gleaming winged firebrand' (86) whose appearance reignites the theme of the city's fiery destruction and the events of the narrative in which Cassandra is most closely implicated. In this passage, then, the land on which Troy is built is literally burning with disastrous activity, while the sea whisks Cassandra backwards through time, taking her back to a moment where Zeus wipes the slate of the earth clean by drowning it in water – and the sound of water – and Cassandra's narrative gains an element of temporal and spatial contextualisation.

Elsewhere in the text, prophetic voices become more deeply implicated in this tension between the land and sea. Cassandra soon returns to the topic of lamenting her homeland:

λεύσσω πάλαι δὴ σπεῖραν ὁλκαίων κακῶν,
σύρουσαν ἅλμῃ κἀπιροιζοῦσαν πάτρᾳ
δεινὰς ἀπειλὰς καὶ πυριφλέκτους βλάβας.

I see from long ago the coil of trailing evils,
dragging its way through the salt sea and shrieking at my fatherland
terrible threats and fire-blazing destruction.   (Lycoph. *Alex.* 216–18)

The 'coil' of events is a bizarrely constructed combination of metaphor and reality: threats to Troy do come from the sea, from Greeks bringing threats and disaster, but the ominous series of evils is not here identified with any specific heroes or events.[41] Instead it brings with it a voice that articulates the coming fiery destruction (πυριφλέκτους βλάβας, 218) with whistles, hisses or shrieks (κἀπιροιζοῦσαν, 217). This verb, *epirroizeō*, is the same

---

[40] *LSJ* s.v. καχλάζω.
[41] Discussed by McNelis and Sens (2016) 18 and 75. Compare Verg. *Aen.* 2.203–27, which may be inspired by this imagery. In the *Aeneid*, Laocoon is threatened by the coils (*immensis orbibus*, 2.204) of a 'real' monster from the sea, whose eyes are suffused with blood and fire. See Chapter 4 for further connections between Laocoon and Cassandra.

as that used to describe the voice of the Furies as they pursue Orestes in Aeschylus' *Eumenides*: Athena asks the chorus of Furies, 'So do you shriek [*epirroizeis*] at this man such a flight?' (Aesch. *Eum.* 424). Later, in other Hellenistic authors (Aratus, Theophrastus), the verb becomes associated with animal noises or songs that can be interpreted to predict changes in the weather.[42] Further on in Lycophron's text, the verb is applied to the activities of the Fates, when Cassandra pauses briefly in her narrative to embrace the voice of these more otherworldly prophetic figures:

> καὶ ταῦτα μὲν μίτοισι χαλκέων πάλαι
> στρόμβων ἐπιρροιζοῦσι γηραιαὶ κόραι.

> And these things from long ago, with their threads
> on bronze spindles, the ancient girls shriek out.
>   (Lycoph. *Alex.* 584–5)

Cassandra attributes the events that she has just vocalised to the shrieking voice of the Fates, who are old-young (γηραιαὶ κόραι, 585) like Cassandra herself. The connection between all these uses of the verb, in Lycophron and beyond, lies in the fact that although the word describes a specific sound, it tends to be used in contexts that explore the prophetic aspect of that sound rather than the sound itself. In its first and strangest appearance in the *Alexandra* (216–18), an anonymously threatening narrative of destiny is not even heard by Cassandra; she 'sees' it (λεύσσω) lurking in the sea, and makes no attempt to reconstruct its sound for her listeners. This prophecy is even more obscure, more untranslatable, than her own voice.

The imagery of the sea provides a space for intermission, then, for delays that encompass ominous journeys and as yet untranslatable murmurings of foreboding or reflection, and set up the fiery activity of mythic events as they are actually enacted and experienced on land by the protagonists. This is not strictly a dichotomy, though, because no mythic event can be detached from the narratives that construct it, whether prophetic or historical. Only a few lines after the passage discussed above, Cassandra returns to this theme:

> μὴ δ' Αἰσακείων οὑμὸς ὤφελεν πατὴρ
> χρησμῶν ἀπῶσαι νυκτίφοιτα δείματα,
> μιᾷ δὲ κρύψαι τοὺς διπλοῦς ὑπὲρ πάτρας
> μοίρᾳ, τεφρώσας γυῖα Λημναίῳ πυρί·
> οὐκ ἂν τοσῶνδε κῦμ' ἐπέκλυσεν κακῶν.

---

[42] *LSJ* s.v. ἐπιρροιζέω: cf. particularly Aratus *Phaen.* 1.969, Thphr. *Sign.* 16.

If only my father had not rejected the night-roaming terrors
of Aesacus' prophetic dream-interpretations,
and instead with one single fate he had buried them both
for our fatherland, burning their bodies to ash with Lemnian fire;
then the wave of such evils would not have flooded over.

(Lycoph. *Alex.* 224–8)

Here Cassandra sets up a plaintive alternative to the narrative as it stands, through a prophecy within a prophecy. In this extended conditional sentence, Cassandra points to the fact that the earlier prophecies of Priam's son Aesacus, who predicted the disasters to come if Hecuba gave birth to Paris, also offered an escape from apparently inevitable doom. In this parallel universe of properly understood prophecies, funerary fire would have destroyed the 'firebrand' that is Paris, and the fluid waves of disaster (228) – the space set up for the formulation and reformulation of narratives that interpret these events – would have been kept away from Troy. Indeed the whole narrative of the *Alexandra* might have been averted, a narrative that may be broadly described as a survey of the tribulations enacted on the two landmasses of Europe and Asia after the sea between them is crossed and recrossed.

A similar combination of hope and despair in Cassandra's formulation of the causal, even circular, relationship between narrative and event occurs almost two hundred lines from the end of the text. Again, Cassandra begins by lamenting the disasters that her fatherland will have to bear (1281–2). She then proceeds to lay a curse upon those she sees as responsible for these disasters. Ὄλοιντο – 'may they perish!' (1291), she declares. The men she refers to are those who engage in the tit-for-tat abductions of Io and Europa in turn, repeatedly crossing the Aegean Sea and inciting hatred between Asia and Europe. This passage, heavily dependent on the opening of Herodotus' *Histories*, is not, however, couched in the form of a prophecy. It cannot be: these events have already happened, being well in the past not just of the readers (according to the conventional irony seen in the other literature of Cassandra's prophecies) but also of Cassandra herself. Cassandra curses men in the past, whose descendants have already seen the results of those men's actions. Cassandra's optative cursing carries a measure of futurity in it, but its application to events in the past only underlines the ironic aspect to Cassandra's prophecies throughout time. The futility of Cassandra's voice is marked by both its truthfulness (the men have indeed perished) and its ineffectiveness (they died too late to affect the disastrous string of consequences triggered by their deeds). And once again her voice becomes tied up with the imagery of the sea-crossing beacons as connections between one story and another, the narratives of one continent and another: the men's first abduction of Io is described as having the result that 'they raised the beacon of enmity [*echthras ... purson*] for the dual continents' (1295).

Gradually Cassandra circles through the myths of Troy leading up to her own time, before finally returning to Paris, the firebrand himself:

λοῖσθος δ᾽ ἐγείρει γρυνὸς ἀρχαίαν ἔριν,
πῦρ εὗδον ἤδη τὸ πρὶν ἐξάπτων φλογί,
ἐπεὶ Πελασγοὺς εἶδε Ῥυνδακοῦ ποτῶν
κρωσσοῖσιν ὀθνείοισι βάψαντας γάνος.
ἡ δ᾽ αὖθις οἰστρήσασα τιμωρουμένη
τριπλᾶς τετραπλᾶς ἀντιτίσεται βλάβας,
πορθοῦσα χώρας ἀντίπορθμον ἠόνα.

So, last of all, the firebrand rouses the ancient strife,
igniting with flame the fire up until then slumbering,
since he [Paris? Asia?] saw the Pelasgians [Argonauts] dipping
into the brightness of the water of Rhyndakos with foreign vessels.
But she [Europe/Greece] in turn, stung into taking vengeance,
will pay back the insult three times and four times,
devastating the land's coastline on the opposite side of the sea.[43]

(Lycoph. *Alex.* 1362–8)

Cassandra zooms in on Paris' role in reigniting the hatred between the Greeks and the Trojans. Where Herodotus' narrative described an inexorable escalation in abductions between the two peoples, Cassandra identifies Paris as taking a more active role in provoking an otherwise dormant enmity between the peoples. Once again the activity of the fiery antagonism between Greeks and Trojans is provoked by the broaching of watery divisions: firstly, the river Rhyndakos is touched by 'foreign vessels' (κρωσσοῖσιν ὀθνείοισι, 1365), then, implicitly after Paris' abduction of Helen, the Aegean Sea is crossed once again as the Greeks aim to wreak vengeance upon the 'opposite side of the sea' (ἀντίπορθμον, 1368).[44] Through these thematic visions, Cassandra swings from the description of Paris' actions in the present, back to the arrival of the Argonauts in Asia, and then forwards to the disasters to come with the Trojan War.

---

[43] For the difficulty in establishing whether an abstract 'Asia' takes over as the subject of line 1364 or whether Paris continues to govern the verb εἶδε ('recreating in his imagination' rather than literally 'seeing' the Argonauts, whose adventures took place before his birth), see Hornblower (2015) 472.

[44] For Lycophron's clustering of words that emphasise the invasion of the 'foreign', including his use of the rare Aeschylean κάρβανος, see Hornblower (2015) 472–3 and McNelis and Sens (2016) 163.

The Greek revenge, multiplied in scale as it will be three and fourfold (τριπλᾶς τετραπλᾶς, 1367) is framed as an escalation of hostilities that perpetuates the entangled chain of future events on the two continents (ἠπείροις διπλαῖς, 1295), and the repeated narration and lament of Troy's fall (στένω σε δισσὰ καὶ τριπλᾶ, 69).

Immediately after this the chain is extended yet further, when Cassandra describes the arrival of Agamemnon in Troy. He will take over the fiery imagery by coming like Zeus with his thunderbolt and burning his enemies' land, and then, Cassandra notes, she will be with him at his end:

σὺν ᾧ θανοῦμαι, κἀν νεκροῖς στροφωμένη
τὰ λοίπ᾽ ἀκούσω ταῦθ᾽, ἃ νῦν μέλλω θροεῖν.

With whom I shall die, and wandering among the dead
I will hear these things, all the rest, which I am now about to voice.
(Lycoph. *Alex.* 1372–3)

In the *Agamemnon*, Cassandra had anticipated her existence after death. She described a scenario in which she would continue to prophesy by the rivers of the underworld, constructing the image from a memory of her childhood growing up by the river Scamander (Aesch. *Ag.* 1160–1). Later, in Euripides' *Trojan Women*, the Scamander echoed the Trojan women's lament over the fall of Troy (Eur. *Tro.* 28–9), building an intertextual theme in which rivers nourish narrative commentary on events. Here in the *Alexandra*, Cassandra offers a dried-up version of these fluvial Trojan outpourings of memory and reaction. She describes what initially appears to be a passive existence in the underworld, not predicting, but merely receiving the narrative of future events – literally 'the rest' (τὰ λοιπά, 1373) – as they take place in the world above.[45] This narrative inactivity is reinforced by the very absence of the rivers of the underworld that accompany Cassandra in her Aeschylean post-mortem prophecies. Then it transpires that the reason for her passivity is that she has already prophesied these events before her death. They are, as she explains, what she is about to utter now: ἃ νῦν μέλλω θροεῖν (1373). Cassandra's 'second' sight, her ever-reduplicating narrative process, gains its most reflexive dimension through the prophet's ability not just to anticipate events, or to articulate those visions, but to visualise her reception of a later narration of those events.

---

[45] Thanks to Helen Van Noorden for pointing out that τὰ λοιπά might mean 'the future' in this context (*LSJ* s.v. λοιπός 3).

Siren Songs

Scholarship on the *Alexandra* has paid close attention to the relationship between Cassandra's authorial voice and the messenger's, so marked at the beginning and end of the text, but less attention has been paid to the poetic voices contained and subsumed within Cassandra's prophecies. These many voices point to a tension similar to that found between Cassandra and the messenger; namely, a blurring of the distinctions between original and response, speaker and interpreter. The voices within Cassandra's narrative are rarely quoted, but their presence can be felt in her oblique references to other laments and songs. They suggest that the process of translating, commenting and ventriloquising that Cassandra performs, and that is in turn performed on her, is part of a wider mythic process of repetition and mimesis, of continued explanation and reformulation. Cassandra's voice encapsulates and exposes this process.

The dissolution of Cassandra's speech by further voices from within builds on several aspects of her characterisation: the riddling incoherence of her speech, the division and repetition of her prophecies and the events of which they tell across different texts, and above all the relationship between her mystic voice and her mortal body. In prophesying her murder in the *Alexandra*, Cassandra moves beyond her earlier portrayals, which halt in front of Agamemnon's house, to survey her final moments in the gory detail that is so very suited to a messenger speech. She describes herself as 'sliced to pieces' by Clytemnestra: *suntethrausmenē* (1109). This recalls the chorus' response to Cassandra in the *Agamemnon*, in which they describe Cassandra's words as 'shattered things' – *thraumat'* (Aesch. *Ag.* 1166). As with the word for 'all mixed up' – *pammigē* (Lycoph. *Alex.* 5), it also echoes an Aeschylean passage from Timotheus' *Persians*, the description of a captured Persian's speech:[46]

> ὁ δ' ἀμφὶ γόνασι περιπλεκεὶς
> ἐλίσσετ', Ἑλλάδ' ἐμπλέκων
> Ἀσιάδι φωνᾷ διάτορον
> σφραγῖδα θραύων στόματος,
> Ἰάονα γλῶσσαν ἐξιχνεύων·

> But he [the Persian], wrapping himself around his [the Greek's] knees
> would beg him, weaving Greek
> with Asian speech, piercingly

[46] Aside from the imagery of shattering, voice and tongue, the use of the term *toros* and reference to tracking a story as a track or trail, *ichnos*, are also Aeschylean: see Aesch. *Ag.* 1062–3; 1184–5, discussed in Chapter 1.

shattering the seal of his mouth
tracking down the Ionian tongue.
(PMG 791: Timoth. Pers. fr. 15, 145–9)

The passage continues with a vivid quotation of the Persian's pidgin-Greek. In the *Alexandra*, Cassandra's language is broken down into riddling Greek throughout, but at the moment of her death her body is fragmented, *suntethrausmenē*, in a horrifying incarnation of her linguistic struggles. The disintegration of her body represents the dissolution of her 'foreign' speech, while her physical shattering also dramatises the fact that not only is her own use of language fragmented, it is also divided up amongst further individual voices in the *Alexandra*.

The first voices to complement Cassandra's are anonymous. The main element lost in Lycophron's text, in its transformation of dramatic material into a more narrative format, is the chorus with its rich metrical and musical variety. The absence of lyric interludes is given a strange spin at certain moments in the Alexandrian text. The following passage follows Cassandra's prediction of Achilles' arrival in Troy:

> καὶ δὴ καταίθει γαῖαν ὀρχηστὴς Ἄρης,
> στρόμβῳ τὸν αἱματηρὸν ἐξάρχων νόμον.
> ἅπασα δὲ χθὼν προὔμμάτων δῃουμένη
> κεῖται, πέφρικαν δ' ὥστε ληΐου γύαι
> λόγχαις ἀποστίλβοντες, οἰμωγὴ δέ μοι
> ἐν ὠσὶ πύργων ἐξ ἄκρων ἰνδάλλεται,
> πρὸς αἰθέρος κυροῦσα νηνέμους ἕδρας,
> γόῳ γυναικῶν καὶ καταρραγαῖς πέπλων,
> ἄλλην ἐπ' ἄλλῃ συμφορὰν δεδεγμένων.

> And now the dancer Ares burns up the land,
> beginning the gory music with his conch.
> And the whole land lies ravaged before my eyes,
> and as if with corn-stalks the fields bristle,
> glittering with spears, and in my ears
> a wailing from the topmost towers seems to sound,
> reaching up to the windless zone of the heavens,
> with groaning of women and tearing of clothes,
> those suffering one disaster after another.
> (Lycoph. Alex. 249–57)

As McNelis and Sens have shown, the story lying behind this passage is ultimately that of the *Iliad*, whose narrative is evoked in theme, metaphor and language.[47] However, the passage is introduced by the appearance of

---

[47] McNelis and Sens (2016) 35–8.

Ares as a dancer (ὀρχηστής, 349), who provides musical accompaniment to the developing story on his conch. His music and dance place the epic narrative within the realm of a more performance-based genre, perhaps even drama. Nor does his work end with the blending of genres. As the divine instigator of war, Ares' song is not just a performance, but is performative in the same way as Cassandra's prophecies are performative: it brings about the events to come. In this sense, Ares is playing the role of a composer or writer who initiates music that is physically damaging, even gory (τὸν αἱματηρὸν ἐξάρχων νόμον, 250), and his power to make things happen, as much as to describe them, is marked by further fiery imagery: he 'burns up the land' (καταίθει γαῖαν, 249). At the same time, Cassandra notes the collective performance of grief that follows Ares' wild dance. He initiates a song of unnamed women's wailing and lamentation, becoming a kind of *chorēgos*. In this section, then, Cassandra's prophecies run their customarily fine line between visionary metaphor and reality, but this time another narrative agent does the main work for her. A divine Ares, whose allegorical role already situates him somewhere between myth and psychological realism, takes a narrative of epic heritage and plays it out through various performance modes even as he transcends the normal boundaries between dancer, musician, actor, poet and producer: his production is unquotable within the unrelenting iambic trimeter, but its power is such as to invoke war and to trigger the (equally unquoted) communal, choral response of the women who suffer through the events narrated.

Other choral responses are elicited by the Furies. In previous texts, the Furies in their own right had provided a choral dimension to Cassandra's solo narrative. In Aeschylus' *Agamemnon*, the Furies' song was tightly bound to Cassandra's prophecies: firstly the chorus claimed that Furies were created by Cassandra's prophecies (Aesch. *Ag.* 1119–20), and then Cassandra had visions of a band of Furies singing a prophetic chant unheard by any but the prophet (1186–93). In the *Trojan Women*, Cassandra claimed to be a Fury herself (Eur. *Tro.* 457). In the *Alexandra*, the Furies emerge from Cassandra's song to underline the ripple effects of her lived experience, and to induce a vocal response from the wider community that suffers those effects. One place where this is highlighted in the *Alexandra* comes in Cassandra's description of her future rape by Locrian Ajax.

Locrian Ajax, at least as Proclus describes him in the Homeric cycle, and according to his dramatic death scene in Homer (*Od.* 4.499–511), is notorious above all for his rape of Cassandra and his ultimate punishment at the hands of Poseidon as he tries to save himself from shipwreck.[48] In the *Alexandra*, it is Ajax's death that Cassandra describes first, in the course of which she describes him with a piling up of multiple and muddled animal associations.[49] He is a 'diving seabird' (Lycoph. *Alex.* 387) that may be identified with a kingfisher; a 'sea bream' (388); a 'cuckoo' (395); a 'dolphin' (397) (or rather, the corpse of a dolphin); and, most strangely of all, a 'decaying preserved fish' (398). The waves that bring Ajax's punishment buffet him as both fish and bird, as a sea and an air dweller, dead and alive: his story transcends the limitations of sea and land. Then, by working backwards from Ajax's curses in death, Cassandra explains the earlier events of his attack on her:

> ἥ μιν παλεύσει δυσλύτοις οἴστρου βρόχοις,
> ἔρωτας οὐκ ἔρωτας, ἀλλ' Ἐρινύων
> πικρὰν ἀποψήλασα κηρουλκὸν πάγην.
> ἅπασα δ' ἄλγη δέξεται κωκυμάτων ...

> She [Aphrodite] who will snare him in the inescapable nets of lust,
> of a love that is not love, but having twanged shut
> the bitter doom-dragging trap of the Furies.
> The whole land will hear the grief in people's howls ...
> (Lycoph. *Alex.* 405–8)

Though Ajax dies as a fish, he is captured with the imagery of bird hunting and in particular with nets, part of Clytemnestra's murderous toolkit as well as the means by which Aphrodite herself was caught in adultery with Ares. Now Aphrodite both prompts Ajax's crime and initiates its punishment, having 'twanged' (ἀποψήλασα, 407) the tripwire of the Furies' trap like the string of a musical instrument.[50] With this – a new musical addition to Ares' trumpeting – Ajax's fate is guaranteed, and this fate is enforced by the Furies. The result is a Greece joined in lament. Communal howls of pain (ἄλγη ... κωκυμάτων, 408) recall once again those echoed by the river Scamander in the *Trojan Women* (πολλοῖς δὲ κωκυτοῖσιν, Eur. *Tro.* 28).

Even without the Furies, a similarly lamenting Greek chorus will return much later in the work, when events are even more explicitly triggered by not just Ajax's assault of Cassandra, but also Agamemnon's:

---

[48] See Chapter 2 for a discussion of whether or not Euripides recognises the story of Ajax's rape of Cassandra.
[49] The list of animals linked to Ajax is exceptional, although in the *Alexandra* heroes are frequently associated with a particular animal as part of the riddling style of the text. See Cusset (2001).
[50] Cf. ψαλάξεις (139–40) and ψάλλουσα (1453), discussed below.

καὶ τοὺς μὲν ἄλγη ποικίλαι τε συμφοραὶ
ἄνοστον αἰάζοντας ἔξουσιν τύχην,
ἐμῶν ἕκατι δυσγάμων ῥυσταγμάτων.

And they [the Greeks] will encounter grief and many different misfortunes
wailing 'aiai' over their luck that keeps them from returning home,
because of my unhappily marrying abductions.

(Lycoph. Alex. 1087–9)

These mourners bewail their fate (αἰάζοντας, 1088; cf. αἰάζωμεν, Eur. *Tro.* 145), using a noise that echoes Cassandra's first word in the text: 'Aiai!' (Lycoph. *Alex.* 31). The cry is also an accusation against the perpetrator of Cassandra's rape, Ajax/*Aias*. For readers who have forgotten this chain of causality, Cassandra reinforces the point in the next line, combining the attacks of Ajax and Agamemnon in referring to her 'unhappily marrying abductions' (δυσγάμων ῥυσταγμάτων, 1089). If in the *Trojan Women* Cassandra welcomed the disastrous local consequences of her 'marriage' to Agamemnon, in the *Alexandra* she embraces the wider destruction of the Greeks – and their vocal response to this – as a consequence of her repeated assaults.

Internal choral voices are also joined by internal epic voices in Cassandra's narration, with Odysseus providing the longest sub-story. Stretching as it does to nearly two hundred lines (648–819), this passage serves as a virtual paraphrase of the *Odyssey* – paraphrase being another important tool in the Alexandrian scholarly tradition.[51] Here the scholarly and the creative interact through the parallels between the voices of the epic Odysseus and the tragic Cassandra. They both have a marked relationship with the ambiguities of language, but are the inverse of each other: where Odysseus is a master of effective but deceitful speech, Cassandra is ineffectively truthful. In the *Trojan Women*, Odysseus is reviled by Hecuba for his 'double tongue' (Eur. *Tro.* 287). In the same text Cassandra also offers a kind of epitome of the *Odyssey*, at the end of which she dismisses her Odyssean narrative curtly as irrelevant in the face of the action she is about to take.[52] Locked away as she is in the *Alexandra*, Cassandra is enforcedly inactive, so the use of epitome necessarily takes on a different tenor. Harking back to her situation in the *Agamemnon*, rather than in the *Trojan Women*, speech or reticence is now all Cassandra has. Cassandra's account of Odysseus' future in the *Alexandra* is therefore all the more combative, and as such

---

[51] Cameron (2004) 82.
[52] See the discussion of συντέμω (Eur. *Tro.* 441) in Chapter 2.

it demonstrates a closer relationship with Odysseus and his narrative aggressions than is even the case in the *Trojan Women*.[53]

For Lycophron, the most marked overlap in the roles of Odysseus and Cassandra occurs at the point of Odysseus' death. There Cassandra notes that Odysseus will also become a seer: μάντιν δὲ νεκρὸν Εὐρυτὰν στέψει λεώς – 'The Eurytanian people will crown him as a prophet when he is dead' (Lycoph. *Alex.* 799). By contrast, in the strange passage quoted in the epigraph to this chapter (1373), Cassandra claims that she will cease to prophesy when she is dead, becoming instead the audience to her own prophecies' fulfilment. So Odysseus receives Cassandra's prophetic mantle after he joins her in the underworld. This connection is pinned to their shared experience of telling their life stories, or having their life stories retold, from one text to another. Cassandra repeatedly laments Troy's fall (στένω σε δισσὰ καὶ τριπλᾶ, 69); Odysseus' (auto)biography is notable for the hero's repeat appearances in the underworld:

> χὼ μὲν τοσούτων θῖνα πημάτων ἰδὼν
> ἄστρεπτον Ἅιδην δύσεται τὸ δεύτερον …
>
> And he, having seen such a pile of sufferings
> will go down a second time to Hades of no return …
> (Lycoph. *Alex.* 812–13)

Odysseus is said to have seen a multitude of sufferings; his visionary understanding of the world in death is defined by his experiences in the past (τοσούτων θῖνα πημάτων ἰδὼν, 812), whereas the young Cassandra sees woes in the future. When Odysseus told of his first visit to the underworld in *Odyssey* 11, he spoke of learning about Cassandra's death from Agamemnon. Now that Cassandra tells Odysseus' story, she focuses on his second and permanent trip to the underworld, revealing the death of the hero that still lies ahead of him. These different temporal perspectives which pivot around Odysseus' and Cassandra's shared narrative talent reinforce the *Alexandra's* emphasis on narrative circularity, in which no event is entirely separable from the many tales that tell of it either before, during or after its occurrence.

The circularity of narrative and event shared between multiple characters is at its most intriguing when Cassandra reaches the story of the

---

[53] Sens (2010) 306 suggests that the dubious veracity of Odysseus' speech (pointed at Lycoph. *Alex.* 764) and its parallelism with Cassandra's speech draws attention to the possibility that Cassandra is not as authoritative as she and the messenger would have their audience believe. McNelis and Sens (2016) 140–1 note that Cassandra in the *Alexandra* and Odysseus in the *Odyssey* both play fast and loose with chronology in their accounts of Odysseus' travels.

Sirens.[54] This story is embedded within her tale of Odysseus' travels and evokes a crucial moment of the *Odyssey* at the very central point of the *Alexandra*. Similarly, the Sirens of the *Odyssey* are found within Odysseus' own account of his travels and at the centre of the poem (*Odyssey* 12), where they serve to evoke the narrative of another epic: the *Iliad*.[55] Cassandra tells of the Sirens' death, an event that offers in and of itself a challenge to mythic time, for until this version is told by Lycophron, these creatures appear to have been imagined as having an immortal existence.[56]

> κτενεῖ δὲ κούρας Τηθύος παιδὸς τριπλᾶς,
> οἵμας μελῳδοῦ μητρὸς ἐκμεμαγμένας,
> αὐτοκτόνοις ῥιφαῖσιν ἐξ ἄκρας σκοπῆς
> Τυρσηνικὸν πρὸς κῦμα δυπτούσας πτεροῖς,
> ὅπου λινεργὴς κλῶσις ἑλκύσει πικρά.

> And he [Odysseus] will kill the triple daughters of Tethys' son,
> who performed impressions of their melodious mother's songs,
> with suicidal plunge from the topmost cliff
> diving into the Tyrrhenian swell with their wings,
> where the bitter flaxen thread of the Fates will drag them.
>   (Lycoph. *Alex.* 712–16)

In Cassandra's representation of the three Sirens' death, she offers a complex reflection on narrative overdetermination. Odysseus is described as killing the creatures, simply by escaping from their captivating narrative. On the other hand, they die by 'suicidal plunge' (αὐτοκτόνοις ῥιφαῖσιν, 714); it is self-inflicted. Then again, their plunge is also seen as part of the plan of the Fates. There is effectively a triple motivation behind their end. Odysseus' escape, the Sirens' suicidal despair (for readers are reminded that they are birds with wings (πτεροῖς, 715) and need not die even as they plunge from their cliff) and the plan of the Fates all pivot around one essential fact: the Sirens' song has failed, according to their set model of communication.

Cassandra claims that the songs are, in fact, repetitions of songs by the creatures' 'melodious mother' (μελῳδοῦ μητρὸς, 713). One tradition has it that the Sirens' mother was one of the Muses, the Muses being the daughters of memory, Mnesmosyne. These Sirens are related to figures of poetic inspiration and creation, though their own songs are imitative

---

[54] Fusillo, Hurst and Paduano (1991) 30; Hornblower (2015) 276, with more on the connection between Cassandra and the Sirens.
[55] Pucci (1979).
[56] *BNP* s.v. 'Sirens'. Hyg. *Fab.* 141 later has the creatures commit suicide, this time because Orpheus, another competitive singer, helps the Argonauts to escape their wiles.

(ἐκμεμαγμένας, 713). As with the Odysseus and Cassandra of the *Alexandra*, they are creatures defined by repetition and doubling. In fact, the archetype of their song, their narrative in the *Odyssey*, shows a similar interest in their imitative communications:

δεῦρ' ἄγ' ἰών, πολύαιν' Ὀδυσεῦ, μέγα κῦδος Ἀχαιῶν,
νῆα κατάστησον, ἵνα νωϊτέρην ὄπ' ἀκούσῃς.
οὐ γάρ πώ τις τῇδε παρήλασε νηῒ μελαίνῃ,
πρίν γ' ἡμέων μελίγηρυν ἀπὸ στομάτων ὄπ' ἀκοῦσαι,
ἀλλ' ὅ γε τερψάμενος νεῖται καὶ πλείονα εἰδώς.
ἴδμεν γάρ τοι πάνθ', ὅσ' ἐνὶ Τροίῃ εὐρείῃ
Ἀργεῖοι Τρῶές τε θεῶν ἰότητι μόγησαν,
ἴδμεν δ' ὅσσα γένηται ἐπὶ χθονὶ πουλυβοτείρῃ.

Come here, renowned Odysseus, great glory of the Achaeans,
anchor your ship, so that you may hear both our voices.
For nobody so far has passed by this way in his black ship
before hearing the sweet-sounding voice from our mouths,
but he who has experienced the delight goes on his way knowing
    even more.
For we know everything, all that in broad Troy
the Argives and Trojans have struggled with, by the will of the gods,
and we know all that happens on the rich earth.

(Hom. *Od.* 12.184–91)

The first line of the Sirens – and there are apparently only two Sirens here, as their use of the dual in the next line will reveal – is almost a quotation of Agamemnon's greeting to Odysseus when the latter returns from visiting Achilles in *Iliad* 9 (another passage with striking use of duals): εἴπ' ἄγε μ' ὦ πολύαιν' Ὀδυσεῦ μέγα κῦδος Ἀχαιῶν ... – 'Come tell me, O renowned Odysseus, great glory of the Achaeans ...' (Hom. *Il.* 9.673). These Sirens go on to promise a song that retells the events that took place in the *Iliad* (Hom. *Od.* 12.189–90). But their repetitions offer much more. As Cicero later points out in *De Finibus*, they promise that their listeners will not only enjoy the song but also proceed on their way knowing more (πλείονα εἰδώς, 12.188).[57] The Sirens claim that they have the capacity to reveal enormous stretches of information. They are not unlike the all-seeing Cassandra, with ability that verges on the prophetic (ἴδμεν δ' ὅσσα γένηται, 12.191).[58] However, these Sirens are also very much

---

[57] Goldhill (1991) 64. Cicero glosses the lines: *multa se scire profitebantur, ut homines ad earum saxa discendi cupiditate adhaerescerent* – 'they claimed to know many things, so men would cling to their rocks out of a desire to learn' (Cic. *Fin.* 5.18).

[58] For the Homeric subjunctive's futurity (its 'prospective' dimension) see Palmer (1962) 149–51.

the daughters of the Muses, at least as Hesiod will describe them (or had already described them), who not only know everything that happens at all times, but also have the ability to control the mix of truth and fiction they deliver to their listeners.[59] For example, the Sirens do not tell Odysseus that their song usually brings about the death of their listeners – though, of course, their omniscience means they must know that this time their listener will continue on his journey unscathed. In fact the Sirens, just like Cassandra, suffer from a communicative malfunction that is embedded in the reception of their song. Though they may initially be understood by their audiences, the communication proves as fruitless as Cassandra's, since their audiences promptly perish. The difference between the Sirens and Cassandra is that the Sirens are willing participants in their communicative malfeasance.

This parallel between the Sirens and Cassandra is at its most complex and interesting when Lycophron retells the story of the Sirens' last song. This episode is marked as an act of repetition from the beginning of the passage, where it is revealed that the two Homeric Sirens have now become three (τριπλᾶς, 712), in an act of literary multiplication. Then Lycophron's Sirens mimic the song of their 'melodious mother' (μελῳδοῦ μητρός, 713), using the syllable μελ- not only to hint at the name of the Muse Melpomene, but also to pick up the description of the original Homeric Sirens' 'sweet-sounding voice' (μελίγηρυν ... ὄπ', Hom. *Od.* 12.187), false etymology notwithstanding.[60] These Alexandrian Sirens evoke a Muse, a mother and a mother-text, all in one. At the same time, Lycophron preserves the mystery embedded in the original song of the Sirens, just as the messenger of the *Alexandra* preserves the complications of Cassandra's voice in his rehearsal of it. In neither the *Odyssey* nor the *Alexandra* does the external audience hear the song of the Sirens, even if the *Odyssey* hints at some of its content at 12.189–91. The external audience's response to the Sirens in the *Alexandra* remains one of titillated frustration, as it is in the *Odyssey*.

The inclusion of the Sirens' suicide in the *Alexandra* adds an important further dimension to the narrative, one that turns Lycophron's Siren song into a swansong. On the one hand, the addition of the sequel privileges their biography, as part of the shifting focalisation of Cassandra's narrative that continues to sustain the lives and narratives of the marginal figures

---

[59] Hes. *Theog.* 32–3, and 27–8.
[60] Hornblower (2015) 293 on the identification with Melpomene.

with whom she identifies. Cassandra pursues these women's voices even after Odysseus, the ostensible 'hero' of their story, has left the stage. But the sequel also reflects the vulnerability of these stories as they are embedded in Cassandra's overarching narrative. According to the myth Cassandra tells, the Sirens are foiled by two acts of internal audience response. One group of listeners (Odysseus' rowers) is deaf to their song, while the other (Odysseus) is constrained by ropes tying him to the mast and, less literally, by a fate whose narrative insists on bringing him home despite all efforts to the contrary.[61] The rowers demonstrate the Sirens' defeat in not being heard, Odysseus their defeat in being heard without the intended result. Bearing in mind the communicative model provided by Cassandra, their narrator, it is surely the latter defeat that induces the Sirens' despair. This is why Cassandra understands, and argues, that Odysseus 'kills' the Sirens (Lycoph. *Alex.* 712).

Yet Odysseus' catalytic function may also be what gives the Sirens a future. The Sirens launch into their overdetermined suicidal plunge when one listener manages to learn their song and, despite its attractions, continues on his way in possession of more knowledge than he had before. Though the song itself remains forever obscured, the single listener, the one whose life experiences will inform his own prophetic ability after death (χὠ μὲν τοσούτων θῖνα πημάτων ἰδών, 812), gives their story an afterlife. The Sirens die because Odysseus has learned their song but, put another way, they *can* die because he has learned their song. Another narrator can now take over their role as singers. It is not inappropriate that the Sirens and their songs are lost at sea, in the ocean where, for Lycophron, historical or prophetic narratives dissolve and reform.

The Sirens' actual song is, indeed, picked up by a new narrator before the end of the work; by Cassandra herself, though she is not the one to make the identification. At the very end of the *Alexandra*, when the messenger once again speaks in his own voice, he describes Cassandra:[62]

> ... ἐν δὲ καρδίᾳ
> Σειρῆνος ἐστέναξε λοίσθιον μέλος,
> Κλάρου Μιμαλλών, ἢ Μελαγκραίρας κόπις

---

[61] On the Sirens as a trope for hearing but not listening in Greek and Latin literature, see Burbidge (2009).

[62] Hornblower (2015) 121 notes that the identification is also hinted at by the messenger at the very beginning of the *Alexandra*. The messenger refers to Cassandra's αἰόλον στόμα – 'shifty speech' (4), which is later picked up in Cassandra's own description of the Sirens' song: αἰόλῳ μέλει – 'shifty song' (671).

Νησοῦς θυγατρός, ἢ τι Φίκιον τέρας
ἑλικτὰ κωτίλλουσα δυσφράστως ἔπη.

... But in her heart
she cried out the last song of the Siren,
like a bacchante of Claros, or a boaster of Melankraira's knowledge
(the daughter of Neso), or the monster Sphinx,
chattering out twisted words, speaking with difficulty.[63]

(Lycoph. *Alex.* 1462–6)

The Sirens have reached out to Cassandra from within her narrative. The messenger claims to have overheard Cassandra, though she spoke with no expectation of reaching an audience. The messenger's verbatim quotation finds an audience, though not a receptive one. But the knowledge of Odysseus' escape from the Sirens, fully understanding their narrative, leaves a glimmer of hope for Cassandra's song, too. There may be one person who yet hears, understands *and* escapes this narrative, who will ensure that Cassandra's final Siren song (Σειρῆνος ... λοίσθιον μέλος, 1463) is not completely lost.

East Meets West

One effect of the slippage between different voices in the *Alexandra* is that the authority of prophetic speech becomes shared between multiple figures. The messenger, Odysseus, the Sirens, all have tested the waters of prophecy by experimenting in and through Cassandra's voice. But Cassandra's literary journey as translator and translated in the *Alexandra* leads her to engage with one particular prophetic successor who will provide a more enduring takeover. As Cassandra's song in the *Alexandra* finally draws to an end, having drifted westwards from narratives of Troy to Greece, and thence to Rome, her voice becomes more firmly associated with a prophet who bears a suspicious resemblance to a sibyl who would come to have profound significance at Rome: the Cumaean Sibyl. This identification, made most recently by Lycophron experts Gutzwiller, Cusset, and McNelis and Sens, and comfortably accepted on the Roman side by Miller, has considerable bearing on our understanding of the authorship of the work.[64] If the function of Cassandra's prophetic voice is indeed

---

[63] For the identifications and discussion of the prophets and places here see Cusset (2004) 55–6.
[64] Parke (1988) 16–17; Gutzwiller (2007). Cusset (2004) reads the Sibyl as a *mise-en-abîme* of Cassandra's narrative process (58), McNelis and Sens (2016) esp. 207. Miller (2009) 135 n. 93 writes 'she (Cassandra) sees herself in the Sibyl'.

being represented as passing on to the prophet whose books will become a legendary source of power for the Roman state, then the shift from east to west in the *Alexandra* refers to a historical as much as a mythographical phenomenon. Italo-Greek voices were believed to be capable of overtaking the Mediterranean, if they were not already in the process of doing so.

Parke has long connected the style of Lycophron's *Alexandra* to the tradition of sibylline prophetic delivery, but he also ties elements specifically to the Cumaean Sibyl.[65] Parke unpicks a passage in pseudo-Aristotle's *De Mirabilibus Auscultationibus* (*c.* third century BCE), which may share a source with the *Alexandra*, and reads: 'in Cumae in Italy there appears to be an underground chamber of the prophet Sibyl, the exceptionally long-lived maiden who they say lived there, who was Erythraean, though by some of the inhabitants of Italy she was called the Cumaean, and by others Melankraira'.[66] The link between the Erythraean Sibyl and the Cumaean is found elsewhere: Servius suggests that the Sibyl of Erythrae was given long life by Apollo but was forced to leave her home and travelled to Cumae (ad Verg. *Aen.* 6.321); Lactantius notes that Erythrae provided the oracles that replaced those of the Cumaean Sibylline Books after they were burned in 83 BCE (Lactant. 1.6.14).[67] Meanwhile, the reference to the name Melankraira helps to explain Lycophron's text. After the messenger of the *Alexandra* compares Cassandra to one of the Sirens, he also compares her prophecies to those of a bacchante of Apollo's shrine at Claros (founded by another prophet and victim of Apollo: Manto, the daughter of Tiresias), and to those of a certain Melankraira, daughter of Neso (Lycoph. *Alex.* 1464–5).[68] This Melankraira must originate in Asia Minor, for her mother Neso can be identified as the daughter of Trojan Teucer, descendant of the river Scamander and wife of Dardanus. Pseudo-Aristotle makes it clear that at least one tradition linked the name Melankraira specifically to the Erythraean/Cumaean Sibyl.[69]

Another passage that offers a yet clearer reference to the Cumaean Sibyl begins as a narrative about rising Trojan power in the west, through the

[65] Parke (1988) 78, followed by Hornblower (2015) 500.
[66] [Aristotle] *Mir. Ausc.* 95, 838a5. Parke suspects that the shared source may be Lycus of Rhegium.
[67] Parke (1988) 78–9. For further discussion see Chapter 4.
[68] On Manto and Claros see Bouché-Leclercq (1879–82) II, 150–1, who notes also the more general confusion between Manto, Cassandra and the Sibyl.
[69] Waszink (1948) 52 argues that the Melankraira of the *Alexandra* refers to the Trojan/Marpessian Sibyl, though in fact the Erythraean Sibyl is not always carefully distinguished from the Trojan Sibyl anyway. Hurst and Kolde (2008) 319, who happily accept the identification of Melankraira with the Cumaean Sibyl, note that the scholia to the *Alexandra* explain the 'black hair' tag with her tendency to obscure (*melainein*) her speech and particularly her oracles, like Cassandra.

actions of pious (*eusebestatos*, rather than *pius*) Aeneas.[70] Cassandra directly links this to the rebirth of her own family fortunes:

γένους δὲ πάππων τῶν ἐμῶν αὖθις κλέος
μέγιστον αὐξήσουσιν ἄμναμοί ποτε,
αἰχμαῖς τὸ πρωτόλειον ἄραντες στέφος,
γῆς καὶ θαλάσσης σκῆπτρα καὶ μοναρχίαν
λαβόντες. οὐδ' ἄμνηστον, ἀθλία πατρίς,
κῦδος μαρανθὲν ἐγκατακρύψεις ζόφῳ.

And some day descendants will once again build up
to the highest degree the fame of my ancestors' family,
winning the garland of victory with their spears,
taking the sceptre and monarchy of earth and sea.
Nor, miserable fatherland, will you hide, forgotten,
your withered glory in the darkness.   (Lycoph. *Alex.* 1226–31)

It is fitting that Cassandra identifies her own ancestors and their descendants with this new power, for Cassandra's physical implication in her dynastic tales is one of the distinctive features of her prophecies. While Cassandra has no biological children to carry on her story further west, her descendants from a common Troy, and her mythographical descendants, will continue to be caught up in events to come. The descendants (ἄμναμοί, 1227) are part of the process that ensures Troy's glory is not forgotten (ἄμνηστον, 1230); as in all of Cassandra's stories, memory is a springboard for the future. Cassandra's constructions of past and future are also always linked to geographical movements: her prophecies have regularly played on a pivotal motion between the land masses on either side of the Aegean, between east and west. Whatever the historical context of the *Alexandra*'s composition, it is entirely consistent with her literary history for an Alexandrian Cassandra now to be looking even further west for a site in which to embed her prophetic future.

This section of Cassandra's prophecies focusing on Rome's foundation legends concludes with a reference to a sibyl in her cave:

… ἔνθα παρθένου
στυγνὸν Σιβύλλης ἐστὶν οἰκητήριον,
γρώνῳ βερέθρῳ συγκατηρεφὲς στέγης.
τοσαῦτα μὲν δύστλητα πείσονται κακὰ
οἱ τὴν ἐμὴν μέλλοντες αἰστώσειν πάτραν.

---

[70] This is the first of the passages identified as tricky to date to the era of Ptolemy Philadelphus. See West (1984) 130, smartly updated by Hornblower (2015) 436.

τί γὰρ ταλαίνῃ μητρὶ τῇ Προμηθέως
ξυνὸν πέφυκε καὶ τροφῷ Σαρπηδόνος ...;

... there exists
the grim abode of the maiden Sibyl,
covered over by the hollowed-out cave of her shelter.
So many unbearable evils will they suffer,
those who are going to destroy my fatherland.
For what is common to both the wretched mother of Prometheus
and to the nurse of Sarpedon ...?   (Lycoph. *Alex.* 1278–84)

Parke notes that the association between sibyls and caves is only attested for the Sibyl at Cumae, so the identification here appears firm.[71] At the end of the work the messenger will compare Cassandra to Melankraira in passing, but here Cassandra makes an inescapable reference to the Cumaean Sibyl in her own voice, using her as the climax to the episode based in Italy. Cassandra leaves her Roman story in the hands – or mouth – of another Greek-speaking prophet, who will patrol the temporal and spatial zones further west.

The lines immediately following the appearance of this sibyl (i.e. from 1281) have been identified as changing direction too abruptly, with the Roman episode insufficiently motivating the reference to Greek sufferings or the swerve into a Herodotus-inspired section of text that explores the conflicts between the divided landmasses of Europe (the 'mother of Prometheus') and Asia (the 'nurse of Sarpedon').[72] In fact, though, this is a shift of focus, not of theme. Cassandra is underlining the fundamental opposition between east and west, at the very moment when she hints that the baton of prophecy itself will move westwards.[73] With the movement from east to west, past to future and, ultimately, myth to history (as the Herodotean notes imply), Greece is now trapped between Cassandra's ancestors to the east and her descendants to the west.[74]

---

[71] Parke (1988) 89, *contra* Waszink (1948); McNelis and Sens (2016) 207. For more on the topography of Lycophron's Cumaean cave, and how it influences Virgil, see Miller (2009) 134–5.
[72] This provides evidence for interpolation, for West (1984) 131, and leads to the insertion of a lacuna after line 1280 by some editors: Scheer (1879) and Hurst and Kolde (2008) 290.
[73] McNelis and Sens (2016) 95–100.
[74] This handover across time is all the more pointed if we read Cassandra as moving from prophecy to curse at this point in the text (see discussion above on ὄλοιντο, Lycoph. *Alex.* 1291). If we read τοσαῦτα (1281) as referring not to previous struggles, but to agonies still to come in Cassandra's speech, this fits the fact that Cassandra is about to begin her cursing of the tit-for-tat abductions between the Trojans and the Greeks. No matter that τοσαῦτα more naturally refers back to what has just been said; who is more likely to confuse what has gone before with what is to come than Cassandra? So she looks forward to the miseries that the Greeks are going to suffer in battles back and forth across the Aegean, leaving the Sibyl in control of the prophetic role in the future Roman state.

Cassandra's last words in the *Alexandra* are not the final words in the text, for the messenger reasserts his presence at the very end, but they bring a sense of closure to her speech by returning to the essential battle between sound and sense, and to the source of her tortured language as well as that of the Cumaean Sibyl, Apollo:

> τί μακρὰ τλήμων εἰς ἀνηκόους πέτρας,
> εἰς κῦμα κωφόν, εἰς νάπας δασπλήτιδας
> βαύζω, κενὸν ψάλλουσα μάστακος κρότον;
> πίστιν γὰρ ἡμῶν Λεψιεὺς ἐνόσφισε,
> ψευδηγόροις φήμαισιν ἐγχρίσας ἔπη
> καὶ θεσφάτων πρόμαντιν ἀψευδῆ φρόνιν,
> λέκτρων στερηθεὶς ὧν ἐκάλχαινεν τυχεῖν.
> θήσει δ' ἀληθῆ. σὺν κακῷ δέ τις μαθών,
> ὅτ' οὐδὲν ἔσται μῆχος ὠφελεῖν πάτραν,
> τὴν φοιβόληπτον αἰνέσει χελιδόνα.

> Why do I yelp to the unlistening rocks,
> to the deaf wave, to the horrifying woods,
> twanging the empty tremolo of my mouth?
> For Lepsieus deprived me of trustworthiness,
> anointing with false-speaking rumours my words
> and the un-false prophetic wisdom of my oracles,
> since he was deprived of the bed for which he was flushed with desire.
> But he will make them true. And having learned it through suffering,
> when there will be no way to help my fatherland,
> someone will praise the Phoebus-inspired swallow.

(Lycoph. Alex. 1451–60)

In a sudden step back from her tortuous narrative, Cassandra adopts a pastoral tone. The conventional topos of deaf nature illustrates her inability to communicate her prophecies, but reminders of the topsy-turvy nature of Cassandra's use of language and genre pervade even this formulaic lament. Through the rare verb βαύζω (1453), 'to bark' or 'to cry *ba ba*', Cassandra gives herself an animalistic association that finally aligns her with the characters peopling her prophecies, for animal descriptions are one of the most common riddling methods she uses.[75] She commits herself to joining the narrative, rather than limiting herself to endless commentary from the sidelines. At the same time, with this verb Cassandra reminds herself of, and then accepts, her characterisation as a babbling barbarian.

---

[75] The verb is also found in Aesch. *Ag.* 449. See Hornblower (2015) 498. On animal imagery in Lycophron, see Cusset (2001) and the discussion of Ajax above.

Cassandra expands on this despairing disparagement of her voice with the extraordinary phrase 'twanging the empty tremolo of my mouth' (κενὸν ψάλλουσα μάστακος κρότον, 1453). Cassandra's Orphic song to the land, the sea and the woods, though it is met not with exceptional response but with deafness, is a bizarre mix of human voice and instrumentation.[76] The line conflates voice and performance on the lyre, a monstrous muddling of musical elements that are supposed to work in concert. Earlier in the work, Cassandra mentions how Aphrodite had 'twanged' (ἀποψήλασα, 407) the tripwire entrapping Ajax in the Furies' toils, and before that Cassandra had accused Paris of 'twanging' a lyre string too:

> τοιγὰρ ψαλάξεις εἰς κενὸν νευρᾶς κτύπον,
> ἄσιτα κἀδώρητα φορμίζων μέλη ...

> And so you will twang, to empty purpose, the sound of a string,
> playing on the lyre fruitless, unrewarding songs ...
> (Lycoph. *Alex.* 139–40)

Paris/Alexandros, the firebrand who sets in motion a string of unstoppable narrative events, is at once the bane of the prophet Cassandra/Alexandra and her match: he acts where his sister comments and laments, and he triggers events where she resists, repeats and rewinds, but he also shares her dubious gift of translating narrative into meaningless music. At the end of the work Cassandra takes this theme to its most surreal extreme, making the sounds of the plucked lyre string emerge from her own mouth. Once again Cassandra's communications are assimilated to noise, not meaning.

In these final lines of Cassandra, Apollo also returns to a position of prominence. No longer Loxias, he is now given the epithet Lepsieus, a *hapax* that the scholia rather desperately guess must come from the Greek word *lepos* – 'the rind (behind which meaning is concealed)'.[77] Apollo certainly remains a tricksy character. While Cassandra makes it clear that he set up her tragic failure to communicate true knowledge, her strange description of him 'anointing' her words 'with false-speaking rumours' (ψευδηγόροις φήμαισιν, 1455) leaves as baffling as ever the question as to where exactly Cassandra's communications are breaking down. Are Cassandra's words flawed – despite her protestation that they are 'un-false' (ἀψευδῆ, 1456) – or is it by means of empty rumours that Apollo has discredited her? Is it Cassandra's speech that is the problem, or the way in which her listeners

---

[76] Crippa (1998) 169.
[77] Hornblower (2015) 432 now offers the more prosaic explanation that there was a sanctuary to Apollo on the island of Lepsia.

are responding to her narrative? Then Cassandra attributes to Apollo the final unravelling of her prophecies, but she does so with one last use of an almost invisible alpha privative that underlines the perversity of its pervasiveness elsewhere in the text: θήσει δ᾽ ἀληθῆ – 'But he will make them true' (1458); ἀ-ληθῆ – 'true', but also 'un-concealed', or perhaps 'un-forgotten'. Will Apollo just make Cassandra's prophecies true, or will he finally make them *recognised* as true, in a way that will leave 'concealment' of her truths behind forever?

This question becomes embedded in perhaps the most intriguing mystery in the text: that concerning the identity of the person, a 'someone' (τις), in line 1458? This person learns, through hard experience, the disasters that will befall Troy. When this anonymous character has processed Cassandra's stories and the events they describe (just as the prophet herself will do after her death, 1372–3), this 'someone' will become the speaker, praising the speech of 'the Phoebus-inspired swallow' (τὴν φοιβόληπτον ... χελιδόνα, 1460). With her adoption of the powerful swallow imagery used by Homer and Aeschylus to describe her linguistic struggles, Lycophron's Cassandra reaches back through literary history to anticipate a reassessment of her language later in the mythical, historical or literary future. This proper valuation of her speech, the identification of the match between word and event, will prove her truth more comprehensively than the enacting of the events themselves.

Can we establish who it could be that Cassandra imagines will be in a position to see her prophecies fulfilled and her ravings vindicated? The anonymous 'someone' who struggles to understand the truth of her narrative (as she admits, the process is painful and achieved 'through suffering' – σὺν κακῷ, 1458) may stand for a range of interpreter-translators, each playing a part in the muddle of characters, speakers and listeners embroiled in this text.[78] One figure who suffers through the narrative events is her immediate audience: that is to say, the messenger who overhears her speech. Then there is also the messenger's audience: her father, Priam. Perhaps she is looking outwards to another audience of the text: to the Cumaean Sibyl (who knows the script and will take it further), or to each and every reader who ventures an interpretation of one of the riddles. Or, maybe, 'someone' is a covert reference to the anonymous writer (or writers) of the text: the one who praises the swallow not by translating her riddles into banal explanations, but by allowing them to stay richly ravelled under the claim of 'literal' quotation, and who obscures his or her own authorial identity in the process.

[78] McNelis and Sens (2016) 100.

Commentary

By any standards the *Alexandra* is an unusual work. Lycophron, or whoever wrote the text, added features from the bookish Alexandrian poetic world to Cassandra's already difficult position within ancient Greek literature. The role of the commentary, although not explicitly referred to anywhere in the text, inspires aspects of this particular presentation of Cassandra. The work, as Cameron points out, demanded a commentary as soon as it left its author's hands, and may even have been furnished with one by the author himself. As Cameron puts it, 'Who else would have known all the answers?'[79] On the other hand, the *Alexandra* also already contains its own commentary of sorts, for Cassandra's voice in all its riddling complexities offers details about peoples and places that under normal circumstances would provide only the 'further background' to a narrative. Instead, in this text, it is the narrative itself that is hard to track down. The *Alexandra* offers a commentary by a young Cassandra that anticipates – even prophesies – her more canonical later narratives. By problematising the notion of explication itself, the work plays with ideas of literary authority. To whom should a reader turn when the text does not open itself up under examination? Whose voice within the text is to be trusted when its author and performance context is so obscured? In the *Alexandra*, the text is demonstrably fragmented between voices, even as those voices overlap and merge and become impossible to separate. Meanwhile the text's confusion of mythic and historical material and its range across such a wide sweep of the Mediterranean gives the impression that it must be the production of an equally tangled mess of voices, of influences. The literal and thematised fragmentation of authority in the *Alexandra* demands that its readers identify the functions of translation, commentary and rewriting at work in the text before they can even begin to reach for a coherent narrative.

[79] Cameron (1995) 224–5. See also Cameron (2004) 82.

CHAPTER 4

Graeco-Roman Sibylline Scripts: Virgil's Aeneid

insanam uatem aspicies, quae rupe sub ima
fata canit foliisque notas et nomina mandat.

You will see a frenzied visionary, who deep in the cave of a cliff
sings the fates to come and commits symbols and words to leaves.
(Verg. *Aen.* 3.443–4)[1]

Over the course of several generations of Greek literature, Cassandra and her prophetic curse provided the focal point for authors and audiences to explore a range of poetic problems. Cassandra's voice first showcased meaningful nonsense (Aeschylus), then it presented disordered emotional literacy (Euripides), before it turned to ventriloquised scholarly scribbling (Lycophron). In settings that regularly placed her in an abject position, she was granted a verbal activity that ranged from speaking silence, through defiant raving, to wilful obfuscation. Across all the varied examples of her vocal efforts in Greek, the function of translation was always implicated at some level, through the manifold acts of interpretation that worked with her obstinately obscure words within and across literary texts.

The Roman literary world was built on cumulative acts of translation. From Livius Andronicus' first rendering of Homer's *Odyssey* into Latin saturnians, with many-turned Odysseus 'turned' (*uersutus*) into Latin, Roman poetry emerged from a cultural and linguistic 'contact zone'.[2] With a combination of humble deference and proud imperialism, Greek myth and Greek literature was imitated, appropriated and assimilated into Latin literature of every mode and genre. From this early rivalry or *aemulatio* came some of the most vigorously allusive literature ever produced, with

---

[1] Quotations from the *Aeneid* are from the edition of Mynors (1969).
[2] In recent scholarship: Traina (1989), Hinds (1998), Most (2003), Barchiesi (2005), Feeney (2005), Sciarrino (2006), Wallace-Hadrill (2008), Bettini (2012), Hutchinson (2013), McElduff (2013), Feeney (2015) and Bartsch (2016). McElduff (2013), esp. 11–16, outlines in broad brushstrokes the relationship between Roman translation practices and the cultural, social and imperial concerns of translation studies.

its own signalling tropes (some of them Greek borrowings in their own right): the Alexandrian footnote; *oppositio in imitando*; expressions of anxiety that would later be characterised as Freudian/Bloomian, or boastings of confident self-canonisation; claims to primacy or belatedness, generic affiliation or innovation; images of the river or the path of literary tradition.[3]

In this context it might be imagined that Cassandra, with all the hermeneutic richness of her speech, would be a figure of fascination to Roman authors as they engaged in their own creative translations. Roman epic in particular needed prophetic voices to rise out of its hexameters, hexameters that were only lately adopted from their Greek models and allegedly invented by inspired prophets in the first place.[4] Such prophetic voices would be crucial to stitching over the seams at the awkward moments when legend and recent history were at risk of coming unstuck, and to offer the sense of predestined teleology that was so closely connected to the self-definition of the Roman state.[5] In practice, however, Cassandra does not play a prominent role in extant Roman literature.[6] The communicative dynamics she provokes in Greek literature are just as pointed and potent in Latin texts, but they are articulated by different prophetic women, whose acts of translation occur as a result of their journeys across the Adriatic Sea, not the Aegean: Virgil's Sibyl, Ovid's Carmentis (also known as Carmenta), Lucan's Phemonoe and Erictho.[7] Just as Lycophron's Alexandrian Cassandra started to look west to Italy, so it is the distance between Rome and Greece, rather than Greece and Asia Minor, that maps the dislocated Latin narratives of past, present and future events. Nonetheless, the paradox of miscommunicated truth-telling that lies

---

[3] The trailblazing scholarship: Conte (1986), Thomas (1986), Hardie (1993), Fowler (1997a) and Hinds (1998).

[4] The legend that Apollo's first priestess at Delphi invented the hexameter is found in Pliny the Elder, Plutarch and Pausanias. See the second section of the Introduction, 'Prophecy as Poetry, Prophets as Poets'.

[5] The essays in Levene and Nelis (2002) explore a range of connections between Roman epic and historiography. As Ash (2002) neatly puts it, the interrelation is cemented by the Roman obsession with warfare, 'whether a historical narrative is dominated by the fabulous or by the rational, or whether an epic is located in a historical or mythological period (or both)' (253). See also Woodman (1988) 98ff.; Hardie (1986); Feeney (1991) 250–312. On the past and Roman identity see Gowing (2005) 2: 'For Romans the past wholly defined the present, and to forget – to disconnect with – the past, at either the level of the individual or of the state, risked the loss of identity and even extinction.'

[6] For an overview of her appearances in early Roman literature see Neblung (1997) 107–27. Extant is the operative word here: Cassandra clearly had a vital role in Ennius' play *Alexander*, which was a sufficiently popular tragedy to be quoted by Cicero at *Div.* 1.66.

[7] See e.g. Feeney (2004) esp. 101–4, on 'seascapes ... crossed and recrossed by so many expeditions and their tracking texts' (88), building on the identification of water as a boundary between individual stories within the *Metamorphoses* by Barchiesi (1997b) 182–3.

beneath Cassandra's speech remains the driving force behind the characterisation of these new prophetic figures, and Cassandra's voice is often tacitly in the background.

If Cassandra is a character influenced by sibylline speech, sibylline characters in Roman literature owe even more to Cassandra's Greek voice.[8] Lycophron had hinted that a moment would come in which Cassandra's prophetic baton would be handed over to a new prophet, when his Trojan prophetess made reference to a sibylline figure whose prophetic domain would be joined to Rome's rising fortunes. This prediction by Lycophron's Cassandra was proven truthful when her vision of a visionary was realised in the writings of Roman poets. From the many descriptions of sibyls in Roman literature, a syncretistic character who could perform Cassandra's role for a new cultural tradition gradually took shape in the form of the Sibyl of Cumae, the most famous sibyl of Roman legend and, at least by the Augustan era, the purported author of Rome's treasured Greek-language Sibylline Books. Embedded in Roman ritual practices and foundational narratives, this sibyl would be protected from many of Cassandra's sufferings, but she could, and did, 'act' Cassandra for a new audience.[9]

The Cumaean Sibyl was a Greek woman who prophesied for Roman male citizens; a speaker whose voice was silenced by 'her' writing; a figure of foundational legend whose words shaped the history of a people. The Sibyl was more influential within the society that cultivated her than Cassandra was in Greece, but the vulnerability of her prophecies to fragmentation, loss and misinterpretation over time made hers an equally troubling voice. In *De divinatione*, Cicero and his brother Quintus wrestle with her mysterious position, hovering as it is somewhere between myth, history and contemporary ritual. In the second book, Marcus Cicero transitions smoothly from criticism of the Sibylline Books' ambiguities in historical practice to dismissal of Cassandra's certainties in the literary domain, concluding with regard to the latter: 'Surely you aren't insisting that I should believe in legendary tales [*fabulis*]?' (*Div.* 2.113).[10] For the poet

---

8   Parke (1988) 16–17; Lightfoot (2007) 8–9. Mazzoldi (2001) 102–7.
9   Parke (1988) notes that Virgil's Sibyl prophesies just like Cassandra: 'the first person is obviously not meant for Apollo but the Sibyl herself, engaging in that use of second sight which is a typical feature in her prophecies as also in those of Cassandra. In fact Virgil is quite consistent in maintaining the picture that this is a Sibyl, not a Pythia, replying to Aeneas. She is inspired by Apollo, but not completely possessed by the god' (79).
10 Quintus Cicero had already admitted straying into the realm of literary myth-making when he discussed Cassandra's voice in the first book of *De divinatione*: 'I seem to be talking about tragedies [*tragoedias*] and legends [*fabulas*]' (*Div.* 1.68). The weight of *fabula* is picked up in Livy's preface (1.pr.6), in the most famous pointing of the myth/historical disjunction: 'Those stories that are told about what happened before the city was founded, or was about to be founded, which are more the

Virgil, however, the Cumaean Sibyl's value to his own writing of legendary material was clear. This was his 'foreign-speaking' prophet, whose Apollo-inspired and dangerously opaque texts tied her as tightly to the poets and poetry that shaped her as Cassandra's voice had tied her to the Greek literary tradition.[11]

Ta(l)king over Cassandra

The connection between Cassandra and a sibyl is implied in Propertius 4.1, in which poem the words of the former prophet appear to follow those of the latter, and are introduced with a pointed evocation of Lycophron's *Alexandra* (*dicam*, Prop. 4.1.87; λέξω, Lycoph. *Alex.* 1).[12] Only a few years beforehand, Virgil's *Aeneid* had become the first fully extant text in which the various sibyls of Greek myth are subsumed within the figure of the Cumaean Sibyl, as well as the first text in which Cassandra's prophecies are comprehensively replaced by those of the Sibyl.

Cassandra's prophecies could have played a central role in the *Aeneid*, with its complicated mytho-historical relationship between past and present.[13] In fact, Cassandra is fundamental to the narrative of the *Aeneid*, but her part is obscured by Virgil's decision to silence her voice, such that evidence of her presence behind the action has to be carefully excavated. When Juno bursts furiously into the first speech of the epic, she offers a justification for her behaviour, and hence for the path of the narrative to come, by alluding to the epic's Homeric backstories. Juno begins with the *Iliad*, punningly mistranslating its first word, Achilles' *mēnin*, in her first word: *mene* (Verg. *Aen.* 1.37). She then leaps into the *Odyssey* with a reference to another

---

material of poetic legends [*poeticis … fabulis*] than of accurate records of achievements [*incorruptis rerum gestarum monumentis*], those stories it is my intention neither to confirm nor dispute.' For nuanced readings of Livy's distinction between *fabula* and *historia* see Feldherr (1998) 75–8 and Miles (1995) 16–19.

[11] The Sibyl was Apollo-inspired at least from Virgil's invention of Deiphobe. On the Cumaean Sibyl's association with Juno before Virgil see Johnston (1998) and Oliensis (2004) 43.

[12] The text is disputed, but Cassandra clearly speaks to Priam from within Propertius' poem: *dicam 'Troia, cades, et Troica Roma, resurges'* – 'I shall say "Troy, you will fall, and Trojan Rome, you will rise again"' (Prop. 4.1.87, with this and line 88 surely rightly placed after line 52). Compare also Carmentis' version of this prophecy in Ovid's *Fasti*: *uicta tamen uinces euersaque, Troia, resurges* – 'though conquered you will nonetheless conquer and though crushed, Troy, you will rise again' (Ov. *Fast.* 1. 523), discussed below in Chapter 5. Heyworth (2009) 420–1 makes an excellent case for the placement of Cassandra's lines of speech after the appearance of the sibylline figure, and he and Hornblower (2015) 438 explore the lines' links with Lycophron, especially Lycoph. *Alex.* 1229. Hutchinson (2006) 70 casts heavier doubt on the lines of Cassandra's speech, but he does support the identification of Propertius' sibyl as the Cumaean Sibyl. Propertius also aligns himself with Cassandra at 3.13.61–end.

[13] Williams (1983) 1–16.

person's anger: that of the goddess Athena. Why, Juno asks, was Athena permitted to burn and drown the Greek fleet on leaving Troy, in retaliation for Locrian Ajax's attempted rape of Cassandra in her temple (*unius ob noxam et furias Aiacis Oilei* – 'on account of the crime and madness of a single man, Ajax son of Oileus', 1.41)? It is this example, with close echoes of Lycophron's account of Ajax's responsibility for thousands of Greek deaths, that has prompted Juno's decision to exact her own revenge on the Trojans.[14] Cassandra's body is, once again, a catalyst for action.

Nor is Cassandra simply a contributor to Juno's resentful jealousy. Cassandra's prophecy that the Trojans should seek a place called Hesperia shapes the first years of the Trojans' travels westwards. Juno, furious once again in *Aeneid* 10, notes that Aeneas went to Italy under the influence of the fates, but that he was actually 'driven on' (*impulsus*, 10.68, rather than *profugus* – 'fleeing', 1.2) by the voice of Cassandra's madness:

> *Italiam petiit fatis auctoribus (esto)*
> *Cassandrae impulsus furiis …*

> He sought Italy with the fates in charge (admittedly),
> driven on by Cassandra's furies …
>
> (Verg. *Aen.* 10.67–8)

Like Jupiter, the Sibyl and other true prophets in the *Aeneid*, Cassandra is aligned with the fates that impel Aeneas and the destiny of the Roman people. So Juno has identified a truth here, but she has also over-simplified in her rage, which comes with selective memory (*ira memor*, 1.4). Cassandra's words are as misunderstood as ever in the *Aeneid*, and nobody, let alone Aeneas, knowingly follows her predictions. Her prophecies do direct the path of the *Aeneid*'s hero and his followers, but without their full understanding. Virgil signals this in his text not by representing a voice of prophetic nonsense or confusion, but by erasing her voice at the very moments when it might be most expected.

When Aeneas recounts to Dido the events of Troy's last hours and his subsequent wanderings, he evokes through dramatic quotation the voices of many other protagonists.[15] This two-book narrative by the hero, in which (not unlike Cassandra herself) he plays both *actor* and *auctor*, shows him as both knowing and vulnerable in his half-control over his story, particularly in the semi-fulfilled prophecies he chooses to reveal and discuss. This was the

---

[14] Lycoph. *Alex.* 365, with Hornblower (2015) 199.

[15] Aeneas' oral narrative is defined by the final lines of *Aeneid* 1, which set the scene for his storytelling and offer the two paradigms between which his performance is poised: the sung tales of Iopas (1.740–6) – see Hardie (1986) 52 – and the conversation shaped by Dido's questions (1.747–52). On the literary heritage of *Aeneid* 2 see Rossi (2002).

chance for Virgil, or rather Aeneas, to create a dramatic speaking character in Cassandra. In the face of her words, Aeneas could have revealed himself to be ruefully and belatedly understanding, or still wilfully obtuse. Instead, in Aeneas' first description of Cassandra, he only gets as far as her opening her mouth, just as the Trojan horse is bumping at the gates into Troy:

> *tunc etiam fatis aperit Cassandra futuris*
> *ora dei iussu non umquam credita Teucris.*

> Even at that moment Cassandra opens her mouth for the
>   fates to come
> by the order of the god never to be believed by the Trojans.
>   (Verg. *Aen.* 2.246–7)

This is pitched as a version of the opening to Lycophron's *Alexandra*. In that work, at a carefully pinpointed moment, just as Paris' ships are setting off for Sparta from Troy, Cassandra 'opens her god-inspired [*entheon*] Bacchic mouth' (Lycoph. *Alex.* 28), before delivering more than a thousand lines of speech. If a similar outpouring might have been expected in the *Aeneid*, it is stymied by Aeneas. In Aeneas' narrative, *dei iussu*, sandwiched as it is between two phrases, points both forwards and backwards in the lines: Apollo's order forces Cassandra to tell the future (*fatis … futuris*) and then ensures that she will not be believed, at least by her immediate audience (*non umquam credita Teucris*). But instead of quoting these incomprehensible words, the actual prophecy, Aeneas moves briskly on to describe the Trojan people in their ignorance dressing the local shrines for celebrations. Neither Aeneas nor his listener, Dido, has to deal with the status of Cassandra's speech. In Aeneas' narrative, the figure of misunderstood prophecy is, instead, Cassandra's brother Laocoon, who delivers the very warnings that in other texts come from Cassandra.[16]

The next time Cassandra appears in the *Aeneid* she has been captured by the Greeks, and Aeneas dwells for some time on the image of her being dragged out of Athena's temple, echoing the scene of Ajax's violation to which Juno had referred in her first speech:

> *heu nihil inuitis fas quemquam fidere diuis!*
> *ecce trahebatur passis Priameia uirgo*
> *crinibus a templo Cassandra adytisque Mineruae*
> *ad caelum tendens ardentia lumina frustra,*
> *lumina, nam teneras arcebant uincula palmas.*

---

[16] Horsfall (2008) 85 cites Apollod. *Epit.* 5.17, where Laocoon backs up Cassandra's warning that the Trojan Horse is full of warriors.

> Oh, it is not advisable for anyone to trust in anything when
>   the gods are reluctant!
> Look, the daughter of Priam was being dragged with her hair flowing
> from the temple and inner sanctum of Minerva; Cassandra,
> turning her blazing eyes to the sky in vain,
> her eyes, for chains were binding her delicate hands.
>
> (Verg. *Aen.* 2.402–6)

Once again Cassandra is silent, and this time she is not only gagged by the text, but also physically bound. Only her eyes can move, staring upwards, perhaps in a perversion of the tradition, told by Lycophron, that Athena's statue gazed at the ceiling during Cassandra's rape.[17] The diction of blazing eyes is probably that of Ennius: *quid oculis rapere uisa est derepente ardentibus?* – 'what did she seem to be suddenly grasping with her blazing eyes?' (Enn. fr. 17 Jocelyn, quoted at Cic. *Div.* 1.66). But an echo of Aeschylus' *Agamemnon* is also audible in this passage. When Cassandra first resisted Clytemnestra's attempts at conversation, she remained silent and still. In baffled fury Clytemnestra had asked Cassandra to speak a kind of sign-language with a hand that is 'foreign' (Aesch. *Ag.* 1061, discussed in Chapter 1), a suggestion that Cassandra appears to reject. In the *Aeneid*, Cassandra's hands are elegiacally delicate (*teneras ... palmas*, Verg. *Aen.* 2.406), not foreign, and they are bound by the Greeks, not by her own resistance. But the forcible constriction of Cassandra's voice and of her body in the *Aeneid* points to the same essential conflict staged in her first arrival in the *Agamemnon*: a conflict between what she understands, and what she fails to communicate. The difference is that Virgil does not go on to allow Cassandra to reveal herself in either word or body, speech or action.

Aeneas also silences Coroebus, Cassandra's suitor. Where Aeneas was driven away from Troy by Cassandra (*Cassandrae impulsus furiis*, 10.68), Coroebus was drawn to the city by her: *uenerat insano Cassandrae incensus amore* – 'he had come aflame with crazed love for Cassandra' (2.343). In his passion for the prophet, Coroebus reflects the literal and symbolic flames of Cassandra's prophetic language, as well as her apparent madness. He also casts Cassandra's communication issues into relief as he demonstrates a fleetingly successful outcome of linguistic confusion, managing to turn a communicative muddle into a temporary success for the Trojans. Aeneas tells of a Greek warrior named Androgeos who accidentally falls among a group of Trojans led by Coroebus. Aeneas gives Androgeos three lines of

---

[17] Lycoph. *Alex.* 361. The gaze of Pallas is explained, though not in this context, by Horsfall (2008) 168.

direct speech in which he addresses the men, encouraging them to join him
in attacking the city. Suddenly he realises that these men are not Greeks:

> *dixit, et extemplo (neque enim reponsa dabantur*
> *fida satis) sensit medios delapsus in hostis.*

> He spoke, and suddenly (for satisfactory replies were not given him)
> he realised that he had fallen into the lap of the enemy.
>
> <div align="right">(Verg. <i>Aen.</i> 2.375–6)</div>

The audience of the monoglot *Aeneid* cannot know that Androgeos had
spoken Greek to the Trojans. They are given a clue, however, when Aeneas
uses a Greek nominative participle in the indirect statement following
his speech (*sensit … delapsus*); this reveals Androgeos' inner thoughts
through the syntax of his native language.[18] Aeneas then obscures the
response of the Trojans. It is impossible to know how, or indeed if, they
replied, but their incomprehensibility reveals Coroebus and his men to
be enemies. Androgeos and his men are promptly killed, and the episode is capped by Coroebus dressing himself in Androgeos' armour, in
a deliberate bid to further the confusion between Greek and Trojan. For
a brief moment the Trojans triumph through misunderstanding. Then,
in the very next scene, Coroebus is faced with the disastrous image of
Cassandra's capture.

If *Aeneid* 2 is the book in which Cassandra's voice is missed, *Aeneid* 3 is
the book in which her prophetic gift is fully squandered and dissipated.
The book shows the Trojans groping for some sense of purpose and direction, after failing to understand Cassandra's basic – but vague – instruction to 'go west'. This failure reduces them to blindly following the
minimalistic utterances of a series of prophets, each one of whom refines
the predictions of the last in a fragmented refashioning of Cassandra's
broad vision. Cassandra's miscommunication has opened a space for other
prophets to offer their voices, with Anchises as interpreter and Aeneas as
narrator further scattering the authority of the message even as they seek
to pin it down.

The disparate prophetic utterances in *Aeneid* 3 are only marginally
more comprehensible to the Trojans than was Cassandra's speech. The
first obscure 'divine instructions' (*auguria diuum*, 3.5) on the shores of
Troy encourage the Trojans to build boats, in which they sail to Thrace
and thence to Delos. On Delos the king Anius presides over an unusual

---

[18] Feeney (2015) 17–44 expands on the rarity of references to foreign language use in epic, but reminds
us of Virgil's reference to the *ora sono discordia* (*Aen.* 2.423) following soon after this episode.

prophecy that comes in the form of a voice sounding directly from Apollo's temple. It tells the Trojans: *antiquam exquirite matrem* – 'seek your ancient mother' (3.96). This prophecy is no less baffling to the Trojans for the fact that it is not ventriloquised by a mortal prophet. Anchises steps in to interpret the phrase, *ueterum uoluens monimenta uirorum* – 'unrolling the records of ancient ancestors' (3.102).[19] This description of 'unrolling' or 'turning over' a narrative echoes Jupiter's preamble to his prophecy to Venus in the first book of the epic, where he claims to reveal (and performatively enact) the mysteries of the future with a similar movement: *uoluens fatorum arcana mouebo* – 'unrolling the secrets of the fates I will set them in motion' (1.262).[20] In both episodes the participle *uoluens* evokes the image of reading a scroll. This visual effect will have been strengthened by the literary imprint of Naevius' Anchises, whom Venus had given 'books containing the future' (*libros futura continentes*, Naev. fr. 9 Strzelecki) in the *Bellum Punicum*. In *Aeneid* 6, too, Anchises will perform a kind of reading (*legere*, Verg. *Aen.* 6.755) of the parade of heroes.[21] Feeney connects this characterisation of Anchises as an interpreter of prophetic scrolls to the role of the *quindecimuiri*, the Roman priests who translated the oracles found in the Sibylline Books.[22] This mediating role is certainly central to Anchises' characterisation throughout the *Aeneid*, and an early hint that these prophecies *en route* are not just harking back to Cassandra's visions, but looking forward to the visions of the Sibyl.

The problem is that despite Anchises' game attempt to translate the voice at Delos, he fails. The Trojans dutifully follow his guesswork and sail to Crete, where they settle briefly before being struck down by a plague. At this point Aeneas is visited by his Phrygian *penates* in a dream, and told that the Trojans should be heading to an ancient land. Before they mention that the country is called *Italia* by its inhabitants, they note: *Hesperiam Grai cognomine dicunt* – 'the Greeks call it by the name Westernland' (3.163). It is not immediately clear why these Phrygian gods, even sent by the Greek Apollo, would feel concerned to add this detail about the Greek

---

[19] For the oddity of the prophecy at Delos see Barchiesi (1994) 439: 'Delos, incidentally, is emphatically not a place of normal mantic activity.' Paschalis (1986) offers more on the importance of Delos and the Sibyl.

[20] Kennedy (1997) 48.

[21] Oliensis (2004) describes how a 'masculine scene of writing and reading, at which the Sibyl is but a silent spectator, resolves the disarray of the Sibyl's leaves into the legible, teachable verse line of Roman history of 6.754–5' (42).

[22] Feeney (1991) 111.

name for Italy.[23] When Aeneas tells his father of his dream, Anchises moves to correct the initial reading he gave on Delos: *agnouit prolem ambiguam geminosque parentis* – 'he recognised that the offspring was ambiguous and the parentage twofold' (3.180). The language of this retraction is packed full of 'double' meanings: it alludes to the twofold stock of the Trojans, confirms that it takes both a Greek and a Latin linguistic perspective to properly encompass this new land, and embraces the ambiguous nature of the previous prophecy and its various possible interpretations.

Cassandra returns to the picture in the course of Anchises' self-correction; her prophetic skill is rehabilitated through the clarification granted by the *penates*. According to Anchises' recollection, Cassandra used the same combination of Greek and Latinate names that the Phrygian *penates* had produced in Aeneas' dream. The disparate prophecies of the Trojans' goal are becoming more focused through a shared multilingualism – or, at least, what Aeneas narrates in terms of a shared multilingualism:

> *tum memorat: 'nate, Iliacis exercite fatis,*
> *sola mihi talis casus Cassandra canebat.*
> *nunc repeto haec generi portendere debita nostro*
> *et saepe Hesperiam, saepe Itala regna uocare.*
> *sed quis ad Hesperiae uenturos litora Teucros*
> *crederet? aut quem tum uates Cassandra moueret?*
> *cedamus Phoebo et moniti meliora sequamur.'*

> Then he remembers: 'Son, battered by the Trojan fates:
> Cassandra alone sang of such events.
> Now I remember that she predicted that these things were
>   destined for our people
> and often named Hesperia, often the Italian realms.
> But who would believe that the Trojans would come to the
>   shores of Hesperia?
> Or whom then could Cassandra, the visionary, convince?
> Let us give in to Phoebus and, informed as we now are, seek
>   a better future.'   (Verg. *Aen.* 3.182–8)

Still without quoting the prophet's words, keeping her at the remove of an indirect statement, Anchises rearticulates Cassandra's prophecies with belated comprehension. Now he strips away the semantic uncertainties of her original speech, as he turns what had been an inspired act of prophecy

---

[23] Macrobius (*Sat.* 1.3.15) and Servius (on *Aen.* 1.530) both feel compelled to explain exactly how the Greek term influenced the name Hesperia for Italy and, ultimately, Spain. According to Macrobius 6.1.11, in the first book of his *Annales* Ennius wrote *est locus, Hesperiam quam mortales perhibebant* – 'there is a place, which mortals used to call Hesperia' (*Ann.* 20 Skutsch).

into a banal act of memory: *tum memorat ... repeto ...* (3.182–4).[24] In the process Anchises not only undercuts the words that had meant so little to him in the past, but he proceeds to go over Cassandra's head to gesture towards the god who had caused the confusion in the first place: Apollo (*cedamus Phoebo*, 3.188). He confidently moves on; with his hortatory conclusion that invites the Trojans to seek 'better things' (*meliora*, 3.188) he looks to pursue not just better outcomes but also, perhaps, better prophecies.

From now on Cassandra's voice is thoroughly scattered. One case makes the point clearly. A prophecy she had uttered in Lycophron's *Alexandra* claimed that the Trojans would have discovered their homeland when they found themselves eating their tables. At that point Cassandra says, rather vaguely, that they will be 'reminded of an ancient prophecy' (Lycoph. *Alex.* 1252). The *Aeneid* plays on the vagueness of this reminder in its reworking of the prophecy's delivery. Roman writers had already variously attributed the prophecy to different figures, including the oracle of Zeus at Dodona and a Greek sibyl from Asia Minor.[25] Virgil has Helenus mention it (Verg. *Aen.* 3.394), but he assigns the main delivery of the prophecy to the leader of the Harpies, Celaeno, whom Virgil describes as *infelix uates* – 'an unlucky visionary' (3.246), and who describes herself as *maxima Furiarum* – 'the greatest of the Furies' (3.252). Both references, to a seer and a Fury, evoke through Celaeno the characterisation of Cassandra in earlier texts; Virgil is deliberately sustaining the prophecy's connection with Cassandra, even as he erases her from his text.[26] Later the prophecy's origins will be even more demonstrably misremembered. When in *Aeneid* 7 Ascanias notices that the Trojans have eaten the bread on which their food had been placed, Aeneas quotes Anchises delivering the original prophecy.[27] This 'nod' on Virgil's part is, in fact, a pointed deletion of Celaeno as author, just as Cassandra had been deleted when Virgil assigned her prophecy to Celaeno in *Aeneid* 3.[28]

---

[24] Aeneas fails to grasp the same prophecy when he 'hears' it from Creusa at 2.781. Hexter (1999) 73 makes the connection.
[25] Takács (2008) 62; Parke (1988) 75. The attribution to Dodona was found in Varro, according to Servius, and in Dionysius of Halicarnassus, while the attribution to either the Erythraean or Marpessian Sibyl is also found in Dionysius of Halicarnassus (the text is uncertain).
[26] Hardie (1991).
[27] Murgia (1987) 52.
[28] In another case Virgil takes the prophecy of Lycophron's Cassandra concerning the portent of the sow with her litter, which was supposed to mark the spot of Alba Longa (Lycoph. *Alex.* 1255–60). In the *Aeneid* it forms part of Helenus' prophecy (Verg. *Aen.* 3.390–3) and is later picked up by the river Tiber (8.42ff.).

Juno, perhaps appropriately, signals the final obliteration of Cassandra's voice in the lead-up to the Sibyl's arrival. She sends Iris, disguised as Beroe, to stir up the Trojan women to burn the ships in *Aeneid* 5. There Iris creates a maliciously fictional 'quotation' of Cassandra:

> *nam mihi Cassandrae per somnum uatis imago*
> *ardentis dare uisa faces: 'hic quaerite Troiam;*
> *hic domus est' inquit uobis.'*

> For the image of Cassandra seemed to offer me
> blazing torches in a dream: she said, 'Seek Troy here;
> this is your home.' (Verg. *Aen.* 5.636–8)

Though the symbolism is fitting for Cassandra (the torches, the boats, the identification of a new home for the Trojans), her appearance in a dream is not the normal mode of her prophetic speech, and is the first clue that Iris is distorting Cassandra's voice. So too is the straightforward message contained within direct speech; the very clarity of expression is another sign of Iris' deceit.[29] Yet, in one further twist, it transpires that Cassandra's value as a prophet still lurks behind this artificial image. Understood retrospectively (as Anchises has shown) Cassandra's words are always proven truthful, and Iris' fiction is no exception to the rule. The women *will* make Sicily their home, another Troy, when their disaffection induces Aeneas to leave them behind with Acestes. The prophecy Iris has invented in Cassandra's name inspires the Trojan women to reach for, and attain, its fulfilment. This performative dimension within speech that is characterised as prophetic will echo through the Roman successors to Cassandra's voice.

Helenus, Halfway

In the *Agamemnon* and other Cassandra-inspired Greek texts, temporal, spatial and communicative shifts were mapped and connected by images of fire kindled from fire. The image is no less potent and polysemous in the *Aeneid*, particularly in Aeneas' description of the fall of Troy.[30] Fire both literal and symbolic presages the ultimate fall of Carthage, and the flames of Dido's funeral pyre guarantee the queen's slow-burning curse, as well as providing an immediate visual signal to the anxious but uncertain

---

[29] For Lelièvre (1971), Iris' deceit is revealed because her impersonation implies what is impossible: that a mortal like Beroe would ever have believed Cassandra.

[30] Knox (1950) notes that Virgil's predilection for sustained metaphor is shared by Aeschylus. On the connection between the *Aeneid* and the *Oresteia* more generally see Hardie (1991). See further Morgan (1998) 190–2.

Aeneas as he sails away (5.1–7). Further flames play around the temples of Iulus (2.681–6), Lavinia (7.71–80) and Augustus on Aeneas' shield (8.680–1), still hinting at violence but also marking out the privileged destiny of those who will be pivotal in founding or nurturing Rome and its urban predecessors, Alba Longa and Lavinium. In these last cases the fire is a strange portent that requires careful interpretation: it is a purely symbolic fire that does not burn, indicating rather than enacting the problematic violence running through the history of Rome's rise.

These different kinds of fire in the *Aeneid* all respond to the imagery of Troy falling into flames and the streams of Greek narrative that are produced in the aftermath of the disaster, but they are now attached to the multiple cities that will take over from Troy as the focus of Roman mytho-history. The narrative of the *Aeneid* itself is structured through its protagonists experiencing, describing, cursing or prophesying the rise – and sometimes fall – of Troy, Carthage, Rome and all the smaller settlements in between. As Cassandra's sweeping prophecy of a journey to Hesperia has been scattered among the voices that guide the Trojans haphazardly from city to city, so the beacons that used to lead her narrative from Troy to Greece are now replaced by the flames of several individual cities by whose fortunes Rome marks her own development and survival.

Sicilian Acesta was tagged as another Troy by Iris, but Greek Buthrotum is an earlier and more pronounced case of a replica Troy, a recreation of the city in both name and form (3.334–6, 349–51).[31] The episode set at Buthrotum forms the emotional climax of Aeneas' narrative to Dido in Carthage, and sits at the mid-point of Aeneas' six-book journey across the Mediterranean. The pivotal role of this city is marked not just by its central placement in the narratives of both Virgil and Aeneas, but also by the behaviour of its inhabitants, who shuttle between past and future. They look to the past through the city's construction and funeral rituals, which maintain the population's ties to ancient Troy and the events of *Aeneid* 2, and to the future through Helenus' prophecy, which is focused on helping Aeneas reach Italy in *Aeneid* 6.[32] This tension appears to be gendered too, with Andromache's grief and longing providing further grist for the argument that in the *Aeneid*, 'where women tend to cling to origins, men are oriented toward ends'.[33] Yet when it comes to inspired prophetic

---

[31] Hershkowitz (1991) and Hardie (1993) 14–18.

[32] On *Aeneid* 3 and the past see Quint (1982) and Bettini (1997). For more connections between *Aeneid* 3 and 6 see Hershkowitz (1991) and Bright (1981).

[33] Oliensis (1997) 303; Smith (2005) 71–7.

speech it is women who are, if anything, the sex that is primarily 'oriented toward ends', and Helenus' characterisation does little to counterbalance this identification.

Virgil's Helenus owes debts to the central male prophets of Greek literature, Homer's Tiresias and (especially) Apollonius' Phineus.[34] However, the temptation to align Helenus exclusively with his male predecessors obscures the fact that his prophetic voice does not fit neatly into the normal male/female patterns of prophecy. Helenus is positioned partway across the Mediterranean and one step along the route traced by the Trojans from *Aeneid* 2 to *Aeneid* 6. Alert to his transitional status, Helenus acknowledges, just as Cassandra had done in Lycophron's *Alexandra*, that his knowledge will cede in time to the prophecies of the Sibyl at Cumae. Helenus cements his place within the genealogy of Apollo's female prophets, sandwiched between the voices of Cassandra and the Sibyl. In addition to this, Helenus, like Laocoon, is a brother of Cassandra. Cicero notes this family connection, marking it through the traditional association of sign-reading with masculinity, and inspiration with femininity: 'Did not Priam, the king of Asia, have both a son, Helenus, and a daughter, Cassandra, who could prophesy [*diuinantes*], the one by means of sign-reading [*auguries*], the other by divine inspiration and excitation of the mind [*mentis incitatione et permotione diuina*]?' (Cic. *Div.* 1.88). Yet the prophetic skills of Virgil's Helenus are not gendered according to the norms identified by Cicero. Helenus' characterisation as a *uates* (Verg. *Aen.* 3.358) plays with both domains of prophecy, masculine sign-reading and feminine inspiration. Helenus' inspiration is not even tempered by the blindness that offsets the unusual visionary skills of male prophets like Tiresias and Phineas.

When Aeneas first addresses Helenus, the hero praises his wide-ranging prophetic abilities. Aeneas mentions Helenus' familiarity with Apollonian tripods and bay leaves, as well as the stars and the songs and flight of birds (3.359–61). Then, when Aeneas comes to making a specific request of the prophet, he invites the application of more modest skills, asking for an interpretation of the oracles he had received earlier in the book. Here Aeneas seems to be expecting Helenus to behave like Anchises; that is, as a pious and intelligent, but flawed, interpreter.[35] Instead Helenus delivers yet one more prophecy to add to the collection in *Aeneid* 3, in a voice that is initially

---

[34] For a thorough discussion see Horsfall (2006) 233–7, including Circe and Tiresias; Nelis (2001) 38–44 addresses Phineas.

[35] Hershkowitz (1991) 69 discusses how Aeneas' interaction with Helenus anticipates his consultation of Anchises in *Aeneid* 6.

described as that of a divinely inspired prophet (*canit diuino ex ore*, 3.373), then later as that of a friend (*ore … amico*, 3.462), and combines new and useful (if limited) information with a straightforward clarity of expression. As he proceeds with his advice to Aeneas, Helenus demonstrates a flexibility and knowingness in his prophetic style that suits his own peculiarly indeterminate prophetic position, and in some ways anticipates that of the Cumaean Sibyl herself.[36]

Through his carefully regulated inspiration, Helenus makes explicit the problems in the fragmented prophecies of *Aeneid* 3. In his opening words he acknowledges the fact that inadequate amounts of information are being conveyed to the Trojans, through his apologetic admission that he will not be able to share as much as he would like:

> *Nate dea (nam te maioribus ire per altum*
> *auspiciis manifesta fides; sic fata deum rex*
> *sortitur uoluitque uices, is uertitur ordo),*
> *pauca tibi e multis, quo tutior hospita lustres*
> *aequora et Ausonio possis considere portu,*
> *expediam dictis; prohibent nam cetera Parcae*
> *scire Helenum farique uetat Saturnia Iuno.*

> Son of a goddess (for there is obvious proof that under greater portents
> you are travelling over the deep; thus the king of the gods lays out
> the fates and rolls out the alternatives, from these the course
>   of events unfolds),
> a few things, out of many, so that you may wander the
>   welcoming waters
> more safely and so that you are able to lay anchor in an Ausonian port,
> I will lay out in spoken words; for the Parcae forbid Helenus
> to know the rest and Saturnian Juno prevents him from speaking.
>   (Verg. *Aen.* 3.374–80)

Helenus begins by casually referring to the several 'greater portents' (*maioribus … auspicibus*, 3.374–5) that exist outside his speech (perhaps with a deliberate echo of Anchises' exhortation, *meliora sequamur*, 3.188). The emphasis here is not on sign-reading exactly, for the portents under consideration remain vague, but Helenus is speculating on the indications of Aeneas' broader destiny as if he were an interpreter in the mould of Anchises, as Aeneas had initially expected.[37] This detached beginning

---

[36] On the peculiar self-consciousness of all sibylline prophecy see Lightfoot (2007) 10, 14.
[37] The phrase *maioribus … auspicibus* is problematically ambiguous. Does it refer to the portents that mark out the greater leader, i.e. Aeneas (as opposed to Anchises), which would explain why

permits Helenus to ponder not just the fragmentation of prophecies and portents, but also the splintering of authority behind them. At first he suggests that individual destinies are shaped by Jupiter, but the king of the gods' control over the fates and their 'alternatives' or 'twists and turns' (*uices*, 3.376) is placed at a further distance by the actual 'course of events' (*ordo*, 3.376). Helenus refuses to uncomplicate the murky partnership between Jupiter and fate. Then, when he moves to outline the parameters of his own prophetic speech, Helenus explains that he will have to limit the information he conveys, blaming both the Fates (the Parcae) and Juno for this unsatisfactory situation. This is an unusual alignment of forces indeed, and an unnecessary one at that: why would Juno need to silence Helenus if he does not even know the material she wishes him to suppress?[38] In emphasising the limits to his prophetic intelligence, as well as its confused origins, Helenus appears to be struggling with shortages of meaning, rather than the excesses that dog Cassandra's prophecies. The theme returns when Juno reappears in Helenus' speech, in his insistence that the Trojans must cultivate her worship at all costs. Helenus drives home this message with an appeal to his hybrid prophetic authority, referring both to his intellectual capacities and his possession by Apollo:

> ... *si qua est Heleno prudentia uati,*
> *si qua fides, animum si ueris implet Apollo ...*
>
> ... if Helenus as prophet has any knowledge,
> any trustworthiness, if Apollo fills his mind with the truth ...
>
> (Verg. *Aen.* 3.433–4)

Even at the end of his prophecy Helenus concludes by reminding Aeneas once again how constrained his speech has been: *haec sunt, quae nostra liceat te uoce moneri* – 'these are the things that my voice is permitted to teach you' (3.461).

Helenus acknowledges that he is short-changing Aeneas in his prophecy, and counters this by trying to rescue Aeneas from the limitations of his successor, the Sibyl. In order to do this he offers a full explanation of her mode of divination, drawing attention to the different kind of fragmentation inherent in her problematic *sortes*:

Helenus' prophecy is addressed to him rather than his father? Or is it supposed to indicate an oracular hierarchy? See Horsfall (2006) 287.

[38] For discussion see O'Hara (1990) 26–31, who (like Horsfall) writes more in terms of what Helenus actually left out: specifically, the death of Anchises. O'Hara leans on the role of Juno throughout Helenus' prophecy, and on the role of malign interference in prophecy in the *Aeneid* more generally. See also Nelis (2001) 40.

huc ubi delatus Cumaeam accesseris urbem
diuinosque lacus et Auerna sonantia siluis,
insanam uatem aspicies, quae rupe sub ima
fata canit foliisque notas et nomina mandat.
quaecumque in foliisque descripsit carmina uirgo
digerit in numerum atque antro seclusa relinquit:
illa manent immota locis neque ab ordine cedunt.
uerum eadem, uerso tenuis cum cardine uentus
impulit et teneras turbauit ianua frondes,
numquam deinde cauo uolitantia prendere saxo
nec reuocare situs aut iungere carmina curat:
inconsulti abeunt sedemque odere Sibyllae.

When you have been brought to this place and have approached
    the Cumaean city
and the immortal lakes and Avernus rustling with woods,
you will see a frenzied visionary who deep in the cave of a cliff
sings the fates to come and commits symbols and words to leaves.
Whatever prophecies she has copied down on the leaves
she lays out in order and leaves them shut away in a cave:
they stay in place, unmoved, and do not fall out of order.
But then, when with the turn of a hinge a light wind
has struck them and the open door has tossed the delicate foliage
    into confusion,
then she never cares to collect them up, return them to their place,
    or reconnect
the prophecies flying around the empty rock:
her petitioners go away unadvised and hate the home of the Sibyl.
                                  (Verg. *Aen.* 3.441–52)

Helenus' prophetic skill places him uncertainly between inspired visionary, sign-reader and amateur interpreter. His Cumaean Sibyl is no more easily pigeonholed. She is frenzied (*insana*, 3.443) and yet also a writer who initially organises her texts with thoughtful deliberation. Within the very same line she sings and produces writing (*fata canit foliisque notas et nomina mandat*, 3.444).[39] According to Helenus, the Sibyl's output is, like his own, limited by an external force, to which the Sibyl fatalistically concedes with as little protest as Helenus. The difference is that the Sibyl does at least grasp and record the meaning of the prophecies in the first

---

[39] Servius marks this unusual versatility by glossing it and even amplifying it: *tribus modis futura praedicit: aut uoce aut scripto aut signis* … – 'she predicts the future in one of three ways: either in speech or in writing, or through signs …'. This contains an echo of Heraclitus' description of Apollo at Delphi as one who 'neither speaks nor conceals, but gives a sign'. See Crippa (1998) 164.

place; it is only at the moment of attempted reception, when the door is opened, that complications arise.

The fragmentation of the Sibyl's prophecies begins with the distinction Helenus draws out between the oral and written elements of her craft. This antithesis (or maybe symbiosis), according to Lowrie, responds to the role of the Augustan poetic *uates* as much as to the prophetic *uates* within Virgil's text: the poetics of Virgilian 'sung' epic and the role of the Sibyl as a proxy for Virgil are designed to explore the kinds of political authenticity and authority to which Virgil and his peers were laying claim. The metapoetic dimension also stretches into the realm of poetic composition and generic affiliation.[40] The genius of the inspired Sibyl, the *insana uates*, is tempered by the artful technique of her compositional style.[41] Her prophecies, which are also poems (*carmina*, 3.445) are written carefully in order (*in numerum*, 3.446) and left for a while, just as Horace advises in his *Ars Poetica*:[42]

> ... *nonumque prematur in annum,*
> *membranis intus positis: delere licebit*
> *quod non edideris; nescit uox missa reuerti.*

> ... let it be put away until the ninth year,
> with the papers stored inside: it is possible to delete
> what you have not published; a voice once sent out cannot be
>   called back.   (Hor. *Ars P.* 388–90)

For Virgil's Sibyl, as for Horace's poet, the writing process prolongs an author's exclusive relationship with his or her material, and Helenus draws this out with overtones of Callimachean slightness: the wind is 'light' (*tenuis ... uentus*, Verg. *Aen.* 3.448) and excites the 'delicate foliage' (*teneras ... frondes*, 3.449). (Cassandra's potentially expressive but bound hands were interestingly also described as 'delicate': *teneras ... palmas*, Verg. *Aen.* 2.406.) The Sibyl is not interested in producing the single work of continuous poetry

---

[40] Lowrie (2009) esp. 1–23.
[41] Oliensis (2004) extends the discussion on *sedes* as 'position within the line' (cf. Hor. *Ars P.* 257) and the pun on *Sibylla/syllaba*.
[42] Helenus also has a claim to Horace's approval:

> *ordinis haec uirtus erit et uenus, aut ego fallor,*
> *ut iam nunc dicat iam nunc debentia dici,*
> *pleraque differat et praesens in tempus omittat.*

> This is the strength and charm of order, unless I am mistaken,
> that one says now what needs to be said now,
> and one postpones and leaves out much for the moment.   (Hor. *Ars P.* 42–4)

condemned by Callimachus in his *Aetia* (*hen aeisma diēnekes*, Call. *Aet.* fr. 1.3, cf. *nec … iungere carmina curat*, Verg. *Aen.* 3.451), nor does she care that the larger body of people who come to consult her leave unsatisfied. When Helenus introduces the Sibyl's written poetry with the slightly dismissive *quaecumque carmina* ('whatever prophecies', 3.445), he perhaps even echoes Catullus' offering to Cornelius Nepos of his neoteric book: *quidquid hoc libelli | qualecumque quidem* ('a little thing of a book, whatever kind of thing it is', Catull. 1.8–9). Catullus' friend Nepos was engaged in writing a universal history of the Italian peoples; Helenus' Sibyl is a Catullan poet writing scraps of Roman history in prophetic reverse.[43]

The elitism of the Sibyl's written compositions may be combated, Helenus suggests, by a demand for more straightforward oral communication: *precibus oracula poscas | ipsa canat uocemque uolens atque ora resoluat* – 'ask, with prayers, | that she herself sing the oracles and willingly release her mouth and voice' (3.455–6).[44] This describes more than a simple shift from writing to speech. It will be a return to the performance mode of epic song (*canat*), even while the 'releasing' of the Sibyl's mouth and voice in Latin (*resoluat*) actually hints at a movement from the constraints of poetic form to something less elevated, maybe something as fluent and 'released' (*solutus*) as prose.[45] Above all, the exchange that will be successful is exactly that: an exchange. It requires that the petitioner make clear demands (*poscas*) and that the Sibyl willingly cooperate in response (*uolens*). This is the very relationship that was gestured to and then avoided in the monolithic, if multilayered, *Alexandra*.

The role of question and answer is key to the Sibyl's adoption of Cassandra's voice within the *Aeneid*, and to Virgil's adoption of the Sibyl's voice. The ability to reply to confused interlocutors, to respond to questions in a way that intends to clarify an original statement, is a form of self-translation and a continued assertion of authorial control. In the case of Cassandra, no matter how many times she revises her statements, her spoken word remains doomed to misunderstanding until events reveal the misapprehensions of her listeners. The process of self-translation appears to complicate, rather than clarify, her speech, compressing as it does too many layers of interpretation into her voice at once. Even when

---

[43] Tibullus reinforces this development of the Sibyl into a more scholarly historian, by turning the historical *chartae* of Nepos (Catullus 1.6) into Sibylline scripts: *sacrae chartae* (Tib. 2.5.17).

[44] This is another echo from Lycophron: ἔλυσε χρησμῶν … αἰόλον στόμα (Lycoph. *Alex.* 3–4). See also the discussion earlier in this chapter of Aeneas' silencing of Cassandra as she opens her mouth at Verg. *Aen.* 2.246–7, with Lycoph. *Alex.* 28.

[45] *OLD* s.v. *solutus* 8 and 9.

her prophecies are reformulated by others, such as Lycophron's messenger (λέξω τὰ πάντα, Lycoph. *Alex.* 1) or Virgil's Anchises (*tum memorat*, Verg. *Aen.* 3.182), her voice continues to baffle. The Cumaean Sibyl demonstrates a similar layering of interpretative processes in her prophecies, though they are less compressed than in Cassandra's case. Rather than all taking place within one human body, the layers of interpretation extend, in stages, from the Sibyl's voice into her writing. The priestess is inspired, writes what she knows, then loses control over what she has written. Her prophecies pass into the realm of question and answer in the form of the Sibylline Books which, detached from their author, are translated instead by the Roman priesthood that had responsibility for them. The fixity and longevity of the Sibyl's writing allows for a regular revisiting of her prophetic text without further input from the prophet herself, a process that will continue to foreground potential misreading until its narrative is correctly 'realised'.[46] Helenus' solution to the danger of misreading is to encourage Aeneas to make the Sibyl respond to him directly, reclaiming her words from the contingencies of reception by generations of Roman priests. The Sibyl's voice will, for once, transcend the confusion imposed on her prophecies by their customary mediation through time and text. It remains to be seen whether this form of self-translation proves any more effective, or any less desperately creative, than Cassandra's attempts to self-translate.

Vaticination, from Voice to Text

Two books of tragi-erotic drama and epic games intervene before the reader of the *Aeneid* learns whether Helenus' suggestion will prove useful to Aeneas. This chapter will pause, too, to offer a glance at the background to the character of the Cumaean Sibyl that Virgil builds in *Aeneid* 6. Her voice emerges as a composite from a web of mythic figures, an extended family of Greek sibyls.[47] At the same time, a historical artefact also lurks behind her characterisation, in the form of the corpus of Sibylline Books that were housed at Rome. In those books a Greek sibylline voice of mysterious origins had already been firmly marshalled towards the interests of

---

[46] Fowler (1997b) 269 discusses 'the stress on the indeterminacy of reception implied by the story of the Sibyl's *folia* – the implication that whatever fixity a text might possess, it disappears in the very act of reading which is necessary to give it meaning'. See also Spentzou (2002) 17.

[47] On the oddity of the singular/plural construction of the sibyl(s) see Crippa (2004) 99. On the Greek origins of sibyls see Parke (1988) 1–22; Potter (1990a) 102ff. As Lightfoot (2007) vii warns, 'the Sibylline tradition is a story of constant invention and reinvention'. For further accounts of the tradition surrounding the appearance of the Sibylline Books see Potter (1990b); Orlin (1997) 76–115; Buitenwerf (2003) 92–123; Keskiaho (2013).

the Roman state, and the production and use of the books were of particular interest to Augustus.

A sibylline voice makes an early appearance in Greek culture via Plutarch, who claims to quote Heraclitus:

> 'The Sibyl, with crazed mouth [*mainomenōi stomati*]', according to Heraclitus, 'uttering unpleasant, undecorated and uncouth material, reaches with her voice through a thousand years, because of the god'.
>
> (Plut. *De Pyth. or.* 397a)

If the quotation is entirely attributed to Heraclitus (there is some debate over how many of the phrases are supposed to belong to him, and how many to Plutarch), readers are encouraged to believe that from very early on in the tradition the Sibyl is inspired to the point of frenzy and speaks through a god's influence, though not *as* a god.[48] There is no suggestion that this figure speaks in response to being consulted; she appears to burst out with her horrific material unprompted. In these several respects, as Lightfoot points out, the traditional sibylline voice was always closely connected to that of Cassandra: the relative autonomy of both voices contrasts with that of the Pythia at Delphi, whose utterance was delivered in the first person of the god Apollo himself, and mainly in response to specific questions by petitioners. As Parke puts it, a sibyl (and Cassandra) is a 'clairvoyante' rather than a 'medium'.[49] However, Heraclitus includes a vital element in his sibyl's characterisation that offers a challenge to Cassandra's prophetic model. Unlike Cassandra, whose life is, if anything, compromised by her vocal powers, this sibyl's voice grants her unusual longevity. She is not immortal, but her thousand years of influence transcend conventional mortality. She is an 'extra-temporal figure – almost a disembodied voice'.[50]

In the next chapter of sibylline history this extra-temporality gains a new element: Heraclitus' single sibyl multiplies. With the emergence of a group of prophetic women, each individually characterised as a sibyl, the voice of a single woman was extended further still through time and space, even as it was split between bodies in a way that expanded the fragmentation experienced by Cassandra's voice. Meanwhile, the bodies of textual material that circulated as 'Sibylline Oracles' offered a physical testimony

---

[48] Maurizio (2013) makes an excellent case for Heraclitus' own identification with the style and authority of the Pythia's voice.

[49] Parke (1988) 10.

[50] Lightfoot (2007) 4 offers an excellent summary of the tradition, from the earliest mentions of 'the' Sibyl in Heraclitus, Aristophanes and in Plato's famous grouping of her with the Pythia in the *Phaedrus*.

to these women's scattered voices; their material durability mirrored the women's longevity.[51] Varro, the great scholar of Virgil's age, attempted to codify the texts and their legendary authors as far as they were understood in the first century BCE. Varro acknowledged that the term 'sibylline' encouraged people to assume that the oracles were written by a single figure, but went on to explain that the single figure of early Greek myth was part of a canon of ten women, associated with different places around the Mediterranean, and in some cases with specific prophecies and specific collections of oracles.[52] By Varro's time a single point of sibylline authority had dissipated, while the catalogue of prophetic material had proliferated.

In fact, from very early in their tradition the prophecies of Greek sibyls had been associated with wandering and with writing. This becomes a point of particular interest to those working within the Roman tradition. Tibullus, for example, mentions the story of the Tiburtine Sibyl, who managed to bring her lots through the river Anio without them getting wet (Tib. 2.5.69–70). Livy has a tantalising reference to the arrival of an unnamed sibyl in Italy, who is anticipated by the appearance of the prophet Carmenta and her son Evander:

> At that time Evander, a refugee [*profugus*] from the Peloponnese, ruled that area more by influence than by formal command, a man revered for the miracle of writing [*uenerabilis uir miraculo litterarum*], a novel thing for men uneducated in the arts [*rudes artium*], and even more revered for the divinity accredited to his mother Carmenta, whom those people had admired as a prophet [*fatiloquam*] before the arrival of the Sibyl in Italy.
>
> (Liv. 1.7.8)

In this narrative, characteristics of sibylline prophecy are transferred to the family who lay the groundwork for a sibyl's arrival: Carmenta's prophetic abilities combine with her son's familiarity with writing to grant Evander unusual authority. Servius (*ad Aen.* 6.321) notes that the Cumaean Sibyl settled at Cumae after leaving Erythrae, and Lightfoot discusses other accounts of the Erythraean Sibyl's wanderings, drawing attention to the way in which this element of her characterisation overlaps with that of Homer.[53] The association with writing specifically is most fully probed, however, in the Roman legend of how the Sibylline Books came to the

---

[51] Parke (1988) 8–9.
[52] Lactant. *Div. Inst.* 1.6.7. Parke (1988) 32 notes that at least two of the sibyls that Lactantius goes on to attribute to Varro's list, the Libyan and Cimmerian, seem to be purely literary fictions (of Euripides and Naevius, respectively).
[53] Lightfoot (2007) 12.

notice of the Roman people under the rule of Tarquinius Superbus, or Tarquinius Priscus.[54] Here is Lactantius relating Varro's account:

> [Varro says that] the seventh sibyl is the Cumaean called Amalthea, who is called Herophile or Demophile by others, and she brought nine books to the king Tarquinius Priscus and demanded three hundred *philips* for them and the king, turning them away at such a huge price, laughed at the woman's craziness [*mulieris insaniam*]; in the sight of the king she burned three books and demanded the same price for those that remained; Tarquinius thought the woman all the crazier [*multo magis insanire mulierem putauisse*]; but when she continued to ask the same price having burned three more books, the king was moved to buy the remaining books for three hundred golden pieces; the number of these oracles was later increased when the Capitol was rebuilt, because from all the Italian and Greek states, particularly from Erythrae, oracles bearing the name of whichever sibyls were collected and brought to Rome ...   (Lactant. *Div. Inst.* 1.6.10–11)

An old woman invites the king to purchase nine books at great expense, and on being rejected burns three of the books. The offer is made and rejected again, but after three more books are burnt the king relents and purchases the final remaining three for the original sum demanded. Varro apparently identified the old woman as the Cumaean Sibyl herself: in this narrative, then, the books are produced, passed on and destroyed, all at the whim – apparently crazy as it is – of their author. Only much later are they supplemented by the written oracles of other sibylline figures.

The legendary acquisition of the Sibylline Books by an Etruscan king of Rome initially involved more texts being lost than gained, and this cherishing of a sibylline voice through evanescent writings was sustained in the way the Roman state came to store and use the Sibylline Books, particularly during the first century BCE. According to Varro, all the collections of sibylline oracles other than the Sibylline Books circulated freely through time and space. Most were collated from the Hellenistic era on and variously updated and added to over the next centuries; to this day there remain considerable remnants of these collections. By contrast, the Sibylline Books were generally (and increasingly) inaccessible to the general public, such that there is now virtually no evidence of their contents.[55]

---

[54] Satterfield (2008) summarises the sources: Dion. Hal. *Ant. Rom.* 4.62; Lactant. *Div. Inst.* 1.6; Servius *ad Aen.* 3.445, 6.72 and 6.336; Lydus *de Mensibus* 4.47; Isidore of Seville *Etymol.* 8.8; Zonaras 7.11; Pliny *NH* 13.88; Solin. 2.16f.; Aulus Gellius *NA* 1.19. Parke (1988) draws the link with the Pisistratidae and their acquisition of oracles to keep on the Acropolis of Athens; there is every reason to believe that Greek oracles were circulating in material form from at least the late sixth century BCE.

[55] Phlegon of Tralles reproduces an oracle about the birth of a hermaphrodite, which he dates to 125 BCE, and an Augustan oracle apparently encouraging the celebration of the *ludi saeculares* (*FGrH* 257 fr. 36.X.A–B and fr. 37.V). See Potter (1994) 71.

The only men allowed to access the text were members of the priesthood of *quindecimuiri sacris faciundis*, the sign-readers of the Sibyl:

> The prophecies [*carmina*] of all these sibyls are well-known and shared [*et feruntur et habentur*], except for those of the Cumaean Sibyl, whose books are kept secret [*occultantur*] by the Romans and cannot be examined by anyone except the *quindecimuiri*. (Lactant. *Div. Inst.* 1.6.13)

Yet the Sibylline Books were, if anything, less firmly fixed than the Sibylline Oracles, and their historical production and destruction echoed the legend that told of how they initially fell into the hands of the Romans. The books were burned in the destruction of the Capitoline temple of Jupiter in 83 BCE, at which point, as Varro explains, another collection was assembled.[56] Under Augustus a different kind of book-burning took place. He had already appropriated the Sibylline Books by transferring them from the Capitol to his complex on the Palatine (probably soon after the dedication of the temple to Apollo, and certainly before the composition of the *Aeneid*). According to Suetonius, Augustus also condemned and had burned a whole range of prophetic texts of dubious authenticity, claiming that only the Sibylline Books had any validity:

> Whatever prophetic books [*fatidicorum librorum*] in Greek or Latin were in public circulation under authorship that was either anonymous or inconsequential [*nullis uel parum idoneis auctoribus*], he burned over two thousand of them collected from all over the empire and kept only the Sibylline Books, and even from these he made a selection; and he placed them in two golden bookcases under the pedestal of Palatine Apollo.[57]
>
> (Suet. *Aug.* 31.1)

In addition to this, Dio notes that in 18 BCE Augustus ordered that the worn text of the Sibylline Books be copied out afresh, insisting that the job be done by the *quindecimuiri* themselves, in order to keep the contents secret.[58]

The process of reconstituting the corpus of Sibylline Books was crucial, then, but it went unscrutinised because of the secrecy in which the

---

[56] For Scheid (1998), this episode shows that the Romans were less exercised by the actual contents of the books than they were by the question of who controlled them.

[57] Suetonius appears to assign all of this to 12 BCE but, *pace* Santangelo (2013) 137, he cannot be entirely right. See Parke (1988) 149 n. 11 and Miller (2009) 240, esp. n. 118. The reference at *Aeneid* 6.71–4 (to the placement of the Sibyl in the temple that 'Aeneas' will dedicate to Apollo) must allude to the placement of the Sibylline Books on the Palatine at an earlier date, as must elements of Tibullus 2.5. See Murgatroyd (1994) 164. It is harder to date Augustus' restoration of the cave of the Sibyl at Cumae.

[58] Dio 54.17.2–3. Parke (1988) 209–10; Santangelo (2013) 3. Potter (1990b) 476 n. 14 argues against the secrecy of the books, but see Orlin (1997) 81–5.

texts were kept. The material objects were treasured, but the contents were strictly limited to the intermediary figures whose role only served to emphasise the very obscurity and inaccessibility of the original words. Tibullus, in a poem composed to celebrate the induction of his patron's son, Messalinus, into the priesthood of *quindecimuiri*, rather oddly invites Apollo to help Messalinus understand the Sibyl's 'singing':

> *Phoebe, sacras Messalinum sine tangere chartas*
> *uatis, et ipse precor quid canat illa doce.*

> Phoebus, allow Messalinus to touch the sacred pages
>   of the seer, and teach him yourself, I pray, what she sings.
>   (Tib. 2.5.17–18)

As Apollo interacts with Messalinus, the Sibyl is virtually erased: her pages are touched, but in the following line her implied voice (*quid canat*, 2.5.18) is transmitted directly from god to *quindecimuir*.[59]

In *De divinatione*, Quintus Cicero describes the priesthood of *decemuiri* (originally *duumuiri*, later, maybe under Sulla, expanded to *quindecimuiri*) as Roman *interpretes* – 'interpreters' or 'translators', who transformed the cryptic Greek poetry of the Sibylline Books into Roman ritual prescriptions for specific situations:[60]

> ... and since they believed that the divination of frenzy [*furoris diuinationem*] was contained chiefly in the Sibylline verses, they decreed that ten men should be chosen from the state to be interpreters [*interpretes*] of those verses.   (Cic. *Div.* 1.4)

The *quindecimuiri* turned Greek mythic material into the stuff of Roman history and politics. As Parke notes, 'the difference from the Sibyls elsewhere in the Greek world was that the Cumaean prophetess became an official state institution, who responded to enquiries instead of issuing spontaneous revelations'.[61] Through the translating priesthood and the application of her voice to answering questions, the Cumaean Sibyl begins to look less like the frenziedly emoting Cassandra and her sister sibyls

---

[59] Murgatroyd (1994) 177–8.
[60] Struck (2004) 167 rightly connects the role of the *quindecimuiri* to that of the interpreting *prophētēs*. Scheid (1998) reconstructs as far as possible the process by which the books were consulted, revealing the considerable amount of reading and paperwork involved, and Février (2004) discusses how the priests transformed the language of Greek prophecy into that of Roman ritual. Tibullus 2.5 adds colour to the picture.
[61] Parke (1988) 93. Note also Bartsch (2016) on the implicitly gendered aspect to the translation of Greek into Latin, which is mirrored in the modification of the female prophet's words by Roman male translators.

around the Mediterranean, and rather more like the responsive Pythia at Delphi.

The multimedia and multiply mediated figure of the Cumaean Sibyl therefore synthesises different modes of prophecy, and writing sits at the heart of her versatility. The codification of the Sibyl's ambiguous prophecies meant that her words could be endlessly redeployed by those questioning or interpreting her, leaving her eternally relevant – but also diminishing her authorial control over time. In the second book of *De divinatione*, Cicero questions the validity of the Sibylline Books on the very grounds of their obvious 'written-ness', which (he argues) casts doubt on their authenticity as products of inspiration. Cicero argues that the acrostics in the Sibylline Books are a case in point: *hoc scriptoris est, non furentis, adhibentis diligentiam, non insani* – 'this is the work of a writer, not of a raving prophet, of someone carefully applying themselves, not someone insane' (*Div.* 2.112).[62] Indeed, Cicero anticipates Virgil's Helenus in describing the artistry of the Sibyl's oracles; he finds that they are written *magis artis et diligentiae quam incitationis et motus* – 'more by means of technique and meticulous work than by inspiration and divine possession' (2.111). The very act of writing even seems to challenge the Sibyl's sex. When Cicero describes the myth of an inspired prophet he allows the Sibyl to be a woman: *Sibyllae uersus obseruamus, quos illa furens fudisse dicitur* – 'we pay careful attention to the verses of the Sibyl, which she is said to have poured out when raving' (2.110). Two sentences later, as Cicero notes the suspicious vagueness that characterises the books' predictions, a masculine relative pronoun emerges:

> *callide enim, qui illa composuit, perfecit, ut, quodcumque accidisset, praedictum uideretur hominum et temporum definitione sublata. adhibuit etiam latebram obscuritatis, ut eidem uersus alias in aliam rem posse accommodari uiderentur.*

> For whoever composed these, he did so very cleverly, so that whatever happened, it would seem to have been predicted but with the specific references to people and places removed. The author added the subterfuge of obscurity, so that the same verses could seem to be matched to different events. (Cic. *Div.* 2.110–11)

It appears that 'authorship' of the Cumaean Sibyl's oracles fluidly transcends language, number and even gender.

---

[62] See Connor (2000) 58. *Contra* Cicero, however, acrostics were exactly what the envoys were told to look for when searching for oracles to be included in the new collection, to replace the Sibylline Books burned in 83 BCE (Dion. Hal. *Ant. Rom.* 4.62, apparently following Varro). See Buitenwerf (2003) 101 n. 34 and Potter (1990b) 473 n. 5.

When Virgil set up Aeneas' meeting with the Sibyl at Cumae he was following a literary precedent stretching at least as far back as Naevius' *Bellum Punicum* and creating a 'magnificent bricolage' in the process, but he was also introducing into his epic a figure that stood for an extraordinary piece of writing – a Roman institution.[63] The Sibylline Books were destroyed by fire in myth and in history, and freely acknowledged to have been re-compiled, but they were nonetheless treasured as if they were a static material collection; they were secret, but appropriated for the service of the whole Roman state (and Augustus in particular); they were confined to specific parts of Rome, but flaunted a broad Greek mythic and linguistic heritage; and they were supposedly a product of one woman's frenzied inspiration, but in practice were both collected and read *post facto* by a revolving cast of translators whose interpretative strategies were applied to a text that was more 'authoritative' than 'authored'.[64]

The Sibylline Books appear to have been conceived of as a canon or anthology, to which multiple authors had unobtrusively contributed. Creative reconstructions of the oracles in the poetry of authors such as Virgil might, then, have been perceived as comparable to the production of the books' real contents.[65] The vacuum created by the secrecy of the contents must have added to the Sibylline Books' appeal for poets. This silence offered a space for radical recreation that could be styled as 'translation'. The space had initially been occupied by the priesthood of *quindecimuiri*, but their role might also be adopted by poets; these poets' work would mirror that of the *quindecimuiri*, in that they would produce a Roman version of a Greek prophecy. At the same time, in composing oracles that posed as the actual words of the Sibyl, epic poets were betraying the function of the *quindecimuiri*, for they were claiming to

---

[63] Horsfall (2006) 479. For the earlier tradition see Waszink (1948), who argues that Virgil is combining the Cimmerian Sibyl from Naevius (which explains the *katabasis* since she lived by Lake Avernus), the Cumaean, and what he identifies as the Trojan Sibyl from Lycophron and Tibullus 2.5. However, the chronological relationship of Tibullus and Virgil is debatable, as is the identification of Tibullus' sibyl. We have already seen, too, that Lycophron's sibyl is Trojan only insofar as the Cumaean Sibyl has Ionian 'ancestry' through her identification with the Erythraean Sibyl, and Cairns (1979) 75–6 argues convincingly that the prophet who speaks to Aeneas in Tibullus 2.5 is also the Erythraean, proto-Cumaean, Sibyl. See also Gowers (2005) 174. Some assume that Naevius' Cimmerian Sibyl had already been assimilated with the Cumaean Sibyl by the time Virgil was writing. There were also traditions of other prophecies received by Aeneas, such as the dream that Cicero found in Fabius Pictor's account (*Div.* 1.21.43).

[64] On the anonymity of the Sibylline Oracles (not Books) see Lightfoot (2007) 54.

[65] The anonymity of the Sibylline Books' authorship parallels the case of the Muses, about whom Spentzou (2002) 21 suggests: 'it is this very shapeless collectivity which lends the Muses' existence to appropriation, as dearth of features prompts and provokes the imagination of poets and critics to fill in the gaps'.

expose the 'secret' hexameters themselves. Tibullus gives this a tongue-in-cheek spin when he records his sibyl's production of 'hidden' prophetic hexameters in a pentameter line of his own poetry: *abdita quae senis fata canit pedibus* – 'the hidden fates that she sings in six-foot rhythm' (Tib. 2.5.16). The poets' delicate relationship with the priestly function neatly fits the re-emergence in the Augustan era of poets' claims to stand in the position of the religio-poetic *uates*. Newly valorised, the term no longer evoked the crude versification and charlatanism of soothsayers, but real religious and cultural authority.[66] Horace, the collector of lyric metres and modes, described himself as *Musarum sacerdos* – 'priest of the Muses' (Hor. *Carm.* 3.1.3): he was a poet whose songs were based on a Greek paradigm but pulled from a silent Latin space – *carmina non prius | audita* – 'poems never heard before' (3.1.2–3) – and destined for a privileged place on the Palatine at Rome.[67] Virgil fashions himself as a priest of, and surrogate for, the Cumaean Sibyl: he reconstructs her powerful voice from obscure scraps of Greek oracular text. In doing so he aligns the silent authority of the Sibylline Books with the loud authority of the *Aeneid* itself, and positions both as equally deserving of their move towards canonisation in the Palatine complex at the heart of Rome.[68]

Responsorial

The translation of the Sibylline Books by the *quindecimuiri* meant that the uncontrolled first person voice of a 'Cassandran' sibyl could be channelled, via a written recording of the voice, into the production of purportedly useful ritual responses. Much of the tension in Virgil's presentation of his Cumaean Sibyl 'live' in *Aeneid* 6 comes from the uncertainty over whether she is still playing the part of a rambling Cassandra, or whether she has become the responsive institution of the Sibylline Books; whether she speaks to the moment, or writes for the interrogation of posterity. Within this tension also lies the question of Virgil's own poetic role in negotiating

---

[66] Newman (1967) 51 investigates the Augustan uses of the word. O'Hara (1990) 176–84 gives a full bibliography and a lucid summary of the term's use and importance: 'The Augustans saw in the unreliability of the *uates* and his associations with deception and illusion a fitting representation of the basic ambiguities and complexities of their work and the troubled political situation of the times' (181). Hardie (1986) 57 offers a more straightforward reading of 'the Augustan romantic construction of the *uates*-concept, in which the poet seeks to compensate for the banal reality of his middle-class status by conforming himself to primitive models of omniscience and omnipotence'. Hinds (1998) 52–63 addresses Ennius' vilification of the *uates* at *Ann.* 206–10 Skutsch.
[67] Horsfall (1993) 62.
[68] Zetzel (1983).

the delivery of her prophecies. Is he quoting a Cassandra or translating a Sibylline text? Does he compose the sibylline *ambages* or 'ambiguities' as a fellow poet, or does he explain them as a scholarly or priestly reader? The composite character of Virgil's Sibyl frames these sets of alternatives.

The introduction of the Cumaean Sibyl in person in the sixth book of the *Aeneid* is prefaced by suggestions that her voice will be relatively unmediated in the scenes to come. In contrast with *Aeneid* 3, layers of narrative control are now being stripped away. In *Aeneid* 3, Aeneas had offered his own selective narrative of events, anxiously hovering in North Africa and dwelling on scenes that took place when he was blundering around the Mediterranean. Within that narrative, Helenus' priestly voice had placed the description of the Sibyl at one further remove. By contrast, the author-narrator Virgil is back in immediate control at the beginning of *Aeneid* 6, steering the Trojans straight to their arrival on the 'Hesperian shore' (Verg. *Aen.* 6.6) which, within a few lines, Aeneas is already confidently calling *Italia* (6.61). The instruction to seek out the Sibyl, delivered by Helenus and repeated by Anchises in a vision (5.735–6), is now turned into narrative event signalled from the very first lines in the book, as Aeneas makes straight for the Sibyl's domain:[69]

> at pius Aeneas arces quibus altus Apollo
> praesidet horrendaeque procul secreta Sibyllae,
> antrum immane, petit, magnam cui mentem animumque
> Delius inspirat uates aperitque futura.

> But dutiful Aeneas seeks out the heights over which great Apollo
> exerts his influence, and the far-off hidden realms, the enormous cave,
> of the terrifying Sibyl, whose great mind and spirit
> the Delian visionary inspires and to whom he reveals the events
>   to come.   (Verg. *Aen.* 6.9–12)

Prophetic power promises to be more direct too. Where in *Aeneid* 3 prophecies were scattered among a range of prophets (with the term *uates* applied to Cassandra, Celaeno, Helenus and the Sibyl herself), here at the beginning of *Aeneid* 6 the authority of the *uates* is found in Delian Apollo himself. The application of the term to a divinity is rare.[70] In fact, virtually every other of the many uses of the term in the rest of the book are applied to the Sibyl, the god's devotee. This early assimilation of the inspiring god and inspired priestess appears to present a more systematic and reliable

---

[69] The setting clearly evokes that of the sibyl in Lycophron's *Alexandra*: 'the grim abode of the Sibyl | covered over by the hollowed-out cave of her shelter' (Lycoph. *Alex.* 1279–80). See Chapter 3.
[70] The *OLD* unconvincingly glosses it as a reference to Apollo's role as mouthpiece of Zeus.

alignment of divine and mortal voices. At the same time, the extension of vatic slipperiness all the way up to the god of inspiration himself hints that the potential for ambiguity and miscommunication now infects the divine as much as the mortal domain.

The next sign that creative constructions of the past and the future are being more firmly harnessed in *Aeneid* 6 comes from another builder of narrative lines: the sculptor Daedalus. Through Daedalus' work, Apollo's influence begins to make itself felt over the artistic efforts of Cumae. His power is established by the material construction of a temple devoted to him, in thanks for Daedalus' safe arrival in Cumae after escaping Minos' rule in Crete. The ekphrastic images on the temple offer a respite from the details of the story of the Trojans' journeying, but they also expose some of the questions of prophetic authority being faced by Aeneas, the Sibyl and Virgil himself.[71] Daedalus' work in honour of Apollo engages with questions of how to represent events through time via a visual medium, how to integrate (auto)biographical experience with artistic creativity and how to showcase the productivity of misunderstanding.

Daedalus had begun by devoting to Apollo his wings, which were already loaded with significance: products of his ingenuity, part of his body and a potential for communication between landmasses but one that proved fatal for a son who had failed to comprehend the danger in their power. The wings had carried Daedalus from Crete to Italy, signalling a move from east to west that mimics, even in its fantastical form, the west-ward travelling of Aeneas.[72] If this were not enough to mark Daedalus' Cretan mythology as paralleling elements of the Trojan story, Daedalus then begins his sculptural work by portraying the death of a certain Androgeos. Ostensibly the son of Minos, the name will strike an attentive reader as being the same as that of a character last seen in Aeneas' narrative in *Aeneid* 2 (and discussed above). That Androgeos was the warrior who exposed the linguistic difference between Greeks and Trojans. The evo-cation, bizarre in its own right, is reinforced by the curious periphrasis used to describe the figure of the Minotaur: *mixtumque genus prolesque*

---

[71] The discussion here is indebted to Fowler (1991), who notes that 'Precisely because ekphrasis represents a pause at the level of narration and cannot be read functionally, the reader is possessed by a strong need to interpret' (27). Putnam (1987) outlines the parallelism between Virgil and Daedalus (and Aeneas). Fitzgerald (1984) points out that this is the only Virgilian ekphrasis in which the subject matter is mythical rather than historical, and in which the artist's biography is depicted. He subtly explores how this illustrates Virgil's interest in the disjunction between myth and history, and his argument underpins my suggestion that Virgil is also exploring the sort of prophetic options that are available in the one, as compared with the other.

[72] Fitzgerald (1984) 52.

biformis – 'of mixed heritage and a double-formed offspring' (6.25). This line in turn echoes Anchises' description of the Trojan origins in *Aeneid* 3 (also discussed above): *prolem ambiguam geminosque parentis* – 'the offspring was ambiguous and the parentage twofold' (3.180).

The themes of doubling and confusion are taken into artistically self-conscious territory in the description of Daedalus' sculpture of the Minotaur's maze.[73] Daedalus is not presented as sculpting the maze itself, with all the confusions he built into the original labyrinth, but rather as replicating the solution to the maze, the way out:

> *Daedalus ipse dolos tecti ambagesque resoluit,*
> *caeca regens filo uestigia.*
>
> Daedalus himself reveals the deceptions and ambiguities of the building,
> guiding blind footsteps with a thread.   (Verg. *Aen.* 6.29–30)

The artist demonstrates a commitment to solving the loci of misunderstanding in his own work, at least under certain circumstances. He does so by foregrounding the power of the *filum*, the guiding thread. The word signals controlled movement through space and time, while also engaging with the mythic imagery of mortal lifespans as they are drawn out by the Fates, as in the case of Lausus in *Aeneid* 10: *extremaque Lauso | Parcae fila legunt* – 'the Parcae take up the final threads of Lausus' life' (10.814–15). A similar semantic overlap can be found in the Fates' spinning in Catullus 64, his own ekphrastic Cretan maze. Daedalus' *filum* operates across reality, metaphor and representation, not unlike Cassandra's beacon fire: it begins as a real thread that rescues Theseus; evokes the thread of Theseus' life, saved as surely by the puppeteer Daedalus as by the Fates; and then resolves into a solid material image of the original thread, carved out as an artistic tribute to the presiding deity, Apollo. The verb the narrator uses to describe Daedalus' 'revealing' or 'releasing' his maze's tricks and deceits (*dolos tecti ambagesque resoluit*, 6.29) is no less loaded. Rarely found before Virgil's time, its usage here is surely a deliberate echo of the verb Helenus used to describe the way in which the Sibyl must 'release' her mouth in her own *ambages* in *Aeneid* 6 (*ora resoluat*, 3.456). Daedalus and the Sibyl are both valuable but tricksy guides through the uncharted spaces of land, air and underworld, as well as through broad expanses of mythic and historical time. They are also competitive; the Sibyl asserts her own priority by snapping at Aeneas for lingering in front of Daedalus' artwork: *non hoc ista sibi tempus spectacula*

---

[73] Putnam (1987) 176 discusses Daedalus' relationship with hybridity, and Fitzgerald (1984) 54 the narrative significance of the repeated return to labyrinth imagery.

poscit – 'this is not the moment for such images' (6.37).[74] Both artists offer
the key to understanding their riddles by moving out of their original mode
of delivery (labyrinthine architecture, writing on leaves) and into a new one
(carving of narrative friezes, direct speech). Before their artistic productions
stands Aeneas, now neither *auctor* nor *actor*, but *auditor*, 'listener', and *spectator*, 'viewer'; the avid consumer of their words and images.[75] Behind them
sits the master engineer, Virgil, using his own text to mediate the words and
images and overlapping characteristics of them all.

Virgil's most famous description of his own artistry in terms of material
culture came in his projection of a poetic temple at the beginning of
Georgics 3, and it is yet one more temple to Apollo that completes the
set-up for his Sibyl's verbal craft in *Aeneid* 6: the temple to Apollo on the
Palatine, built by Augustus.[76] In the *Aeneid* the reference to this temple
shows that the Sibyl's biography is as important to her skill and control
over time-defying narratives as Daedalus' biography is to his. At the Sibyl's
instigation, Aeneas prays to Apollo, Hecate and the Sibyl herself, including
the following promises:

> 'tum Phoebo et Triuiae solido de marmore templum
> instituam festosque dies de nomine Phoebi.
> te quoque magna manent regnis penetralia nostris:
> hic ego namque tuas sortis arcanaque fata
> dicta meae genti ponam, lectosque sacrabo,
> alma, uiros. foliis tantum ne carmina manda,
> ne turbata uolent rapidis ludibria uentis;
> ipsa canas oro.' finem dedit ore loquendi.

> 'Then to Phoebus and Trivia I shall dedicate a temple
> of solid marble as well as festival days named after Phoebus.
> A magnificent sanctuary awaits you in our realm:
> for here I shall lay your predictions and hidden fates
> spoken to my people, and I shall appoint chosen men as priests,
> dear protector. Only I beg that you do not commit your
>   prophecies to leaves
> lest they are disturbed and fly away, play things for the swift winds;
> I beg that you actually sing.' He stopped his speech.
>   (Verg. *Aen.* 6.69–76)

[74] Barchiesi (1997a) 274.
[75] If Smith (1997) 180 offers the correct interpretation of *perlegerent* (*Aen.* 6.34), Aeneas is also a *lector*, 'reader', of Daedalus' script.
[76] On the echo of *Georgics* 3 see Miller (2009) 140–1.

This historically loaded passage prophesies the future of the Sibyl's prophecies, and in doing so highlights the unusual relationship between the character of the Sibyl and the text that she will become. The prayer promises the establishment of religious spaces and activities that were either Augustan in origin or had long been part of Roman tradition, beginning with a reference to the construction of Apollo's temple on the Palatine (dedicated in 28 BCE) and the *ludi Apollinares* (established in 212 BCE, according to instruction from the Sibylline Books, among other oracular sources), with hints at the approaching *ludi saeculares* in 17 BCE.[77] It then goes on to mention the settlement of the Sibylline Books at Rome, and the creation of the priesthood of *quindecimuiri*.

Throughout this passage Aeneas is clearly synthesising the prophet and her books. When he tells the Sibyl that 'a magnificent sanctuary awaits you' (*te quoque magna manent … penetralia*, 6.71), 'you' must refer to the actual body of sibylline prophecies that is destined to live beneath the statue to Apollo in his temple on the Palatine, the very temple that the hero has just mentioned.[78] Aeneas goes on to create further syntheses of sibylline body and text through the ambiguity of the terms *sortes* and *fata*, both of which can refer to prophecies (particularly written prophecies, in the case of *sortes* or 'lots') or to an individual or people's destiny. Aeneas' reference to the Sibyl's *sortes* is modified by a loaded possessive: when Aeneas describes *tuas sortis* (6.72) he is talking of both 'your written oracles' and 'your destiny'.

It is clear that the Sibyl of *Aeneid* 6 is more bound up in her own prophecies than Helenus' portrait of her in *Aeneid* 3 had suggested. Far from writing and then ignoring her texts, she is, like Cassandra, a prophet who ultimately cannot escape her own fates, at least when she is corralled into Rome's temples and aligned with the city's imperial destiny. Writing and speech are not separable aspects of the Sibyl's prophecies. Aeneas slides from addressing the Sibyl in bodily form (*te*, 6.71) to describing her prophecies in a way that seems to refer to their written form: the term *sortes* (6.72) implies this materiality, as does Aeneas' promise to 'place' (*ponam*, 6.73) these items in the temple a thousand years later. At the same time, when Aeneas mentions the 'hidden fates' (*arcana fata*, 6.72) contained within these prophecies, he refers to their original articulation by the Sibyl herself (*dicta meae genti*, 6.73). The prophecies are conceptualised as having been vocal utterances, once upon a time.[79] At the end of his prayer, it is to this

---

[77] See Horsfall (2013) and Austin (1986) ad loc. for details and bibliography, with Merkelbach (1961) and Miller (2009) 97 on the possible overtones of the secular games.

[78] Miller (2009) 97.

[79] Compare Helenus' *expediam dictis* – 'I will lay out in spoken words' (3.379).

'original' vocal utterance that Aeneas returns, demanding just such a performance for his own immediate needs: *foliis tantum ne carmina manda …
ipsa canas oro* (6.74–6).

Virgil sustains the tension between the Sibyl's body, speech and writings
when he grants his readers a vivid description of the prophet's inspiration.
The process of the Sibyl's gradual submission to Apollo encircles Aeneas'
prayer, surrounding and contrasting with his promise to root her prophecies in the formal settings of Roman ritualised oracle reading. This Sibyl
is vitally alive and uncontrolled; her body makes the static rocks come
alive with their hundred mouths. Indeed, as she stands on the threshold of
her cave she offers one of the most powerful illustrations of a mortal body
channelling the inspiration of a god and passing it through to the very
earth on which she stands:[80]

> *excisum Euboicae latus ingens rupis in antrum,*
> *quo lati ducunt aditus centum, ostia centum,*
> *unde ruunt totidem uoces, responsa Sibyllae.*
> *uentum erat ad limen, cum uirgo 'poscere fata*
> *tempus' ait; 'deus ecce deus!' cui talia fanti*
> *ante fores subito non uultus, non color unus,*
> *non comptae mansere comae; sed pectus anhelum,*
> *et rabie fera corda tument, maiorque uideri*
> *nec mortale sonans, adflata est numine quando*
> *iam propiore dei. 'cessas in uota precesque,*
> *Tros' ait 'Aenea? cessas? neque enim ante dehiscent*
> *attonitae magna ora domus.' Et talia fata*
> *conticuit.*
> …
> *At Phoebi nondum patiens immanis in antro*
> *bacchatur uates, magnum si pectore possit*
> *excusisse deum; tanto magis ille fatigat*
> *os rabidum, fera corda domans, fingitque premendo.*
> *ostia iamque domus patuere ingentia centum*
> *sponte sua uatisque ferunt responsa per auras …*

The side of the Euboian rock is cut away to create a huge cave,
   to which one hundred wide entrances lead the way, one
      hundred mouths,
whence rush out the same number of voices, the responses of the Sibyl.
They had arrived at the threshold, when the virgin said:
'It is time to ask your fate. The god! Look, the god!' As she
      said this

---

[80] On her body's permeability see Fowler (2002) 149.

in front of the doors suddenly her expression, her complexion,
    fluctuated,
her hair sprang out wildly; but her chest was panting,
and her wild heart swelled with frenzy, and she seemed to grow larger
making inhuman noises, breathed into by the rapidly approaching
spirit of the god. 'Do you delay making your vows and prayers,
Trojan Aeneas?' she said. 'Do you delay? Not before then will the
    great mouth
of this divinely struck house open up.' And so saying
she was silent.
    ...

But no longer suffering Phoebus, the visionary went Bacchic-wild
in the huge cave, as if she were trying to shake the great god
from her chest; all the more did he keep pressing on against her
maddened mouth, conquering her wild heart, and he shaped
    her by force.
And finally the hundred huge mouths of the house spontaneously
    opened up
and brought the responses of the visionary through the air ...
                                   (Verg. *Aen.* 6.42–54, 77–82)

In these famous passages the Sibyl passes through a two-stage process
of inspiration by Apollo. In the first passage her physical frame responds
to the initial onslaught of Apollo, who spontaneously begins his inspiration of the Sibyl without any encouragement from Aeneas beyond
his animal sacrifices. As the Sibyl responds to the vision of Apollo, her
symptoms evoke the physical responses to erotic love that Sappho suffers
in fr. 31, and which Catullus suffers again in his translation of that poem.
In those lyric pieces the presence of a perceived god (φαίνεταί μοι κῆνος
ἴσος θέοισιν | ἔμμεν' ὤνηρ – 'that man appears to me to be equal to the
gods', Sappho *LP* fr. 31.1–2; *mi par esse deo uidetur* – 'he appears to me
to be equal to a god', Catull. 51.1) triggers a poetic reconstruction of the
ripple of physical effects caused by the poets' desire for the object of
their love, their inspiration. These descriptions pivot around the actions
of either the poet or the 'god' watching and listening to their beloved
(ὑπακούει ... ἴδω – 'he listens ... I see', Sappho *LP* fr. 31.4 ... 7; *spectat
et audit* – 'he sees and hears', Catull. 51.4), and around the poet losing
control over speech and body (ἀλλ' ἄκαν μὲν γλῶσσα †ἔαγε – 'but my
tongue has silently splintered', Sappho *LP* fr. 31.9; *lingua sed torpet* – 'but
my tongue is frozen', Catull. 51.9).

The connection between these scenes goes deeper. In all three poems
the triangular dynamics of inspirer (Apollo, beloved), inspired (Sibyl,
poet) and invested spectator (Aeneas, love rival) grow in complexity and

potency: in each poem the reader is challenged to reconstruct the scenario as it develops. The fragmenting body of the inspired poet or prophet remains central to the action in all cases; the language of erotic physicality reinforces the argument that the Sibyl is undergoing a sexualised experience, one that becomes all the more apparent in the second stage of her inspiration.[81] The layers of lyric influence also complicate the gender roles represented by Virgil's scene of prophecy. Catullus' heterosexual co-opting of Sappho's lesbian desire is itself co-opted by the Sibyl, who reasserts female authorship but is now inspired (or rather, coerced) by a male divinity. This is, as Spentzou and Fowler point out, a bold inversion of the paradigm whereby a male poet is inspired by a female muse or Muse.[82] In addition to this, the lyric poets set up a contradiction in which apparent physical decline belies taut control over the poetic medium and, particularly in Catullus' translation, in which the illusion of spontaneous performance is undercut by the complexity and polish of the poetry's form. The same tension between self-abandon and control underpins Virgil's Sibyl as she descends into inspired mania. Just as Catullus cannot be describing an unfiltered reality in his poetic replication of Sappho's (equally literary) desire, so the poetry-writing Sibyl cannot completely forget the Callimachean-Catullan learned skill that she has agreed to temporarily shelve. Another lyric poet would approve the implied combination:

> ... *ego nec studium sine diuite uena*
> *nec rude quid prosit uideo ingenium.*

> ... I do not see any good in bookishness without a divine spark
> or in uncultivated inspiration.   (Hor. *Ars P.* 409–10)

The second stage of the Sibyl's inspiration appears to push her prophecies further into the realm of the spoken word, exposing the function not of a lyric tongue, but of a prophet's raving mouth (*os rabidum*, 6.80). Here too, as with her abnormal lifespan and her existence as both woman and book,

---

[81] See Norden (1916) ad loc., Horsfall (2006) 478 and (2013) 117, with Fowler (2002).

[82] Spentzou (2002) and Fowler (2002) focus on the scene from slightly different angles. For Spentzou the scene constitutes an effacement of the Sibyl's voice: 'would it have made any difference if the prophecy had come out of the Sibyl's own mouth, in her own voice and words, according to Aeneas' request ...? ... has the text briefly opened up to the possibility of a distinctively female voice which, however, never slips through Apollo's and Virgil's text?' (18–19). Fowler is concerned about what the sexualised portrayal of the Sibyl means for a male poet: 'if the Sibyl's inspiration is like the poet's, and inspiration is figured as sexual assault, where does that leave the creative artist?' (149). Lightfoot (2007) 11 draws attention to some interesting features of the Sibylline Oracles in which their authorial voices seem to appropriate features of the Muses, and she points out (22 n. 110) that Plutarch (*Mor.* 398c) describes the Delphic Sibyl as originally reared by the Muses of Mount Helicon.

the Sibyl's body expands beyond normal parameters. As Virgil develops his description of the delivery of the Sibyl's prophecies, it becomes clear that her mouth is just one small part of the fantastic space she inhabits, for her cave possesses one hundred mouths (*ostia centum*). The words are repeated in ring composition at *Aeneid* 6.43 and again at 6.81, and appear once more towards the end of the book when the echo of the earlier phrases ironically undercuts the disingenuous poetic cliché to which the Sibyl resorts, when she claims that she could not list all the torments suffered in the underworld, *mihi si linguae centum sint oraque centum* – 'even if I had one hundred tongues, one hundred mouths' (6.625).[83] It is these one hundred mouths of stone, rather than the Sibyl's single mouth, that are twice described as delivering the prophetic 'responses': *unde ruunt totidem uoces, responsa Sibyllae* (6.44); *uatisque ferunt responsa per auras* (6.82). But will the multiplicity of mouths available to the Sibyl add to her powers of communication (as implied by her appeal to the 'hundred mouths cliché' in the underworld), or will they undermine her message by fragmenting it and threatening disorder, in the same way as do the leaves on which she writes?

The ring composition provided by the reference to her one hundred mouths introduces the actual prophecy of the Sibyl. The mouths tell of the trials awaiting Aeneas (*horrida bella* – 'dreadful wars', 6.86), and the skeleton of the story that Virgil will fill out in the following six books of epic poetry, as Virgil himself later claims: *dicam horrida bella* – 'I shall tell of dreadful wars' (7.41).[84] The prophecy turns out to be neither powerful nor fragmented. It lacks ambition or mystery, stretching no further than Aeneas' lifespan; even the hero notes that he has learned nothing new:

> ... *non ulla laborum,*
> *o uirgo, noua mi facies inopinaue surgit;*
> *omnia praecepi atque animo mecum ante peregi.*

---

[83] Gowers (2005); Hinds (1998) 35ff., 45. The first version of the expression comes in Homer (*Il.* 2.488–93), in which the narrator claims that ten mouths would not be enough to describe the entire multitude of Greeks, before he then launches into the catalogue of ships. It is then reignited by Ennius, Hostius, Lucretius and by Virgil once again in his *Georgics*. On openings before and after the action moves into the underworld, Oliensis (2004) offers a fascinating contrast between the Sibyl 'Deiphobe' and the mutilated 'Deiphobus' in the underworld, whose mutilation's 'extra' orifices produce a more cogent narrative.

[84] Doubtless it is true that the *horrida bella* promised by the Sibyl and by Virgil must have been interpreted by Augustan readers as a reference to the recent civil wars, too. See Miller (2009) 143–4.

... O virgin, not one of these labours
presents a novel or unexpected appearance to me;
I have anticipated everything and already endured it in my mind.
(Verg. *Aen.* 6.103–5)

The Sibyl's prophecy has proved as underwhelming for her interlocutor as Cassandra's entangled prophecies were for her audience.[85]

The Sibyl's prophetic words to Aeneas are blandly coherent not because they are vocalised rather than written, but because, as Virgil emphasises twice here, they are responses rather than spontaneous proclamations: *responsa Sibyllae* (6.44, 6.82; the term *responsa* is never used with reference to her prophecies in *Aeneid* 3). This is not a sibyl whose prophecies are wildly undirected or solipsistic, as they would be if they fitted the normal sibylline model. This is a sibyl who offers sensible answers, like the institutionalised Sibylline Books. Her first answer of this kind comes to Aeneas, the petitioner whose pious prayer promises the arrival of priestly translators who will enable further sibylline answers in the future. They will be able to turn her text back into voice – the 'hidden fates | spoken to my people' (6.72–3) – and to do so in a way that aims to correct the contingency of reception exemplified by her scattered leaves. Aeneas' promise, as oddly time-travelling as the Sibyl herself, means he cannot benefit from the process by which the later generations of *quindecimuiri* will read, translate and reformulate aloud the Sibylline Books for the benefit of all Romans. He can, however, receive an early demonstration of the translation process surrounding the Sibylline Books, performed by the Sibyl alone. She offers a response to the questions surrounding his own immediate fate, a response that is spoken in Latin, and mediated by the one hundred mouths that the prophet herself causes to open.

The Sibyl's prophecy, so pointedly spoken and so pointedly Latin, does not ignore her Greek heritage. In *Aeneid* 2 Androgeos had been the exception that proved the rule whereby epic, like tragedy, avoids representing foreign speech. The Sibyl's interactions with Aeneas make no mention of the fact that her preferred language is Greek, or that the 'hidden fates' of the Romans will be recorded in Greek. Her vocal prophecy helps to sustain this impression of a shared language. Virgil's Roman audience would doubtless have found it jarring to be presented with a scene of prophecies being read from a book in Latin hexameters, when the text was known to have been composed of Greek hexameters. A scene of reading might also have looked worryingly like a betrayal of the secrecy of the books, whereas a scene of inspired utterance offers more of a reconstructed aetiology of

---

[85] Lowrie (2009) 4.

their composition. Nonetheless, translation between Greek and Latin remains part of the Sibyl's story. Perhaps unsurprisingly, the Greek prophet emphasises Greek characters: *alius ... Achilles* – 'another Achilles' (6.89) will challenge the Trojans, and crucial help will come from Evander's Greek city (*Graia ... urbe*, 6.97) on the site of Rome. Also, in summarising the second half of the *Aeneid*, her prophetic narrative tells an Iliadic tale that echoes the Sirens' Iliadic narrative embedded in the *Odyssey*.[86] In other words, the Sibyl, who translates her own Greek for Aeneas, tells of Graeco-Trojan interactions to be faced by the hero as he settles in Italy, and Graeco-Latin interactions to be forged by Virgil in his Homerically inspired epic.

So, finally, the Sibyl's prophecy evokes Virgil himself, the visionary behind all the visionaries in *Aeneid* 6. Aeneas' interactions with the Sibyl force a woman with the lifespan of a recorded and carefully preserved text to revert to her 'original' voice for a single moment of prophecy – a limited prophecy for and about a hero with a limited lifespan.[87] Virgil crafts this move back through time, returning the Sibylline Books to their legendary author, and in the process turning the secret Greek writing into a straightforward Latin speech, like a *quindecimuir* delivering a controlled fragment of the Sibyl's voice. Virgil's act of translation has its own complications, though. Even if the Latin *speech* of the Sibyl avoids the charge that it is a direct transcription and revelation of the Sibylline Books' secret Greek oracles, the *text* that Virgil wrote and that sits before all its readers still exists in perennial defiance of Helenus' (and Aeneas') instructions that this prophecy is not to be written down. The oracles have indeed been translated back, one further time, onto the page.

Once the Sibyl's 'speech' is over, Virgil makes this point explicit:

> *Talibus ex adyto dictis Cumaea Sibylla*
> *horrendas canit ambages antroque remugit,*
> *obscuris uera inuoluens.*

> With such speech from her shrine the Cumaean Sibyl
> sings her terrifying ambiguities and bellows them back around the cave,
> wrapping the truth in obscurities.   (Verg. *Aen.* 6.98–100)

The Sibyl's meaning was not at all obscure, but Virgil rightly identifies her prophecies as *ambages* nonetheless. Their riddling aspect is found in

---

[86] On the Sirens' narrative, see Chapter 3.
[87] Following Jupiter's reference to his three years of settlement: *Aen.* 1.265–6.

the unusual mode of delivery and, linked, in the obscured authorship of the prophecy. Like Cassandra with her animal noises (twittering in Aeschylus' *Agamemnon*, barking at the end of Lycophron's *Alexandra*), the Sibyl bellows or 'moos' back (*re-mugit*, 6.99) in a reduplicated voice that mirrors the layers of vocal authority lying behind the Sibylline Books: the Apollonian inspiration, the myth of the Cumaean Sibyl's utterance through the mouths of her cave and the pronouncements of the *quindecimuiri*. The layers of sibylline writing and lost writing are exposed, too: the inscription on leaves, the nine books ruthlessly reduced to three during their sale to the Romans, then the various acts of compilation and augmentation, transcription and translation. If Jupiter's prophecy in *Aeneid* 1 was produced through an obliquely referenced act of unrolling a scroll and reading the book of the fates (*uoluens fatorum arcana*, 1.262), the Sibyl's prophecy in *Aeneid* 6 is an inversion of this. When Virgil describes her 'wrapping the truth in obscurities' (*obscuris uera inuoluens*, 6.100) it is because her oracular speech is being 'rolled up' in the textuality of books.[88] Are these the Sibylline Books, which make use of the 'subterfuge of obscurity' (*latebram obscuritatis*, *Div.* 2.111) that Cicero had condemned as a sign of the fraudulence of the Sibyl's words? Unlikely, for this episode is defined by the very fact that her words are spoken only once to Aeneas and *not* destined for the Sibylline Books. The book that wraps up the Sibyl's truth in obscurity is the same one that will tell the story she predicted for Aeneas: the *Aeneid* itself. As Katz has cleverly noticed, the many mouths contained within the story are also embedded in an acrostic in the text itself that occurs as the Sibyl's inspiration takes hold: A-B-E-O-O-S-O-S (Verg. *Aen.* 6.77–84) – 'I am transformed [*abeo*], a mouth [*os*], a mouth [*os*].'[89] Katz notes that 'it is Virgil who is the authorial force behind the visible, written acrostic'.[90] Virgil has taken prophetic obscurity away from the Sibyl, whose responsive voice maps so neatly and clearly onto the second half of the *Aeneid*, and instead he has invited his readers to find the rich obscurity buried in his own poetry. His written text, no less than the Sibylline Books, will reward careful – if imperfect – translation from the readers who come to it looking for answers.

---

[88] Cf. Virgil's address to the Muse: *et mecum ingentis oras euoluere belli* – 'and unroll with me the great outlines of the war' (9.528) and Ennius' rhetorical question: *quis potis ingentis oras euoluere belli?* – 'who can unroll the great outlines of the war?' (*Ann.* 164 Skutsch), discussed in Feeney (1991) 186.

[89] Katz (2013) 6–10, Katz's translations.

[90] Katz (2013) 9.

Sibylline Postscripts, from Text to Voice

From the silent scrolls of the Sibylline Books, Virgil resuscitated a speaking Sibyl whose authority and ambiguity he then channelled back into his own books. As is so often the case, a resistant early imperial response to the poem helps to reinforce and sharpen the point. Ovid has Aeneas revisit the Sibyl in *Metamorphoses* 14, a twisted version of *Aeneid* 6 that forms a substantial part of his 'little *Aeneid*'. Ovid uses this episode to reflect on how Virgil had co-opted the voice of the Cumaean Sibyl as an aetiology for the production of the Sibylline Books, and as an analogy for the production of his own Virgilian Books. In the process, Ovid shows how the Sibyl's biography, and particularly her longevity, could also help Virgil's successors to define their own position within the Roman epic tradition.[91]

There is barely a single speaker within Ovid's poetry who does not channel elements of the self-conscious and pseudo-autobiographical external narrator.[92] In the *Metamorphoses*, Ovid tends to take as his avatars characters, often women, who parade their meta-literariness.[93] Indeed, as characters' fluid forms in the *Metamorphoses* often pivot around a name, which stands as a clue to the character's latent identity or to his or her role as the paradigm or progenitor of a species, so Ovid chooses to highlight the stories of speakers, singers and writers who are pointedly named: Byblis in *Metamorphoses* 9, for example, or Canens in *Metamorphoses* 14.[94] Most famous is Echo in *Metamorphoses* 3. As Hinds has shown, in Echo's case the reader is explicitly being reminded that Ovid's layers of narration also represent layers of poetic influence, whose 'echoes' can be read in Ovid's own verses.[95]

Metapoetic prophets are peppered throughout Ovid's work: Ocyroe in *Metamorphoses* 2, Pythagoras in *Metamorphoses* 15 and, in close relation to his Sibyl, Carmentis in *Fasti* 1.[96] Cassandra, however, is as pointedly effaced

---

[91] On the 'successiveness' of Ovid's *Metamorphoses* in relation to Virgil's *Aeneid* see especially Solodow (1988) 136–56; Hardie (1993); Tissol (1993); Myers (1994) 98–104; Smith (1997).

[92] Keith (1992) dissects the complexities of a selection of Ovid's embedded narrators, and more general comments and bibliography can be found in Myers (1994) 61–94 and Wheeler (1999).

[93] Pavlock (2009).

[94] On identity and naming in the *Metamorphoses* see Von Glinski (2012) esp. 26–33.

[95] Hinds (1998) 8.

[96] See Livy's mention of her as Carmenta, the mother of Evander, discussed above. Ovid's Carmentis engages closely with the poetic dynamics of prophets' engagement with literary time: she anticipates in her prophecy the prophecies of Virgil's Sibyl, just as the younger (earlier) Cassandra of Greek literature had anticipated the later Cassandras of a previous literary period. Ovid's Carmentis also reflects on Virgil's inability to prophesy beyond his own period in time (as parodied by Auden's poem, 'Secondary Epic'): *talibus ut dictis nostros descendit in annos, | substitit in medio praescia lingua*

in Ovid's poetry as she is in Virgil's. Her absence from the *Metamorphoses* is no accidental parallel with the *Aeneid*, for where she is mentioned it is obvious that her scenes have been translated directly from her shadowy role in the *Aeneid*, rather than from any specific Greek source.[97] In the *Metamorphoses*, as in the *Aeneid*, she has no speech by which the reader may judge her linguistic ability. When she first joins the action, she is replaying the very scene in which Virgil had introduced her in *Aeneid* 2 (discussed above). Aeneas had described a dishevelled Cassandra being dragged away (*trahebatur passis ... crinibus*, Verg. *Aen.* 2.403–4), looking upwards in supplication, 'turning [*tendens*] her blazing eyes to the sky [*ad caelum*] in vain, | her eyes, for chains were binding her delicate hands [*teneras ... palmas*]' (2.405–6). In the *Metamorphoses* exactly the same features are highlighted – the dragging, the hair, the hands – and while Ovid allows Cassandra to gesture up to the heavens, her appeal is no less doomed to failure:

> ... *tractata comis antistita Phoebi*
> *non profecturas tendebat ad aethera palmas* ...

> ... dragged by her hair, Phoebus' assistant
> was stretching her hands, in vain, to the heavens ...
> (Ov. *Met.* 13.410–11)[98]

In Ovid's version of the story, it is again the assault by the lesser Ajax on Cassandra's body that triggers the disastrous narratives of return:

> *Naryciusque heros, a uirgine uirgine rapta,*
> *quam meruit poenam solus, digessit in omnes* ...

> And the hero of Narycia [Locri], because he raped the maiden
>   [Cassandra],
> spread among everyone the maiden's [Athena's] punishment that he
>   alone deserved ... (Ov. *Met.* 14.468–9)

In the *Aeneid*, it was Juno who had posited Cassandra as the reason for the ill-fated *nostoi* of the Greeks (Verg. *Aen.* 1.41); here in the *Metamorphoses*, Diomedes gives the explanation while he is justifying his decision not to help the Latins against the Trojan invasion. Once again, Cassandra's

---

sono – 'as she reached our times with these words, | her prescient tongue stopped mid-sentence' (Ov. *Fast.* 1.537–8).

[97] Though Curley (2013) 104 rightly points out the influence of Euripides' *Hecabe* and *Trojan Women* more generally in *Metamorphoses* 13. For another shadowy absence in the *Metamorphoses* see Hinds (2011) 10 on Oedipus in *Metamorphoses* 3 and 4, with bibliography at n. 10.

[98] Quotations from the *Metamorphoses* are from the edition of Tarrant (2004).

prophetic power is displaced in favour of a series of manipulations based on the symbolic power of her violated body, not her voice.

As in the *Aeneid*, too, the Cumaean Sibyl replaces Cassandra as the central prophetic figure of the Trojan narrative. This is a natural result of Ovid's decision to focus on the events of books 3 and 6 of the *Aeneid*, as he targets and magnifies Virgil's compressed episodes and elides the more elaborate ones.[99] The prominence of the Sibyl is marked all the more strongly by the almost total erasure of the underworld episode in which Anchises had escalated the prophetic voice in *Aeneid* 6. Yet Ovid's Sibyl does not operate in isolation. She appears as one voice in a cluster of programmatic stories that show Ovid excavating the *Aeneid* for 'other voices' that reflect on the power of speech, text and time.[100]

Directly before the appearance of his Sibyl, Ovid tells the bizarre story of Pithecusae, named, as the narrator explains, after its monkey (*pithēkos*) inhabitants (14.90). According to this myth, Jupiter was infuriated by the fraudulent speech of the Cercopians. As punishment he transformed them into liminal figures, into animals that look like humans. He shortened their limbs (14.95) and 'ploughed old women's wrinkles [*rugis ... anilibus*] into their faces' (14.96). Above all, he banished them to the island on which they now live, and stripped them of their language:

> *misit in has sedes nec non prius abstulit usum*
> *uerborum et natae dira in periuria linguae;*
> *posse queri tantum rauco stridore reliquit.*

> He sent them to this place, but not before he took away their
>   power of speech
> and the tongues that existed only to produce terrible lies;
> he left them just the ability to complain in a raucous shriek.
>   (Ov. *Met.* 14.98–100)

This is a story of verbal trickery capped with bodily constraint, physical decline and an existence that is both mortal and non-mortal; in this case, bestial. As such, it evokes several of the themes that are explored in the literature of sibylline utterance and inform the following episode.

After passing Pithecusae, Aeneas arrives at Cumae and enters the cave of the Sibyl, who is described as 'long-lived' (*uiuacis*, 14.104). From the start,

---

[99] See Myers (1994) 99 on Ovid's transformation of *Aeneid* 3 and 6, with bibliography.
[100] Myers (1994) 102–3. For other examples of free speech constrained or punished in Ovid's *Metamorphoses* see Keith (1992) *passim*, particularly on the long-lived and prophetic crow. Feeney (1992) offers a broader account of Ovid's approach to free speech in the more obviously political domain of the *Fasti* and the Roman calendar.

the extreme old age of this Sibyl is her defining feature; it demonstrates her unique relationship to time and to mortality itself. It is also a feature that engages with the dynamics of literary tradition. In the move from the *Aeneid* to the *Metamorphoses* there has been no shift in the time frame for the narrative: Aeneas meets the Sibyl at the same point in his (and presumably her) story. Yet this is not exactly the same story, and the events are not strictly synchronic. The first temporal tweak relates to the ordering of the narrative. Virgil's Aeneas and his Sibyl had conversed most during the preparations for their underworld visit and on their way down towards the Elysian Fields, with the return described (and implicitly achieved) brusquely and obscurely. Ovid moves the extended exchange between hero and prophet to their journey back up from the underworld, a slow return that is marked by the hero's exhaustion:

> *inde ferens lassos auerso tramite passus*
> *cum duce Cumaea mollit sermone laborem ...*
>
> As he retraced his weary paces on the return journey
> he eased the effort through conversation with his Cumaean guide ...
> (Ov. *Met.* 14.120–1)

The challenge posed by this return journey had already been pointed out in the *Aeneid: facilis descensus Auerno:* | ... *sed reuocare gradum superasque euadere ad auras* | *hoc opus, hic labor est* – 'the descent to Avernus is easy | ... but to recall your step and escape into the breezes above – | this is the challenge, this is the real task' (Verg. *Aen.* 6.126–9). The fatigue of both characters on their way back from the underworld in the *Metamorphoses* reflects the more fundamental exhaustion of the later Sibyl, who is repeating the very journey she undertook with Aeneas in the *Aeneid*. While in the *Metamorphoses* the Sibyl's old age cannot reflect the passing of time between Virgil's plot and that of Ovid, it does suggest that there has been a more fundamental shift in the temporal perspective, and that it has been embedded in the lived experience of the woman whose prophecies make her abnormally sensitive to time's passing. In implying that the Sibyl has aged between one poem and its successor, Ovid sets up the composition of the two epics in terms of the passing of literary history. The Sibyl is, now, a tired old trope.[101]

---

[101] Statius writes a postscript to this postscript with a newly rejuvenated Sibyl for Domitian's era in *Siluae* 4.3. See Pillinger (forthcoming). Petronius takes the tradition in a different direction, reducing the Sibyl's voice to a commentary on her shrunken existence, with Trimalchio quoting her in a bottle saying simply: *apothanein thelō* – 'I want to die' (Petron. *Sat.* 48, evoking Phineus' request for death in Apollonius' *Argonautica* (2.446)). Though the episode is carefully embedded in the *cena Trimalchionis*, in the middle of Petronius' Latin novel, Trimalchio uses his few words of Greek to quote the Sibyl so that her voice remains interestingly untranslated. The quotation occurs only

The exchanges between Aeneas and the Sibyl in the *Metamorphoses* also involve thematic inversions of Virgil's *Aeneid* that transform the effect of both characters' words. Aeneas promises a temple in retrospective thanks for the Sibyl's help in taking him to the underworld (Ov. *Met.* 14.127–8), not as an enticing bribe to bring about her prophetic speech. The Sibyl, in turn, offers nothing by way of useful prophecy to Aeneas, but instead focuses single-mindedly on her autobiography, particularly on events from her past.[102] The tale that the Sibyl tells is one of Apollo's thwarted love, a version that fits her abnormal longevity into a Cassandran narrative of half-fulfilled or backhanded gifts from Apollo.[103] Having been granted as many years of life as there are grains of sand in a pile, the Sibyl refused Apollo's advances and hence failed to secure youth to accompany her one thousand years of life. She announces that she is now seven hundred years old, marking in precise terms her place in her not-quite-immortal biography. As she insists, *nec dea sum* – 'I am not a goddess' (14.130). She applies her prophetic skills not to mapping out the three more years of Aeneas' future, but to the three centuries remaining to her:

> ... *sed iam felicior aetas*
> *terga dedit, tremuloque gradu uenit aegra senectus,*
> *quae patienda diu est. nam iam mihi saecula septem*
> *acta, tamen superest, numeros ut pulueris aequem,*
> *ter centum messes, ter centum musta uidere.*

> ... but now my blessed youth has fled,
> and with tottering step weak old age approaches,
> which must be suffered for a long time. For now seven centuries
>   of my life
> have passed but, until I can match the number of grains of sand,
>   I still have
> three hundred harvests, three hundred vintages to see.
>   (Ov. *Met.* 14.142–6)

At this point the voice of Ovid's Sibyl begins to comment closely on Virgil's version of her biography, as she spells out what exactly will happen to her during the coming three hundred years. Like the monkeys

---

a few lines after Trimalchio boasts of owning both Greek and Latin libraries, further highlighting the Sibyl's own curious position between cultures.

[102] Myers (1994) 102.

[103] Miller (2009) 141 n. 114 makes the connection with Cassandra. He suggests that the myth of the Sibyl's history with Apollo must predate Ovid's *Metamorphoses*, and probably predates Virgil's *Aeneid*.

of Pithecusae, her limbs will shrivel (14.147), and ultimately her body will give way completely, leaving only her voice:

> *usque adeo mutata ferar nullique uidenda,*
> *uoce tamen noscar; uocem mihi fata relinquent.*

> I will be so much changed and visible to nobody,
> however I shall be known by my voice; the fates will leave
>   me my voice.   (Ov. *Met.* 14.152–3)

The Sibyl's bodily disintegration here in the *Metamorphoses* represents a development of Virgil's suggestion that the living Cumaean Sibyl of the *Aeneid* was co-extensive with the *corpus* of Sibylline Books stored on the Palatine. That body of work was fragile, inchoate and largely invisible, but its materiality was conceptually vital for the Roman state and for Virgil's new poetic project. Ovid now allows the Sibyl's materiality to fall into even further obscurity (*nulli uidenda*, 14.152), reconstructing Heraclitus' version of a sibyl whose voice lasts for one thousand years (Plut. *De Pyth. or.* 397A, discussed above). Yet while the Sibyl may be known by a voice (*uoce noscar*, 14.153), it is unclear how this voice is produced, now that its body has gone.[104] Ovid's Cassandra was a body without a voice; his Sibyl is a voice without a body.

In elucidating her forthcoming existential crisis, the Sibyl has also lost her prophetic edge. Virgil's Sibyl had offered a fairly disappointing prophecy to Aeneas, but Ovid's Sibyl does not voice any fate at all beyond her own destiny; in fact the situation is reversed, as it is the fates that let her have a voice (*uocem mihi fata relinquent*, 14.153). As with Virgil's Sibyl, what matters is not so much the content of the prophecies, but the way in which they are packaged by the text that contains them. For Ovid, though, a sibylline *voice* is as important to his poem as sibylline *books* were to Virgil's poem, because he identifies the value of his poem as lying less in the production of the complex text, and more in its reception and public performance(s).

The *Metamorphoses* encompasses mythic, legendary and historical time, but above all it defines itself by its reception in Ovid's present. Ovid had ensured that the teleological trajectory of the poem is understood as culminating in the contemporary world in which he lived and wrote. The gods inspiring the poet were addressed with a specific request: *ad mea perpetuum deducite tempora carmen* – 'draw the endless poem down to my era' (1.4); alternatively,

---

[104] See Connor (2000), especially his introduction and opening chapter, on voices dissociated from bodies. Crippa (1998) 165ff. continues the discussion of sibylline voices without bodies.

bearing in mind that the first word of Ovid's *Fasti* is *tempora*: 'draw the endless poem down to my *Fasti*'.[105] The *Fasti*'s endlessly repeatable account of (half) the year's passing reminds the reader that against the relentless forward drive of the *Metamorphoses* time also passes in the circular repetitions of the calendrical year. The theme is picked up again at the end of the *Metamorphoses* in Pythagoras' divinely inspired vision of a metempsychotic universe (*deus ora mouet* – 'a god controls my mouth', 15.143).[106] Ovid's poetic literary universe, at least, is designed for eternal repetition, for rearticulating and reliving year after year. This is made all the more clear in the penultimate prophecy of the *Metamorphoses*, Jupiter's prophecy to the anxious Venus. Virgil had hinted at Jupiter 'unrolling' written scrolls in order to deliver his prophecy to Venus in *Aeneid* 1. Ovid has Jupiter describe to Venus her family's fates, as they are inscribed on the tablets found in the house of the Fates:

> *inuenies illic incisa adamante perenni*
> *fata tui generis; legi ipse animoque notaui*
> *et referam …*

> You will find there inscribed on eternal adamant
> the fates of your family; I myself have read and noted them in
>   my mind
> and I will relate their contents …   (Ov. *Met.* 15.813–15)

Jupiter explicitly reads from the tablets, mentally 'transcribes' their details, then repeats their contents out loud.[107] The prophecy is wrapped up with a pun: *uix ea fatus erat* – 'scarcely had he spoken …' (15.843), playing on the etymological connection between what Jupiter has spoken (*fatus*) and what has been fated (*fata*).[108] The future is once again proven to be that which has been performatively spoken, and Ovid emphasises the fact that this performance can take place time after time with the help of written records, as is proven by Jupiter's prophecies to Venus, repeated as they are over multiple epics.

Along with this comes Ovid's final projection of his own future immortality. Just as in the case of the Sibyl's body, Ovid predicts that time will ultimately have power over only his material form: *nil nisi corporis huius | ius habet* – 'it governs nothing but this body' (15.873–4). Instead, his name

---

[105] On the oxymoronic Callimacheanism see Hinds (1987a) 19. On the double (or triple) meaning of *tempora* throughout Ovid's work see Hinds (1987b).

[106] Wheeler (1999) 190–1 discusses Ovid's escalation of the problematically 'optimistic prophecy' that O'Hara (1990) finds in the *Aeneid*, particularly in Pythagoras' speech in *Metamorphoses* 15 and its replaying of Helenus' prophecy.

[107] Wheeler (1999) 56, 192.

[108] Commager (1981) 101.

will live on: *nomenque erit indelebile nostrum* – 'my name will be indelible' (15.876). As Hardie elegantly puts it, 'When the poet is reduced to his name, a word whose only substance is the poetry, words, attached to that name, then at last the name, an empty sign detached from this or that living human instantiation, is charged with the fullness of an immutable and eternal being.'[109] While his name will have no 'human instantiation', Ovid will survive in the human voices that endlessly rearticulate his poetry:

> *ore legar populi, perque omnia saecula fama,*
> *(siquid habent ueri uatum praesagia) uiuam.*

> I will be read on the mouth of the people, and through my fame
> (if the prophecies of visionaries have any truth) I will live for
>   all time.   (Ov. *Met.* 15.878–9)

The poet who aligns his authorship with the materiality of tablets and scrolls in virtually all his poems continues to rely upon the theme in his closing lines of the *Metamorphoses*.[110] Ovid predicts that he will ultimately become co-extensive with the text of the *Metamorphoses*, like Virgil and Virgil's Sibyl with their great books of poetry. He even embeds anonymous seers to back up his own 'performative prayer', as Lowrie describes it (*siquid habent ueri uatum praesagia*, 15.879).[111] However, in his epic work Ovid appears less interested in the inscription of a living voice into text, and more in the revoicing of his utterance by future readers of his text. It is the 'mouth of the people' which will, he predicts, ultimately extend and ratify the voice of Ovid and the characters embedded in his poem, including the evanescent Sibyl herself. As the Sibyl herself had boasted: 'the fates [*fata*] will leave me my voice' (14.153); in the light of Jupiter's prophecy, this might also be translated 'the things said out loud [*fata*] will leave me my voice'. Ovid has provided an oracular poetic manuscript that, like the Sibylline Books as they are represented in the literature of the early empire, prophesies and enacts its author's immortality through every translation of his or her voice from the ancient page into live performance. Where

---

[109] Hardie (1993) 94.

[110] Ovid consistently imagines his material books of poetry shuttling between author and audience, along with all the lived experience that is contained within them: his amatory exploits that he hopes will prove instructive to young lovers in the *Ars Amatoria*; the 'interviews' he appeared to conduct with divinities in order to bring to life the day-to-day ritual activities of his Roman readers in his version of the inscribed *Fasti*; and the endless claims to the 'real' suffering that lies behind the writing of the *Heroides* and his letters from exile and that will only be appreciated (and possibly rectified) by a sympathetic reception of the letters' contents. See e.g. Hinds (1985).

[111] Lowrie (2009) 278: 'he calls attention to the bardic nature of his prediction of future immortality with "uatum" in the poem's last line. For future readers such as ourselves, this prediction has come true, but the performative prayer in 861ff. is now merely a record of the past.'

Virgil's epic draws upon the myth of the Sibylline Books' compositional process and obscurity to reinforce the status and complexity of the *Aeneid*, Ovid's epic plays upon on the traditions of the Sibylline Books' use in the contemporary Roman world to enhance the *Metamorphoses'* claim to eternal relevance through performance.

CHAPTER 5

Cassandra Translated: Seneca's Agamemnon

Ca: Veniet et uobis furor.

Cassandra: Madness will come to you too.
(Sen. *Ag.* 1012)[1]

Cassandra's literary descendants make a range of appearances in Roman poetry of the later Augustan age and the decades that follow it. A cluster of Greek prophets, bearing features of Cassandra's prophetic-linguistic dislocations but largely filtered through the powerful influence of the Virgilian Sibyl, can be traced in Latin works of the early empire: Ovid's Arcadian Carmentis in the *Fasti*, Lucan's Thessalian Erictho and Delphic Phemonoe in the *Bellum Ciuile*, and Statius' Neapolitan Sibyl in the *Siluae*.[2] The figure of Cassandra herself is almost entirely dissipated among these new or revived figures, except in one case. This is the resuscitation of her voice by Seneca in his *Agamemnon*, several decades after Virgil wrote the *Aeneid*.

In several respects Seneca's *Agamemnon* conveniently brings the Cassandran tradition back to a starting point of sorts. The story returns to the theatre: to the trappings of dramatic production, if not to the stage itself.[3] Seneca tells the prophet's story as it unfolds during her climactic final hours in Greece, that is, the very moments that are staged by Aeschylus in his *Agamemnon*. Despite not appearing until the second half, Cassandra has

---

[1] Quotations from Seneca's *Agamemnon* are from Fitch (2004), except where noted.
[2] Thoughts on some of these characters can be found in Pillinger (2012) and (forthcoming). Cassandra does reappear in some interesting scenes from Greek literature of the Roman Empire, notably in Triphiodorus and Quintus Smyrnaeus. See Neblung (1997) 216–29; Clausen (1987) 35.
[3] Whether or not Senecan drama was performed remains an unanswered question, though Kelly (1979) and Zanobi (2014) offer some imaginative suggestions for possible forms and contexts of performance, and Slaney (2016) shows how, regardless of their original performance context, the theatrical aspects of Senecan tragic writing inspired a distinctive tradition of dramatic staging over the centuries to come. The question does not bear strongly on the discussion in this chapter, except when it comes to the relationship between actors and audience, but even here the dynamics between the two can be constructed equally well in terms of a performance on stage, a recitation or a private interaction between a theatrically literate reader and writer.

195

the most substantial role in Seneca's play, and she functions as the strongest link between Aeschylus' Greek and Seneca's Latin *Agamemnon*.[4] The connection between the two plays is, in other respects, not straightforward. Seneca is not translating Aeschylus' work in any conventional way; the plots are divergent, let alone the diction. The intervening Greek and Roman literary traditions clearly influenced the development of Seneca's play, though much of that intermediary dramatic material is no longer extant and difficult to reconstruct.[5] For those interested in the development of Cassandra's prophecies it is, nonetheless, a disappointment to find that Seneca has not made any attempt to replicate the extraordinary richness and obscurity of her Aeschylean Greek. Instead Seneca appears to be aiming for the heavy and clear irony of Euripidean tragedy, and for arch self-consciousness; doubtless the kind of writing found in Ovid's influential tragedy, *Medea*.[6]

All the same, it would be wrong to suggest that Seneca has completely avoided the thematics of translation in turning Cassandra's prophetic words from their original Greek (or indeed Trojan) into Latin. In fact Seneca uses the very clarity of Cassandra's Latin to develop a new take on the metaphorical dimensions to her linguistic difference. Where Cassandra's voice was previously implicated in marking the difficulties involved in straddling wide reaches of literal and literary time and space, she now appears in a play that claustrophobically closes those distances before they are even identifiable. Straightforward Latin tells the Roman audience of people and events based in Greece, while that Greek story continuously harks back to the action that took place a little earlier in Troy. The result is the creation of a non-specific tragic setting that mirrors not only the global reach of the Roman Empire, but also the cosmopolitanism of Stoic philosophy, in which mortals are conceived of as citizens of the whole world as well as of their local *polis* or state.[7] Meanwhile the self-conscious allusiveness

---

[4] Tarrant (1976) 3; Calder (1976) 32; Lavery (2004b) 192. Motto and Clark (1988) 165–6 resist the notion that Cassandra brings any unity to Seneca's play, let alone to the combination of the two plays.

[5] Tarrant (1976) 8–18.

[6] On Seneca's eclecticism see Littlewood (2004) 6–7. For Seneca's dependence on Ovidian tragedy see Hinds (2011), esp. 22–28, now with Curley (2013). Hinds (2011) 6 sums up the relationship: 'for Seneca, as for many later writers, poetic Ovidianism involves engagement with a tradition in which issues of genre, representation and literary self-fashioning, along with questions of interplay between mythic and literary historical memory, are already thoroughly explored and thematized'. See also Schiesaro (2003) 221–4 and (1992) 62–3.

[7] Schofield (1991). On the distancing effect Seneca manages to achieve in his Greek-based stories see Tarrant (1995). Siebengartner (2012) offers an example of earlier Roman-Stoic 'globalisation' through literary translation in his analysis of Cicero's Latin version of Aratus' *Phaenomena*: he argues that Cicero aligns himself with his audience as common viewers and students of the heavenly – but also now distinctively Roman – zodiac.

of the text creates a synchronous jumble of Greek and Roman literary history to match the universal dramatic setting.[8] As a seer whose vision encompasses an abnormally wide spectrum of time and space and brings with it a kind of fatalism, Cassandra aligns now more than ever with the poet who writes her story, whose Stoicism imposes a determinist reading of events.[9] Indeed, in Seneca's *Agamemnon* Cassandra all the more obviously closes the gap between the poet's show of authority and his characters' dramatic agency, as she directs many of the most significant shifts in perspective in the play.[10] At the same time, she fails to assert the exclusivity of her knowledge, leaving a disconcerting vacuum, an absence of the normal impression that Cassandra has access to more information than the other characters around her, even if she cannot communicate it. As Fitch puts it, 'Authority is decentred both in the events of the play and in ways of understanding them.'[11]

The lack of firm spatial, temporal or linguistic distinctions in Seneca's *Agamemnon* means that the drama spreads out of the sphere of the action and into the world of the contemporary audience. In Seneca's world – defined by a single despotic ruler, by a sprawling empire and by a philosophy that now preaches the ineluctability of fate in the language of its Roman imperial rulers – there are no alternatives, no escape routes; nothing is 'other'.[12] Everything foreign has been brought under the control of a higher political power, while a sense of alienation has become embedded in the system itself. For Seneca's Cassandra there is no room for the creative misunderstandings that defined her appearance in earlier works. Instead the productive 'surplus' of Cassandra's voice is found in a newly global appreciation of her prophetic paradox and, ultimately, in the shared experience of what it means to be resistant but unheard, to approach madness in trying to comprehend and resist implication in the worlds – real and dramatic – of imperial tyranny. As Cassandra tells her internal and external audience at the end of the play,

---

[8] Hinds (2011) 9: 'dramatic space in Seneca is always intertextual space … the mythological system within which Seneca's tragic plots are mobilized is a system always already constituted by previous literary texts'.

[9] Sellars (2006) 99–104 discusses the difficulty in establishing Stoic beliefs when it comes to fate and providence.

[10] For Cassandra as poet, '*uates* and quasi-messenger', see Trinacty (2014) 199–214, drawing the parallels with e.g. the Bacchic poetics of Hor. *Carm.* 3.25.

[11] Fitch (2004) 119. See also Trinacty (2014) 199.

[12] On the brief moment in the first century CE in which philosophy seems as at home in Latin as in Greek, see Inwood (1995), esp. 67–8. Brunt (1975) delineates the uncomfortable relationship between Stoicism and Roman imperial authority.

the crazed inspiration is overflowing: *Veniet et uobis furor* – 'madness will come to you too' (1012).

Monoglot Multiculturalism

Seneca parades his interest in the workings of literary tradition with post-Ovidian brio. In his tragedies he does not limit his metapoetic conscious-ness to passages of narrative or choral commentary, but allows it to pervade the language of even the most central characters in his plays. They reflect explicitly on their story's rehearsal and development over time, and on the way in which their current behaviour is informed by previous layers of character-drawing and myth-making. This can be seen clearly in Seneca's *Medea*. His Medea traces her gradual metamorphosis into the character shaped by earlier Medeas, ultimately delivering the triumphant claim that she has grown into herself: *Medea nunc sum* – 'now I am Medea' (Sen. *Med.* 910). Here and in other tragedies by Seneca, horrific actions are regularly framed as greater than those seen in the past, trumping the efforts of both the character's earlier instantiations and the poet's own predecessors in the literary world.[13] In the *Agamemnon*, Clytemnestra promises an escalation of her own family's story: she will cast the actions of her sister Helen into the shade by means of a *maius nefas* – 'greater sin' (Sen. *Ag.* 124). In designing her vengeance, Clytemnestra will be inspired by the actions of increasingly specific female literary characters that have preceded her. She goes from citing anonymous adulterous wives (117), then generic stepmothers (118), then Medea herself (*uirgo ... Phasiaca fugiens regna Thessalica trabe* – 'the girl ... fleeing the Phasian realms on a Thessalian boat', 120). In each of these cases Cassandra tells herself to consider the examples by 'unrolling' their plots – *tecum ... euolue femineos dolos* – 'unroll for yourself the fem-inine deceits' (116). Once again the Latin adopts a version of the verb *uoluo*, which implies reading a text as well as thinking something over.[14] In the process, Clytemnestra inverts Jupiter's promise to 'unroll' the scrolls of the fates in his prophecy to Venus in *Aeneid* 1 (*uoluens fatorum arcana mouebo*, 1.262, discussed in Chapter 4). Clytemnestra's promise is to learn from the stories of the past, rather than the future.

[13] E.g. *maius his, maius parat* | *Medea monstrum* – 'Medea is preparing a greater horror than these, | a greater one' (Sen. *Med.* 674–5). On the theme in the *Thyestes* see Seidensticker (1985) and Schiesaro (2003) 31–6, 130–1, and for further explorations of the intertextuality in *Phaedra* and *Medea* see Trinacty (2014) 62–126.

[14] Tarrant (1976) 196 points out that *tecum* discourages the translation of *euolue* as 'unroll' or 'narrate', but he acknowledges that the echoes are there.

In Seneca's *Agamemnon* more generally it is not so much the case that characters trace their personal development through literary time, as Medea does in Seneca's *Medea*, but that one character bleeds unsettlingly into another, as Clytemnestra does here with Medea. This echoing of actions and motivations is part of a more general layering of Trojan and Greek stories and a doubling of roles across both peoples in the 'hybrid world' of the play.[15] Even the chorus is doubled, with an Argive and a Trojan group scattering the narrative focalisation between them.

The process begins at the very start of the play, with the prologue delivered by the shifty ghost of Thyestes. As the ghost points out, his actions have muddled the normal relationships within his family:

> ... *uersa natura est retro:*
> *auo parentem (pro nefas!), patri uirum,*
> *natis nepotes miscui – nocti diem.*

> Nature has been turned back on itself:
> I have mixed up parent with grandparent (the sin of it!),
>   husband with father,
> grandchildren with children – day with night.   (Sen. *Ag.* 34–6)

The Argive Thyestes also plays the part of the Trojan Cassandra who is yet to appear, by introducing the action to come with ominous predictions that bear the weight of prophecy. Thyestes' appearance begins by mimicking and inverting Cassandra's spatial and temporal mobility. His ghost leaves the underworld, the place in which Cassandra had anticipated spending her afterlife (Aesch. *Ag.* 1156–61; Lycoph. *Alex.* 1372–73) and to which she will look forward once again at the end of Seneca's play (Sen. *Ag.* 1004–11). For Cassandra the underworld is a refuge where, safely removed from events, she will hear the future played out as a repetition of her prophecies. As Thyestes emerges from the underworld he too feels the pull of the place: *libet reuerti* – 'I want to go back' (12), but for Thyestes the world of the dead to which he longs to return is also the world of the past. As he leaves it he is entering a scene above ground that has been shaped by historical crimes (the whole trail of the gory strife within the house of Atreus that culminated in Thyestes being tricked into consuming his own children), but is now the domain of the next generation. Thyestes has to correct himself, to move into the present from a house he originally associated with his father: *uideo paternos, immo fraternos lares* – 'I see my father's home – no, my brother's' (6). Continuing this reluctant

---

move forwards in time and upwards in space, Thyestes anticipates the vengeance that will be enacted by the new generation inhabiting this place. He displays the prophetic vision of Cassandra, seeing the weapons of Agamemnon's death scene in advance: *enses secures tela ... uideo* – 'I see swords, axes, spears' (45–6).[16]

As with Cassandra's prophecies, Thyestes' words are loaded with performative power because his message is aligned with a divine authority that guarantees the acts of vengeance to come. Indeed, in this play Thyestes commits himself more fully to the god Apollo than does Cassandra.[17] He rapes his daughter Pelopia at the behest of Apollo's oracle in order to conceive Aegisthus, the agent of his vengeance, and the entire plot is pitched as the fulfilment of this oracle:

> *Sed sera tandem respicit fessos malis*
> *post fata demum sortis incertae fides.*
>
> But at last, belatedly and after my death, the realisation of the
>   uncertain oracle
> looks to those exhausted by their troubles.
>
> (Sen. Ag. 37–8)

Apollo is not just the facilitator of prophetic visions in this play; he is, according to Thyestes, the very agent of the play's action. Thyestes' speech, like Cassandra's, turns out to be another temporary deferral of Apollo's plan, which delays the drama as successfully as Cassandra's nonsense delayed events in the Greek plays. The difference is that Thyestes has no enthusiasm for delay and concludes his speech by invoking Apollo's activity, associating him with the sun and its rising: *Phoebum moramur. redde iam mundo diem* – 'We are delaying Phoebus. It is time to restore daylight to the world' (56).

If Thyestes introduces the play with hints of the voice that Cassandra will produce later, more thematic linking and doubling occurs at the very centre of the drama. The first half of the play focuses on events within Agamemnon's household, and the second half places these events within the broader context of events surrounding the Trojan War.[18] In the middle, Eurybates delivers a lengthy messenger speech to Clytemnestra, a speech that links the first and second halves of the play both through its placement

---

[16] Schiesaro (2003) 180–1.

[17] Boyle (1997) 36–7 notes that although Apollo is implicated in much of the play, he proves a morally destabilising character.

[18] Tarrant (1976) 4–5. Motto and Clark (1988) 167: 'The play appears to commence upon one foot, and then rather shufflingly to shift the centre of gravity and to stand upon the other.'

within the drama and through its themes.[19] Eurybates tells of the various *nostoi* of the Greek warriors returning from Troy, and also embraces within his narrative the experiences of the fleeing Trojans, synthesising Greek and Roman mythographical priorities. Throughout this speech, the Greeks and Trojans are aligned, rather than opposed. As storms rise, their laments are shared:

> *in uota miseros ultimus cogit timor,*
> *eademque superos Troes et Danai rogant.*
> *quid fata possunt! inuidet Pyrrhus patri,*
> *Aiaci Vlixes, Hectori Atrides minor,*
> *Agamemno Priamo: quisquis ad Troiam iacet*
> *felix uocatur …*

> Extreme fear drove the poor sufferers to prayers
> and the Trojans and the Danaans ask the gods for the same thing.
> What a turn of events the fates can bring about! Pyrrhus envies
>   his father,
> Ulysses envies Ajax, the younger son of Atreus envies Hector,
> Agamemnon envies Priam: whoever lies dead at Troy
> is called lucky …   (Sen. *Ag.* 510–15)

The Greeks and Trojans make the same prayers to the same gods, and the Greek heroes envy all who died in the Trojan War, whether they were family members, comrades within the Greek ranks or enemies from among the just-conquered Trojans. Back in the *Odyssey*, Homer's Odysseus had expressed the wish that he had fallen with the Greeks who were killed at Troy, rather than escaped to suffer the horrors at sea: 'Three and four times blessed [*tris makares … kai tetrakis*] are the Danaans who died back then in wide Troy' (Hom. *Od.* 5.306–7). Aeneas made the same lament in Virgil's *Aeneid*, but he identifies with the dead Trojans whose parents could watch the fighting from the city: 'O three and four times blessed [*o terque quaterque beati*], those whose fate it was to die before their fathers' eyes, under the high walls of Troy' (Verg. *Aen.* 1.94–6). In Seneca's *Agamemnon* the Greek cry becomes a communal one, limited to neither Greeks nor Trojans: Ajax, Hector and Priam are equally envied, as 'whoever lies dead at Troy | is called lucky' (514–15). The Greeks go on to beg for mercy on the grounds that the Trojans are also sailing the same seas: *sistite infestum mare: | uehit ista Danaos classis, et Troas uehit!* – 'Calm the raging sea: | this fleet is carrying Greeks as well as Trojans!' (525–6). Virgil had drawn out the

---

[19] On the length of the messenger speeches in Seneca, and their difference from the messenger speeches in classical Greek tragedy, see Zanobi (2014) III.

synchrony of Aeneas' and Odysseus' journeys across the Mediterranean, particularly through the Trojans' rescue of Achaemenides in *Aeneid* 3, but it takes Seneca to create heroes with such a self-conscious understanding of how their enmities have been codified by converging literary traditions that they can reflect on and appeal to their shared travails.

Another external voice synthesises Greek and Roman narratives in Seneca's play, and that is the voice of the Trojan chorus accompanying Cassandra. The language of deception found in this chorus also plays on the confusion of Greek and Trojan characters, often by evoking moments of ambiguity in the *Aeneid*. For example, Seneca's chorus describes Patroclus as a 'false Achilles' (*falsus Achilles*, 618) when he fights in Achilles' armour. The phrase picks up on the language of the Sibyl in the *Aeneid* when she warned Aeneas that he would have to face 'another Achilles' (*alius … Achilles*, Verg. *Aen.* 6.89).[20] There the Sibyl was ostensibly referring to Turnus, though her turn of phrase also foreshadowed the confusion between the heroic roles of Turnus and Aeneas that builds towards the end of the epic, as both men become increasingly identifiable as a furious Achilles.[21]

In fact, Seneca's Trojan chorus laments the fall of Troy with particularly strong echoes of the deceits and confusions brought out in Aeneas' description of the city's fall in *Aeneid* 2, which in turn had anticipated the fatal confusion of native (Latin/Italian) and other (barbarian/Trojan) in the second half of the epic.[22] The chorus' description of the 'pregnant' (*gestans*, Sen. *Ag.* 631) Trojan horse hesitating on the threshold of the city evokes Aeneas' narrative in *Aeneid* 2, where he repeatedly characterises the horse as pregnant, with five references to the soldiers hidden within the horse's 'womb' (*uterus*). Seneca's chorus then avoids the lines delivered by Aeneas that refer to – without quoting – Cassandra's warnings concerning the arrival of the Trojan horse (Verg. *Aen.* 2.246–7). Instead the chorus emphasises a different opportunity offered by the horse that was missed by the Trojans at that precise point in time:

> *et licuit dolos uersare ut ipsi*
> *fraude sua caderent Pelasgi …*

> And we could have rolled the deceit back on them, to make
> the Pelasgians fall by their own trickery …   (Sen. *Ag.* 632–3)

---

[20] Tarrant also compares Ovid *Her.* 1.17.
[21] Anderson (1957).
[22] Calder (1976) 34, with n. 54.

The language here is that found in Aeneas' introduction of Sinon in *Aeneid* 2, an episode described by Hexter as 'the primal scene of narration and misinterpretation in the *Aeneid*'.[23] (It is also, surely not incidentally, a scene that contains the most remarkably pronounced echo of the opening lines to Lycophron's *Alexandra*.)[24] Sinon was introduced with the claim that he was ready for two dramatic alternatives: *seu uersare dolos seu certae occumbere morti* – 'either to roll his deceit into action or to fall in certain death' (Verg. *Aen.* 2.62). As his scene develops, Sinon's pretended shift of loyalty to the Trojans is couched in a relentless stream of conditionals that play on the name *Si-non*, 'If-not', and on his story's debt to Odysseus, *Outis*, 'No-one'.[25] Sinon's threat that if the Trojans accept the Greek horse they will conquer the Greeks' descendants (2.189–94) is, of course, ultimately true, viewed from the perspective of contemporary Rome, but it is a fatal deceit for his immediate interlocutors. When Seneca's Trojan chorus channels Sinon's language they are longing for the reversal of Greek and Trojan fortunes to take place earlier, for the basic truth of Sinon's prophecy to have been proven in their own day. In their wishful thinking the Greeks' language of trickery is appropriated by the Trojans, and the destruction of the Greeks is achieved well before the Trojans become Romans.[26]

The most pervasive twinning of people and places and blurring of allegiances develops around the new generation of the house of Atreus, particularly with the introduction of Cassandra and her double visions, including her two forms of speech, one inspired and one explanatory.[27] Cassandra begins by questioning what she can now claim as her own: *quae patria restat, quis pater, quae iam soror?* – 'what land, what father, what sister, remains to me now?' (Sen. *Ag.* 699). This question turns out to be less rhetorical than it might initially seem, as Cassandra proceeds to replace the terrible losses she suffered at Troy with some of the individual people and

---

[23] Hexter (1990) 109.

[24] *Cuncta equidem tibi, rex, fuerit quodcumque, fatebor | uera* – 'I will tell you everything truthfully, king, yes I will, whatever happens' (Verg. *Aen.* 2.77–8); cf. Λέξω τὰ πάντα νητρεκῶς, ἅ μ' ἱστορεῖς, | ἀρχῆς ἀπ' ἄκρας – 'I will tell everything exactly, all that you inquire about, | from the very beginning (Lycoph. *Alex.* 1–2). See Fusillo, Hurst and Paduano (1991) 43. With *equidem*, an intensifier of the first-person voice (*OLD* s.v. *equidem* 1), Sinon emphasises his role as the latest deliverer of profoundly complex and misleading narrative.

[25] Hexter (1990) 113–14.

[26] Motto and Clark (1988) 170 note the significance of the Trojan chorus to the Roman audience: 'this is symptomatic of a Roman predilection, one that identifies with the underdog Dardanians and, of course, through Aeneas, with future Romans'.

[27] Trinacty (2014) 199–200.

places that surround her in Greece, sustaining in the process her global perspective on events. Cassandra's first main speech signals this double vision:

> *sed ecce gemino sole praefulget dies*
> *geminumque duplices Argos attollit domos.*
>
> But look, the day shines bright with a twin sun
> and a twin Argos brings forth double houses.   (Sen. *Ag.* 728–9)

The language of Dionysiac inspiration in the passage means that Cassandra's speech does a mad dash to Carthage and back to Greece. The prophet's diction is filtered through the description of the increasingly maddened Dido in *Aeneid* 4, whom Virgil was aligning with Euripides' Pentheus (among other figures of Greek myth): *solem geminum et duplices se ostendere Thebas* – 'a twin sun and double Thebes appear' (Verg. *Aen.* 4.470; cf. Eur. *Bacch.* 918–19).[28] Cassandra takes this double vision even further. She sees Argos as a second Troy (Sen. *Ag.* 794–5), Aegisthus as a second Paris (730–3) and Clytemnestra as a hybrid figure whose Spartan dress is paired with Amazonian weaponry (734–6). Even once Cassandra's transports have faded away and she engages in an antilabic back and forth with Agamemnon, she continues to identify Agamemnon as Priam (794) and then Clytemnestra as Helen (795).[29] At this point Agamemnon appears to be communicating reasonably well with Cassandra, but he fails to see the significance in her layering of one city's and one family's tragedy upon another; he keeps a fatal confidence in the distinction between his ancestral home (*patrios lares*, 782) and the conquered Trojans (*barbarae ... gentes*, 783–4). This simplistic identification of 'here and there', his 'us and them' triumphalism, contrasts not only with Cassandra's global worldview, but also with Thyestes' earlier revelation that time, as much as space, can complicate the concept of home: *uideo paternos, immo fraternos lares* – 'I see my father's home – no, my brother's' (6).

In fact Cassandra's vision only reveals the doubling already at the heart of the family of Atreus and Thyestes, the incest, murder and cannibalism that keep implanting one member of the family within another. This had been foregrounded by Thyestes' early reference to his sickening confusion of the roles of father and husband in his devotion to Apollo and fathering of Aegisthus with Pelopia (34–6). Electra sees the problem too: she describes Aegisthus, ironically, as a second Agamemnon (*alter Agamemnon*, 962). In turn Electra aligns herself righteously with the perceptive outsider;

---

[28] Schiesaro (2003) 206–7.
[29] Boyle (1997) 35–6.

she begs Cassandra to share the protection of her priestly adornments, claiming that they face the same fate:[30]

> *... Patere me uittis tuis,*
> *Cassandra, iungi paria metuentem tibi.*

> ... Allow me to share your priestly headbands,
> Cassandra, since I fear the same things as you.   (Sen. *Ag.* 951–2)

The doubling was also already at work in the Argives' anticipation of Cassandra's arrival. When Aegisthus describes the prophet Cassandra in the first half of the play, before her appearance onstage, he plays up her sexual competition with Clytemnestra. He claims that Agamemnon's mistresses throng around the king, one taller than the rest: *sola sed turba eminet | tenetque regem famula ueridici dei* – 'But one alone stands out from the crowd | and clings to the king, the servant of the truth-telling god' (254–5). Once more Cassandra's appearance evokes Dido, the famous foreign sexual threat to Rome, a woman who towered over her attendants like Diana among her divine nymphs: *gradiensque deas supereminet omnis* – 'as she walks she stands taller than all the other goddesses' (Verg. *Aen.* 1.501). When Cassandra does arrive, Clytemnestra revives the image in her description of the miserable Trojan chorus of women (*turba tristis*, Sen. *Ag.* 586), among whom Cassandra stands out:

> *... quas super celso gradu*
> *effrena Phoebas entheas laurus quatit.*

> ... towering over them with high step
> the unbridled priestess of Phoebus shakes her divinely
>   inspired laurels.   (Sen. *Ag.* 587–8)

The difference is that Cassandra is not a Diana/Phoebe, but a Phoebas, a devotee of the goddess' brother Apollo.

At the same time, the definition of the priestess as 'unbridled' and towering over mortals foreshadows the more extended description of Cassandra's ravings in terms that align them pointedly with Virgil's Sibyl at the peak of her inspiration (*maiorque uideri* – 'she seemed to grow larger', Verg. *Aen.* 6.49; *frena furenti | concutit ... Apollo* – 'Apollo violently shakes the raving prophet's bridle', 6.100–1).[31] If the Sibyl takes over from Cassandra as the main voice of prophecy in the *Aeneid*, Cassandra wrests back the role in Seneca's *Agamemnon*. The description of the Sibyl's

---

[30] On Electra's parallels with Cassandra see Paschalis (2010) 224–5.
[31] Tarrant (1976) on 710ff.

inspiration is delivered by the narrator of the *Aeneid* in two separate
passages (6.46–54; 6.77–101); this is taken over by Seneca's Trojan chorus
in its description of Cassandra's physical transformation (Sen. *Ag.* 710–
19) and then by the bystander Agamemnon (786–91; 800–1). Once again
Dionysiac poetics play a part. Cassandra's gradual descent into the role of
Bacchic prophetess, *maenas impatiens dei* – 'a maenad refusing to suffer the
god' (719), echoes the language of the Sibyl's inspiration: *Phoebi nondum
patiens … bacchatur uates* – 'no longer suffering Phoebus, the visionary
went Bacchic-wild' (Verg. *Aen.* 6.77–8), while the Euripidean Cassandra's
Bacchic revelry also lies in the background (βακχεύματα, Eur. *Tro.* 367,
developed also at 169–72 and 408).[32] Seneca's Cassandra, like Virgil's Sibyl,
is characterised by bristling hair (*horrescit coma*, Sen. *Ag.* 712), panting
(*anhela corda*, 713), resistance to the god (*excutiat deum*, 800) and a strange
tallness (*graditurque celsa*, 717). The chorus also focuses on the prophet's
gaze, however, her manically rolling eyes: *incerta nutant lumina et uersi
retro | torquentur oculi* – 'her eyes dart about uncertainly, and her eyeballs
| roll back into her head', 714–15). The tortured gaze is explicitly limited
to Cassandra in the *Aeneid* (2.405–6), when her arms are tied during the
capture of Troy's inhabitants.

When her visions take her into the underworld, Cassandra more actively
participates in this mimicry of the Virgilian Sibyl. She exposes the secrets
of the underworld and describes its inhabitants in the manner of the Sibyl
as Aeneas' tour guide in *Aeneid* 6. She even includes a Deiphobus whose
mutilated features confuse identities yet further and whose name, as he
is addressed here in the vocative, is virtually that of the Sibyl Deiphobe
(the quantity of the final 'e' aside): *incertos geris, | Deiphobe, uultus* – 'you
wear an uncertain face, | Deiphobus' (Sen. *Ag.* 749, modifying Verg. *Aen.*
6.494ff.). In this scene, delivered in her own voice, Cassandra also begins
to combine with another figure from the *Aeneid*: Aeneas himself, the man
who first addressed Deiphobus in the *Aeneid* (Verg. *Aen.* 6.500).[33] Like
Aeneas, Cassandra pursues her father (*te sequor, … pater*, Sen. *Ag.* 742),
and she exults in the imagery of fate operating in reverse, just as Anchises
had revealed it in its futurity to Aeneas through the parade of heroes: *spec-
tate, miseri: fata se uertunt retro!* – 'Watch, you poor sufferers: the fates are

---

[32] Littlewood (2004) 216; Zanobi (2014) 101–3. Paschalis (2010) 215 explores in depth the language of
Cassandra's *furor*.
[33] Littlewood (2004) 217–18 draws some important distinctions between Aeneas and Cassandra, and
notes Cassandra's commonalities with Atreus at this juncture.

turning back on themselves!' (758).[34] Cassandra's brother, Hector, appears to her in his wounded form (*uideo … | lacera membra et saucios uinclo graui | illos lacertos* – 'I see … torn limbs and those arms wounded by heavy fetters', 746–7), just as he had appeared to Aeneas in the dream he narrated to Dido in *Aeneid* 2.[35] The first-person description of this scene seals the association between the Senecan Trojan prophet and the Virgilian Trojan hero, both narrators of their visions.

Cassandra's final description of the murder of Agamemnon reframes it as a Trojan victory, a victory over the Greeks that is not quite as early as that longed for by the chorus when it regretted not having 'rolled the deceit back on them' (631) when the Trojan horse entered the city, but nor is it as late as that offered by the rise of Rome itself. In her fantasy of the underworld at lines 741–58, Cassandra imagines those involved in the events at Argos as travelling together along the river Styx, the conquerors and the conquered alike (*uictamque uictricemque*, 754). When she later turns to describe the climactic events that will send these protagonists to the underworld, the murder of Agamemnon, she inverts the winners and the losers:

> … *uicimus uicti Phryges.*
> *bene est, resurges, Troia; traxisti iacens*
> *pares Mycenas, terga dat uictor tuus!*

> … we conquered Phrygians have conquered.
> It is good, you are rising again, Troy; in your fallen state you
>   have dragged down
> your equal match, Mycenae, and your conqueror surrenders!
>
> (Sen. *Ag.* 869–71)

The perverse triumphalism is Euripidean and the trope of 'ironic reversal' is a Greek and Latin commonplace, but the language also taps into a specifically Roman vein of political poetry.[36]

---

[34] The way in which Cassandra tracks the temporal shifts here is odd but not 'un-Stoic'. As Schiesaro (2003) 29 points out, to 'follow' nature or destiny is the mark of a sage. In this case, Cassandra's dutiful following of her father Priam is imbued with the Roman piety of Aeneas treading in his father's footsteps, literally and metaphorically. The forthcoming events that Cassandra then describes as a 'reversal' of fate are not incited by the prophet (*pace* Schiesaro, who reads Cassandra as a force of *nefas* dedicated to undermining fate's rightful progression), but simply a fated transformation of the Trojans' fortunes which she follows with relief and enjoyment. Fate appears to be operating in reverse because the horrors of the back and forth between Troy and Greece are not teleological; Cassandra is aligning her language with the cosmic instability that defines the universe she inhabits.

[35] Tarrant (1976) 311 points out that this scene might in turn have been anticipated by Cassandra's prophecies in Euripides' *Alexandra*.

[36] Tarrant (1976) 337.

The Augustan poets address the possibilities of such reversals, often from within a prophetic framework, to define the city of Rome's place in the world and in history.[37] Horace, for example, has Juno threaten the Romans of the consequences if they allow Troy to rise again on Roman turf:

> *ter si resurgat murus aeneus*
> *auctore Phoebo, ter pereat meis*
> *excisus Argiuis ...*

> If the bronze wall rises for a third time
> under Apollo's protection, for the third time it will be destroyed,
> cut down by my Argives ...   (Hor. *Carm.* 3.3.65–7)

Virgil too has Juno emphasise the importance of not imposing Trojan behaviour on the Italians, turning directly to the issue of linguistic and cultural translation:

> *ne uetus indigenas nomen mutare Latinos*
> *neu Troas fieri iubeas Teucrosque uocari*
> *aut uocem mutare uiros aut uertere uestem.*

> [I beg] that you do not order the indigenous Latins to change
> their ancient name, or be Trojan, or be called Teucrians,
> or that the men change their language or adopt a different dress.
>   (Verg. *Aen.* 12.823–5)

Ovid's later version of such reversals is less troubled by the potential rebirth of Troy. He has another Greek-speaking prophetic woman, Carmentis, describe the situation for her son Evander, the Greek colonist friendly to the proto-Roman Trojans, in language even closer to that adopted by Seneca: *uicta tamen uinces euersaque, Troia, resurges* – 'though conquered you will nonetheless conquer and though crushed, Troy, you will rise again' (Ovid *Fast.* 1.523). Meanwhile the polyptoton (*uicta ... uinces*) revives the language of literary competition as best expressed by Horace in the famous tag in his letter to Augustus (*capta ... cepit*):

> *... Graecia capta ferum uictorem cepit, et artes*
> *intulit agresti Latio.*

> ... Captured Greece caught its wild conqueror, and brought
> the arts into a rustic Latium.   (Hor. *Ep.* 2.156–7)

Cassandra's narration of the terrible events taking place in Greece, filtered as it is through her revisionist prophecies in the 'future reflexive' tense, is

---

[37] For the contemporary political edge, see Nisbet and Rudd (2007) 36–8.

thus an early assertion both of Trojan-Roman imperial supremacy and of Latin literary power.

The events of the play, at least as they are viewed through Cassandra's macroscopic perspective, are staged by Greek characters who mimic Trojans and Trojan characters who anticipate Romans, and they take place in a Greek space that is overlaid by events that have happened at Troy and events that will happen in Italy. Nothing is allowed to sit solely within the narrowly Greek mytho-historical tradition. Seneca's insistence on reminding the audience of the Trojan-Roman dimension to the action sandwiches the Greek *nostoi* within a broader narrative sweep that reaches deeper into the past and further into the future. It takes the events from a story of Greek family vengeance, as Thyestes constructs it, to one of global power struggle, as Cassandra portrays it.[38] In addition to this political reframing of events, the play insists that its mythology does not belong simply to the Greek literary tradition, but to the Roman one too, as it has been filtered through the transformative narratives of poets such as Virgil, Horace and Ovid. The Roman audience of Seneca's Graeco-Latin tragedy is to be no more – or no less – alienated from the events onstage than the Athenian audience of a Trojan-Greek tragedy.

Composing, Connecting, Collapsing the Cosmos

If messenger speech constructs Lycophron's *Alexandra*, it glues together the episodic and thematically fragmented drama of Seneca's *Agamemnon*. Though Cassandra's story has theoretically returned to a theatrical setting, Seneca's play leans heavily on speeches that replace performance with narrative – narrative being that which normally marks action as taking place at a distance in time and space from the here and now of the utterance. Messengers normally relate historic events for internal and external audiences, in the process affirming the audience's understanding that these events, no matter how welcome or dreadful, have passed out of the realm of enacted experience and into the realm of story. In fact, though, the messengers in Seneca's *Agamemnon* do as much to blur the distinctions between dramatic action and narrative as they do to reinforce them. It is not clear that the events described by Seneca's messengers can be so comfortably consigned to the world of his storytelling.

---

[38] See Tarrant (1976) 334 on the shift from Thyestes' story of revenge to the broader Trojan perspective on events.

There are two characters that act as messengers in the play. The first, Eurybates, establishes the idea that action and description of action are not necessarily mutually exclusive modes, through his reformulation of the beacon fire imagery from the Greek tragedies preceding Seneca's play and his reworking of much of Cassandra's performatively prophetic material from previous texts.[39] The second messenger is Cassandra herself, who tells of Agamemnon's murder in her main final speech.[40] In this monologue Cassandra builds on the way in which dramatic action trumps narrative symbolism in Eurybates' tale; events overtake Cassandra's narrative so that what should have been visionary prophecy becomes a vivid description of contemporary, and adjacent, action.

The messenger speech at the centre of Seneca's *Agamemnon* (421–578), in which Eurybates tells of the returns of the Greeks after the fall of Troy, gives a dramatic verbal account of the journeys across the Aegean that were mapped out by the beacon fires in Aeschylus' *Agamemnon*. Fire still punctuates this narrative, linking the stories of Asia to those of Europe, but it is fire that is produced by individual events. Nor are those events simply the fall of Troy, as in Euripides' *Trojan Women*, or even the communication of that fall, as in Aeschylus' *Agamemnon*.[41] Eurybates' story does begin with the fire of Troy (*Pergamum omne Dorica cecidit face* – 'the whole of Pergamum fell to Doric flame', 421), until this fades to a signifying smoke in the eyes of the Greeks sailing away: *Iliacus atra fumus apparet nota* – 'the Trojan smoke appears in the form of black marks' (459). Next this gives way to the lightning of the storms at sea:

> ... *excidunt ignes tamen*
> *et nube dirum fulmen elisa micat* ...
>
> ... but the fires fall to earth
> and terrifying lightning flashes through the shredded cloud ...
> (Sen. *Ag.* 494–5)

Then the beacon theme is developed at length with the extraordinary description of the lesser Ajax as a human torch:

> ... *solus inuictus malis*
> *luctatur Aiax. uela cogentem hunc sua*

---

[39] The parallel that forms between Eurybates and Cassandra in Seneca's play echoes Talthybius' commonalities with Cassandra in Euripides' *Trojan Women*.

[40] On Cassandra as a tragic messenger see Calder (1976) 32; Trinacty (2014) 199–214.

[41] Shelton (1983) 168 notes that Eurybates' speech also moves the play from the realms of metaphor to action in its transformation of storm imagery to the reality of the storms that afflicted the Greek fleet.

> *tento rudente flamma perstrinxit cadens.*
> *libratur aliud fulmen: hoc toto impetu*
> *certum reducta Pallas excussit manu,*
> *imitata patrem. transit Aiacem et ratem*
> *ratisque partem secum et Aiacem tulit.*
> *nil ille motus, ardua ut cautes, salo*
> *ambustus exstat, dirimit insanum mare*
> *fluctusque rumpit pectore, et nauem manu*
> *complexus ignes traxit et caeco mari*
> *conlucet Aiax; omne resplendet fretum.*
> *tandem occupata rupe furibundum intonat:*
> *'superasse me nunc pelagus atque ignes iuuat,*
> *uicisse caelum Palladem fulmen mare.'*

> … Ajax alone, unconquered by his troubles,
> battled on. As he hauled on the sails, tautening their rope,
> the flame fell and grazed him.
> Another lightning bolt was poised: Pallas hurled it in sure aim
> and full force, with her arm drawn back,
> in imitation of her father. It passed through Ajax and his boat
> and tore away with it part of the boat and Ajax.
> Unmoved, like a towering crag, he stood out from the salt water
> smouldering, he parted the raging sea
> and burst out of the waves chest-first, and grabbing hold
> of the ship Ajax caught on fire and lit up
> the dark sea; the whole strait shone bright.
> Finally he made it to a rock and from it he thundered in fury:
> 'I rejoice at having overcome sea and fire,
> at having conquered sky, Pallas, lightning, sea.'   (Sen. *Ag.* 532–46)

Lycophron's messenger/jailor told how Cassandra had described Ajax's death scene by comparing the warrior to animals of both the sea and the sky (discussed in Chapter 3). Seneca's messenger has Ajax speak for himself, boasting his dominance over not just sea and sky, but also over the very bolt of lightning fire that travels from heaven to earth through his own body. Ajax's language embraces all the elements of the earth's power, while Athena's punishment impels him to join those natural forces surrounding him: initially unscathed by the first lightning bolt, he rears up from the sea like a craggy outcrop (*ardua ut cautes*, 539), he thunders (*intonat*, 544), before catching the lightning fire from his boat and illuminating the sea around him (*conlucet Aiax; omne resplendet fretum*, 543). Burning on a rock in the sea, between the landmasses of Europe and Asia and at almost the exact centre point of Seneca's play, Ajax's failed *nostos* is glossed with the imagery of beacon fire that stands for all the Greeks' *nostoi*, and for all the narratives that trace their progress from Troy to Greece.[42] At the same time, Ajax's fiery death makes the hero into the producer of his own narrative, as he fuels the fire itself. Ajax's actions all ended up having powerful repercussions: his rape of Cassandra triggered the rage of Athena, justified the actions of Juno in the *Aeneid* and foreshadowed Agamemnon's abduction of the prophet. Eurybates reminds his audience that it is the hero who provides the agency, who fans the flames of his own life – and death – story.

Eurybates' speech ends by offsetting Ajax's experience with more flames. Firstly, Eurybates mentions the 'deceitful beacon fire' (*perfida ... face*, 570) set by Palamedes' father, Nauplius. This flame was designed to bring to a premature end the *nostoi* of other Greeks responsible for Palamedes' death, and was doubtless a vital part of Euripides' *Palamedes*, the second play in the Trojan trilogy that began with the *Alexander* and ended with the *Trojan Women* (see Chapter 2). Seneca takes care to mark this event as occurring at a space in the Aegean that is as pivotal as – and more specific than – the location of Ajax's death scene. Cape Caphereus gets a detailed description that marks its point between two seas: *arx imminet praerupta quae spectat mare | utrimque geminum* – 'a rugged headland overhangs which looks out at both seas | one on each side' (562–3). The false message sent by Nauplius' beacon is another seam between east and west, between Trojan and Greek disaster. It is also the exception proving the rule that fire in Eurybates' speech emerges from acts of destruction, not from a desire to communicate. This one case of beacon fire is designed as a form of communication, but it is a communication whose message proves to be as false as the fires themselves are real. Finally, events are calmed, but not concluded, by the appearance of the sun as a new day dawns: *Phoebus redit* – 'Phoebus returns' (577). The flames of this beacon in the sky neither create nor signal disaster, but reveal it in all its reality: *damna noctis tristis ostendit dies* – 'the miserable day showed the damage done in the night' (578).

Cassandra's version of a messenger speech, at lines 867–909, offers an even stranger combination of action and revelation. Instead of Eurybates' description of the *nostoi* that took place over ten years of Greek suffering, she describes the brief moments of Agamemnon's death at home as a fair reprisal for the time spent destroying Troy: *res agitur intus magna, par annis decem* – 'a great act is taking place inside, a match for the previous ten years' (867). In place of events scattered over the Mediterranean, she tells of those that happen inside the house of Atreus, the house that exerts such a powerful push-pull force on Cassandra in the previous versions

---

[42] Tarrant (1976) 278 notes Seneca's vagueness concerning Ajax's precise location.

of her story. Contracting the scope of the messenger's speech to focus on events taking place within this narrow domestic domain, and overlaying her speech with the trappings of inspired prophecy even though, as will become clear, the events she describes take place at the very same time she tells of them, Cassandra reveals an even more claustrophobically involved approach to narrative than did Eurybates.

At this point in the play all the gaps normally straddled by Cassandra's prophetic abilities are closed. The vividness or *enargeia* of what Cassandra sees takes her beyond even her customary abilities and places her simultaneously in the roles of actor, messenger and audience:

> *tam clara numquam prouidae mentis furor*
> *ostendit oculis: uideo et intersum et fruor;*
> *imago uisus dubia non fallit meos.*
> *spectemus!*

> Never has the madness of my prophetic mind presented such
>   clear visions
> before my eyes: I see and I am involved and I am revelling in it;
> no uncertain image is tricking my sight.
> Let us watch!   (Sen. *Ag.* 872–5)

As she begins to articulate her description of Agamemnon's murder, Cassandra is drawn into the very events she describes with such enjoyment (*intersum et fruor*, 873). In fact she has already spun these events in terms of a more general Trojan action: *uicimus uicti Phryges* – 'we conquered Phrygians have conquered' (869, discussed above). At the same time, Cassandra's prophetic *furor* is externalised, which marks her as an appreciative observer of what she describes (*ostendit oculis; uideo; uisus ... meos*, 873–4).[43] This is reinforced by her exhortation, *spectemus!* (875), in which the use of the plural is striking. Cassandra appears to be addressing the Trojan chorus whose ode has just ended. Rather than keeping the chorus on the receiving end of her verbal narrative, as the audience to her messenger speech, Cassandra invites the women to join her in a shared viewing of the images she conjures up. By extension, the members of the wider audience watching the play are also being encouraged to consider themselves as Cassandra's peers, watching events alongside her rather than listening to her words.

Interpretation of this scene depends to a considerable degree on the language that relates to its staging, or at least to its implied staging. Cassandra

---

[43] Littlewood (2004) 220–1.

describes her visions as arising from her prophetic ability (*prouida mens*, 872), but the actions she relates are virtually, if not completely, simultaneous with her narrative.[44] She uses verbs in the present tense and explains that the events are happening in a different space, not a different time: *res agitur intus magna* – 'a great act is taking place inside' (867). Paschalis suggests that *intus* here refers not just to the house in which the murder is taking place, but to the specific space behind the *skēnē*, towards which Cassandra is directing her gaze.[45] Cassandra is describing events that are taking place backstage, actions that are visible to her but not her audience, purely because of the sightline from the spot she is occupying on the stage. Her mantic ability to transcend time and space has been reduced to the point where her speech is that of neither a real messenger nor a real prophet: she has no temporal and little spatial distance from the action she relates, and can lay claim to nothing more than a privileged space onstage. For Zanobi, by contrast, *intus* locates Cassandra's visions inside her mind.[46] These are then brought into the realm of more conventional spectatorship through her exhortation to her audience to watch with her as she describes them, evoking the narrations of pantomime performance. This allows Cassandra to sustain a display of divinely privileged knowledge, though she remains only minimally separated from the action and from her audience.

These two 'messenger' speeches of Eurybates and Cassandra each construct a narrative in which the action threatens to overpower the normal distancing process of storytelling. Eurybates connects the landmasses of Asia and Europe through his account of Greek and Trojan journeys that do not trace the path of the beacon fire, but actually replace it, generating their own light – firelight and sunlight – that proves to be revelatory and destructive in equal measure as everything proceeds inexorably westwards. Cassandra connects the spaces inside and outside the house of Atreus, identified with the spaces off- and onstage, by relaying events that are occurring at exactly the same time as her narrative. With Cassandra neither prophesying the future nor relating the past, the scene of Agamemnon's murder generates its own simultaneous narrative. In both cases the messengers strip away from their speech the very elements that suggest that their narration of events, no matter how vivid, keeps those events at a safe distance from

---

[44] Zanobi (2014) 121.

[45] Paschalis (2010), leaning on the absence of the verb *cerno*, which he argues would be more appropriate to describe prophetic vision than *specto*.

[46] Zanobi (2014) 121. Tarrant (1976) 335–6 also reads this scene as one of clairvoyancy, and suspects the influence of a post-Euripidean work.

an audience that cannot see them, or cannot bear to see them. Instead Eurybates and Cassandra create a discomfiting sense of proximity in time and space to the action they describe.

Spreading the Word

Cassandra brings onstage the action that is purportedly taking place back-stage. Her all-too-vivid voice also takes the action to the theatrical front of house, not quite breaking the fourth wall but still breaching the barrier between her visions and the experience of the external audience. Cassandra's visions may not be strictly prophetic in this play, but her unusual perception allows her to manipulate the different perspectives from which the action is appreciated, and to shape the degree to which the audience feels implicated in the action.[47]

Cassandra begins by asserting her unique independence within the play. This includes detaching herself from the chorus of her Trojan fellow captives, even though she will later invite them to share her visions. The chorus encourages a communal response to the terrors surrounding them: *lacrimas lacrimis miscere iuuat* – 'It is comforting to mingle tears with tears' (664). Cassandra rejects such an approach, spurning the community closest to her and the mode of support that it offers:

> *Cohibete lacrimas omne quas tempus petet,*
> *Troades, et ipsae uestra lamentabili*
> *lugete gemitu funera: aerumnae meae*
> *socium recusant. cladibus questus meis*
> *remouete: nostris ipsa sufficiam malis.*

> Restrain the tears that every future age will demand,
> Trojan women, and grieve the deaths of your own
> with mournful cry: my tribulations
> reject company. Keep your laments away
> from my misfortunes: I shall be enough for my troubles.
> (Sen. *Ag.* 659–63)

With the tears 'that every future age will demand', Cassandra hints at Hecuba's self-conscious reference to her tragedy 'providing themes to the Muses of later mortals' in Euripides' *Trojan Women* (Eur. *Tro.* 1245). Cassandra's self-isolation here also evokes features of Euripides' stubbornly independent version of the prophet, but Seneca's Cassandra does not reject

[47] For detailed studies of the gaze as a focalising instrument for the audience see Feldherr (2010) 123–59 on Ovid's *Metamorphoses* and Fitzgerald (1995) 140–68 on Catullus 64.

the pain of grief itself as Euripides' did. She prefers, rather, to lay claim to a grief and a perspective that does not depend on the sympathy of others, at least not that of her fellows in captivity. Her isolation, her determination to be her own best audience, removes her from the need to persuade her immediate onstage audience and draws her away from the clinging interests of any single group.

Though the Trojan chorus tries to persuade Cassandra that her solo lament cannot possibly be sufficient to encompass her grief, it ultimately only reinforces the notion that Cassandra's life experience is as resistant to an adequate response as are her prophecies. The chorus adduces several mythic narratives of frenzied grief, such as that of the Corybantic Galli, and activates with particular emphasis the metaphors of tragically lamenting birdsong that have already become peculiarly associated with Cassandra's experience. First they invoke the songs of Procne and Philomela. This myth, one with which Aeschylus toyed in his *Agamemnon* to explore Cassandra's incomprehensible utterances, had become increasingly polyvalent over time: confusion reigned over whether Procne was transformed into the nightingale and Philomela into the swallow (as in Aeschylus' play), or vice versa. Ovid reinforces the ambiguity when he addresses the myth's moment of metamorphosis – *quarum petit altera siluas,* | *altera tecta subit* – 'of whom one heads for the woods, | the other goes under the roof' (Ov. *Met.* 6.668–9) – and seems to have been building on Augustan poets' general uncertainty over the details of the myth.[48] The flexibility of association continues to play a part in Seneca's version of the story. Here the nightingale continues to sing the name 'Itys' (still in the accusative, *Ityn*, as at Aesch. *Ag.* 1144), but it is the swallow that now chatters about a husband's outrage (the swallow is described as *garrula* – 'chatty' (Sen. *Ag.* 275), like Ovid's fruitlessly prophetic *cornix* at *Met.* 2.547–50, and quite inappropriate for the silenced Philomela).[49] The nightingale's song is described as a *mobile carmen* – 'changeable song' (Sen. *Ag.* 670), reflecting in its modulations the uncertainty within the tradition as to which song Procne or Philomela will sing, and to which voice Cassandra's is best assimilated.[50] The chorus then extends the list of mythological exempla, adducing more

[48] Morgan (1999) 208–9 offers a helpful exploration of the tradition as it relates to Virgil.
[49] On Ovid's crow and her metapoetic garrulousness see Keith (1992) 39–61.
[50] Fitch (2004) leans towards the inversion of Aeschylus' identification, assuming that the nightingale lamenting Itys is now Philomela and that Procne, as the garrulous swallow, is lamenting her husband's horrors. Though he notes the ambiguities and vagueness of this passage, Tarrant (1976) infers the opposite: Procne remains the nightingale, while Philomela is the swallow chattering about Tereus, who is both her attacker and her sister's husband. Martial 14.75 calls Philomela a *garrula ... auis*, which implies that he too is keeping Aeschylus' original associations.

birds whose metamorphosis came from unbearable human grief: the swan (679) and the halcyons (681).

In the end, in the collective view of the Trojan chorus, none of these songs is sufficient to describe the expression of grief, no matter how the myths' details are presented. But just as there is no end to the expression of Cassandra's trauma, so there is no end to that of the other Trojan women of the chorus, who reaffirm their affinity with Cassandra through their grief:

> *non est lacrimis, Cassandra, modus,*
> *quia quae patimur uicere modum.*

> There is no limit, Cassandra, to our tears,
> for our sufferings have conquered any limit.   (Sen. *Ag.* 691–2)

The lack of any 'limit' (*modus*), not just to Cassandra's tears but also to the tears of all the captive women, is the failure of any limit; it is a reinforcement of the lack of boundaries in this play, be they personal, geographical, mythic or linguistic. The absence of this limit is also the failure of song, of *modus* in its meaning of τὸ μέτρον – 'metre', the means by which the women's experience can be translated into meaningful sound. As Trinacty notes, Cassandra will go on to demonstrate that her song is unconstrained by normal metrical limits when she shifts from one metre to another within her inspired utterance at lines 720–74.[51] With the chorus women's reference to their own grief and suffering as also having overwhelmed the normal building blocks of expression (*uicere modum*), the chorus describes its particular Senecan version of the unspecific chirruping 'unmusical music' (νόμον ἄνομον, Aesch. *Ag.* 1142) that Aeschylus' chorus had identified with Cassandra's lament. Seneca's chorus insists that it shares in Cassandra's experience of vocal excess.

Seneca's Cassandra begins by operating within her own isolated world of grief, then, but this position is modified as her interactions with other characters develop. Nothing Cassandra says appears to be particularly incomprehensible to others, and the inadequacy of language to express the events that she experiences is an inadequacy shared by the Trojan chorus. As the play goes on, Cassandra begins to welcome other communities sharing her visionary experience with all its exhilarations and frustrations, even if they cannot share her exact understanding of the future ahead. From the Trojan chorus, Cassandra reaches out to the Greek protagonists, and then even further, to the play's Roman audience.

---

[51] *OLD* s.v. *modus* 7, with Trinacty (2014) 201 and Tarrant (1976) 314.

After Cassandra experiences her vision of the underworld, she prays to its spirits that the underworld be uncovered and exposed to the world above. Her ostensible goal is to let the crowd of dead Trojans peer out (*prospiciat*, 757) from the underworld to see the world in which vengeance is being enacted. In her last line of iambic speech, before she ratchets up her vocal production into a lyric invocation of the Furies, she addresses the dead: *spectate, miseri: fata se uertunt retro!* – 'Watch, you poor sufferers: the fates are turning back on themselves!' (758). The theme of cosmic reversal began right at the beginning of the play, during Thyestes' first appearance from the underworld. There he noted how he had begun the work of inverting nature (*uersa natura est retro*, 34) and experienced his own visions of the events that would follow (46).[52] The theme is now all the more firmly linked to the work of observing events unfold. Cassandra's eyes, as always the focal point for her visionary experience of the future in terms of the present, have already been seen rolling 'back' in the chorus' description of her mania: *uersi retro | torquentur oculi* (714–15).[53] Now inverted spectatorship joins the inversion of what is fated: the dead are no longer just the object of Cassandra's visions, but join Thyestes in looking out at the living and anticipating the reversal of past events. Cassandra's imperative, *spectate* (758), instructs the protagonists of the past to become viewers of the present, just as she will soon invite other audiences to share in her vision of the actions that are taking place within the house: *spectemus!* (875). As she notes in that scene, all the anticipation and reflection that she normally masterminds is collapsing into an appreciation of this present moment, in this particular place: *uenere fata* – 'The fates have arrived' (885). In both these cases, Cassandra mobilises Trojans – Trojans who are either dead in the underworld or captive in the chorus – to provide a triumphant viewing audience from the past and from the east, looking in upon the Argive present onstage. At the same time, Cassandra is turning those Trojans into an avatar for the Roman theatre audience that resides in the future and in the west, an audience that is also looking in on the events onstage. Both audiences watch the events unfolding in a shared act of spectatorship that takes place simultaneously in the world of the theatre, and yet at a millennium's and a sea's distance in mytho-historical terms.

Cassandra also manages to turn the main actors in the drama circling around her into puppets whose actions are no longer strictly their own, but

---

[52] The theme is explored by Schiesaro (2003) 202–4.
[53] Schiesaro (2003) 203.

are manipulated by Cassandra and her sympathisers. She does so by evoking the modes of communication and action that she used in previous versions of her story to wrestle with her predetermined mythic trajectory. In the literary tradition, Cassandra's paradoxical knowledge and disempowerment is always most vividly illustrated when her body takes over from her voice. In Aeschylus' *Agamemnon*, Clytemnestra suggests that Cassandra gesticulates with her hands; in Virgil's *Aeneid*, Cassandra uses her eyes rather than her hands to reach to the heavens; and in Ovid's *Metamorphoses*, her hands stretch upwards again in a futile appeal. In Seneca's *Agamemnon*, hands and eyes become the focal points for action and appeal in Cassandra's narrative of the final moments of Agamemnon, but they are not the prophet's own hands and eyes. They are the physical tools of the agents upon whose violence and trauma she looks, and asks others to look.[54]

It is Clytemnestra who begins this process. According to Cassandra's vision of the action inside, in which she gleefully half-participates (*uideo et intersum et fruor*, 873), Clytemnestra cajoles Agamemnon to change out of his foreign outfit (*cultus … hostiles*, 881) into something that is homemade: *coniugis fidae manu | textos amictus* – 'a cloak woven | by the hand of his faithful wife' (882–3). This garment turns out to be deadly, partly because its folds constrain the hands of the king (*exitum manibus negant*, 888). For a brief moment Aegisthus' hands take over: he makes a pathetic attempt to stab Agamemnon in the side with a trembling hand (*trementi … dextra*, 890), but the wound is insufficiently deep. Now Clytemnestra's hands return to the action (*armat bipenni Tyndaris dextram furens* – 'mad Tyndaris takes an axe in her right hand', 897) and, while eyeing up her victim like someone about to make an animal sacrifice (*designat oculis*, 899), she aims the weapon with 'impious' hand (*sic huc et illuc impiam librat manum*, 900). The hands and eyes of a prophet held captive by Greeks and by fate itself have become, in that prophet's narrative of fate's ineluctable fulfilment, the hands and eyes of Greeks turned against each other.

Cassandra's direction of the frenzied 'arming' and 'disarming' surrounding Agamemnon does not end with a final stroke of death. Instead, in her simultaneous narration of his last moments, Cassandra skips to the second after that fatal blow, the point when it is clear that Agamemnon is dead. Here she suddenly adopts the language of Roman gladiatorial games: *habet, peractum est!* – 'He's had it, it's all over!' (901).[55] Cassandra's gladiatorial

---

[54] On the 'speaking hands' of pantomime see Lada-Richards (2007) esp. 44–8.
[55] *OLD* s.v. *habeo* 16.d.

idiom evokes a peculiarly Roman kind of spectatorship, and one of which Seneca clearly disapproves in his letters, not because of the violence itself, but because it pervades and corrupts its viewers.[56] The ambivalence inherent in this gleeful portrayal of Agamemnon's murder pivots on Cassandra's shifting roles (author, performer, audience member), which straddle the many aspects of literary and theatrical production. Cassandra's narrative highlights the bodily instruments she associates with her own death and appeal in past instantiations; here they have become the violent hands of the killers and constrained hands of the victim Agamemnon. With these gestures Cassandra supplies the focal point at which the violence takes place, constructing the scenario with an impresario's sense of drama. But even as she directs the focus of the action, her visions and her language of spectatorship here also position her as a proxy viewer. Littlewood describes her detachment (compared to her earlier frenzied visions of the underworld) as 'the self-possession of a spectator without pity'.[57] Her account of the scenario with gladiatorial overtones emphasises the fact that her corrupting vision is being conveyed further afield, to a still wider, and Roman, audience. This audience is no less morally implicated in the cruelty being described than are the spectators at a human bloodbath in the amphitheatre, whose thirst for violence stages the horror in the first place and whose thumbs, turned up or down, determine the wretched protagonists' fate.

Cassandra's narrative concludes with an image reinforcing the impression that she has deliberately manipulated the direction of gaze and locus of action throughout this 'prophecy'. She turns to the sun, and notes that it seems unsure as to how to proceed through the heavens:

> *stat ecce Titan, dubius emerito die*
> *suane currat an Thyestea uia.*

> Look, the Titan stops still, uncertain now his day is over
> whether he should run along his own route or the route of Thyestes.

> (Sen. *Ag.* 908–9)

---

[56] See e.g. Sen. *Ep.* 7. The issue is explored in Edwards (2007) 46–77. This is not quite the same as the question regarding the implication of audiences in Senecan drama and the difficulties in reconciling this with Stoic dogma, but it is not unrelated. Seneca himself notes that poetry ignites the emotions: *carmina poetarum, quae adfectibus nostris facem subdant* – 'the songs of the poets, which inflame our emotions' (Sen. *Ep.* 115.12). See further Schiesaro (2003) esp. 228–43 and Staley (2009) esp. 28–34, 60–4.

[57] Littlewood (2004) 223.

In Seneca's *Agamemnon*, the sun has already risen once to reveal a terrible day at the end of Eurybates' messenger speech (*Phoebus redit … damna noctis … ostendit*, 577–8). The sun now also brings to a close Cassandra's strange messenger speech, in which the prophet measures the horror of her narrative by the solar scale originally established when Agamemnon's father, Atreus, forced Thyestes to eat his own children. During that scene, described vividly in choral song in Seneca's *Thyestes* (Sen. *Thy.* 789–884) and referred to in his *Agamemnon* (Sen. *Ag.* 295–7), the sun had fled from the sky in its disgust at the sight, censoring the vision in case it might implicate other viewers. A generation later, Cassandra suspends her narrative at the point where she notes that the sun is left poised midway through the air, neither sinking to the east nor the west, glaring at events in moral confusion and replicating the uneasy sense of responsibility that may be felt by the narrator who is both illuminating the scene and watching it as a part of the avid audience.

The sun's pause picks up on Eurybates' imagery, then, and the imagery found in the previous generation of the house of Atreus. It also harks back to the earlier literary generation, to Aeschylus' *Agamemnon*. The last images that Cassandra had constructed in that play, the shadows and the scribble that stand for human activity in all its enacted and refracted variations (Aesch. *Ag.* 1328–9), had been placed in the light of the sun setting in the west: 'and facing the last light of the sun, I pray …' (Aesch. *Ag.* 1323–4). This was the point at which Aeschylus' Cassandra handed over to future avengers, to the shadows and scribbles that would be produced under a new sun. The hovering sun described by Seneca's Cassandra also marks the end of one story and the transition to another, but the nature of that transition is as undecided as the motion of the sun. Without the sun's clear movement from east to west, without a promise that it will set on the human action onstage, Cassandra presages the lack of closure that marks the last lines of Seneca's *Agamemnon*. Her themes will spill out beyond the story, the setting and the stage.

Immediately after Cassandra's reflection on the paused sun, which ends her barely prophetic 'messenger' speech, there is a curious interlude – a pause in its own right – in which Electra and Orestes appear onstage, fully apprised of the events that have just taken place inside the house. Orestes escapes with Strophius and Pylades, who were conveniently passing by, and Electra spars with her mother and Aegisthus until she is condemned to imprisonment. The play finally returns to Cassandra, with Clytemnestra furiously rounding on the prophet. Clytemnestra orders her to be dragged away (*trahite*, Sen. *Ag.* 1003) so that the prophet may follow Agamemnon (*sequatur*, 1003). Cassandra's response sums up her role as the figure around

whom the action revolves, and around whose body the action is to be forever viewed and reformulated:

> *Ne trahite, uestros ipsa praecedam gradus.*
> *perferre prima nuntium Phrygibus meis*
> *propero: repletum ratibus euersis mare,*
> *captas Mycenas, mille ductorem ducum,*
> *ut paria fata Troicis lueret malis,*
> *perisse dono, feminae stupro, dolo.*
> *nihil moramur, rapite, quin grates ago:*
> *iam, iam iuuat uixisse post Troiam, iuuat.*

> Do not drag me off; I shall proceed ahead of your footsteps.
> I am eager to be the first to bring the news to my Phrygians:
> that the sea has overflowed with shipwrecked boats,
> that Mycenae has been captured, that the leader of one
>   thousand leaders,
> in order to pay for the Trojan troubles with equal doom,
> has perished by a gift, by the depravity of a woman, by trickery.
> I am not holding back, take me away, indeed I thank you:
> now, finally, I rejoice – rejoice! – to have lived beyond the
>   fall of Troy.   (Sen. *Ag.* 1004–11)

Rather than 'following' the events that she had prophesied in real time,
Cassandra insists that she will anticipate her murderers (*uestros … praecedam
gradus*, 1004). With the haste of Euripides' Cassandra, she rushes to transcend
the boundary between the living and the dead (*propero … nihil moramur*,
1006, 1010). Her goal is not just to move into the underworld, but to take
her narrative there and become the first to narrate to the triumphant Trojans
the story of the disastrous *nostoi* and the terrible events at Mycenae. At the
moment her death becomes imminent, Cassandra celebrates the precise length
of her life, a length that is defined by her survival past Troy's fall, the tradition-
ally longed-for point of death ('whoever lies dead at Troy | is called lucky', 514–
15). Cassandra's joy in her life's coda, another kind of 'excess', has come now
(*iam, iam*, 1011) in a space and time beyond the fall of Troy (*post Troiam*, 1011).

At this moment Cassandra is as suspended as the sun she sees hovering
uncertainly in the sky: paused between life and death; post-Troy and pre-
underworld; thinking ahead to how she will embark on yet another tale
of Greek disasters from the retrospective rather than prospective angle, for
the benefit of the dead Trojans who will happily believe her history from
beyond the grave. This transitional position allows Cassandra to facilitate
one last perspectival shift that again transfers the burden of her prophetic
understanding away from her immediate audience on the stage, and this
time hands it over to the external, contemporary, Roman audience.

Clytemnestra's anger bursts out in one final exclamation: *Furiosa, morere!* – 'Die, mad as you are!' (1012). Cassandra's response provides the last words in the play: *Veniet et uobis furor* – 'Madness will come to you too' (1012). The exchange appears to be limited to these two protagonists who have been left hurling insults at each other at the end of the play. Cassandra and Clytemnestra each accuse the other of *furor* ('madness'), a passion that has pervaded the play and has characterised the extreme lows of Ajax's behaviour as well as the extreme highs of Cassandra.[58] The word encapsulates the Stoic horror of any overwhelming or distorting emotion that defies a rational response to the workings of the cosmos. Cassandra's prophetic *furor*, though technically aligned with fate, is perceived as a kind of madness. The prophet makes no effort to correct Clytemnestra's characterisation of her in such a way, when Clytemnestra describes her as *furiosa*. Instead, however, Cassandra suggests that *furor* is more widely shared than Clytemnestra imagines.

This is not the first time that Cassandra has inspired such a notion of shared *furor*. After Cassandra's first frenzied vision of the underworld, the chorus had noted that her *furor* appeared to be mobile: *iam peruagatus ipse se fregit furor* – 'Now her madness has run its full course and spent itself' (775). With the word *peruagatus* the chorus describes how Cassandra's visionary inspiration, manifesting as madness, appears to move through and out of her body: it diffuses itself and dissipates beyond the limits of her physical form. In the last phrase of the play, *Veniet et uobis furor*, Cassandra returns to this idea. The prophet's riposte to Clytemnestra gives her *furor* an even stronger motion: she threatens that it will travel away from Cassandra and towards her addressees. The conventional assumption is that with this fresh *furor* Cassandra refers to the vengeance of Orestes, which will be visited upon both Clytemnestra and Aegisthus. Yet this is not quite as simple a back-and-forth exchange as the combative *antilabe* between the two women would suggest. Cassandra had used the second person plural in her previous speech (*ne trahite ... rapite ...* , 1004, 1010), in which she refers not to Clytemnestra and Aegisthus, but to the orderlies who had been ordered by Clytemnestra to drag her away (*trahite*, 1003). The second person plural in Cassandra's final phrase may also be assumed to spill out beyond the main female protagonists. The silence that follows that final

---

[58] *Furor* takes the form of prophetic inspiration, vengeance and the more generalised chaos of the failed *nostoi*. Paschalis (2010) finds twenty occurrences of the word in Seneca's *Agamemnon* and notes that this number is surpassed only in *Hercules Furens* and *Phaedra*. For Boyle (1997) 43, it is Cassandra's longing for death itself that is characterised as *furor*, picking up on Calder (1976) 36.

phrase, and the expectation that the noise to follow can come only from the audience response to the play, suggests that *uobis* is neither limited to Clytemnestra and Aegisthus, nor even to the collection of characters onstage. The 'you' on whom Cassandra promises that *furor* will descend is the 'you' before whom the words and action have just stopped: the audience 'you' who must respond to Cassandra's last phrase. Like the mysterious figure in the last lines of Lycophron's *Alexandra*, the 'someone' who will finally grasp Cassandra's riddles with a painful level of understanding (Lycoph. *Alex.* 1458), so Seneca's 'you' embraces all those who use their own suffering to translate, share and understand Cassandra's experience of tyranny, beginning with her Roman audience.

Seneca's Cassandra has been the pivot for action and reaction onstage and offstage. She has brought narratives from east to west, from the land of the living to the world of the dead, from the inside of the house of Atreus out to the choral audience onstage and thence to the live audience in the theatre or auditorium. She has taken part in the action and shaped its narrative form, while she has also embraced the role of spectator and invited her Trojan comrades dead and alive as well as her Roman descendants to share that viewing experience with her. In her final words, she reminds the external audience that they are implicated in the events that they have seen on stage or heard in recitation by pointing out how the mad possession that normally characterises Cassandra alone will spread to them too.

The shared emotion of *furor* is a passionate response to events that takes hold of its sufferer and dispossesses it of self-control. Cassandra's prophetic voice has created a sympathetic community of understanding that spills beyond the conventional theatrical boundaries, a community of audience members who are as impotent to enact change as is the prophet herself. The *furor* of Cassandra's audience takes over from that of the prophet in the form of an equally passionate but futile comprehension of the logic of authoritarian force in the cosmos. This force exists within the theatre as an echo of the reality outside it, in the same way that Agamemnon's murder is narrated in the form of a vision by Cassandra onstage while it actually takes place backstage. There are powerful and productive currents of communication within the world of Neronian theatre, as Bartsch has shown, but the frustrations of the all-seeing Cassandra and her followers demonstrate that these currents do not necessarily translate into philosophical or political empowerment in the world outside the theatre.[59] Though

---

[59] Bartsch (1994). As Staley (2009) 22–3 points out, Seneca's plays are best read as representations of human passions, not as guides to Stoic ethics. It should also be noted that we cannot be confident that Seneca's *Agamemnon* is Neronian.

Cassandra ultimately reaches out to share her vision with many communities, she dismisses the healing possibilities of communal lament when the Trojan chorus offers its support. The process of acknowledging the tyranny of fate, and the fate imposed by a tyrannical regime, is as isolating as if the text were being consumed (as it may indeed have been) in the context of a private recitation or a silent personal reading.

Cassandra's mediating function has disappeared in the very success of her communication with her audiences within and outside Seneca's drama. She has few of the problems faced in earlier versions of her story, problems that had mostly been embedded in the impossibility of transcending spatial, temporal, or linguistic distance. In Seneca's *Agamemnon*, events occur with such proximity to her narrative that her claims to prophecy are barely necessary. She engages in less stylistic obscurity than ever before, and layers of literary influence are brutally exposed whenever they threaten to complicate the narrative. The creativity occurs in Cassandra's insistence on drawing greater and greater numbers of people into the madness of her futile understanding: she glues events to their narratives, narratives to their interpretation, and forces her entire audience into a brutally clear understanding of fate while reinforcing their sense of powerlessness. By the end of the play Cassandra has been fully translated and the drama, irresistible and predestined as it is, has been expanded to embrace past, present, future; Troy, Greece, Rome; backstage, onstage and audience; tragic performance, song-and-dance pantomime, personal reading. Seneca's Medea noted the process by which she had grown into herself: *Medea nunc sum* – 'now I am Medea' (Sen. *Med.* 910). Seneca's Cassandra and her audiences could reformulate that line to describe their freshly shared experience of the prophet's paradoxical combination of understanding and disempowerment: *Cassandra nunc sumus* – 'Now we are Cassandra.'

Conclusion
Transposing Cassandra

In her various appearances across half a millennium of Greek and Latin poetry, Cassandra – along with her alter ego, the Cumaean Sibyl – blazes a trail of linguistic confusion that defies and transcends communicative norms. Apollo's twofold imposition, his gift and his curse, creates what the introduction to this book described as Cassandra's 'prophetic paradox': at the very moment Cassandra utters (or inscribes) truths about the future, she becomes incomprehensible to those around her. The result is that she must resign the reconstruction of her meaning to the imaginative guesswork of her audience(s). The 'foreignising' function within Cassandra's prophetic speech, her defamiliarisation of a known language, makes for ambiguities and deficiencies in her meaning and tone. Yet these apparent failures of communication take place within a basically comprehensible linguistic system; the prophet's words are still recognisable as language, even as a particular language (e.g. Greek), so they cannot be dismissed as gibberish. This means that while Cassandra's prophecies resist precise construal, they still demand attention: their frustrations seed a supplementary interpretative response in an audience that hears tantalising fragments of sense within her garbled words. Cassandra's prophetic language presents itself as a flawed translation of the narrative of future events, a translation that invites further acts of translation to reconstruct the original (but yet-to-happen) story. In engaging with these semantic processes the prophet and her audiences explore more or less explicitly many of the oppositional elements on which all human communications are founded: sound and silence, knowledge and ignorance, repetition and adaptation, literalism and symbolism, performance and description, empathy and enmity, trust and suspicion, power and vulnerability. Those audience members who make the effort to grapple seriously with Cassandra's prophetic paradox learn, or reveal, more about the possibilities of human language(s) than they could ever have done with a more straightforward narrative of future events.

A fresh exposition of Cassandra's relationship with language can be found in a creative response written only a few years ago. In her collection of poetry entitled *Hapax*, published in 2006, A. E. Stallings includes a poem she calls 'Cassandra'.[1] The collection as a whole is intriguingly named. A *hapax legomenon* is a word 'spoken once': a word that is found only in a single attestation within a work or, in an extreme case, a word that appears only once across the entire extant corpus of classical literature. In order to excavate the meaning of a lonely *hapax legomenon*, readers must extrapolate from the context, exercise their knowledge of etymology and cognate words, compare the word's usage in other works (if it appears elsewhere) and then take a leap of faith in their translation from the ancient source. Deconstructionists might argue that we take a similar leap of faith when we claim to understand any word in any language, but when a word exists in one solitary citation even its very claim to belong to the specific language world in which it is embedded is put under pressure, and its translatability is brought into particular question. In this respect, the 'hapax' sits perilously close to nonsense, jostling for position on the edge of the language of its author.[2]

Stallings is a poet, classicist and translator; her writings are influenced by an intimate familiarity with some of the more rebarbative literature of ancient Greece and Rome, and shaped by the challenges of constraining contemporary English within formal poetic limits – challenges which she tackles as a native English speaker living in Greek-speaking Athens.[3] The poem 'Cassandra' sits at the very centre of the collection *Hapax*, and it unpicks various elements of Cassandra's prophetic paradox. Stallings' Cassandra speaks in the first person throughout the poem, and she pins her prophetic struggles on the treacheries of linguistic elements both literal and metaphorical, citing the alphabet, grammar, syntax, translation, paraphrase and riddles.

Cassandra

If I may have failed to follow
Your instructions, Lord Apollo,
So all my harping lies unstrung,
I blame it on the human tongue.

---

[1] Stallings (2006) 44.
[2] On Cassandra and nonsense see Chapter 1.
[3] Stallings' other works include translations of Lucretius' *De Rerum Natura* and Hesiod's *Works and Days*.

Our speech ever was at odds
With the utterance of gods:
Tenses have no paradigm
For those translated out of time.

Perhaps mortals should rejoice
To conjugate in passive voice –
The alphabet to which I go
Is suffering, and ends in O.

Paraphrase can only worsen:
For you, there is no second person,
'I want' the same verb as 'must be,'
'Love,' construed as 'yield to me,'

The homonym of 'curse' and 'give,'
No mood but the infinitive.   (A. E. Stallings *Hapax*, 44)

Stallings' Cassandra begins her poem on a conditional note – 'If I may have failed' – which sets a tone of ambivalence that runs throughout and is reinforced halfway through with 'Perhaps ...'. This construction echoes the conditionals that appear when prophets in ancient works want to appeal to Apollo's influence as proof of their speech's veracity. Such an example can be found in the *Trojan Women* in Cassandra's prediction of Agamemnon's downfall, εἰ γὰρ ἔστι Λοξίας – 'if Loxias exists' (Eur. *Tro.* 356), and it appears again when Helenus, who is about to give the Trojans his most essential piece of advice for their future success, justifies his advisory role: *animum si ueris implet Apollo* – 'if Apollo fills [my] mind with the truth' (Verg. *Aen.* 3.434). In both these cases the conditional presumes to present an axiom concerning the god's authority that guarantees the truth of the claims to come, but the syntax introduces a note of mild doubt over Apollo's reliability that is appropriate to prophets' ever-equivocal utterances. In Stallings' poem, Cassandra shifts the doubt from god to prophet: she uses the conditional not to appeal to Apollo's authority over her truthful speech, but to measure her own distorting effect on Apollo's words and intents. Cassandra is exploring her defiance of Apollo's 'instructions', instructions that might refer either to his sexual approaches or to his prophetic guidance, or to both. This defiance Cassandra attributes to the flawed nature of language itself, 'the human tongue'.

Avoiding mention of a specific language, Cassandra's reference to 'the human tongue' pits not barbarian against native speaker, but mortal against divine. 'I blame it on the human tongue', evoking the idiom 'she's only human', projects an appearance of ingenuousness and vulnerability regarding her own mortal speech that is underscored by the deceptively simple singsong form of the poem. It is composed of lines in four regular beats, marshalled into stanzas of four lines each, four of which stanzas – plus a bonus couplet – make up the entirety of the poem. This strict form is further regimented by the rhyming couplets that run throughout the poem. However, within this tight structure there is complexity and nuance: for example, the four-beat lines slip between flowing and conversational iambic tetrameters and more aggressively confrontational trochaic tetrameters. This can be seen at work in the second stanza: 'Our speech ever was at odds | With the utterance of gods'. The emphases in the first line are particularly dissonant, but appropriately so: though 'speech' is the subject of the sentence, and though it is frontloaded within the line and the stanza, the syncopated feel of the catalectic trochaic tetrameter diminishes its emphasis in favour of 'Our', 'ever', 'was' and 'odds'. 'Our' flawed speech then contrasts with the more comfortably stressed 'utterance of gods', while the placement of these two phrases at the opposite ends of the rhyming couplet highlights the difficulty involved in communicating across the divide between these languages. This carefully structured poem in 'human tongue' then goes on to compare the radical lawlessness of divine language. The gods' immortal existence is unconstrained by the normal limitations of past, present and future – they are 'translated out of time' – and they prove to be as liberated from the grammatical models of mortal language as they are from the awkward emphases of this poem's metre: their 'Tenses have no paradigm'.

At the heart of the poem, however, lies the suggestion that Cassandra's experience with language differs not only from that of the gods, but also from that of other mortal speakers. In other words, as this book has argued, although she translates the language of the gods into a 'human tongue', her translation requires further translation. In the third stanza Cassandra speculates on the advantages that exist for mortals who 'conjugate in passive voice' – who speak without agency, accepting fate as it comes. Can this include Cassandra, whose prophecies are fatalistic but furiously defiant at the same time? If Cassandra is alluding to the benefit of taking a more submissive 'conjugal' approach to Apollo, she is certainly drawing a contrast with her own resistance and the language-related punishment that follows. Indeed, the stanza goes on to dwell on that punishment, as Cassandra shows how her unique predicament forces her to experience language in a truly unusual way: in the fragmented form of the letters of the alphabet. Here, finally, Stallings' Cassandra alludes to the specific human language in which she is purportedly operating, as the 'alphabet' that 'ends in O' (Ω – omega) must be Greek. But, as is the case with all the grammatical and syntactic forms described within the poem, this reference to the foundational elements of a particular language stands for more than the articulation of meaning in that single language. This fully disintegrated set of letters 'Is suffering', and it culminates in a universal expression of pain: 'O' ('Oh'). An account of future suffering is what Cassandra is always endeavouring to shape from pained cries into words, while her attempts to form those words and their failure to convince create in turn a new tale of suffering. With the exclamation of that final letter 'O', Stallings' Cassandra harks back to her first appearance in Aeschylus' *Agamemnon*. There her initial stutterings, beginning with the short 'o' (O – omicron), expand into a pained invocation of Apollo, where Cassandra stretches the first letter of the god's name (A – alpha), also the first letter of the alphabet, into a cry that becomes the final letter of the alphabet (Ω – omega): ὀτοτοτοτοῖ ποποῖ δᾶ· | ὤπολλον ὤπολλον – 'Otototototoi popoi da; | Ahpollo Ahpollo' (Aesch. *Ag.* 1076–7).

Throughout Stallings' poem Cassandra addresses her twisted relationship with sound and sense, and the way in which her utterance embraces the extremes of both as it ranges from twittering to truth-telling. Stallings' Cassandra admits that for her the sounds of the alphabet, though designed to encode verbal language, have always expressed her emotion better than they have her message. She also alludes to another communication system that by its very nature leans more heavily on sound than sense, and to which Cassandra's utterances have so often been assimilated in the works discussed earlier in this book: music. Although in the first stanza of the poem Cassandra puts the blame for her communicative failures on the general inadequacy of human language, she chooses a musical metaphor to describe the shortcomings of her utterance. Her suggestion that 'all my harping lies unstrung' hints at the prosaic English idiom 'to harp on' about something, and indeed fruitless repetition – with its female-gendered association with nagging – bears no little part in Cassandra's characteristic speech. At the same time, the phrase evokes the elevated and allusive ancient depictions of her voice in terms of lyrical sound and song. Lycophron's Cassandra describes her speech as a form of music-making: κενὸν ψάλλουσα μάστακος κρότον – 'twanging the empty tremolo of my mouth' (Lycoph. *Alex.* 1453). This surreally compressed aural imagery synthesises performance on a stringed musical instrument such as the lyre (ψάλλουσα) with Cassandra's rattling vocal utterance (μάστακος κρότον), while it still underlines the futility of the sound she produces (κενὸν). Aeschylus explores a version of Cassandra's 'lawless' approach to music's formal structures when the chorus of the *Agamemnon* characterises her sound with a splendid oxymoron: θροεῖς | νόμον ἄνομον – 'you voice | unmusical music' (Aesch. *Ag.* 1141–2). Even when Cassandra has been speaking to the chorus of Euripides' *Trojan Women*, and doing so with relative clarity, it still addresses her as a singer of confusing songs: μέλπεις θ' ἃ μέλπουσ᾽ οὐ σαφῆ δείξεις ἴσως – 'you sing things that perhaps, through your singing, you will show to be unclear' (Eur. *Tro.* 407). Virgil's Sibyl is presented as singing her riddling truths despite being characterised as a habitual writer; her mysterious words are confined neither to the world of inspired song nor to the page on which she (or in this case, Virgil) writes: *horrendas canit ambages ...* | *obscuris uera inuoluens* – 'she sings her terrifying riddles ...* | wrapping the truth in obscurities' (Verg. *Aen.* 6.99–100). Finally, Seneca's Trojan chorus point out to Cassandra their common transcendence of song: *quae patimur uicere modum* – 'our sufferings have conquered any limit [rhythm/melody]' (Sen. *Ag.* 692); they combine the notion that suffering desires a language in which it can be expressed ('The alphabet to which I go | Is suffering') with the recognition that some suffering can be too great for even the formal building blocks (*modi*) of song to convey.

Moreover, as Stallings' Cassandra goes on to argue, 'paraphrase can only worsen'. This is borne out in every one of the ancient works that deals with her voice. Cassandra's prophecies fail to strip the future of its mystery; her versions of events remain too entangled in a narrative that normal humans find impenetrable. Any further attempt to translate Cassandra's speech into a more easily grasped message or a more palatable soundscape, no matter how creative, is doomed to take the listener even further from her intended meaning. Cassandra's words are functionally unglossable; they are only quotable, as the guard-messenger of Lycophron's *Alexandra* illustrates most explicitly with his literal report: Λέξω τὰ πάντα νητρεκῶς – 'I will tell everything exactly' (Lycoph. *Alex.* 1).

In the fourth stanza of Stallings' poem Cassandra cycles back to her original addressee, Apollo, whose association with the lyre offered merely a hint of his role in inspiring Cassandra's 'harping' in stanza one. Now, though, Apollo is not so easily absolved of his responsibility for Cassandra's communicative difficulties, and his persecution of the prophet is more openly acknowledged. The power imbalance between Cassandra and Apollo is clear from her accusation that 'For you, there is no second person.' Unlike Cassandra, Apollo is incapable of valuing, or even recognising, diversity in people's use of language. He distorts language in his own way, a way that casts Cassandra's distortions into relief: where Cassandra says one thing that lends itself to multiple interpretations, Apollo insists that different words mean the same thing according to his whim. In order to demonstrate this, the poem draws connections between words or phrases that are neither grammatically nor semantically identical, but whose meaning is reduced to the same thing in Apollo's solipsistic language world: ' "I want" the same verb as "must be," | "Love," construed as "yield to me" '. Apollo's divine power makes his prophetic speech performative, guaranteeing its outcome and overriding mortal attempts to read and influence the future according to their various interests. As Lucan wonders in his own scathing account of the god's influence at Delphi, perhaps it is not that Apollo sings what is fated, but the opposite: *quod iubet ille canendo | fit fatum* – 'what he orders in his singing, | becomes fate' (Luc. *B.C.* 5.92–3). Cassandra cannot escape taking on the performativity of Apollo's voice when she delivers her prophecies, but just as she successfully resisted the god's sexual attack, refusing his insistence that she 'yield to me', so the incomprehensibility of her prophetic speech in the world of human communications reintroduces the possibility that her interpreters may also take on an element of her resistance to Apollo when their confusion leads them to deny, at least temporarily, the narrative of events to come.

The steady flow of the poem's four four-line stanzas is disrupted by the final abrupt couplet. Expanding on the dubiously analogous phrases of Apollo that she had given as examples of the god's oppression in the previous stanza, Cassandra begins the last lines with another verbal pairing: 'The homonym of "curse" and "give" '. This sums up the horrible dichotomy behind Apollo's infliction of the prophetic paradox on Cassandra, while it also illustrates Apollo's tendency to conflate different concepts in order to impose his monolithic will. The final line, 'No mood but the infinitive', continues with this acknowledgement of Apollo's power, as his affiliation with 'the infinitive' suggests that he has no interest whatsoever in the range of first, second and third persons with which Cassandra has populated the poem. Yet Cassandra surely has another motive in ending her speech, and the poem, on the word 'infinitive'. It may describe Apollo's selfishly limiting approach to mortal life and language, but it also embraces Cassandra's own profoundly unselfish speech. In her knowledge of her guaranteed failure to convince and the inevitability of her own demise, Cassandra's every utterance from Aeschylus' play through to Stallings' poem shows her disinterested openness to the endless translation work that will be performed on her speech: each interpretation is bound to be inaccurate, but from every flawed reprise there will emerge a new reading. Cassandra's prophecies are 'infinite' in several dimensions: her understanding stretches far into the past and future; her voice travels endlessly through time; and countless listeners continue to translate her prophecies. In this context the final couplet can be read both as a catalectic interruption – a description of Apollo's cruel limitation of Cassandra's speech and his own inescapable imposition of fate as he pleases; and as an addition to the four-square poem – a surplus or remainder that arises from the unendingly rich complexity of Cassandra's utterance.

Stallings' Cassandra is idiomatically English-speaking, but she is very much a product of the Graeco-Roman tradition. In fact, the poem is only one of many works of modern reception that engage with the prophet's voice in ways that reach beyond the cliché of gloomy doom-mongering and respond instead to the complexities of her ancient portraits. Her story appears in works ranging from reworkings of ancient tragedy to Victorian burlesque, from visual art to contemporary dance, from the essay to the novel and across various genres of music.[4] In so many of these cases Cassandra's voice once again manifests as valuable, not because it represents the poignancy of failed communication (though it does that too), but because its failures create a space for more unorthodox communications that build new bridges between individuals and communities.

Just a few examples taken from music and from critical and fictional prose will suffice to show Cassandra's travails with language at work in some of the creative modes that exist beyond poetry. Firstly, the Cassandra of Hector Berlioz's *Les Troyens*, an opera based on the first books of the *Aeneid*. There the prophet laments her incomprehensibility (*tu ne m'écoutes pas* – 'you aren't listening to me') to a rhythm resonant of the Latin hexametric beat. From her silence in the *Aeneid* she has emerged to become the musical essence of *Les Troyens'* epic ambitions. Her situation inspires the composer to draw an analogy between her unheard truths and the fluctuating fortunes of contemporary music in the 1850s, writing in *Evenings with the Orchestra*: 'It is Virgil's Cassandra, the inspired virgin over whom Greeks and Trojans fight, whose prophetic speech [*les paroles prophétiques*] is never listened to and who raises her eyes towards heaven, only her eyes,

---

[4] Neblung (1997) 216–29; Reid and Rohmann (1993) 1, 285–8; Monrós Gaspar and Reece (2011); Goudot (1999a). For a recent dance project see Ludovic Ondiviela's *Cassandra*, a study in the incomprehensibility of madness commissioned by and performed at the Royal Ballet in October–November 2014. The Cumaean Sibyl, too, continues to make herself heard or read, in some form, as her prophecies adapt to the demands of Christian writers from late antiquity and the medieval ages onwards; see Bouquet and Morzadec (2004).

for her hands are bound by chains.'⁵ As Berlioz's music became less popular, so the composer increasingly identified with Cassandra.

More than a century later, Iannis Xenakis, a composer whose work was considerably more iconoclastic than that of Berlioz and whose life as an exile in Paris after the Greek civil war gave him more legitimate reason to feel rejected by the establishment, wrote a very short piece called *Kassandra* (1987). In this extraordinary work a male singer plays the part of both female prophet and male chorus, with the lines of Greek taken directly from Aeschylus' *Agamemnon*. As the exchanges between Cassandra and the chorus grow more frantic, the musical directions make it increasingly difficult for the singer to sustain the distinction between the different characters he is playing. At one point, as his voice leaps and cracks, the singer is instructed to deliver a glissando of a cry that is marked as crossing from the treble clef to the bass clef: the singer must soar from a falsetto scream down to a baritone roar. With this it becomes clear that Cassandra's voice is no longer purely that of a woman facing a chorus of men, or even simply that of an individual facing a community. Instead the broken voice of the single singer shares the fragile power of Cassandra's voice with the members of the chorus, the audience that engages with her. Xenakis had his own devotees who will have well understood this representation of shared pain. Even before *Kassandra* was written, Milan Kundera had dubbed Xenakis a *prophète de l'insensibilité* – 'prophet of emotionlessness', whose brutal but unhistrionic and highly abstract representations of violence granted the Czech writer a strange kind of comfort among the turmoil of the post-war years in Eastern Europe.⁶

Cassandra makes her mark in the world of the essay with the burgeoning feminist movement.⁷ In a particularly close engagement with the classical material, Virginia Woolf turns to Cassandra's voice in her famous essay of the mid-1920s, 'On Not Knowing Greek'. In her discussion of how to translate Aeschylus' impossible Greek, Woolf pounces once again on Cassandra's first stuttering *otototototoi* in the *Agamemnon*, identifying it as a 'naked cry' that represents the epitome of sound triumphing over sense.⁸ Here the incomprehensible voice of the prophet becomes a way for the

---

⁵ My translation of Berlioz (1968 [1854]) 383, a passage that is closely modelled on the language of *Aeneid* 2.402–6. See further Pillinger (2010). For another nineteenth-century French representation of Cassandra turning her eyes to the heavens, but this time in the visual domain, and in response to Ajax's rape, see Jérôme-Martin Langlois' painting of 1810, 'Cassandre implorant la vengeance de Minerve contre Ajax' (cover art).

⁶ Kundera (1981).

⁷ For example, she gives her name to Florence Nightingale's passionate and lengthy mid-nineteenth-century essay on women's energy and abilities going unrecognised. See Monrós Gaspar (2008).

⁸ Woolf (1984 [1925]) 31, with Prins (2005), Dalgarno (2001) and (2012), Pillinger (2017).

author – a woman in a man's world of classical scholarship – to explore the productive borderline between academic translation and creative writing, as Woolf delves into the mysterious poetic moments in which 'meaning is just on the far side of language'.[9]

At the other end of the twentieth century, Christa Wolf allows Cassandra's voice to expand fully from essay into novel, creating in the process one of the most powerful reception works based on the prophet's story. Wolf's *Kassandra* (1983) is composed of four diverse essays and a short novel, all originally delivered as a series of lectures for the Frankfurter Poetik-Vorlesungen (1982).[10] The project, designed as an exploration of alternative literary approaches to the male-dominated cultural tradition, emerged partly from Wolf's surprised sense of dislocation when she visited Athens from East Germany during the Cold War. The author explains that she is preoccupied above all else by 'the sinister effects of alienation [*Entfremdungserscheinungen*]'.[11] In the novel the titular character's prophecies have been transformed into a retrospective and introspective assessment of all the events leading up to her arrival in Argos, a city where 'they do not know that I speak their language'.[12] The work consists of an internal monologue that Cassandra runs through in the moments before her death; the prophet wryly describes herself as having 'Nothing left to describe the world but the language of the past [*Vergangenheitssprache*]'.[13] But with this reversal of her prophetic skills comes a powerful account of the Trojan War that challenges the narratives that have traditionally focused on male heroes. Wolf's Cassandra offers a subjective account that gives a voice, and a measure of resistance, to the women who operate on the margins of a repressive and self-defeating patriarchal state. Cassandra even briefly considers asking Clytemnestra for her help in recording this female counterpoint to the received version of events:

> Send me a scribe, or better yet a young slave woman with a keen memory and a powerful voice [*mit scharfem Gedächtnis und kraftvoller Stimme*]. Ordain that she may repeat to her daughter what she hears from me. That the daughter in turn may pass it on to her daughter, and so on. So that alongside the river of heroic songs this tiny rivulet, too, may reach those faraway, perhaps happier people who will live in times to come.[14]

---

[9] Woolf (1984 [1925]) 31.
[10] The significance of Wolf's spoken delivery of *Kassandra* was reinforced by the work's transformation into a 'spoken opera' by Michael Jarrell in 1994.
[11] Wolf (1984) 142. For the original German see Wolf (2008 [1983]) 11. See also Paul (2009) 200.
[12] Wolf (1984) 5.
[13] Wolf (1984) 14; original German: Wolf (2014 [1984]) 21.
[14] Wolf (1984) 81; original German: Wolf (2014 [1984]) 95.

The prophet imagines a chain of female authorship that carries her voice into the future. Through this hopeful projection Wolf's Cassandra develops, with a feminist twist, a claim that Hecuba makes in Euripides' *Trojan Women*. There the queen acknowledges that the horrors through which she has lived will inspire poets to tell her story in the future. Hecuba is self-consciously aware of her role, as well as that of the other Trojan women, in these tales to come: μούσαις ἀοιδὰς δόντες ὑστέρων βροτῶν – 'providing themes to the Muses of later mortals' (Eur. *Tro.* 1245). Wolf's Cassandra goes a step further: she does not simply predict her part in the stories that will be told, she makes an effort to shape the telling of those stories and to sustain a distinctively female narrative.

What unites these ancient and modern translations of Cassandra's voice is their understanding that they all emerge from, and then replicate, the space of confusion left by the prophet's uniquely thwarted speech. Whether they present themselves as sequels or prequels, whether they retell Cassandra's story or transplant elements of her prophetic mode into another figure such as the Cumaean Sibyl, whether they imagine an autobiography or comment on a biography, they all enact a version of the interpretative process Cassandra invites from her immediate audiences: a translation of her speech that offers a new angle on the events described while sustaining enough of her obscurity to demand further interpretation. From Cassandra's perspective, then, every audience member is a potential link in a chain of reception, a means to her survival as a narrative, if not as a person. Every time Cassandra explicitly addresses her audience, even as she acknowledges its failure to grasp her immediate point, she is affirming the power of her flawed speech to endure through repeated, flawed, translation.

Every one of the ancient texts discussed in this book offers at least one moment in which Cassandra confronts her immediate audience with their responsibility: a responsibility not necessarily to understand her message, but to recognise, and then to perpetuate, the rich combination of truth and obfuscation in her speech. These moments suggest that even if Cassandra and her audience do not reach a point of perfect communication, they will at least share an imperfect kind of communion. In Aeschylus' *Agamemnon*, Cassandra addresses the chorus, the men who, along with the rest of the audience in the theatre, watch her walk to her death:

> καὶ τῶνδ' ὁμοῖον εἴ τι μὴ πείθω· τί γάρ;
> τὸ μέλλον ἥξει, καὶ σύ μ' ἐν τάχει παρὼν
> ἄγαν γ' ἀληθόμαντιν οἰκτίρας ἐρεῖς.

And yet it is all the same if I fail to convince in any of these
    things: what of it?
The future will come, and very soon, right here,
you will pity me and describe me as all too accurate a prophet.
                             (Aesch. *Ag.* 1239–41)

At the moment when the chorus recognises the truth of Cassandra's prophecies, it will find its own voice to replicate her words. The prophet who
later claims that she understands Greek 'only too well' (ἄγαν, 1254), will
become the subject of a chorus that will describe her as 'all too accurate' a
prophet (ἄγαν γ' ἀληθόμαντιν ... ἐρεῖς, 1241).

In the *Trojan Women*, Cassandra asks Hecuba to be the judge of her
emotional state, and if necessary to urge on her daughter:

καὶ πέμπε, κἂν μὴ τἀμά σοι πρόθυμά γ' ἦι
ὤθει βιαίως ...

See me off, and if my own self does not seem enthusiastic enough to you,
force me along ...   (Eur. *Tro.* 355–6)

In a play where her emotions and actions appear to be more baffling
than her words, Cassandra is encouraging Hecuba to demand even
more enthusiasm of the prophet than she has already displayed, and
to chivvy her along as she takes her first steps down the route towards
ensuring the Greeks' destruction. She is asking Hecuba, and by extension all the Trojan women, to recognise her eager commitment to her
fate in this play and to magnify her bizarre characterisation yet further
in response.

In the *Alexandra*, as befits her isolated situation, Cassandra's appeal to a
receptive audience does not come through a direct address in the second
person, but she gropes towards a point of human contact nonetheless:

... σὺν κακῷ δέ τις μαθών,
ὅτ' οὐδὲν ἔσται μῆχος ὠφελεῖν πάτραν,
τὴν φοιβόληπτον αἰνέσει χελιδόνα.

... And having learned it through suffering,
when there will be no way to help my fatherland,
someone will praise the Phoebus-inspired swallow.
                        (Lycoph. *Alex.* 1458–60)

'Someone' – anyone emerging from any of the layers of audience listening
in on Cassandra's speech – will join the prophet in her suffering and in
understanding the futility of any resistance to fate. At that point they

will open their mouths to praise her inspired twittering, just as she had
predicted, in the *Agamemnon*, that the chorus would ultimately proclaim
her exceptional truthfulness.

In the *Aeneid*, the second person address returns in a passage designed to
mark the Cumaean Sibyl's position as a recognised authority, but this time
the address is directed at the prophet herself:

> *te quoque magna manent regnis penetralia nostris:*
> *hic ego namque tuas sortis arcanaque fata*
> *dicta meae genti ponam …*
>
> Magnificent sacred inner shrines await you in our realm:
> for here I shall lay your predictions and hidden fates
> spoken to my people …   (Verg. *Aen.* 6.71–3)

Appropriately enough for a prophet who is reluctant to cater to her audience beyond sending out scattered scribblings, it is the hero Aeneas who
must drag her into some kind of responsive engagement with the audience
who will perpetuate her voice. Here the second person may be applied to
the Sibyl, but the context remains one that celebrates her reception. 'You',
here, refers to the Sibyl in the form of the Sibylline Books that contain her
riddling voice, and will become a treasured and much-translated resource
for a Roman audience reaching down to Virgil's time and beyond.

Finally, in Seneca's *Agamemnon*, Cassandra returns with a vengeance,
addressing not a singular but a plural 'you' that embraces Clytemnestra,
Aegisthus, the chorus(es) and the theatre audience. Indeed, hers is not an
address, but a threat: *Veniet et uobis furor* – 'Madness will come to you too'
(Sen. *Ag.* 1012). Cassandra's audience will not simply align itself with the
prophet's hopeless truth-telling, but will become a vital part of it, replicating the controlled chaos of her voice. Nobody will escape her suffering.

The acts of translation that Cassandra demands of herself and her audience are transformative. The effort required for Cassandra to describe
the future in her tangled speech, and for her audience to grapple with
that description, changes not only the message but also every person who
engages with it. For both Cassandra and the Cumaean Sibyl, the transformation is one that sees an immortal voice, an utterance that grows in value
(if not in clarity) through time, emerging from each of their mortal bodies.
For the prophets' audiences, the transformation consists in their growing
awareness that no matter how they translate the prophetic utterance,
whether they accept its truth or not and whether they welcome their own
agency or not, their very act of interpretation implicates them in the construction of the utterance's meaning as well as its ultimate realisation.

Each stage in the chain of translations emphasises the relative importance of a message's conduit over that of its source. Cassandra's magnetic incoherence pulls the focus towards herself as the bearer, at most the shaper, of prophecy, rather than its genitor, and the scenes in which she acts represent the value of imperfect exchange, not pure monologue. As this process extends beyond Cassandra's interactions with her immediate audience and into the wider audiences of the works in which she is constructed, the possibility for radical interpretations of her words becomes the opportunity for new receptions of her biography. The translation of her words expands into the translation of her life story, often transposed into a relative key as her representation crosses into new media.

For all the painters, composers, writers and choreographers who follow the poets in portraying Cassandra and her prophecies, the core of their representation must lie in reconstructing a voice and a body whose incomprehensibility offers a version of the 'foreignising' function in linguistic translation, a function that challenges the audience to work ever harder to reach some understanding of the strange prophet. Enigmatic silences, blank stillnesses, inarticulate sounds, glares at the heavens or at visions, baffling riddles and incongruous metaphors, explosive physical gestures; Cassandra's responses to the traumatising world around her, behind her and in front of her never offer a clear translation of what she knows, no matter the language or medium in which she performs. Nonetheless, as communities gather in their attempts to translate her mysterious output, Cassandra becomes the inspiration for a more profound, extensive and above all *human* kind of understanding. This understanding is based on sympathy for another's suffering, respect for another's perspective and energetic engagement with another's creativity, no matter how alien it appears.

Bibliography

The titles of modern journals are abbreviated as in *L'Année philologique*.

BNP = H. Cancik, H. Schneider and C. F. Salazar (eds.) (2002–) *Brill's New Pauly*. Brill.

OCD = S. Hornblower, A. Spawforth and E. Eidinow (eds.) (2012) *Oxford Classical Dictionary*, 4th edn. Oxford University Press.

OLD = P. G. W. Glare (ed.) (2012) *Oxford Latin Dictionary*, 2nd edn. Oxford University Press.

LP = E. Lobel and D. Page (eds.) (1955) *Poetarum Lesbiorum Fragmenta*. Oxford University Press.

LSJ = H. G. Liddle and R. Scott. Rev. (eds.) (1996) *A Greek-English Lexicon*, augm. H. S. Jones, with the assistance of R. McKenzie. Oxford University Press.

PMG = D. L. Page (ed.) (1962) *Poetae Melici Graeci*. Oxford University Press.

RE = A. Pauly and G. Wissowa (eds.) (1893–1980) *Real-Encyclopädie der classischen Altertumswissenschaft*. Metzler.

Adams, J. N. (2003) *Bilingualism and the Latin Language*. Cambridge University Press.

Adams, J. N., Janse, M. and Swain, S. (eds.) (2002) *Bilingualism in Ancient Society: Language Contact and the Written Text*. Oxford University Press.

Aélion, R. (1982) 'Silence et personnages silencieux chez les Tragiques', *Euphrosyne* 12: 31–52.

(1983) *Euripide, héritier d'Eschyle*. 2 vols. Les Belles Lettres.

Ahl, F. (1984) 'The art of safe criticism in Greece and Rome', *AJPh* 105.2: 174–208.

Alexiou, M. (1974) *The Ritual Lament in Greek Tradition*. Cambridge University Press.

Anderson, W. S. (1957) 'Vergil's second *Iliad*', *TAPhA* 88: 17–30.

Ash, R. (2002) 'Epic encounters? Ancient historical battle narratives and the epic tradition', in D. S. Levene and D. P. Nelis (eds.), 253–73.

Austin, J. L. (1975) [1962] *How to Do Things with Words*, 2nd edn. J. O. Urmson and M. Sbisà (eds.). Harvard University Press.

Austin, R. G. (1986) *P. Vergili Maronis Aeneidos Liber Sextus*. Oxford University Press.

Barchiesi, A. (1993) 'Future reflexive: two models of allusion and Ovid's *Heroides*', *HSPh* 95: 333–65.

(1994) 'Immovable Delos: *Aeneid* 3.73–98 and the *Hymns* of Callimachus', *CQ* 44.2: 438–43.

(1997a) 'Virgilian narrative: ecphrasis', in C. Martindale (ed.), 271–81.

(1997b) 'Endgames: Ovid's *Metamorphoses* 15 and *Fasti 6*', in D. H. Roberts, F. M. Dunn and D. Fowler (eds.) *Classical Closure: Reading the End in Greek and Latin Literature.* Princeton University Press, 181–208.

(2005) 'Centre and periphery', in S. Harrison (ed.) *A Companion to Latin Literature.* Blackwell, 394–405.

Barker, A. (2004) 'Transforming the nightingale: aspects of Athenian musical discourse in the late fifth century', in P. Murray and P. Wilson (eds.) *Music and the Muses: The Culture of* mousikê *in the Classical Athenian City.* Oxford University Press, 185–204.

Bartsch, S. (1994) *Actors in the Audience: Theatricality and Doublespeak from Nero to Hadrian.* Harvard University Press.

(2016) 'Roman literature: translation, metaphor, and empire', *Daedalus* 145.2: 30–9.

Benjamin, A. (1989) *Translation and the Nature of Philosophy.* Routledge.

Benjamin, W. (1999) [1923] 'The task of the translator', trans. H. Zorn, in *Illuminations.* Introduction H. Arendt. Pimlico, 70–82.

Bergren, A. (1983) 'Language and the female in early Greek thought', *Arethusa* 16.1/2: 69–95.

Berlioz, H. (1968) [1854] *Les Soirées de l'orchestre*, 2nd edn. Ed. L. Guichard. Gründ.

Bermann, S. and Wood, M. (eds.) (2005) *Nation, Language, and the Ethics of Translation.* Princeton University Press.

Bettini, M. (1997) 'Ghosts of exile: doubles and nostalgia in Vergil's *parva Troia* (*Aeneid* 3.294ff.)', *ClAnt* 16: 8–33.

(2008) *Voci: antropologia sonora del mondo antico.* Einaudi.

(2012) *Vertere: un'antropologia della traduzione nella cultura antica.* Einaudi.

Bing, P. (1988) *The Well-Read Muse: Present and Past in Callimachus and the Hellenistic Poets.* Vandenhoeck and Ruprecht.

Bloom, H. (1997) [1973] *The Anxiety of Influence: A Theory of Poetry*, 2nd edn. Oxford University Press.

(2003) [1975] *A Map of Misreading.* Oxford University Press.

Bouché-Leclercq, A. (1879–82) *Histoire de la divination dans l'antiquité.* 4 vols. E. Leroux.

Bouquet, M. and Morzadec, F. (eds.) (2004) *La Sibylle: parole et représentation.* Rennes University Press.

Boyle, A. J. (1997) *Tragic Seneca: An Essay in the Theatrical Tradition.* Routledge.

Brault, P.-A. (1990) *Prophetess Doomed: Cassandra and the Representation of Truth.* PhD thesis, New York University.

Bremmer, J. N. (1996) 'The status and symbolic capital of the seer', in R. Hägg (ed.) *The Role of Religion in the Early Greek Polis.* Proceedings of the Third International Seminar on Ancient Greek Cult: Organised by the Swedish Institute at Athens, 16–18 October 1992. Svenska institutet I Athen, 97–109.

Bright, D. F. (1981) 'Aeneas' other nekyia', *Vergilius* 27: 40–7.

Brisson, L. (1976) *Le mythe de Tirésias: essai d'analyse structurale.* Brill.

Brock, S. (1979) 'Aspects of translation technique in antiquity', *GRBS* 20: 69–87.

Brunt, P. (1975) 'Stoicism and the Principate', *PBSR* 43: 7–35.

Buitenwerf, R. (2003) *Book III of the* Sibylline Oracles *and its Social Setting*. Brill.

Burbidge, J. (2009) 'Dido, Anna and the Sirens', *MD* 62: 105–28.

Burkert, W. (1983) *Homo Necans: The Anthropology of Ancient Greek Sacrificial Ritual and Myth*, trans. P. Bing. University of California Press (= *Homo necans: Interpretationen altgriechischer Opferriten und Mythen*. De Gruyter. 1972).

  (1991) *Oedipus, Oracles, Meaning: From Sophocles to Umberto Eco*. University of Toronto Press.

Buxton, R. G. A. (1982) *Persuasion in Greek Tragedy: A Study of Peitho*. Cambridge University Press.

Cairns, F. (1979) *Tibullus: A Hellenistic Poet at Rome*. Cambridge University Press.

Calame, C. (1995) *The Craft of Poetic Speech in Ancient Greece*, trans. J. Orion. Preface J.-C. Coquet. Cornell University Press (= *Le récit en Grèce ancienne: énonciations et représentations de poètes*. Méridiens Klincksieck. 1986).

Calder, W. M. III (1976) 'Seneca's *Agamemnon*', *CPh* 71: 27–36.

Cameron, A. (1995) *Callimachus and his Critics*. Princeton University Press.

  (2004) *Greek Mythography in the Roman World*. Oxford University Press.

Chaudhuri, S. (1999) *Translation and Understanding*. Oxford University Press.

Clausen, W. (1987) *Virgil's* Aeneid *and the Tradition of Hellenistic Poetry*. Sather Classical Lectures 51. University of California Press.

Commager, S. (1981) 'Fateful words. Some conversations in *Aeneid* IV', *Arethusa* 14: 101–14.

Connelly, J. B. (1993) 'Narrative and image in Attic vase painting: Ajax and Kassandra at the Trojan Palladion', in P. J. Holliday (ed.) *Narrative and Event in Ancient Art*. Cambridge University Press, 88–129.

Connor, S. (2000) *Dumbstruck: A Cultural History of Ventriloquism*. Oxford University Press.

Conte, G. B. (1986) *The Rhetoric of Imitation: Genre and Poetic Memory in Virgil and Other Latin Poets*. Cornell University Press.

Craik, E. (1990) 'Sexual imagery and innuendo in *Troades*', in A. Powell (ed.) *Euripides, Women and Sexuality*. Routledge, 1–15.

Crippa, S. (1990) 'Glossolalia. Il linguaggio di Cassandra', *SILTA* 19: 487–508.

  (1998) 'La voce e la visione: il linguaggio oracolare', in I. Chirassi Colombo and T. Seppilli (eds.) *Sibille e linguaggi oracolari: mito, sotira, tradizizone: atti del convegno Macerata-Norcia, settembre 1994*. Istituti editoriali e poligrafici internazionali, 159–89.

  (1999) 'Cassandre, figure sonore', in M. Goudot (ed.), 81–91.

  (2004) 'Figures du σιβυλλαίνειν', in M. Bouquet and F. Morzadec (eds.), 99–108.

Croally, N. T. (1994) *Euripidean Polemic:* The Trojan Women *and the Function of Tragedy*. Cambridge University Press.

Curley, D. (2013) *Tragedy in Ovid: Theater, Metatheater, and the Transformation of a Genre*. Cambridge University Press.

Cusset, C. (2001) 'Le bestiaire de Lycophron: entre chien et loup', *Anthropozoologica* 33–4: 61–72.

(2004) 'Cassandre et/ou la Sibylle', in M. Bouquet and F. Morzadec (eds.), 53–60.

(2006) 'Dit et non-dit dans l'*Alexandre* de Lycophron', in M. A. Harder, R. F. Regtuit and G. C. Wakker, (eds.) *Beyond the Canon.* Hellenistica Groningana 11. Peeters, 43–60.

Cusset, C. and Prioux, E. (eds.) (2009) *Lycophron: éclats d'obscurité: actes du colloque international de Lyon et Saint-Etienne, 18–20 janvier 2007.* Publications de l'Université de Saint-Etienne.

Dalgarno, E. (2001) *Virginia Woolf and the Visible World.* Cambridge University Press.

(2012) *Virginia Woolf and the Migrations of Language.* Cambridge University Press.

Davreux, J. (1942) *La légende de la prophétesse Cassandre d'après les textes et les monuments.* Bibliothèque de la faculté de philosophie et lettres de l'Université de Liège, 94. Droz.

Debnar, P. (2010) 'The sexual status of Aeschylus' Cassandra', *CPh* 105.2: 129–43

Depew, M. and Obbink, D. (eds.) (2000) *Matrices of Genre: Authors, Canons, and Society.* Harvard University Press.

Derrida, J. (1979) 'Living on: border lines', trans. J. Hulbert, in H. Bloom (ed.) *Deconstruction and Criticism.* Continuum, 62–142.

Detienne, M. (1996). *The Masters of Truth in Archaic Greece*, trans. J. Lloyd. Foreword P. Vidal-Naquet. Zone Books (= *Les maîtres de vérité dans la Grèce archaïque.* Maspero. 1967).

Diggle, J. (1981a) *Euripidis Fabulae, Vol. II.* Oxford University Press.

(1981b) *Studies on the Text of Euripides:* Supplices, Electra, Heracles, Troades, Iphigenia in Tauris, Ion. Oxford University Press.

Dodds, E. R. (1951) *The Greeks and the Irrational.* University of California Press.

Dué, C. (2006) *The Captive Woman's Lament in Greek Tragedy.* University of Texas Press.

Dunn, F. M. (1993) 'Beginning at the end in Euripides' *Trojan Women*', *RhM* 136.1: 22–35.

(1996) *Tragedy's End: Closure and Innovation in Euripidean Drama.* Oxford University Press.

Edwards, C. (2007) *Death in Ancient Rome.* Yale University Press.

Ekbom, M. (2013) *The Sortes Vergilianae: A Philological Study.* PhD thesis, Uppsala Universitet.

Ertel, E. (2011) 'Derrida on translation and his (mis)reception in America', *Trahir* 2: 1–18.

Faraone, C. A. (2011) 'Hexametrical incantations as oral and written phenomena', in A. P. M. H. Lardinois, J. H. Blok and M. G. M. van der Poel (eds.), 191–203.

Feeney, D. C. (1991) *The Gods in Epic: Poets and Critics of the Classical Tradition.* Oxford University Press.

(1992) '*Si licet et fas est*: Ovid's *Fasti* and the problem of free speech under the Principate', in A. Powell (ed.) *Roman Poetry and Propaganda in the Age of Augustus.* Bristol Classical Press, 1–25.

(2004) '*Tenui ... latens discrimine*: spotting the differences in Statius' *Achilleid*', *MD* 52: 85–105.

(2005) 'The beginnings of a literature in Latin', *JRS* 95: 226–40.

(2015) *Beyond Greek: The Beginnings of Latin Literature*. Harvard University Press.

Feldherr, A. (1998) *Spectacle and Society in Livy's History*. University of California Press.

(2010) *Playing Gods: Ovid's* Metamorphoses *and the Politics of Fiction*. Princeton University Press.

Février, C. (2004) 'Le double langage de la Sibylle: de l'oracle grec au rituel romain', in M. Bouquet and F. Morzadec (eds.), 17–27.

Fitch, J. G. (2004) *Seneca Tragedies: II*. Loeb Classical Libraries 78. Harvard University Press.

Fitzgerald, W. (1984) 'Aeneas, Daedalus and the labyrinth', *Arethusa* 17.1: 51–64.

(1995) *Catullan Provocations: Lyric Poetry and the Drama of Position*. University of California Press.

Fleming, T. J. (1977) 'The musical nomos in Aeschylus' *Oresteia*', *CJ* 72.3: 222–33.

Flower, M. (2008) *The Seer in Ancient Greece*. University of California Press.

Foley, H. P. (1998) 'Antigone as moral agent', in M. Silk (ed.), 49–73.

(2001) *Female Acts in Greek Tragedy*. Princeton University Press.

Ford, A. (2002) *The Origins of Criticism: Literary Culture and Poetic Theory in Classical Greece*. Princeton University Press.

Fowler, D. (1991) 'Narrate and describe: the problem of ekphrasis', *JRS* 81: 21–35.

(1997a) 'On the shoulders of giants: intertextuality and classical studies', in S. Hinds and D. Fowler (eds.) *Memoria, arte allusiva, intertestualità: Memory, Allusion, Intertextuality*. Istituti editoriali e poligrafici internazionali, 1–39.

(1997b) 'Virgilian narrative: story-telling', in C. Martindale (ed.), 259–70.

(2002) 'Masculinity under threat? The poetics and politics of inspiration in Latin poetry', in E. Spentzou and D. Fowler (eds.), 141–59.

Fraenkel, E. (1950) *Aeschylus*: Agamemnon. Oxford University Press.

Franke, W. (2011) 'On doing the truth in time: the *Aeneid*'s invention of poetic prophecy', *Arion* 19.1: 53–63.

Fraser, P. M. (1979) 'Lycophron on Cyprus', *RDAC*: 328–43.

Fusillo, M. (1984) 'L'*Alessandra* di Licofrone: racconto epico e discorso drammatico', *ASNP* 14.2: 495–525.

Fusillo, M., Hurst, A., and Paduano, G. (eds.) (1991) *Licofrone*: Alessandra. Guerini.

Gantz, T. (1982) 'Inherited guilt in Aischylos', *CJ* 78.1: 1–23.

Gera, D. (2003) *Ancient Greek Ideas on Speech, Language and Civilization*. Oxford University Press.

Goff, B. (2009) *Euripides: Trojan Women*. Duckworth.

Goldhill, S. (1984a) *Language, Sexuality, Narrative: the* Oresteia. Cambridge University Press.

(1984b) 'Two notes on telos and related words in the *Oresteia*', *JHS* 104: 169–76.

(1986) *Reading Greek Tragedy*. Cambridge University Press.

(1991) *The Poet's Voice: Essays on Poetics and Greek Literature*. Cambridge University Press.

(1998) 'Collectivity and otherness – the authority of the tragic chorus: response to Gould', in M. Silk (ed.), 244–56.

(2004) *Aeschylus: the* Oresteia, 2nd edn. Cambridge University Press.

(2006) 'The language of tragedy: rhetoric and communication', in P. E. Easterling (ed.) *The Cambridge Companion to Greek Tragedy*. Cambridge University Press, 127–50.

Goudot, M. (ed.) (1999a) *Cassandre. Figures mythiques*. Editions Autrement.

(1999b) 'Enquête sur une énigme bien gardée', in M. Goudot (ed.), 7–14.

Gould, J. (1998) 'Tragedy and collective experience', in M. Silk (ed.), 217–43.

Gowers, E. (2005) 'Virgil's Sibyl and the "many mouths" cliché (*Aen.* 6.625–7)', *CQ* 55.1: 170–82.

Gowing, A. M. (2005) *Empire and Memory: The Representation of the Roman Republic in Imperial Culture*. Cambridge University Press.

Graf, F. (1985) *Nordionische Kulte: Religionsgeschichtliche und epigraphische Untersuchungen zu den Kulten von Chios, Erythrai, Klazomenai und Phokaia*. Bibliotheca Helvetica Romana.

Gregory, J. (1997) *Euripides and the Instruction of the Athenians*. University of Michigan Press.

Gutzwiller, K. (2007) *A Guide to Hellenistic Literature*. Blackwell.

Hall, E. (1991) *Inventing the Barbarian: Greek Self-definition through Tragedy*. Oxford University Press.

(1999) 'Actor's song in tragedy', in S. Goldhill and R. Osborne (eds.) *Performance Culture and Athenian Democracy*. Cambridge University Press, 96–122.

(2002) 'The singing actors of antiquity', in P. Easterling and E. Hall (eds.) *Greek and Roman Actors*. Cambridge University Press, 3–38.

(2010) *Greek Tragedy*. Oxford University Press.

Hallett, J. P. and Skinner, M. B. (eds.) (1997) *Roman Sexualities*. Princeton University Press.

Hardie, P. R. (1986) *Virgil's Aeneid: Cosmos and Imperium*. Oxford University Press.

(1991) 'The *Aeneid* and the *Oresteia*', *PVS* 20: 29–45.

(1993) *The Epic Successors of Virgil: A Study in the Dynamics of a Tradition*. Cambridge University Press.

(2014) *The Last Trojan Hero: A Cultural History of Virgil's Aeneid*. I. B. Tauris.

Hartog, F. (1988) *The Mirror of Herodotus: The Representation of the Other in the Writing of History*, trans. J. Lloyd. University of California Press (= *Le miroir d'Hérodote: essai sur la représentation de l'autre*. Gallimard. 1980).

Heath, J. (2005) *The Talking Greeks: Speech, Animals and the Other in Homer, Aeschylus and Plato*. Cambridge University Press.

Heirman, L. J. (1975) 'Kassandra's glossolalia', *Mnemosyne* 28.3: 257–67.

Henrichs, A. (1995) ' "Why should I dance?" Choral self-referentiality in Greek tragedy', *Arion* 3.1: 56–111.

Hershkowitz, D. (1991) 'The *Aeneid* in *Aeneid* 3', *Vergilius* 37: 69–76.

Heyworth, S. J. (2009) *Cynthia: A Companion to the Text of Propertius*. Oxford University Press.

Hexter, R. J. (1990) 'What was the Trojan horse made of? Interpreting Virgil's *Aeneid*', *YJC* 3.2: 109–31.

(1999) 'Imitating Troy: a reading of *Aeneid* 3', in C. G. Perkell (ed.) *Reading Vergil's* Aeneid: *An Interpretative Guide.* University of Oklahoma Press, 64–79.

Hinds, S. E. (1985) 'Booking the return trip: Ovid and *Tristia* 1', *PCPhS* 31: 13–32.

(1987a) *The Metamorphoses of Persephone: Ovid and the Self-Conscious Muse.* Cambridge University Press.

(1987b) 'Generalizing about Ovid', *Ramus* 16: 4–31.

(1998) *Allusion and Intertext: Dynamics of Appropriation in Roman Poetry.* Cambridge University Press.

(2011) 'Seneca's Ovidian *Loci*', *SIFC* 9.1: 5–63.

Hornblower, S. (2014) 'Lykophron and epigraphy: the value and function of cult epithets in the *Alexandra*', *CQ* 64.1: 91–120.

(2015) *Lykophron: Alexandra.* Oxford University Press.

Horsfall, N. (1993) 'Empty shelves on the Palatine', *G&R* 40.1: 58–67.

(2005) 'Lycophron and the *Aeneid*, again', *ICS* 30: 35–40.

(2006) *Virgil,* Aeneid *3: A Commentary.* Mnem. Suppl. 273. Brill.

(2008) *Virgil,* Aeneid *2: A Commentary.* Mnem. Suppl. 299. Brill.

(2013) *Virgil,* Aeneid *6: A Commentary.* 2 vols. De Gruyter.

Hunter, R. L. (2006) *The Shadow of Callimachus: Studies in the Reception of Hellenistic Poetry at Rome.* Cambridge University Press.

Hunter, R. L. and Fantuzzi, M. (2004) *Tradition and Innovation in Hellenistic Poetry.* Cambridge University Press.

Hurst, A. and Kolde, A. (eds.) (2008) *Lycophron,* Alexandra. Les Belles Lettres.

Hutchinson, G. O. (1988) *Hellenistic Poetry.* Oxford University Press.

(2006) *Propertius Elegies Book IV.* Cambridge University Press.

(2013) *Greek to Latin: Frameworks and Contexts for Intertextuality.* Oxford University Press.

Inwood, B. (1995) 'Seneca in his philosophical milieu', *HSCPh* 67: 63–76.

Iriarte, A. (1999) 'Le chant interdit de la clairvoyance', in M. Goudot (ed.), 42–64.

Jakobson, R. (1959) 'On linguistic aspects of translation', in R. A. Brower (ed.) *On Translation.* Harvard University Press, 232–39.

Jocelyn, H. D. (1967) *The Tragedies of Ennius: The Fragments.* Cambridge University Press.

Johnson, W. A. (2000) 'Musical evenings in the early empire: new evidence from a Greek papyrus with musical notation', *JHS* 120: 57–85.

Johnston, P. A. (1998) 'Juno's anger and the Sibyl at Cumae', *Vergilius* 44: 13–22.

Jones, J. (1962) *On Aristotle and Greek Tragedy.* Chatto and Windus.

Josifović, S. (1968) 'Lykophron', *RE* Suppl. 11, 888–930.

Karanika, A. (2011) 'Homeric verses and divination in the *homeromanteion*', in A. P. M. H. Lardinois, J. H. Blok and M. G. M. van der Poel (eds.), 255–77.

(2014) *Voices at Work: Women, Performance, and Labor in Ancient Greece.* Johns Hopkins University Press.

Katz, J. (2013) 'The muse at play: an introduction', in J. Kwapisz, D. Petrain and M. Szymański (eds.), 1–30.

Keith, A. M. (1992) *The Play of Fictions: Studies in Ovid's* Metamorphoses *Book 2.* University of Michigan Press.

Kelly, H. A. (1979) 'Tragedy and the performance of tragedy in late Roman antiquity', *Traditio* 35: 21–44.

Kennedy, D. (1997) 'Modern receptions and their interpretative implications', in C. Martindale (ed.), 38–55.

Keskiaho, J. (2013) 'Re-visiting the *Libri Sibyllini*: some remarks on their nature in Roman legend and experience', in M. Kajava (ed.) *Studies in Ancient Oracles and Divination*. Acta Instituti Romani Finlandiae, 40. Institutum Romandum Finlandiae, 145–72.

Knox, B. (1950) 'The serpent and the flame: the imagery of the second book of the *Aeneid*', *AJP* 71.4: 379–400.

    (1979) *Word and Action: Essays on the Ancient Theater*. Johns Hopkins University Press.

Kolde, A. (2009) 'Parodie et ironie chez Lycophron: un mode de dialogue avec la tradition?', in C. Cusset and E. Prioux (eds.), 39–57.

Kosmetatou, E. (2000) 'Lycophron's *Alexandra* reconsidered: the Attalid connection', *Hermes* 128: 32–53.

Kovacs, D. (1999) *Euripides:* Trojan Women, Iphigenia Among the Taurians, Ion. Loeb Classical Libraries 10. Harvard University Press.

Kwapisz, J., Petrain D. and Szymanski, M. (eds.) (2013) *The Muse at Play: Riddles and Wordplay in Greek and Latin Poetry*. De Gruyter.

Kytzler, B. (1989) '*Fidus interpres:* the theory and practice of translation in classical antiquity', *Antichthon* 23: 42–50.

Kundera, M. (1981) 'Xenakis «prophète de l'insensibilité»', in M. Fleuret (ed.) *Regards sur Iannis Xenakis*. Stock, 21–4.

Lada-Richards, I. (2007) *Silent Eloquence: Lucian and Pantomime Dancing*. Duckworth.

Lape, S. (2010) *Race and Citizen Identity in the Classical Athenian Democracy*. Cambridge University Press.

Lardinois, A. P. M. H., Blok, J. H. and van der Poel, M. G. M. (eds.) (2011) *Sacred Words: Orality, Literacy and Religion*. Orality and Literacy in the Ancient World, Vol. VIII. Mnem. Suppl. 332. Brill.

Lavery, J. F. (2004a) 'Aeschylus *Agamemnon* 1180–2: a booster?', *Hermes* 132: 1–19.

    (2004b) 'Some Aeschylean influences on Seneca's *Agamemnon*', *MD* 53: 183–94.

Lebeck, A. (1971) The Oresteia: *A Study in Language and Structure*. Harvard University Press.

Lecercle, J.-J. (1990) *The Violence of Language*. Routledge.

Lee, K. H. (1976) *Euripides:* Troades. Macmillan.

Lelièvre, F. J. (1971) 'Two supernatural incidents in the *Aeneid*', *PVS* 11: 74–7.

Lesky, A. (1961) *Göttliche und menschliche Motivation im homerischen Epos*. C. Winter.

LeVen, P. A. (2014) *The Many-Headed Muse: Tradition and Innovation in Late Classical Greek Lyric Poetry*. Cambridge University Press.

Levene, D. S. and Nelis, D. P. (eds.) (2002) *Clio and the Poets: Augustan Poetry and the Traditions of Ancient Historiography*. Mnem. Suppl. 224, Brill.

Lightfoot, J. L. (2007) *The Sibylline Oracles: With Introduction, Translation, and Commentary on the First and Second Books.* Oxford University Press.

Littlewood, C. A. J. (2004) *Self-Representation and Illusion in Senecan Tragedy.* Oxford University Press.

Loraux, N. (1987) *Tragic Ways of Killing a Woman*, trans. A. Forster. Harvard University Press (= *Façons tragiques de tuer une femme.* Hachette. 1985).

(2002) *The Mourning Voice: An Essay on Greek Tragedy*, trans. E. Trapnell Rawlings. Cornell University Press

Lowe, N. J. (2004) 'Lycophron', in R. J. F. de Jong, R. Nünlist and A. Bowie (eds.) *Narrators, Narratees, and Narratives in Ancient Greek Literature.* Brill, 307–14.

Lowrie, M. (2009) *Writing, Performance, and Authority in Augustan Rome.* Oxford University Press.

Martin, R. P. (1992) 'Hesiod's metanastic poetics', *Ramus* 21.1: 11–33.

Martindale, C. (ed.) (1997) *The Cambridge Companion to Virgil.* Cambridge University Press.

Mason, P. G. (1959) 'Kassandra', *JHS* 79: 80–93.

Maurizio, L. (1995) 'Anthropology and spirit possession: a reconsideration of the Pythia's role at Delphi', *JHS* 115: 69–86.

(2013) '*Technopaegnia* in Heraclitus and the Delphic oracles', in J. Kwapisz, D. Petrain and M. Szymanski (eds.), 100–20.

Mazzoldi, S. (2001) *Cassandra, la vergine e l'indovina: identità di un personaggio da Omero all'Ellenismo.* Filologia e critica 88. Istituti editoriali e poligrafici internazionali.

(2002) 'Cassandra's prophecy between ecstasy and rational mediation', *Kernos* 15: 145–54.

McClure, L. (1999) *Spoken Like a Woman: Speech and Gender in Athenian Drama.* Princeton University Press.

McElduff, S. (2013) *Roman Theories of Translation: Surpassing the Source.* Routledge.

McNelis, C. and Sens, A. (2016) *The* Alexandra *of Lycophron: A Literary Study.* Oxford University Press.

Merkelbach, R. (1961) 'Aeneas in Cumae', *MH* 18: 83–99.

Miles, G. B. (1995) *Livy: Reconstructing Early Rome.* Cornell University Press.

Miller, J. F. (2009) *Apollo, Augustus, and the Poets.* Cambridge University Press.

Mitchell-Boyask, R. (2006) 'The marriage of Cassandra and the *Oresteia*: text, image, performance', *TAPhA* 136.2: 269–97.

(2009) *Aeschylus: Eumenides.* Duckworth.

Moberly, R. W. L. (2006) *Prophecy and Discernment.* Cambridge University Press.

Momigliano, A. (1942) 'Terra marique', *JRS* 32: 53–64.

Monrós Gaspar, L. (2008) 'The voice of Cassandra: Florence Nightingale's *Cassandra* (1852) and the Victorian woman', *New Voices in Classical Reception Studies* 3: 61–76.

Monrós Gaspar, L. and Reece, R. (2011) *Cassandra, the Fortune-Teller: Prophets, Gipsies and Victorian Burlesque.* Levante.

Montiglio, S. (2000) *Silence in the Land of Logos.* Princeton University Press.

(2005) *Wandering in Ancient Greek Culture.* University of Chicago Press.

Moreau, A. (1989) 'Les ambivalences de Cassandre', in A.-F. Laurens (ed.) *Entre hommes et dieux. Le convive, le héros, le prophète.* Annales littéraires de l'Université de Besançon. Les Belles Lettres, 145–67.

Morgan, K. A. (1994) 'Apollo's favorites', *GRBS* 35.2: 121–43.

Morgan, Ll. (1998) 'Assimilation and civil war: Hercules and Cacus', in H.-P. Stahl (ed.) *Vergil's* Aeneid: *Augustan Epic and Political Context.* Duckworth/The Classical Press of Wales, 175–97.

 (1999) *Patterns of Redemption in Virgil's* Georgics. Cambridge University Press.

Most, G. W. (2003) 'Violets in crucibles: translating, traducing, transmuting', *TAPhA* 133.2: 381–90.

 (ed.) (1999) *Commentaries = Kommentare.* Vandenhoeck and Ruprecht.

Motto, A. L. and Clark, J. R. (1988) *Senecan Tragedy.* Hakkert.

Mullen, A. (2012) 'Introduction: multiple languages, multiple identities', in A. Mullen and P. James (eds.) *Multilingualism in the Graeco-Roman Worlds.* Cambridge University Press, 1–35.

Murgatroyd, P. (1994) *Tibullus,* Elegies *II.* Oxford University Press.

Murgia, C. (1987) 'Dido's Puns', *CPh* 82: 50–9.

Murray, P. (1996) *Plato on Poetry.* Cambridge University Press.

Myers, K. S. (1994) *Ovid's Causes: Cosmogony and Aetiology in the* Metamorphoses. University of Michigan Press.

Mynors, R. A. B. (1969) *P. Vergili Maronis Opera.* Oxford University Press.

Nagy, G. (1989) 'Early Greek views of poets and poetry', in G. A. Kennedy (ed.) *The Cambridge History of Literary Criticism, Vol. I.* Cambridge University Press, 1–77.

 (1990) 'Ancient Greek poetry, prophecy, and concepts of theory', in J. L. Kugel (ed.) *Poetry and Prophecy: The Beginnings of a Literary Tradition.* Cornell University Press.

 (1996) *Poetry as Performance: Homer and Beyond.* Cambridge University Press.

Neblung, D. (1997) *Die Gestalt der Kassandra in der antiken Literatur.* B. G. Teubner.

Nelis, D. (2001) *Vergil's* Aeneid *and the* Argonautica *of Apollonius Rhodius.* Francis Cairns.

Newman, J. K. (1967) *The Concept of* Vates *in Augustan Poetry.* Collection Latomus.

Niranjana, S. (1992) *Siting Translation: History, Post-Structuralism, and the Colonial Context.* University of California Press.

Nisbet, R. G. M and Rudd, N. (2007) *A Commentary on Horace,* Odes, *Book III.* Oxford University Press.

Norden, E. (1916) *P. Vergilius Maro Aeneis Buch VI,* 2nd edn. B. G. Teubner.

O'Hara, J. J. (1990) *Death and the Optimistic Prophecy in Vergil's* Aeneid. Princeton University Press.

Oliensis, E. (1997) 'Sons and lovers: sexuality and gender in Virgil's poetry', in C. Martindale (ed.), 294–311.

 (2004) 'Sibylline syllables: the intratextual *Aeneid*', *PCPhS* 50: 29–45.

Orlin, E. M. (1997) *Temples, Religion and Politics in the Roman Republic.* Brill.

Padel, R. (1992) *In and Out of the Mind: Greek Images of the Tragic Self.* Princeton University Press.

Page, D. L. (1972) *Aeschyli septem quae supersunt tragoedias*. Oxford University Press.

Palmer, L. H. (1962) 'The language of Homer', in A. J. B. Wace and F. H. Stubbings (eds.) *A Companion to Homer*. Macmillan, 75–178.

Papadopoulou, T. (2000) 'Cassandra's radiant vigour and the ironic optimism of Euripides' *Troades*', *Mnemosyne* 53.5: 513–27.

Parke, H. W. (1988) *Sibyls and Sibylline Prophecy in Classical Antiquity*. Ed. B. C. McGing. Routledge.

Parker, R. (1983) *Miasma: Pollution and Purification in Early Greek Religion*. Oxford University Press.

Paschalis, M. (1986) 'Virgil and the Delphic Oracle', *Philologus* 130: 44–68.

(2010) 'Cassandra and the passionate lucidity of *furor* in Seneca's *Agamemnon*', in S. Tsitsiride (ed.) *Parachoregema: Studies on Ancient Theatre in Honour of Professor Gregory M. Sifakis*. Crete University Press, 209–28.

Paul, G. (2009) *Perspectives on Gender in Post-1945 German Literature*. Camden House.

Pavlock, B. (2009) *The Image of the Poet in Ovid's* Metamorphoses. University of Wisconsin Press.

Pillinger, E. (2010) 'Translating classical visions in Berlioz's *Les Troyens*', *Arion* 18.2: 65–103.

(2012) '*And the gods dread to hear another poem*: the repetitive poetics of witch-craft from Virgil to Lucan', *MD* 68: 103–43.

(2017) 'Finding asylum for Virginia Woolf's classical visions', in V. Zajko and H. Hoyle (eds.) *A Handbook to the Reception of Classical Mythology*, Wiley-Blackwell, 271–84.

(forthcoming) 'A walk in Virgil's footsteps: Statius on the Via Domitiana', in B. Gladhill and M. Y. Myers (eds.) *Walking Through Elysium*: Aeneid *6 and Its Cultural Reception* (under contract, University of Toronto Press).

Poole, A. (1976) 'Total disaster: Euripides' *The Trojan Women*', *Arion* 3: 257–87.

Potter, D. S. (1990a) *Prophecy and History in the Crisis of the Roman Empire: A Historical Commentary on the Thirteenth Sibylline Oracle*. Oxford University Press.

(1990b) 'Sibyls in the Greek and Roman world', *JRA* 3: 471–83.

(1994) *Prophets and Emperors: Human and Divine Authority from Augustus to Theodosius*. Harvard University Press.

Prins, Y. (1991) 'The power of the speech act: Aeschylus' Furies and their binding song', *Aresthusa* 24.2: 177–95.

(2005) 'OTOTOTOI: Virginia Woolf and "the naked cry" of Cassandra', in F. Macintosh, P. Michelakis, E. Hall and O. Taplin (eds.) Agamemnon *in Performance: 458 BC to AD 2004*. Oxford University Press, 163–85.

Pucci, P. (1979) 'The song of the Sirens', *Arethusa* 12.2: 121–32.

Putnam, M. C. J. (1987) 'Daedalus, Virgil and the end of art', *AHPh* 108.2: 173–98.

Quint, D. (1982) 'Painful memories: *Aeneid* 3 and the problem of the past', *CJ* 78.1:30–8.

Rabinowitz, N. S. (1993) *Anxiety Veiled: Euripides and the Traffic in Women*, Cornell University Press.

Racine, R. (2003) *Le mythe littéraire de Cassandre. Vingt apparitions de la prophétesse Troyenne: entre perte et recherche d'identité*, PhD thesis, Université Paris IV – Sorbonne.

Raeburn, D. and Thomas, O. (2011) *The Agamemnon of Aeschylus: A Commentary for Students*. Oxford University Press.

Rehm, R. (1994) *Marriage to Death: The Conflation of Wedding and Funeral Rituals in Greek Tragedy*. Princeton University Press.

(2002) *The Play of Space: Spatial Transformation in Greek Tragedy*. Princeton University Press.

Reid, J. D. and Rohmann, C. (eds.) (1993) *The Oxford Guide to Classical Mythology in the Arts, 1300–1990s*. 2 vols. Oxford University Press.

Richardson, N. (1993) *The Iliad: A Commentary. Vol. VI: Books 21–24*. Cambridge University Press.

Robinson, D. (1997) *Translation and Empire: Postcolonial Theories Explained*. St Jerome Publishing.

Rosenmeyer, T. G. (1982) *The Art of Aeschylus*. University of California Press.

Ross, S. (2005) '*Barbarophonos*: language and panhellenism in the *Iliad*', *CPh* 100.4: 299–316.

Rossi, A. (2002) 'The fall of Troy: between tradition and genre', in D. S. Levene and D. P. Nelis (eds.), 231–51.

Rutherford, R. B. (2012) *Greek Tragic Style: Form, Language and Interpretation*. Oxford University Press.

Santangelo, F. (2013) *Divination, Prediction and the End of the Roman Republic*. Cambridge University Press.

Satterfield, S. (2008) *Rome's Own Sibyl: The Sibylline Books in the Roman Republic and Early Empire*. PhD thesis, Princeton University.

Scheer, E. (1879) 'Die Ueberlieferung der *Alexandra* des Lykophron', *RhM* 34: 272–91, 442–73.

Scheid, J. (1998) 'Les livres sibyllins et les archives des quindécimvirs', in C. Moatti (ed.) *La mémoire perdue. Recherches sur l'administration romaine*. L'Ecole Française de Rome, 11–26.

Schein, S. L. (1982) 'The Cassandra scene in Aeschylus' *Agamemnon*', *G&R* 29: 11–16.

Schiesaro, A. (1992) 'Forms of Senecan intertextuality', *Vergilius* 38: 56–63.

(2003) *The Passions in Play:* Thyestes *and the Dynamics of Senecan Drama*. Cambridge University Press.

Schofield, M. (1991) *The Stoic Idea of the City*. Cambridge University Press.

Sciarrino, E. (2006) 'The introduction of epic in Rome: cultural thefts and social contests', *Arethusa* 39.3: 449–69.

Scodel, R. (1980) *The Trojan Trilogy of Euripides*. Vandenhoeck and Ruprecht.

Seidensticker, B. (1985) '*Maius Solito*. Senecas Thyestes und die tragoedia rhetorica', *A&A* 31: 116–36.

Segal, C. (1993a) *Euripides and the Poetics of Sorrow: Art, Gender, and Commemoration in* Alcestis, Hippolytus *and* Hecuba. Duke University Press.

(1993b). 'The female voice and its contradictions: from Homer to tragedy', in J. Dalfen, G. Petersmann and F. F. Schwarz (eds.) *Religio Graeco-Romana: Festschrift für Walter Pötscher*. Grazer Beiträge Suppl. 5. Berger, 57–75.

Sellars, J. (2006) *Stoicism*. University of California Press.

Sens, A. (2010) 'Hellenistic Tragedy and Lycophron's *Alexandra*', in J. J. Clauss and M. Cuypers (eds.) *A Companion to Hellenistic Literature*. Wiley-Blackwell, 297–313.

Seremetakis, C. N. (1991) *The Last Word: Women, Death, and Divination in Inner Mani*. University of Chicago Press.

Sewell-Rutter, N. J. (2007) *Guilt by Descent: Moral Inheritance and Decision Making in Greek Tragedy*. Oxford University Press.

Shelton, J.-A. (1983) 'Revenge or resignation: Seneca's *Agamemnon*', in A. J. Boyle (ed.) *Seneca Tragicus: Ramus Essays on Senecan Drama*. Aureal, 159–83.

Siebengartner, A. W. (2012) 'Stoically seeing and being seen in Cicero's *Aratea*', in J. Glucker and C. Burnett (eds.) *Greek into Latin from Antiquity until the Nineteenth Century*. Warburg Institute, 97–115.

Sienkewicz, T. J. (1978) 'Euripides' *Trojan Women*: an interpretation', *Helios* 6.1: 81–95.

Silk, M. S. (ed.) (1998) *Tragedy and the Tragic: Greek Theatre and Beyond*. Oxford University Press.

Sissa, G. (1990) *Greek Virginity*, trans. A. Goldhammer. Harvard University Press (= *Le corps virginale: la virginité féminine en Grèce ancienne*. Librairie philosophique Vrin. 1987).

Skutsch, O. (1985) *The* Annals *of Quintus Ennius*. Oxford University Press.

Slaney, H. (2016) *The Senecan Aesthetic: A Performance History*. Oxford University Press.

Sluiter, I. (1998) 'Metatexts and the principle of charity', in P. Schmitter and M. V. D. Wal (eds.) *Metahistoriography: Theoretical and Methodological Aspects of the Historiography of Linguistics*. Nodus Publikationen, 11–27.

　(2000) 'The dialectics of genre: some aspects of secondary literature and genre in antiquity', in M. Depew and D. Obbink (eds.), 183–203.

Smith, R. A. (1997) *Poetic Allusion and Poetic Embrace in Ovid and Virgil*. University of Michigan Press.

　(2005) *The Primacy of Vision in Virgil's* Aeneid. University of Texas Press.

Solodow, J. B. (1988) *The World of Ovid's* Metamorphoses. University of North Carolina Press.

Sommerstein, A. H. (2008) *Aeschylus:* Oresteia. Loeb Classical Libraries 146. Harvard University Press.

Sourvinou-Inwood, C. (1997) 'Medea at a shifting distance: images and Euripidean tragedy', in J. J. Clauss and S. I. Johnston (eds.) *Medea: Essays on Medea in Myth, Literature, Philosophy, and Art*. Princeton University Press, 253–96.

Spentzou, E. (2002) 'Introduction: secularizing the Muse', in E. Spentzou and D. Fowler (eds.), 1–28.

Spentzou, E. and Fowler, D. (eds.) (2002) *Cultivating the Muse: Struggles for Power and Inspiration in Classical Literature*. Oxford University Press.

Staley, G. A. (2009) *Seneca and the Idea of Tragedy*. Oxford University Press.

Stallings, A. E. (2006) *Hapax: Poems*. Northwestern University Press.

Steiner, G. (1998) [1975] *After Babel: Aspects of Language and Translation*, 3rd edn. Oxford University Press.

Strzelecki, W. (1964) *Cn. Naevii* Belli Punici *Carmen*. B. G. Teubner.

Struck, P. T. (2004) *Birth of the Symbol: Ancient Readers at the Limits of their Texts.* Princeton University Press.

Stephens, S. (2003) *Seeing Double: Intercultural Poetics in Ptolemaic Alexandria.* University of California Press.

Suter, A. (2003) 'Lament in Euripides' *Trojan Women*', *Mnemosyne* 56.1: 1–28.

Takács, S. (2008) *Vestal Virgins, Sibyls, and Matrons: Women in Roman Religion.* University of Texas Press.

Taplin, O. (1972) 'Aeschylean silences and silences in Aeschylus', *HSPh* 76: 57–97.
  (1977) *The Stagecraft of Aeschylus: The Dramatic Use of Exits and Entrances in Greek Tragedy.* Oxford University Press.
  (2003) [1978] *Greek Tragedy in Action.* Routledge.

Tarrant, R. J. (1976) *Seneca:* Agamemnon. Cambridge University Press.
  (1995) 'Greek and Roman in Seneca's tragedies', *HSCPh* 97: 215–30.

Thalmann, W. G. (1985) 'Speech and silence in the *Oresteia*', *Phoenix* 39: 99–118 and 221–37.

Thomas, R. F. (1986) 'Vergil's *Georgics* and the art of reference', *HSPh* 90: 171–98.

Tissol, G. (1993) 'Ovid's little *Aeneid* and the thematic integrity of the *Metamorphoses*', *Helios* 20: 69–79.

Torrance, I. (2013) *Metapoetry in Euripides.* Oxford University Press.

Tracy, S. V. (1986) 'Darkness from light: the beacon fire in the *Agamemnon*', *CQ* 36: 257–60.

Traina, A. (1989) 'Le traduzioni', in G. Cavallo, P. Fedeli and A. Giardina (eds.) *Lo spazio letterario di Roma antica, Vol. II.* Salerno, 93–123.

Trinacty, C. V. (2014) *Senecan Tragedy and the Reception of Augustan Poetry.* Oxford University Press.

Venuti, L. (1995) *The Translator's Invisibility: A History of Translation.* Routledge.
  (1998) *The Scandals of Translation: Towards an Ethics of Difference.* Routledge.
  (2008) 'Translation, interpretation, canon formation', in A. Lianeri and V. Zajko (eds.) *Translation and the Classic: Identity as Change in the History of Culture.* Oxford University Press, 27–51.

Vernant, J.-P. (1990) 'Tensions and ambiguities in Greek tragedy', in J. P. Vernant and P. Vidal-Naquet (eds.) *Myth and Tragedy in Ancient Greece*, trans. J. Lloyd. Zone Books, 29–48 (= *Mythe et tragédie en Grèce ancienne*. Maspero. 1972 and 1986).

Verrall, A. W. (1904) *The* Agamemnon *of Aeschylus*. Macmillan.

Van Sickle, J. (1980) 'The book-roll and some conventions of the poetic book', *Arethusa* 13.1: 5–42.

Volk, K. (2002) *The Poetics of Latin Didactic: Lucretius, Vergil, Ovid, Manilius.* Oxford University Press.

Von Glinski, M. L. (2012) *Simile and Identity in Ovid's* Metamorphoses. Cambridge University Press.

Wallace-Hadrill, A. (2008) *Rome's Cultural Revolution.* Cambridge University Press.

Waszink, J. H. (1948) 'Vergil and the Sibyl of Cumae', *Mnemosyne* 1.43–58.

West, M. L. (1991) *Aeschyli* Agamemnon. B. G. Teubner.

(1997) *The East Face of Helicon: West Asiatic Elements in Greek Poetry and Myth*. Oxford University Press.

West, S. R. (1984) 'Lycophron Italicized', *JHS* 104: 127–51.

(2000) 'Lycophron's *Alexandra*: "Hindsight as Foresight Makes No Sense"?', in M. Depew and D. Obbink (eds.), 153–66.

Wheeler, S. M. (1999) *A Discourse of Wonders: Audience and Performance in Ovid's* Metamorphoses. University of Pennsylvania Press.

Whitehorne, J. (2005) 'O city of Kranaos! Athenian identity in Aristophanes' *Acharnians*', *G&R* 52.1: 34–44.

Whitmarsh, T. (2004) *Ancient Greek Literature*. Polity.

Willi, A. (2002) 'Languages on stage: Aristophanic language, cultural history, and Athenian identity', in A. Willi (ed.) *The Language of Greek Comedy*. Oxford University Press, 111–50.

Williams, G. (1983) *Technique and Ideas in the* Aeneid. Yale University Press.

Winnington-Ingram, R. P. (1948) 'Clytemnestra and the vote of Athena', *JHS* 68: 130–47.

Wohl, V. (1998) *Intimate Commerce: Exchange, Gender and Subjectivity in Greek Tragedy*. University of Texas Press.

Wolf, C. (1984) *Cassandra: A Novel and Four Essays*, trans. J. Van Heurck. Farrar, Straus and Giroux.

(2008) [1983] *Voraussetzungen einer Erzählung: Kassandra. Frankfurter Poetik-Vorlesungen*. Suhrkamp Verlag.

(2014) [1983] *Kassandra: Erzählung*. Text und Kommentar, ed. S. Hilzinger. Suhrkamp Verlag.

Wood, M. (2003) *The Road to Delphi: The Life and Afterlife of Oracles*. Farrar, Straus and Giroux.

(2005) *Literature and the Taste of Knowledge*. Cambridge University Press.

Woodman, A. J. (1988) *Rhetoric in Classical Historiography: Four Studies*. Croom Helm.

Woolf, V. (1984) [1925] 'On not knowing Greek', in *The Common Reader: First Series*, Harvest edn. Harcourt.

Zanker, G. (1987) *Realism in Alexandrian Poetry: A Literature and its Audience*. Croom Helm.

Zanobi, A. (2014) *Seneca's Tragedies and the Aesthetics of Pantomime*. Bloomsbury.

Zeitlin, F. I. (1965) 'The motif of the corrupted sacrifice in Aeschylus' *Oresteia*', *TAPhA* 96: 436–508.

(1996) *Playing the Other: Gender and Society in Classical Greek Literature*. University of Chicago Press.

(2009) 'Troy and tragedy: the conscience of Hellas', in U. Dill and C. Walde (eds.) *Antike Mythen: Medien, Transformationen und Konstruktionen*. De Gruyter, 709–26.

Zetzel, J. E. G. (1983) 'Re-creating the canon: Augustan poetry and the Alexandrian past', *Critical Inquiry* 10.1: 83–105.

Ziegler, K. (1927) 'Lykophron der Tragiker und die Alexandra Frage', *RE* 13.2: 2316–81.

Index Locorum

257

General Index